Scales of Governance and Indigenous Peoples' Rights

This book takes an interdisciplinary approach to the complicated power relations surrounding the recognition and implementation of Indigenous Peoples' rights at multiple scales.

The adoption of the United Nations Declaration on the Rights of Indigenous Peoples in 2007 was heralded as the beginning of a new era for Indigenous Peoples' participation in global governance bodies, as well as for the realization of their rights – in particular, the right to self-determination. These rights are defined and agreed upon internationally, but must be enacted at regional, national, and local scales. Can the global movement to promote Indigenous Peoples' rights change the experience of communities at the local level? Or are the concepts that it mobilizes, around rights and political tools, essentially a discourse circulating internationally, relatively disconnected from practical situations? Are the categories and processes associated with Indigenous Peoples simply an extension of colonial categories and processes, or do they challenge existing norms and structures? This collection draws together the works of anthropologists, political scientists, and legal scholars to address such questions. Examining the legal, historical, political, economic, and cultural dimensions of the Indigenous Peoples' rights movement, at global, regional, national, and local levels, the chapters present a series of case studies that reveal the complex power relations that inform the ongoing struggles of Indigenous Peoples to secure their human rights.

The book will be of interest to social scientists and legal scholars studying Indigenous Peoples' rights, and international human rights movements in general.

Irène Bellier, is a senior research director at the French National Center for Scientific Research (CNRS) and teaches at the Graduate School of Social Sciences (Ecole des Hautes Études en Sciences Sociales, EHESS) in Paris. She is the director of the Laboratory of the Anthropology of Institutions and Social Organizations (LAIOS) at Interdisciplinary Institute for Contemporary Anthropology (IIAC).

Jennifer Hays is an associate professor of social anthropology in the Department of Social Sciences (ISS) at UiT the Arctic University of Norway, in Tromsø.

Part of the Indigenous Peoples and the Law series
Series editors
Dr Mark A. Harris, University of British Columbia, Canada
Professor Denise Ferreira da Silva, University of British Columbia, Canada
Dr Claire Charters, University of Auckland, New Zealand
Dr Glen Coulthard, University of British Columbia, Canada

SOGIP

Scales of Governance & Indigenous Peoples

For information about the series and details of previous and forthcoming titles, see https://www.routledge.com/law/series/INDPPL

Scales of Governance and Indigenous Peoples' Rights

Edited by
Irène Bellier and Jennifer Hays

Routledge
Taylor & Francis Group
a GlassHouse Book

First published 2020
by Routledge
2 Park Square, Milton Park, Abingdon, Oxon OX14 4RN

and by Routledge
605 Third Avenue, New York, NY 10017

First issued in paperback 2021

Routledge is an imprint of the Taylor & Francis Group, an informa business

A GlassHouse Book

Publisher's Note
The publisher has gone to great lengths to ensure the quality of this reprint but points out that some imperfections in the original copies may be apparent.

British Library Cataloguing-in-Publication Data
A catalogue record for this book is available from the British Library

Library of Congress Cataloging-in-Publication Data
Names: Bellier, Irène, editor. | Hays, Jennifer, editor.
Title: Scales of governance and indigenous peoples' rights /
Edited by Irène Bellier, Jennifer Hays.
Description: New York: Routledge, 2019. |
Series: Indigenous peoples and the law | Includes bibliographical references and index.
Identifiers: LCCN 2019028248 (print) | LCCN 2019028249 (ebook) |
ISBN 9781138944480 (hardback) | ISBN 9781315671888 (ebook)
Subjects: LCSH: Indigenous peoples—Civil rights. | Indigenous peoples—Legal status, laws, etc. | Indigenous peoples (International law) |
Self-determination, National.
Classification: LCC K3247 .S33 2019 (print) | LCC K3247 (ebook) |
DDC 342.08/72—dc23
LC record available at https://lccn.loc.gov/2019028248
LC ebook record available at https://lccn.loc.gov/2019028249

ISBN 13: 978-1-03-208852-5 (pbk)
ISBN 13: 978-1-138-94448-0 (hbk)

Typeset in Galliard
by codeMantra

Contents

Contributors

Irène Bellier, a senior research director at the CNRS (National Center for Scientific Research), is an anthropologist and teaches at the Graduate School of Social Sciences (Ecole des Hautes Études en Sciences Sociales, EHESS) in Paris. Since 2001, she has been studying the international movement of Indigenous Peoples and its interactions with the United Nations system. Since 2010, she has coordinated global and comparative research, first as the director of the project SOGIP *Scales of Governance – The United Nations, the States, and Indigenous Peoples: Self-determination in the time of globalization* (www.sogip.ehess.fr), for which she received support from an Advanced Grant of the European Research Council (ERC). She is currently coordinating the Thematic Research Network JUSTIP (Justice and Indigenous Peoples), supported by the CNRS and partner institutions (https://justip.hypotheses.org/). Her many publications on indigenous issues are available on the website http://www.iiac.cnrs.fr/article1295.html#autochtone.

Caroline F. Butler is the research and planning coordinator for the Gitxaala Fisheries Program. A cultural anthropologist, she has conducted collaborative research with the Gitxaala Nation for 18 years and has been an employee of the Gitxaala First Nation government for ten years. She has written about Gitxaala research methods and traditional ecological knowledge and has forthcoming publications on Gitxaala conservation and marine planning initiatives.

Leslie Cloud is a legal scholar specializing in the rights of Indigenous Peoples and the right of asylum. She lived for more than ten years in a Mapuche community in Chile, where she worked on Mapuche conceptions of law and the relationship between the Mapuche and the State Justice. She has also published articles on the right of the Rapa Nui people to their cultural heritage. She continues her research on the rights of Indigenous Peoples in Chile, on justice, and legal pluralism, which she enriches from a perspective related to the right of asylum. She collaborated to the research project SOGIP, supported by the European Research Council, and is a member of the International Thematic Network, JUSTIP.

Verónica González González is a member of the Mexican National System of Researchers and a university lecturer in France and Mexico. She has focused mainly on Indigenous Peoples' rights in Mexico and at the international level, in particular, the implementation of the UN Declaration on Rights of Indigenous Peoples, an issue she worked on as a member of the SOGIP research team. She has a PhD in sociology from the Institute of Latin American Studies in Paris, and she has developed her work from an interdisciplinary approach that includes political science, law, and anthropology. Her current work looks at the challenges that climate change involves for the realization of Indigenous Peoples' rights, and she is a consultant for UNESCO in projects promoting the inclusion of indigenous knowledge on weather and climate into climate change adaptation policies.

Stéphanie Guyon is an assistant professor of political science in the University of Picardie Jules Verne and a member of the University Research Centre on Public Action and Politics (Centre Universitaire de Récherche sur l'Action Publique et le Politique CURAPP-ESS / CNRS). She has been working on French Guiana for 15 years. Her PhD thesis dealt with the colonial legacy in local contemporary politics in French Guiana, in particular, the politicization process of minoritized groups of French Guiana (Amerindians and Maroons). Since 1946, as a member of the SOGIP research project, she has been focusing on the design and implementation of public indigenous policies in French Guiana. From 2014 to 2018, she also studied family justice in French Guiana, especially relationships between indigenous populations and the State justice stystem, in the project of the National Agency for Indigenous Research (l'Agence nationale de la récherche, ANR).

Jennifer Hays is an associate professor of social anthropology at UiT the Arctic University of Norway, in Tromsø. She has been working in southern Africa for over two decades, both as a researcher and as a consultant for community-based education and development initiatives, and on Indigenous Peoples' rights projects in Botswana and Namibia. She has published extensively on the theoretical and practical issues at the intersections of development and Indigenous Peoples' rights, and she recently founded the Research and Advocacy Group on Hunter Gatherer Education (https://site.uit.no/hg-education/). Jennifer was a member of the SOGIP research team, and she is currently a member of the international thematic network JUSTIP.

Neal B. Keating is an associate professor of Anthropology at The College at Brockport, State University of New York (SUNY), with research interests in political ecology and culture theory. At the suggestion of a Cayuga beadwork artist, he began a study of Indigenous Peoples' rights-making at the UN Permanent Forum on Indigenous Issues (UNPFII) in 2007. In 2010, this study led to fieldwork in Cambodia to better understand the relations between rights-making at the UN, and observable conditions of life in the territories of Indigenous Peoples. He has published on the struggles for land rights that involved

Kuy and Bunong peoples. He is currently working with indigenous communities in Cambodia and Vietnam on a transnational project to revitalize the Bunong language. He has also collaborated with Haudenosaunee artists, resulting in a book, numerous exhibits, and a short film.

Justin Kenrick is a senior policy advisor at the Forest Peoples Programme, which supports forest peoples in their efforts to determine their own futures. He has a PhD in anthropology from Edinburgh University, where he is also currently a research fellow. His work is mostly in Kenya, the DRC, and Scotland, at the intersection between community land rights, ecological needs, and sustainable livelihoods. He has been engaged with various international mechanisms, including the Whakatane Mechanism of the IUCN, the World Bank safeguards, and REDD+. He also works on land reform and related issues of self-determination in Scotland, where he is a director of Edinburgh Portobello's Transition Town, of Life Mosaic, and of Action Porty. He has been working intensively with the Elgon Ogiek and the Sengwer since 2011.

Laurent Lacroix is a sociologist and has published numerous articles in Europe and Latin America on indigenous issues in Bolivia and the genesis of the Plurinational state, on the making of Indigenous Peoples' rights at global levels, and the processes of change in Bolivia. From 2006 to 2009, he was the scientific coordinator of the international team "Governance and Gender" at the Graduate Institute of International and Development Studies under the North-South NCCR program, and he chaired the Bolivian Studies Association from 2011 to 2015. He is a member of the Francophone section of the International Work Group for Indigenous Affairs (IWGIA). Laurent was a member of the SOGIP project from 2010 to 2015.

Fabien Le Bonniec has a doctorate of Anthropology from the Graduate School of Social Sciences (Ecole des Hautes Études en Sciences Sociales, EHESS) and is a professor of Anthropology at the Catholic University of Temuco, in Chile, where he is also a researcher at the Research Center for Interethnic and Intercultural Studies (Núcleo de Investigación en Estudios Interétnicos e Interculturales). He is also an associate researcher at the Interdisciplinary Institute of Social Issues (Institut de Recherche Interdisciplinaire Sur Les Enjeux Sociaux (IRIS), Paris, France. He is a member of the International Thematic Network JUSTIP, coordinated by Irène Bellier, and he is currently working on the issues of Mapuche territories and justice.

Charles R. Menzies is a member of Gitxaała Nation (an Indigenous nation on the north west coast of Canada) and a professor in the Department of Anthropology at the University of British Columbia. His research projects deploy techniques including ethnographic film, coastal and alpine archaeology, and ethnography within an Indigenous intellectual tradition. Menzies current research explores practices of cultural resurgence in the mountainous coast of Gitxaała territory.

Martin Préaud is an anthropologist, a member of the SOGIP team, and a research adjunct at James Cook University; he also contributes to the "Anthropology of perception" team at the CNRS Laboratory of Social Anthropology. Since 2002, he has been working with Aboriginal groups in Australia, particularly in the Kimberley region and also at an international level. His work focuses on the relational dynamics that shape indigeneity in Australia and beyond, questioning and analyzing the mechanisms of settler colonialism and the tensions between *indigeneity* and *creolization*. He has published many articles and chapters on these topics. Martin was a member of the SOGIP research team from 2010 to 2015.

Brian Thom, an associate professor of Anthropology at the University of Victoria, has worked for over 25 years with Coast Salish communities in British Columbia, Canada. He has focused on the recognition of Indigenous land rights and jurisdictions, attending to the cultural and political priorities of their engagements with the ongoing legacies of colonialism. From 1994–1997 to 2000–2010, he worked as a researcher, a senior advisor, and a negotiator for several Indigenous communities involved in comprehensive land claims negotiations. In 2010, he founded the University of Victoria's Ethnographic Mapping Lab (http://ethnographicmapping.uvic.ca). His publications attend critically to state-reinforced discourses of overlapping claims. He also published an ethnography examining political ontology in reconciling land rights. Thom has been associated to the SOGIP project and is a current member of the JUSTIP network (led by Irene Bellier). He is part of the Centre for Indigenous Conservation and Development Alternatives (http://cicada.world).

Acknowledgments

This work is the fruit of collective research conducted by the project SOGIP, led by Irène Bellier, director of research at CNRS (National Center of Scientific Research) in Paris, from 2010 to 2015. The complete title of the project indicates the scope of the research in which we engaged: *Scales of Governance – The United Nations, the States, and Indigenous Peoples: Self-Determination in the time of Globalization.* The motivation behind launching SOGIP was to investigate the potential for the UN of the Declaration on the Rights of Indigenous Peoples (UNDRIP), as a new international norm adopted in 2007, to change the situation of Indigenous Peoples around the world. Toward this end, our research team worked in a dozen countries on four continents, to better understand the links between the "scales of governance" in different regions and situations. SOGIP was funded by the European Research Council, in the 7th program framework of the European Community (FP7/2007–2013 *Grant Agreement* n° 249236, www.sogip.ehess.fr).

This book is a collection of contributions from several members of this interdisciplinary research team (Irène Bellier, Leslie Cloud, Verónica González González, Stéphanie Guyon, Jennifer Hays, Laurent Lacroix, Martin Préaud), and from other colleagues who participated in a scientific panel organized by Bellier and Hays in 2013, at the American Anthropological Association (AAA) meetings: *Anthropological Engagement with Indigenous Peoples' Rights: Following the trails from global to local and back again in search of sustainable futures* (Neal B. Keating, Justin Kenrick, Charles Menzies, Brian Thom). The chapters in this book are the product of an extremely enriching bilingual exercise undertaken in order to achieve simultaneous publication in two languages. Six chapters were delivered in English, and five in French, and each one was translated into the other language – this made for very complex editorial work. The coordinators of this volume would like to thank all of the authors for their patient participation in this process. We also acknowledge the translators (whose names appear in footnotes of the translated chapters). We also thank the publishers at Routledge (for the English version) and L'Harmattan (for the French version) for their support in the production this book.

Indigenous peoples' rights

Global circulation, colonial heritage, and resistance

Irène Bellier and Jennifer Hays

Introduction

The adoption of the United Nations Declaration on the Rights of Indigenous Peoples (UNDRIP) on the 13th of September, 2007 marks a turning point in the global recognition of indigenous peoples and their rights. This remarkable achievement is, however, embedded in a long process of negotiations – one that, as the chapters in this book make clear, is still ongoing. This book seeks to contribute to a deeper understanding of these processes, and how they are taking shape at different scales of governance.

Although it is impossible to identify a clear starting point for the international movement for indigenous peoples' rights, highlighting certain key events over recent decades gives us a sense of the course of this important global social movement, which challenges current economic and political power structures. In the 1970s, a series of meetings organized in Geneva by the United Nations Committee on Non-Governmental Organizations (NGO Committee) on racism and racial discrimination, apartheid, and decolonization raised awareness within the UN about the concerns of indigenous peoples. In September 1977, the first conference on discrimination against indigenous peoples in the Americas took place. Representatives from 60 nations attended (activists from other countries having been blocked by their governments), including peoples from 16 countries in the Americas, and almost 50 international NGOs (Morin 2005, 2006). This conference was followed by the UN Conference on Racism (1978), the fourth session of the Russel Tribunal in Rotterdam (1980), and the UN Conference on Indigenous Peoples and the Land (1981). At these meetings and others, indigenous peoples addressed the United Nations with the aim of putting an end to the various activities that had been robbing them, exploiting them, treating them like incapable minors, and causing them to disappear as distinct cultures and languages. They requested the creation of a UN working group to examine their situations and to develop standards of protection.[1]

1 This history is described in greater detail in Bellier, Cloud, and Lacroix (2017). See also the film produced by indigenous youth in 2013, sponsored by the Indigenous Peoples Centre for Documentation, Research and Information (DOCIP), which has served as the technical secretariat for indigenous people at the UN since 1978. https://www.docip.org/en/oral-history-and-memory/youth-empowerment/ (last accessed 3 February 2019).

In meetings of the World Council of Indigenous Peoples (1972–1996), indigenous representatives elaborated a list of 14 principles, formalized at the Panama Conference (1984), that laid out the terms that would be discussed at the UN Working Group on Indigenous Populations (WGIP). A quarter of a century later, these principles would become the Declaration on the Rights of Indigenous Peoples (Daes 2008: 13). This was the beginning of a global movement that started in the Americas and spread to the other continents. The aim of the movement was to recognize and promote the rights of these social groups, who are scorned by the dominant social groups and more powerful actors. Currently, UN estimates are that there are approximately 370 million indigenous people, living in 90 countries (UN-SOWIP 2009: 12). These groups are subject to various forms of recognition (or more often, denial) in countries where they reside (Bellier 2013).

In 2007, the United Nations Declaration on the Rights of Indigenous Peoples (UNDRIP) became the first declaration of the UN General Assembly to have been drafted and finalized in direct negotiation with representatives of the rights-holders themselves – indigenous peoples. Intensely negotiated with representatives of national governments for over 25 years, UNDRIP complements the focus on the rights of the individual elaborated in the Universal Declaration of Human Rights, by articulating the collective rights of indigenous peoples. It recognizes the right of indigenous peoples to govern themselves – in other words, the right to self-determination (Charters and Stavenhagen 2009). Indigenous peoples are therefore new subjects of international law (Anaya 2000).

The recognition of this right marks the beginning of a new era for indigenous peoples' participation in global governance bodies. It also marks the beginning of a series of studies on the various rights that the UNDRIP articulates, on the means to implement them (Hartley, Joffe, and Preston 2010; Allen and Xanthaki 2011), and on the situations of indigenous peoples with regard to certain rights, in particular land rights, cultural rights, and political rights (Bellier, Cloud, and Lacroix 2017). An important aspect of these studies is the urgent need to connect the very local situations of indigenous peoples, with international legal standards and processes. Most of these studies focus primarily on one level, for example, on how UN mechanisms address indigenous issues (Rodríguez-Piñero Royo 2009), or how indigenous peoples' rights are interpreted in a region, for example, by the Inter-American Court of Human Rights (Rodríguez-Piñero Royo 2006; Rinaldi 2012), or by the African Court of Human and Peoples Rights (Baldwyn and Morel 2013). These studies provide critical insight into how these rights were defined, and how they are interpreted. This in turn allows us to understand the progress, or setbacks, that we observe following political and governmental changes. Many studies also examine the struggles of indigenous peoples to protect their territories, to resist large-scale development projects, or regarding public policies that affect them, such as in education or health, for example.

In the context of these transformations connected to the recognition of the rights of indigenous peoples in international human rights law, a question surfaced for jurists and anthropologists alike: that of how such an international apparatus, universal in scope, is translated locally. The research project SOGIP (*Scales of Governance: the United Nations, the States, and the Indigenous Peoples, 2010–2015*),[2] coordinated by Irène Bellier, worked to better understand how the principles and concepts relating to the rights of indigenous peoples circulated between several scales – from the United Nations spaces where the various actors associated with indigenous issues meet, to the level of the most remote villages. This circulation can be understood as an effect of the present phase of globalization, but it also bears witness to something else that is particular *to* globalization, which integrates the economic, political, and the legal, while simultaneously exacerbating the contradictions between the affirmation of identities and integration into a global space. To better grasp this phenomenon, SOGIP launched a large-scale comparative study, involving several countries on four continents. The research project assembled an interdisciplinary team including sociologists, political scientists, a jurist, and several anthropologists. Each of these disciplines regards the situation of these highly marginalized, stateless peoples from a different angle, and the data collected by members of the team allowed us to establish a common analytical framework, both through comparativism and through the resonance generated by the analysis (Bellier 2007).

Although the project was grounded in an ethnographic approach, the object was not to document cultural content of indigenous groups, but to understand their situations and their relations with the state and international organizations, in articulation with what was happening on the "sites" of international negotiations and discussions concerning the rights of indigenous peoples. The "global" is often contrasted with the "local." Over the last few decades, however, the borders between these spaces have been called in to question, and when we examine this distinction in regard to indigenous peoples, we find a dual phenomenon. On the one hand, international agencies are increasingly present on the "local" ground for various activities (such as humanitarian aid, or development and education projects); analysis of their modes of operation feeds the analytical streams of the anthropology of institutions (see, for example, Müller 2013). On the other hand, indigenous people are traveling to the United Nations and other places of international governance, in order to make their voices heard, and possibly to benefit from the projects decided upon within these bodies (Brysk 2000). Working at the intersections of these two dynamics, the SOGIP team examined the processes of recognition, the legacies of colonialism, issues of territory and land ownership, education, development, and other issues at the heart of the indigenous peoples' rights movement.

This book is one output of the project SOGIP. The majority of the case studies presented here include those from the project's major areas of research on scales of governance, by scholars from the SOGIP research team. Some of the

2 Research funded by the European Research Council, in the 7th program framework (FP7/2007-2013 Grant Agreement ERC, 249 236). The team of 12 researchers engaged in collaborative research at the level of the UN and in ten countries on four continents. http://www.sogip.ehess.fr/?lang=en (last accessed 20 February 2019).

chapters are also based on the research of other anthropologists from the network that the project expanded. Each author is a specialist in indigenous issues in the country they are describing, and each chapter explores a particular case, closely examining its specific cultural, historical, political, and social contexts. The common context for all of these chapters is the extreme political, economic, and social marginalization faced by indigenous peoples today. This context, and its implications for research, is highlighted in the sections that follow.

Indigenous peoples' rights – the global and the local

Indigenous peoples' concerns often seem to be but an epiphenomenon of current global crises – economic crises, climate change, mass migration, fears of terrorism, food crises, water shortages, general uncertainty, local conflicts – the list is long. Although their concerns relating to environmental destruction, forced displacement, food security, water, and physical safety are at the heart of many current global issues, the problems experienced by indigenous peoples themselves are generally not a high priority for governments, nor are they fully addressed by international institutions.

Research over the past two decades (see, for example, Sutherland 2003; Gorenflo et al. 2012) has demonstrated a clear link between human cultural and linguistic diversity, and biodiversity, indicating that the future of humanity on this planet is intimately bound up with that of the environment and other species – and our own diversity.[3] A critical component of the indigenous peoples' rights movement is about establishing the right to maintain this diversity, through land and resource rights, and the rights to maintain or establish systems of governance that protect indigenous culture and languages. Because their ways of life are grounded in spiritual and material relationships with the territories and natural resources from which they gain their subsistence, indigenous peoples are also particularly concerned about environmental protection. This concern connects them to another global movement, that seeking "environmental rights." In this arena, indigenous peoples promote their image as guardians of nature and protectors of diversity, and on these grounds they resist both their expulsion from protected areas, and disputes over land titles that protect the territories where they live. There is a strong argument to be made that protecting indigenous peoples' rights is in the interest of all of humanity, along with environmental protection. Unfortunately, this is not the dominant global perspective; as Keating

3 UNESCO has recognized this link since the Declaration on Cultural Diversity in 2001. The Director General, Koïchiro Matsuura emphasizes that the declaration "elevates cultural diversity to the level of a "common heritage of humanity," "as necessary for the human race as biodiversity is for the order of life," and makes its defense an ethical imperative, inseparable from respect for the dignity of the human person" (https://unesdoc.unesco.org/ark:/48223/pf0000127162_fre). This connection is reaffirmed by UNESCO as it relates endangered languages: http://www.unesco.org/new/en/culture/themes/endangered-languages/biodiversity-and-linguistic-diversity/ (last accessed 4 February 2019).

puts it in his chapter in this volume: "It is a tragic irony that, in a time when it is becoming clear that the dominant socioeconomic forces are driving the planet to a global ecological disaster, peoples whose world-making practices constitute truly sustainable life-systems are considered by the powerful to be inferior and expendable" (130).

The perception that indigenous peoples and their lifeways are of lesser value is not new, and it is not by chance. The concept of indigenous peoples' rights threatens the immediate interests of powerful political, economic, and social actors, at different levels (see the chapters of Hays, Keating, Thom, Préaud, Cloud and LeBonniec, Kenrick). Respect for indigenous peoples' rights threatens the interest of global corporations who have everything to gain from plundering local resources – including those of indigenous peoples (the most problematic sectors in the eyes of the international indigenous peoples' movement are the forestry industry, the mining industry, and agribusiness). The opposition that arises from the movement of indigenous peoples and its allies, especially environmentalists, threatens the interests of governments and national actors who benefit from the control of these resources, and who gain by ceding their exploitation to multinational companies. At the local level, stronger, more numerous, or more daring neighbors encroach on indigenous territories – even when these lands are protected legally. Some of these are also primarily seeking basic livelihood needs, and very often this encroachment is ultimately driven by the same forces that are pushing for expansion into all exploitable terrain.

Since the colonial era, the portrayal of indigenous peoples and their lifestyles as "primitive" or "inferior," "immoral," and even "nonexistent" has underpinned the discourse of domination. This denigration has supported – consciously or not – the displacement or slaughter of people, the spoliation of their territories, and the appropriation of their resources. Although the outright murder of people is less acceptable now than it was in previous centuries, there is a worrying and growing number of killings of indigenous leaders and environmental advocates (Forst 2017). The forced displacement of people and communities (which leads to the appropriation of territories), the denigration of livelihoods (often deemed illegal), and the criminalization of indigenous acts of resistance (and the application of anti-terrorism laws) are still part of a process of elimination of indigenous peoples. To complement these alarming facts, existing statistics[4] clearly indicate that indigenous populations are under severe pressure in terms of simple respect for fundamental rights, such as basic health, housing, social, and economic needs.

In Australia, for example, according to figures available in 2016, the life expectancy of Aborigines is 10.6 years lower than the national average; 59% of aboriginal students finish secondary school, in contrast to 85% of non-indigenous students;[5] 18% of Aboriginals are unemployed – a figure three times higher than

4 The collection of such statistics is only possible when ethnic statistics are not authorized by the state, in other cases data must be gathered or estimated by other means.

5 https://www.creativespirits.info/aboriginalculture/education (accessed 4 February 2019).

that for non-Aboriginals;[6] 75% of Aboriginal youth are under judicial control, compared to 3% of non-Aboriginal youth; and Aborigines, who represent 2.8% of the population, constitute 26% of the prison population.[7] In French Guiana, the number of Wayana and Wayampi suicides is currently nearly 25 times higher than in the metropolis, and ten times higher than that of the Guianese coast.[8] Alarming indicators such as these bear testimony to an extreme social, economic, and political marginalization that is found in virtually every state whose population includes indigenous peoples.

Indigenous peoples are not passive in this dynamic. In a global economy driven by access to natural resources, they fight against the forces seeking to monopolize the resources on their territories, especially large extraction projects (of wood, gas, petrol, and gold, among other resources) and large-scale development (mega-dams, road, rail, or river infrastructures) trigger opposition. Such operations are usually carried out without the consultation – and therefore without the consent – of the populations concerned, triggering a resistance that is a major force behind the recent growth of the indigenous peoples' rights movement.

This movement is in many ways, and at different scales, engaged in a struggle against a global hegemonic order. Such struggles are by nature not clearly defined. They are diffuse and local and they are taking place on multiple stages – but they are also increasing globally, and we can observe similar forms around the world, patterns that can be traced to common driving forces. For example, deforestation affects forest peoples of the Amazon, the Congo Basin, or in Asia; large infrastructural projects and mines are responsible for similar ecological disasters from one territory to another. Struggles against these forces are taking place on the ground, in active resistance to projects for which the peoples concerned were not consulted prior to their realization. They also take place on a discursive level, for example, in negotiations at governmental, non-governmental, and international forums about the definition of terms to describe "autochthony" or "indigeneity"; in relation to the elaboration of laws and policies; or in regulations defining the participation of representatives of indigenous peoples in the work of national and global institutions.

Each chapter of this book explores how the international indigenous peoples' rights movement works in a specific locality, and at different levels. Each provides a close look at a particular case and examines from that perspective the struggle of indigenous peoples when they come up against more powerful systems that have the power to define the terms of debate. These include the United Nations system (Bellier, Hays, González-González, Keating), the state system (Guyon, Lacroix, Préaud), the legal system (Thom, Cloud and Le Bonniec), the conservationist system (Kenrick), or the university system (Menzies and Butler).

6 https://www.creativespirits.info/aboriginalculture/economy (accessed 4 February 2019).
7 https://www.creativespirits.info/aboriginalculture/law (accessed 4 February 2019).
8 http://www.leparisien.fr/societe/nouvelle-vague-de-suicides-chez-les-amerindiens-de-guyane-04-12-2018-7960299.php (accessed 4 February2019).

Human Rights norms are defined in global offices and are universal in scope. These efforts are, however, strongly influenced by Europe and the Americas, reflecting the existence of more developed regional human rights systems in these regions than in Africa and Asia (Bellier, Cloud, and Lacroix 2017). These global norms are intended to affect the circumstances of (sometimes very small) groups of people around the world, living in a very wide variety of situations. In order to do this, they must pass through national legislative systems and also gain acceptance by governmental and nongovernmental stakeholders at various levels within any given country. How does this happen? Anthropologist Sally Engle Merry (2006) asks how transnational ideas on human rights are adopted in local social settings, and how they "move across the gap between a cosmopolitan awareness of human rights and local sociocultural understandings" (2006: 38). All the chapters in this book address the ways in which transnational approaches to human rights meet local preconceptions, at different levels, and the ways in which these cultures, values, and approaches at regional, national, and local levels are reflected in international approaches to indigenous peoples' rights.

Indigenous peoples and the postcolonial

The category of *indigenous peoples* does not have a substantive definition, neither legally nor in the UNDRIP – the declaration that concerns them and that serves as a reference in various spaces of global government (including frameworks of international human rights, of climate change, or the sustainable development goals). As a political category, it is *relational* (Saugestad 2001; Bellier 2012), defined not by specific characteristics attached to a large group of humans, but by the relations that they have with other social groups and institutions of power. Locally, this context is defined according to relations with neighboring groups (indigenous and non-indigenous). The relational context extends to local and national institutions, and is reconfigured in the global context by the way in which these international institutions (and the various branches of the UN family) understand the issue and construct their programs of action.

An earlier work of the SOGIP team focused on identifying the conditions of the emergence of this category in international law, and its reception on all the continents (Bellier 2013). Here we would like to simply recall that this relational category is also defined by the dispossession, historically and ongoing, of indigenous peoples. This dispossession is characterized by the exercise of violence and the displacement of certain groups, by the control of individuals placed on the margins of citizenship, by racism, and by socioeconomic and political marginalization. These practices have been legally and morally justified by concepts such as *terra nullius*, and in previous eras, they were supported by a (religious–scientific) framework that considered indigenous peoples as less than human; and by a vision of "progress" that invalidated forms of organization and livelihood other than what the western model had developed. Within the social sciences and in the modern era of human rights, the legal, religious, and moral assumptions that justified colonialism are generally considered scientifically invalid.

We read in the preamble of the UNDRIP:

> *Affirming further* that all doctrines, policies and practices based on or advocating superiority of peoples or individuals on the basis of national origin or racial, religious, ethnic or cultural differences are racist, scientifically false, legally invalid, morally condemnable and socially unjust.

Nonetheless, the structures that these views and practices underpinned are largely still in place, and the assumptions of the colonialist era are still reflected in the dominant discourses of many governments, and even development organizations. The overall result is the general de-valorization and structural marginalization of indigenous peoples everywhere – even in countries that have legislation in place specifically dealing with indigenous peoples' rights (see especially the chapters of Lacroix and Préaud).

Can the global movement of indigenous peoples change the experience of communities at the local level? Or are the concepts that it mobilizes, around rights and political tools, essentially a discourse circulating internationally, relatively disconnected from practical situations? To what extent are current categories and processes an extension of colonial categories and processes? The questions raised by indigenous peoples, locally and internationally, put into tension different legalities and call us to question the relative weight assigned to them. What, for example, is the weight of human rights, in the face of the weight of commercial rights, or the weight of contract law? In the colonial era, indigenous peoples were threatened primarily by governments and their legislation – this is no longer the case. A major question today is whether the principles of the indigenous peoples' rights movement can hold in the face of powerful multi-national corporations, and others interested in exploiting the resources on indigenous territories. In what ways are these issues linked to broader human and environmental concerns?

To answer these questions, it is necessary to examine global and national structures and institutions, and the individuals who navigate these arenas in order to promote the interests of their communities. We need to understand the international language that is being used, and the conditions of its reception and reproduction in the national cultures, to ultimately see how indigenous representatives – as colonized subjects who were largely left out of the changes initiated at the various stages of decolonization – appropriate the available tools. These are not the fields of classic anthropological study, and this book is the fruit of a multidisciplinary approach that combines the methods of anthropology (in order to get a deep understanding of *culture* and cultural contact) with the perspectives of sociology, history, law, and political science (in order to grasp the social and political dynamics in their temporal thickness) and finally with law (which provides both a grammar for ordering pluralism [Delmas-Marty 2006] and a promise of protection, in this case of indigenous peoples).

Structure of this book

This volume consists of 11 chapters, each addressing an aspect of indigenous peoples' rights and "postcolonial" law, using case studies from different parts of the world and the international arena. All of the chapters consider constraints on indigenous agency associated with both indigenous *participation in*, and *exclusion from* national and international frameworks, and the implications thereof. A common underlying question has to do with the ways in which international human rights norms and mechanisms are strategically mobilized by different actors, for highly divergent ends. Indigenous peoples' rights are defined and agreed upon internationally, but must be enacted at regional, national, and local scales. The interactions between these different scales are at the heart of this volume.

Each chapter describes an empirical case, from the UN, Namibia, Mexico, Cambodia, French Guiana, Peru, Canada, Australia, Chile, and Kenya. The majority of the chapters (Bellier, Hays, González-González, Guyon, Lacroix, Préaud, Cloud and Le Bonniec) are by researchers affiliated to the SOGIP project, and who conducted research directly under the auspices of this project, using various methods but grounded in ethnography. These chapters are complemented by four papers from scholars in our network who participated in a panel organized by the editors of this volume at the annual meeting of the American Anthropological Association (AAA) in November 2013 (Keating, Thom, Kenrick, and Menzies and Butler).[9] A central question of the AAA panel was the role of anthropologists in the indigenous peoples' rights movement, in recognition that anthropologists were among the first to alert the UN about the serious violations of human rights against these populations. It was anthropologists, for example, who in the late 1960s founded the first organizations to support the rights of indigenous peoples, including the International Working Group for Indigenous Affairs (IWGIA), Survival International, and Cultural Survival (see Morin 2005, 2006). Fifty years later, anthropologists continue to play various roles in the global movement towards the recognition of indigenous peoples and their rights – a movement that has had multiple consequences and that confounds simple analysis.

What methodologies do we use to gain a clearer picture of where exactly the problems and potential solutions lie? How do – and should – researchers and indigenous people collaborate, and in which contexts? Many chapters address this issue explicitly. The chapters of González-González and Guyon point out the historical role of anthropologists and other academics in defining the terms and shaping policy toward indigenous peoples. Some of the authors are explicitly supporting indigenous peoples in their efforts to overcome severe historical and current injustice. Keating, Thom, and Kenrick all describe different ways

9 The executive panel organized by Bellier and Hays at the AAA was titled "Anthropological Engagement with Indigenous Peoples' Rights: Following the trails from global to local and back again in search of sustainable futures."

in which they have engaged with indigenous communities, organizations, and individuals – as a fellow activist, an advisor, or a facilitator.

This kind of participant observation yields rich insights into the complexities of the movement, and what indigenous peoples are up against in their struggles for self-determination. Since 2001, Bellier has participated in the UN international negotiation scene alongside indigenous peoples. This perspective from the inside, close to the actors engaged in a series of claims, has proven highly fruitful for understanding the nature of relations between states and indigenous peoples, ways of overcoming colonial history, and the role of UN officials in this complex apparatus. Hays has conducted research as a consultant for local and international organizations advocating for indigenous peoples' rights in southern Africa since 1999. Menzies and Butler address more precisely in their chapter what collaboration between the university and Aboriginal communities means. By reversing the relationships between researched and researchers, and by rethinking ways of collaborating to produce knowledge for both, they highlight the biases inherent in the traditional relationship between academics and indigenous peoples and describe a model for collaboration between universities and indigenous communities.

A central theme of the SOGIP project and the panel was *scales of governance*. Each author followed a thread between scales – from global institutions, to national governments, to local situations – examining how a particular aspect of indigenous peoples' rights takes shape in a particular geographical area. The strong resonance between our observations from different field sites became obvious, and this comparative approach greatly enriched the research of the project. Questions addressed include the following: How can community decision-making processes and leadership practices interface with the hierarchical and bureaucratic structures of national and international governments and organizations? In what ways must indigenous peoples learn – and conform to – national and international systems? In what ways are their demands also shaping these systems?

This approach highlighted the ways in which the terms used to refer to indigenous peoples, and the discourses around the diverse peoples that are included in this category, take on a special significance in these areas of dialogue and negotiation. These terms are not merely interchangeable labels but express underlying philosophies about the peoples themselves, their place in society, and in some cases their legal status (see Hays, Guyon, Préaud). In effect, the international term *indigenous peoples* reflects simultaneously their recognized status as peoples (with collective rights) and the structural nature of the extreme marginalization, and sometimes violence, that such peoples continue to experience. In some cases, discourses and definitions contribute to the characterization of indigenous peoples within a country as terrorists or otherwise criminals (Cloud and Le Bonniec), negate their identities (Préaud), or in some cases even render them non-existent (Kenrick) – thus effectively excluding them from participation in decision-making processes.

Likewise, political terms describing national approaches to ethnic and economic diversity encapsulate philosophies about inclusion and exclusion, self-determination, and assimilation. These terms and their meanings are also negotiated at national and international levels (Bellier, González-González, Lacroix). At the UN, in the forums that accept them as observers and that give them the floor, indigenous peoples' representatives work to master the specific discourse of this global institution, in order to be able to advocate for their rights – and in some cases to change that discourse itself (Bellier, Keating). As they do so, they escape from the conditions in which they are dominated in the local or national arena, to manifest themselves as actors at the international level.

This book on scales of governance and indigenous peoples' rights has been organized into three sections. The first section examines the ways that ideas and individuals circulate among the different scales; the dynamic of rights-making at global, national, and local levels; and the relations between these levels. The second examines the ways in which colonial legacies continue to play out in countries that consider themselves to be "post-colonial" and the implications of this for contemporary indigenous peoples. The third part traces processes of "invisibilization" that indigenous peoples experience, and the ways in which they are resisting these processes. Most of the papers touch on all of these topics, which are inherent in the dominant structure of global politics and central to indigenous peoples' realities.

Section I: Circulating between the scales

The global indigenous peoples' rights movement has taken shape largely within the structures of the UN. Originally, indigenous peoples sought to bypass antagonistic states and to appeal to international law, in order to make their voices heard. In practice, operating at the international level has meant that indigenous representatives (individuals and organizations) have been required to conform to the procedural and behavioral requirements of the UN, including, for example, the use of one of the six authorized languages (Arabic, Chinese, English, French, Russian, and Spanish) and the discursive forms of the UN milieu. At the same time, indigenous leaders and representatives have brought their own forms of discourse and codes to the international level. Some indigenous leaders, and even entire peoples, have pointedly chosen to remain outside this process, which they view as being dictated by interests (for example, of states or corporations) that go against the aims and spirit of indigenous peoples' rights. An example of this is the Zapatista movement in Mexico, which seeks the autonomy of these peoples and their structures at the local level in Chiapas, and the emancipation of the people included in this group.

What impact has the indigenous peoples' rights movement had on the articulation and circulation of these representatives and individuals as political subjects? How have the individuals and organizations involved in the movement overcome racial and colonial stereotypes and legal prejudices? On the one hand, we can see that participation in UN dialogues and the movement between the different platforms of action have had a powerful transformative effect on individuals, who are gradually converted by these institutions into "legitimate interlocutors." On the other hand, it is through this participation and by learning the workings of power, that indigenous representatives introduce new subjects into the international agenda.

These men and women are participating because of their own particular situations, but their concerns are much broader, and in some cases extend to all of humanity. For example, in the 1970s, early recognition of climate change led Inuit peoples to create a cross-border organization – the Inuit Circumpolar Conference (ICC) – to address the impact of global warming on their livelihoods, and to alert the States to this phenomenon. This was the beginning of a growing awareness within the Western world of the global nature of the problem. The work that we are trying to describe – this articulation of specific indigenous issues with the great world debates – is the product of a movement that, in a certain way, is very pragmatic. For any given topic discussed at the UN, for instance, within the sustainable development goals (i.e., poverty, gender, education, climate), indigenous delegates must remind decision-makers that they exist, that they are affected, that they have rights, and that they have a collective voice – which States and the international system must learn to hear and respect. Our observation of international scenes over a period of 20 years reveals the extent to which international and national categories and legal systems have evolved to respond to indigenous warnings and demands.

The participation of indigenous peoples in the international sphere necessarily is at the level of individuals, who travel to the global centers as representatives of their communities and are then charged with taking information back to their home countries and communities. These individuals are the "middlemen" described by Merry (2006), whose work straddles disparate worlds and vocabularies. They function as translators, not only of words but of concepts, values, philosophies, and cultural assumptions. These international norms must also be interpreted in the context of regional discourses, which in turn influence and are in communication with national discourses. Even though we can observe changes over time, the concept of indigeneity is firmly established on the American continent (see Cloud, Gonzalez, and Lacroix, 2013). This is not the case, however for Africa or for Asia, two continents with a large number of such peoples.

Hays describes the particular wariness around the concept of indigeneity in Africa, which international organizations seeking to promote indigenous peoples' rights in the region must navigate. Keating notes how the Asian context influences the acceptance of the Cambodian (and other Asian) governments of the principles of indigenous peoples' rights. González-González details the regional political trends in approaches to indigenous peoples in Latin America, and how the circulation of concepts and approaches at the regional level influenced the activities of UN organizations on the ground in Mexico.

The first chapter of this book addresses the participation of indigenous peoples in matters that concern them. This question is of particular interest to Irène Bellier, who argues that this participation is a direct consequence of the adoption of the UNDRIP – the negotiations of which she observed at the UN. According to this declaration, indigenous peoples have the right to their own institutions, including those that represent them. Bellier's research provides a window into the complexity of the UN system and highlights the current limits of the status of indigenous participation. She identifies a core within this system, that she calls the "matrix" and that was the home of the early movement advocating for indigenous peoples' rights. This "matrix" is made up of key institutions for this movement and continues to gather representatives of states and indigenous peoples on a regular basis: it is a key point of articulation of indigenous issues in the international system. Bellier illustrates how indigenous peoples have defined, within this space, political modes of action and organizational forms; these forms also frame their participation in other major events underpinned by the UN, such as Global Summits, in which indigenous peoples participate as one of the nine sections of international civil society (i.e., the "major groups"). Representatives of indigenous peoples request recognition of their own representative organizations, rather than the current model of accreditation in which they are recognized as constituting non-government organizations, and Bellier describes the tension that the demand for this alternative form of participation evokes from the "club of states." Such negotiations have been made possible by the recognition of the right of indigenous peoples to self-determination, and testify to the importance of the UN in this regard. But the states continuously delay the resolution of this complex issue, expressing particular concern about the diversity and the number of indigenous peoples. This is a clear indication that indigenous affairs are always matters of ongoing negotiation, and that different states, with their different cultures, do not share a common vision.

In the following chapter, Jennifer Hays examines the International Labour Organization (ILO) Convention 169 on Indigenous and Tribal Peoples (C169), the only binding international mechanism on indigenous peoples' rights. She describes the strategies used by the ILO to promote the principles of indigenous peoples' rights in Namibia. The particular characteristics of the colonial experience in Africa in general, and especially in southern Africa, have resulted in a situation in which the concept of indigeneity is highly contested. Although it has some of the most progressive policies and laws in the region, the Namibian government resists the term "indigenous peoples," referring instead to "marginalized minorities" – a difference in terminology that reflects divergent cultural perspectives and political priorities and results in very different approaches to "development." This chapter examines the complications involved with promoting international mechanisms regarding the rights of indigenous peoples, on a continent where the concept itself is often seen as a neo-colonial imposition.

Mexico, on the other hand, has been an influential role-player in the definition of indigenous peoples' rights at national and international levels, as well as in the Latin American region. As González-González demonstrates in Chapter 3, which analyzes the role of the UN in defining the political position of indigenous peoples in the country, Mexico has also itself been greatly influenced by the historical patterns and the politics of the region, and the approach of the UN. González-González traces these patterns and policies: from the assimilationist approaches of the first decades of the twentieth century, through the regional trend toward multiculturalism in the 1980s and 1990s. She describes a certain convergence of public policies with a global governance system, now founded in the right to self-determination for indigenous peoples, and participation in matters that concern them. She argues that, in order to analyze the ability of the UN to promote indigenous peoples' rights, we must take a close look at the ways in which the institution interacts with national structures and populations. This, she argues, "is central to a better understanding of the complex, multi-level dynamics in which the UN operates, and the opportunities and challenges these dynamics create for the implementation of international policies regarding indigenous peoples." In this chapter, we see the ways in which the "global" penetrates the "local."

In the following chapter, Neal Keating examines the UN structures from another perspective – that of rural Cambodian activists seeking support for their claims of violations of indigenous peoples' rights from which they are suffering. Here we see how the "local" penetrates the "global." The case study described in this chapter about Cambodian activists and their efforts to deliver a statement at the United Nations Permanent Forum on Indigenous Issues (UNPFII) provides a detailed exploration of the circulation of both people and ideas between the many levels. The "transplantation" (cf. Merry 2006) of indigenous peoples' rights has so far proven difficult to achieve in Asia, not only because of states' lack of political will, but also because of conflicted understandings of collective indigenous identities and human rights that extend across and within different scales of rights-making. Cambodia is so far the only nation-state in mainland Southeast Asia to formally acknowledge the existence of indigenous peoples as distinct groups with collective land rights; however, this recognition is highly ambivalent and uncertain. Keating makes clear the complex situation in which these activists find themselves trying to harmonize the three main scales of indigenous peoples' rights: the international where the concepts are generated, the national at which states choose to recognize or ignore human rights, and the local scale, the daily lives of indigenous peoples.

These complexities are further bound up with the heritage of colonialism. Although the dominant perception today is that we are living in a postcolonial world, this history continues to reverberate throughout the politics, policies, discourses, and interventions aimed at indigenous peoples. The chapters in the next section provide detailed illustrations of the ways in which this happens.

Section II: Colonial legacies

The four chapters in this section bring to the fore both continuities and discontinuities with previous colonial and racist structures, practices, and realities by looking at policies and government structures that are formulated with the specific intention of addressing indigenous peoples' concerns or representing their interests. In some cases, indigenous peoples are a numerical and/or political majority, as in Bolivia; in others they are marginal, as in French Guiana, Canada, and Australia. The chapters in this section address the ways in which indigenous peoples remain subject to particular kinds of force at local and national levels, sometimes disguised and sometimes overt, that limit their ability to advocate for their rights.

These chapters examine the constraints on indigenous agency at the local or national level, including cases in which these constraints are framed within a positive discourse about the rights of indigenous peoples, and with reference to the international framework. In what ways – and in what contexts – are states and other parties (such as multinational corporations) able to ignore, circumvent, or manipulate international mechanisms, and what impact does this have on indigenous peoples' rights? How are concepts of "rights" used as discursive tools for promoting and/or undermining indigenous interests? What mechanisms do states use to dispossess, incorporate, maintain control over, or oppress indigenous citizens, and how do indigenous peoples respond? How does the global notion of *indigenous peoples* circulate and stimulate new policies?

The chapter of Stéphanie Guyon examines the various ways in which the indigenous peoples of French Guiana (and other local inhabitants of the overseas territory) have been governed throughout the last century. Much of this history is reflected in the various categorizations of groups, and the labels that were used by the political and administrative authorities. In tracing the terms used to designate the Amerindians, and the descendants of the "Maroons," from 1946 to the present, she illustrates how these are related to the public policies applied to them within a "postcolonial" framework. Guyon highlights the role of ethnologists in these processes of defining categories and public policies toward indigenous peoples in French Guiana, noting also the ways in which the ethnologists' own approaches were in turn defined by the politics of the time. This historical dimension allows us to better understand how the indigenous communities of French Guiana engage with the indigenous peoples' rights movement today.

In the following chapter, Laurent Lacroix explores the enormous challenges of introducing a completely new normative framework founded in decolonization, and giving indigenous peoples a central place in the definition of the state. Bolivia made history in 2005 with the election of the president Evo Morales, who claimed indigenous descent, and who proceeded to reform the constitution to advance the construction of a "Unitary Social State of Pluri-national Communitarian Law"[10] and to incorporate UNDRIP. Although the plurinational state project firmly locates itself within a "postcolonial" perspective, Lacroix examines numerous contradictions – in particular the absence of any real involvement by most indigenous peoples in the national government – and highlights the mechanisms through which the colonial past still asserts itself.

One of the most destructive legacies of colonialism was the acquisition of indigenous lands, and their redefinition as private property. In Chapter 7,

10 As defined in the Bolivian Constitution of 2009: https://www.constituteproject.org/constitution/Bolivia_2009.

Brian Thom examines this issue and highlights a set of vexing challenges at the intersection between Canadian property rights and policies toward indigenous peoples. He focuses on a case that, since 2007, has been heard by the Inter-American Commission on Human Rights. In dispute is the absolute reluctance of the state to engage in titling and demarcation of indigenous titles on land that is privately held by third parties. In the absence of binding forms of international intervention, Thom examines the prospects for intervention by the international community and discusses the strategies indigenous peoples have developed to implement the political and moral will of the international community. He focuses both on the choice made by the indigenous peoples of British Columbia to employ international arguments regarding human rights, and on the legal constraints that they are operating under. Based on the experiences of the Coastal Salish, Thom considers the broader implications for indigenous peoples looking to the international community for resolution and reconciliation that are elusive within national legal frameworks.

Australia shares with Canada the experience of being a former British colony, and in Chapter 8 Martin Préaud questions the claim that Australia is post-colonial. In particular, he illustrates how development processes allow the structure of colonial domination to be reproduced in the context of the promotion of the rights of indigenous peoples. Focusing on a mining-related industrial project involving a consortium of multinational companies, he analyzes the ways in which the different stakeholders positioned themselves around three "competing" legal regimes: aboriginal law or customary rights; Australian law; and indigenous peoples' rights. Préaud explores how the different terms employed, and conditions imposed, put aboriginal Australians in an extremely vulnerable position, noting that they "take up the defense of their rights at their own risk (p. 210)." His analysis shows that, within Australia, "far from being abolished or eradicated, the colonial institutions continue to operate deep down [and] to structure social and power relations (p. 205)." Préaud also describes how within these relations, claims of fulfilling indigenous peoples' rights become tools of repression under "the cultural logic of elimination" that is characteristic of settler states.

This aspect of the repression of indigenous peoples – that which renders them less visible at the national and international levels – and the ways in which this invisibilization is countered are at the center of the chapters of the next section.

Section III: Resisting processes of invisibilization

For many indigenous communities, dispossession and occupation of their territories; intervention in their private, family, and community lives; and a high rate of detention of individuals are all part of their daily realities. In this context, the role of multinational corporations – particularly extractive industries – is increasingly problematic and results in the displacement of indigenous peoples, the contamination of their lands and waters, and the destruction of their livelihood bases.

Decisions made by distant, powerful actors (who are completely disconnected from the local situation) affect the livelihoods, health, and rights of indigenous communities, who often have little or no recourse. Since the colonial era, specialists from the social sciences have played an important role, sometimes defending indigenous peoples and their rights, and sometimes defining them in ways that suited the interests of colonial powers. In either case, the research and its results have almost always been controlled by the researchers – not indigenous communities themselves.

Considering this state of affairs, these authors identify the means indigenous peoples have available to them to mobilize the mechanisms of international law, in order to mediate their relations with multinational corporations. They also reflect upon the power relations that underlie negotiations – between indigenous peoples and their communities, and states, multinational corporations, international legal structures, and universities. In what contexts do laws permit the use of physical force to control indigenous peoples today? How do environmental protection projects or research programs exert violence, symbolic or real, over indigenous communities? This in turn requires consideration of the mechanisms of inclusion and exclusion in the context of the rights of indigenous peoples.

In Chile, the Mapuche are striving to recover lands – which they claim never to have surrendered – and to have the right to be different (Gros 1999). In this context, Leslie Cloud and Fabien Le Bonniec analyze the dual dynamics of *criminalization* of the Mapuche by public authorities, and *judicialization*, which has become part of the indigenous peoples' rights movements' repertoire of action in this country. The state does not constitutionally recognize its indigenous peoples, but an "indigenous" law identifies them as "ethnic groups" (a category much criticized in Latin America today) and recognizes their right to form "communities" or "associations." In order to delegitimize their claims based on indigenous peoples' rights, the state has adopted the strategy of criminalizing their activities by transforming Mapuche activists into "terrorists." In addition, for almost 20 years, the territorial disputes between Mapuche, private land owners, multinational corporations, and the Chilean government have been characterized by a two-way process of increasing judicialization. In the face of numerous threats, in order to protect their land and environment the Mapuche have made use of the justice system and international mechanisms. However, within this same context, they are also prosecuted in special tribunals, through the imposition of security legislation. This chapter analyzes the strategies implemented by each party in terms of procedures and interpretation of rights and identifies the limits and challenges of intercultural dialogue in the Chilean judicial system. In the case of Chile – where the Mapuche territory was reduced to 5% of what it was prior to conquest – we see how difficult it is for indigenous peoples to be fully recognized because the issue of territorial control is at the very heart of the conflictual relations with the state, and with private enterprises.

The following chapter shows how a similar logic of denial is employed by the state authorities in Kenya, but in quite another way. Justin Kenrick describes the ongoing case of Sengwer evictions from the Embobut Forest, in Kenya. Recent evidence indicates that the continuing habitation of forest peoples like the Sengwer is beneficial to the forest. Kenrick points out, however, that these evictions, enacted by the Kenya Forest Service (KFS, the forest guards of Kenya), are taking place under the auspices of conservation projects funded by important international and national donors. He argues that these evictions, which are often brutal, are human rights violations that are deeply embedded in the global structure and discourse of conservation. Without specific attention to indigenous peoples' rights within such projects, he argues, people like the Sengwer are not only the victims of discrimination, they are "rendered invisible" as their very existence is denied by those who stand to immediately benefit from their evictions.

The final chapter of this book, by Charles Menzies and Caroline Butler, focuses not on indigenous peoples' rights mechanisms per se, but on another globalized institution – the university. Based on a long-standing collaborative experience in Gitxaała, British Columbia, the authors argue that traditional relationships between researchers and indigenous communities define indigenous community members as lacking in "capacity" and in need of "development." In such paradigms, the real capacity and deep knowledge of indigenous communities and individuals is rendered invisible. This chapter describes an innovative collaborative program designed to invert these hierarchies and re-define the research relationship. The authors do not argue against research – to the contrary, they clearly recognize the need for good collaborative research efforts that draw upon the capacity, knowledge, and strengths of both community and academic institution. But these need to be carefully defined, because, they ask, "how can we document indigenous land rights if we cannot concede a community's jurisdiction over our research?"

This dilemma described by Menzies and Butler – the structurally unequal relationships between researchers and indigenous communities – is one that the authors of this book were all attuned to. Some of the authors were working in close collaboration with indigenous individuals toward the aims that they had defined. Others have worked closely with indigenous organizations or with international and local human rights organizations, contributing their research to larger projects designed to promote indigenous peoples' rights. Still others have conducted interviews, legal research, and archival research in an effort to better understand the political, economic, and historical contexts in which indigenous peoples' rights efforts are being played out today. The authors share the view that research can – and should – help to understand the struggles of indigenous peoples, whose universal dimension concerns us all. Such understanding is important and necessary, in large part because these groups still need support from civil society in order to resolve the disputes that pit them against states and corporations like agroindustry and mines. Understanding how people and discourses move, and evolve, between the different levels at which their rights are being contested is critical to this effort.

Conclusion

We are living in a moment in history that is defined by an immense contradiction between a global trend toward the recognition of the rights of indigenous peoples, and a global race to exploit the wealth of the territories they occupy and use for their economic and cultural livelihood. This book aims to show the extent to which, in such a context, indigenous societies, peoples, and nations can rely on international law to protect their right to self-determination. The chapters presented here highlight how, in this context, different courses of action are decided at different scales. The very possibility to observe this movement of people between the scales of law and politics, and to witness how this circulation can change circumstances of oppression, is itself a particular characteristic of the international indigenous peoples' movement. If the potential positive effects of legal and political instruments describing indigenous peoples' rights were to become manifest, an era of denunciations could give way to an era of recognition. But history teaches us that "progress" is reversible and that the process of democratization of states, which allows indigenous peoples to benefit from certain forms of recognition of their fundamental rights, is never guaranteed. The vision of human rights, including indigenous peoples' rights, is one whose achievement threatens the powerful forces that are driving the brutal exploitation of lands, territories, and resources – and the human beings engaged in organic and vital relations with them.

In 2012, on the twentieth anniversary of the Rio Conference on Sustainable Development, indigenous peoples advocated for the inclusion of the concept of *culture* alongside the three pillars of sustainable development (economic, social, and environmental) in the declaration "The future we want."[11] Ultimately their proposal was not retained in the text that was adopted by the Heads of State and Government, primarily because of a narrow interpretation of the concept of *culture*.[12] In this specific arena, however, *culture* is synonymous with *life*. For the human species, as for all species, the diversity of life forms is what allows for adaptation to new circumstances – such as those that the future certainly holds for us – and to reproduce. Ultimately, the maintenance of this diversity of life and cultures, to which indigenous peoples belong and of which they are the expression, enriches us all. The research presented in this book informs global, national, regional, and local processes, all of which affect the lives of local communities. The authors seek to contribute to an understanding of how indigenous peoples' rights, as they are invoked in global governance today, might define a more just and sustainable future for humanity, by creating a space for those peoples that are striving to preserve our rich diversity.

11 https://sustainabledevelopment.un.org/content/documents/733FutureWeWant.pdf (last accessed 20 February 2019).

12 Voir Bellier (2015).

References

Anaya, James. 2000. *Indigenous Peoples in International Law*. New York: Oxford University Press.

Allen, Stephen, and Alexandra Xanthaki, eds. 2011. *Reflections on the UN Declaration on the Rights of Indigenous Peoples*. Oxford: Hart Publishing.

Baldwyn, Clive, and Cynthia Morel. 2013. "Recourir à la Déclaration des Nations unies sur les droits des peuples autochtones dans des actions en justice" In *Peuples autochtones dans le monde. Les enjeux de la reconnaissance*, edited by Irène Bellier, 265–290. Paris: L'Harmattan.

Bellier, Irène, ed. 2007. "La mesure de la mondialisation." *Cahier du Gemdev* 31.

Bellier, Irène. 2012. "Les peuples autochtones aux Nations unies: un nouvel acteur dans la fabrique de normes internationals." *Critique internationale* 54: 61–80.

Bellier, Irène, ed. 2013. *Peuples autochtones dans le monde. Les enjeux de la reconnaissance*. Paris: L'Harmattan.

Bellier, Irène. 2015, "L'avenir que veulent les peuples autochtones. Stratégies institutionnelles, mobilisations collectives et force de négociation, à Rio +20" In *Regards croisés sur Rio+20: La modernisation écologique à l'épreuve*, edited by Jean Foyer, 259–279. Paris: Editions du CNRS.

Bellier, Irène, Leslie Cloud, and Laurent Lacroix. 2017. *Les droits des peuples autochtones. Des Nations uies aux sociétés locales*. Paris: L'Harmattan.

Brysk, Allison. 2000. *From Tribal Village to Global Village: Indian Rights and International Relations in Latin America*. Stanford, CA: Stanford University Press. https://books.google.fr/books?hl=en&lr=&id=Q9q04JD4NBMC&oi=fnd&pg=PR9&dq=info:JZMfPwevjq0J:scholar.google.com&ots=LpB1farOC_&sig=2zTydL9gYjjNLF7k-DlWdKzf4LOg&redir_esc=y#v=onepage&q&f=false (accessed 28 January 2019).

Charters, Claire, and Rodolfo Stavenhagen, eds. 2009. *Making the Declaration Work: The United Nations Declaration on the Rights of Indigenous Peoples*. Copenhagen: IWGIA.

Daes, Erica-Irene. 2008. "An Overview of the History of Indigenous Peoples: Self-determination and the United Nations." *Cambridge Review of International Affairs* 21 (1). http://www.sfu.ca/~palys/Daes-2008-HistoryOfIndigPeoplesAndSelf-Determination.pdf (accessed 25 January 2019).

Delmas-Marty, Mireille. 2006. *Les forces imaginantes du droit (II). Le pluralisme ordonné*. Paris: ed du Seuil.

Forst, Michel. 2017. Report of the Special Rapporteur on the Situation of Human Rights Defenders. UN Doc: A/HRC/34/52. https://documents-dds-ny.un.org/doc/UNDOC/GEN/G17/011/75/PDF/G1701175.pdf?OpenElement (accessed 23 February 2019).

Gorenflo, Larry J., Suzanne Romaine, Russell A. Mittermeier, and Kristen Walker-Painemilla. 2012. "Co-occurrence of Linguistic and Biological Diversity in Biodiversity Hotspots and High Biodiversity Wilderness Areas." *Proceedings of the National Academy of Sciences* 109 (21): 8032–8037. https://www.pnas.org/content/109/21/8032 (consulté le 21 janvier 2019).

Gros, Christian. 1999. "Ser diferente por (para) ser moderno, o las paradojas de la identidad." *Análisis político* 36: 3–20.

Hartley, Jackie, Paul Joffe, and Jennifer Preston, eds. 2010. *Realizing the UN Declaration on the Rights of Indigenous Peoples: Triumph, Hope, and Action*. Saskatoo: Purich Pub.

Merry, Sally Engle. 2006. "Transnational Human Rights and Local Activism: Mapping the Middle." *American Anthropologist* 108 (1): 38–51.

Morin, Françoise. 2005. "L'ONU comme creuset de l'autochtonie." *Parcours anthropologiques* 5: 35–42.

Morin, Françoise. 2006. "Les Nations unies à l'épreuve des peuples autochtones." In *Être indien dans les Amériques*, edited by Christian Gros and Marie-Claude Strigler, 43–54. Paris: Éditions de l'Institut des Amériques.

Müller, Birgit. 2013. *The Gloss of Harmony. The Politics of Policy Making in Multilateral Organizations.* London: PlutoPress.

Rinaldi, Karine. 2012. *Les Droits des sociétés traditionnelles dans la jurisprudence de la Cour interaméricaine des droits de l'homme. Le modèle interaméricain de l'interprétation multi- culturelle des droits.* Doctoral thesis in International Public Law, Université de Nice Sophia-Antipolis.

Rodríguez-Piñero Royo, Luis. 2006. "El sistema interamericano de derechos humanos y los pueblos indígenas." In *Pueblos indígenas y derechos humanos*, edited by Mikel Berraondo López, 153–203. Bilbao: Éditions de l'université de Deusto.

Rodríguez-Piñero Royo, Luis. 2009. "'Where Appropriate': Monitoring/Implementing of Indigenous Peoples' Rights under the Declaration." In *Making the Declaration Work: the United Nations Declaration on the Rights of Indigenous Peoples*, edited by Claire Charters and Rudolfo Stavenhagen, 314–343. Copenhagen: IWGIA.

Saugestad, Sidsel. 2001. "Contested Images: 'First Peoples' or 'Marginalized Minorities' in Africa?" In *Africa's Indigenous Peoples. First Peoples or Marginalized Minorities?*, edited by Alan Barnard and Justin Kenrick, 299–322. Edinburgh: Centre for African Studies, University of Edinburgh.

Sutherland, William. 2003. "Parallel Extinction Risk and Global Distribution of Languages and Species." *Nature* 243: 276–279.

UN-SOWIP. 2009. *State of the World's Indigenous Peoples.* New York: United Nations Department of Economic and Social Affairs (UNDESA). https://www.un.org/esa/socdev/unpfii/documents/SOWIP/en/SOWIP_web.pdf (accessed 24 Febraury 2019).

Part I

Circulating between the scales

The global, the national, and the local

1 Participation of indigenous peoples in issues affecting them

A matter of negotiation at the United Nations

Irène Bellier[1]

The United Nations (UN) holds a unique place in the constellation of stakeholders in an international movement that aims to secure the representation of indigenous peoples, and their "participation in issues affecting them."[2] This ultimate global institution, where visitors meet the diversity of the world, is an extremely complex space, far removed from any indigenous environment, with its own regulations and a vast labyrinth of action networks, interconnected mechanisms and decision-making bodies to which only international officials hold the keys. Nonetheless, indigenous peoples that participate in UN meetings – whether as experts or delegates, involved for many years in international talks or simply as occasional visitors – think they can have some influence at the UN. This is because, in the late 1970s, the UN established structures for examining issues affecting indigenous peoples, which opened up an epistemological and legal political space for considering the definition of this particular category, and handling of these questions. Since the early 1980s, the participation of indigenous peoples has been the object of renewed discussion, and since 2010 the issue has been under consideration by the United Nations General Assembly (UNGA). This chapter examines the various ways in which indigenous peoples' representatives have been involved in issues that are affecting them since they first appealed to the UN to define their rights. I will concentrate on the changes that have occurred since the adoption of the UN Declaration on the rights of indigenous peoples, in 2007.

Background

Several UN bodies welcome indigenous delegations, who represent 90 countries, some 5,000 languages, and an estimated 400 million people.[3] The examples

1 Translated by Cadenza Academic Translations, revised by Jennifer Hays, and the author.
2 This expression is commonly used at the United Nations.
3 The UN calculated the figure of 370 million people in the 1980s, but their services were unable to carry out a precise global census. The Scales of Governance & Indigenous Peoples (SOGIP) website hosts a map showing the world distribution of indigenous peoples, with information on the names of these peoples, and their demography compared to state or regional populations,

I will present in this chapter bear the hallmarks of the protocols defined by the UN member states, but function according to modalities that differ from those of national politics. These examples depict representatives of indigenous peoples, men and women, young and old, holding discussions with representatives of member states, and in particular with those from their own states. Indigenous delegates work with international officials, participate in global dialogue, and establish alliances with non-indigenous organizations. During the last decade or so, some have taken on major responsibilities including the roles of UN Special Rapporteur and President of the UN Voluntary Fund for Indigenous Peoples, as well as acquiring membership of UN Programme administrative boards.

The UN Declaration on the Rights of Indigenous Peoples (UNDRIP) was developed and negotiated at length within the sector of the institution focused on human rights and was finally adopted by the UNGA in September 2007 (Charters and Stavenhagen 2009; Bellier 2012a). Based on my observations,[4] I consider the part of the UN where indigenous issues are at the heart of debate as a kind of "matrix" in which the participation of indigenous peoples is the driving force of developments – in this paper, the term *matrix* refers to this specific space. This space represents a model that the most senior indigenous delegates desire to both improve and reproduce within the UN.

In addition, since the first Earth Summit (Rio Conference, 1992), indigenous delegations have been actively engaged in discussions about the future of the planet, including debates surrounding sustainable development and climate change, in their capacity as one of the nine major groups of "civil society" consulted by "the international community" (the member states) on a regular basis. In this wider context, they mobilize techniques of participation and internal decision-making developed in the matrix, but are also confronted by the inherent limits of these conferences, in which they are only one of many stakeholders. Although indigenous delegations are indeed consulted, their members have great difficulty securing involvement with preliminary proceedings (the drafting of outcome documents, for example) and struggle to assert their desires in negotiations controlled by the representatives of member states. The final

based on data provided by the official sites (national census) or by various non-governmental organizations such as the International Work Group for Indigenous Affairs (IWGIA), in instances where such data is not available. View the map at http://www.sogip.ehess.fr/ and http://www.sogip.ehess.fr/squelettes/cartes_sources.pdf.

4 In my academic work on indigenous peoples' rights, I have followed (and continue to follow) the annual meetings of several UN bodies, for working sessions lasting one to two weeks: in Geneva, from 2002 to 2006, the Working Group on Indigenous Populations (WGIP), created in 1982, and the Working Group on the Draft Declaration (WGDD), created in 1995, both of which were dissolved after the adoption of UNDRIP by the Human Rights Council in 2006; in New York, since 2002, the United Nations Permanent Forum on Indigenous Issues (UNPFII); and in Geneva, since 2008, the Expert Mechanism on the Rights of Indigenous Peoples (EMRIP). This work has involved participating in plenary sessions, parallel events, and indigenous assemblies (caucuses) which are an informal part of the United Nations but have been essential in building the international indigenous movement and developing a shared knowledge base.

outcome documents sometimes contain only one of the numerous points that indigenous representatives wanted to include. In negotiations over the content of such documents, the symbolic fight for the inclusion of terms carrying global significance, such as "the rights of indigenous peoples," is extremely fierce.

In 2010, the UNGA decided to hold a high-level plenary session on indigenous peoples as part of the conclusion of the Second International Decade of the World's Indigenous People. This project, announced at the tenth session of the UN Permanent Forum on Indigenous Issues (UNPFII), in 2011, provoked a strong reaction from indigenous peoples. Bolstered by the advances resulting from UNDRIP and the right to self-determination that it recognized, they called for the conference to be organized with indigenous representatives, using the slogan "Never again without us." This resulted in a meeting of the General Assembly that, for the first time in the history of the UN, was organized with the "full and complete participation" (in UN language) of indigenous peoples. The full description of this conference was the "High-Level Plenary meeting to be known as the World Conference on Indigenous Peoples" (HLPM/WCIP).[5] This act of undeniable symbolic power turned over a new page in the history of the relationship of indigenous peoples with the international community. This conference resulted in an "outcome document," which was adopted in September 2014 (UN 2014), and which completes the provisions of the UNDRIP for involving member states as well as the whole UN system – its agencies, programs, and funds – in the global implementation of the rights of indigenous peoples. The two declarations have the same legal value and complement each other, and they expressly mention the issue of participation to meetings "on issues affecting them": in Article 41 of UNDRIP, and in paragraph 33 of the document adopted by the HLPM/WCIP.[6]

Through an exploration of these different situations involving the international movement of indigenous peoples, and the current debates about how their participation might be improved, this chapter seeks to explain the organizational forms of the movement and examines in more detail the general characteristics of the participation of indigenous delegates in relevant decision-making processes, and the policy domains in which they are involved. The first section locates the UN space dedicated to the examination of "issues affecting them" and outlines the kind of alliance that indigenous delegates can form there with state, non-state, and international actors. The second section deals with the modes of

5 This long expression comes from the UN lexicon, and its terms specify the hybrid character of the organization to which the international movement has demanded and obtained association.

6 Article 41 of the UNDRIP says: "The organs and specialized institutions of the United Nations system and of other intergovernmental organizations contribute to the full implementation of the provisions of the present Declaration through, in particular, the mobilization of financial cooperation and technical assistance. The methods of ensuring the participation of indigenous peoples in discussions of issues affecting them must be put in place."

Paragraph 31 of the outcome document says: "We commit to consider, at the 70th session of General Assembly, ways to enable the participation of indigenous peoples' representatives and institutions in meetings of relevant United Nations bodies on issues affecting them, including any concrete proposals made by the Secretary General in response to the request in OP40."

participation of indigenous peoples in discussions held by the UN in the areas of sustainable development and the fight against climate change. The third section considers the implications of the HLPM/WCIP for indigenous peoples' "participation in issues affecting them," which, since September 2015, has been the object of an intense consultation process and of debates held by UNGA itself.

The UN: an experimental matrix for indigenous peoples

The indigenous peoples' movement, which emerged at the end of the 1970s, strives for recognition of the rights of populations formerly or currently dominated by colonial states, and for their implementation as outlined in UNDRIP. Its development has required the establishment of a base of understanding regarding the definition of *indigenous peoples* and identification of the problems they face, both of which are grounded in the pioneering study led by Ecuadorian sociologist José Martínez Cobo, who in 1971 was named Special Rapporteur of the United Nations on the problem of discrimination against indigenous populations by the former Commission on Human Rights.[7] This work was followed by studies carried out by members of the Sub-Commission on Prevention of Discrimination and Protection of Minorities,[8] as part of the Working Group on Indigenous Populations (WGIP). A number of reports issued by this body focus on the particularly complex themes raised by the status of indigenous populations, who are neither state actors nor strong economic actors, and not simply "minorities" or sections of civil society. Of particular note was the "Study on Treaties, Agreements and other Constructive Arrangements between States and Indigenous Populations" (Martínez 1999) and the report "Indigenous Peoples' Permanent Sovereignty over Natural Resources" (Daes 2004), which raised the issue of relationship to the land.[9] The Martínez report explores the validity of the "nation to nation" relation involving the treaties signed between representative powers of the current state and its (still living) peoples on the territory to which they apply. The Daes report focuses on *sovereignty*, a politically sensitive term recalling that, by law, the member states cannot deprive peoples of resources that are necessary to their existence. These two reports, in particular, examine the nature of the relationship between these populations and the notion

7 The Commission on Human Rights was, from 1946 to 2006, the principal organ of the United Nations Economic and Social Council charged with human rights issues. It was composed of 53 members. It has been superseded by the Human Rights Council, which is composed of 47 members directly elected by the UNGA.

8 This body changed its name in 1999 to become the Sub-Commission on the Promotion and Protection of Human Rights. It was dissolved in 2006 as part of the reform which led to the establishment of the Human Rights Council.

9 The relationship to the land, examined by the UN and elsewhere at a judicial and political level, manifests itself as a series of imagined ontological projections of relation between man and nature, which indigenous peoples link to "spirituality" and thus establish their symbolic link with "Mother Earth" (cf. Bellier and González 2015). This link establishes the relation between "life" and "culture" that indigenous delegations desire to see handled at a political level.

of *territory* in the light of international law, as well as the current value of the relations established by acts that were legal at the time of conquest or invasion.[10] Both go straight to the heart of the issue of recognition by member states and the international system of these populations as "indigenous peoples," a term proposed by Martinez Cobo in the first working definition.

Birth of a relational political category

The work carried out between 1973 and 1986 by Augusto Willemsen-Diaz, a Guatemalan official at the UN who helped Martínez Cobo to identify the problem, was presented in five volumes and led to a working definition.[11] This definition was based on a multi-criteria approach capable of resisting the essentialist paradigm of "the indigene;"[12] in particular, it recognized the existence of indigenous "cultural patterns," "legal systems," and "social institutions." They are, as the rapporteur says:

> peoples and nations ... which, having a historical continuity with pre-invasion and pre-colonial societies that developed on their territories, consider themselves distinct from other sectors of the societies now prevailing on those territories, or parts of them ... [and which] are determined to preserve, develop and transmit to future generations their ancestral territories, and their ethnic identity, as the basis of their continued existence as peoples, in accordance with their own cultural patterns, social institutions and legal system. (Martínez Cobo 1986)

These notions of patterns, systems and institutions are important to recall, because the states have based their domination of indigenous peoples on the denial of exactly such forms of organization.

The International Labour Organization (ILO) had already produced elements of this definition, but its Convention 107, passed in 1957, is marred by a vocabulary now seen as outdated and assimilationist (see also Hays, and González González, both in this volume). It was reworked into Convention 169 (C.169), which became, in 1989, the first legally binding tool recognizing a series of rights held by indigenous and tribal peoples. C.169 does not define indigenous and tribal peoples per se, but it does provide criteria for identifying the peoples that it aims to protect. Self-identification is considered as a fundamental criterion,

10 See also the study carried out by Tonya Gonnella Frichner on the Doctrine of Discovery, at the request of the UN Permanent Forum (Gonnella Frichner 2010).

11 This pioneering study within the United Nations system, on the theme of discrimination against indigenous populations, was ordered by the Economic and Social Council in 1971 and completed in 1985. The main chapters derive from the reflections of the WGIP, from 1982, and the collection was then published by the United Nations. It can be consulted in facsimile form.

12 For more on the semantic charge of the terms "indigenous" and "autochthon" as utterances, see Bellier (2009a, 2009b).

as are the following elements indicated by the ILO publication *Indigenous and Tribal Peoples in Practice: A guide to the Convention 169*:

> Elements of *tribal* peoples include: Culture, social organization, economic conditions and way of life differ from other segments of the national population, e.g. in their ways of making a living, language, etc.; [they have their] own traditions and customs and/or special legal recognition.
>
> Elements of *indigenous* peoples include: Historical continuity, i.e. they are pre-conquest/colonization societies; Territorial connection (their ancestors inhabited the country or region); Distinct social, economic, cultural and political institutions (they retain some or all of their own institutions). (ILO 2009: 9; my emphasis)[13]

The ILO C169, as well as following legal instruments such as UNDRIP in 2007 and the outcome document of the HLPM/WCIP in 2014, highlight the existence of "their own social organizations" and "their own political institutions," in addition to "traditional customs and laws"; three elements on which this chapter will focus attention.

The study of the discrimination against indigenous populations and the work of the ILO led to the emergence of two characteristics that are important for our examination of participation. First, the international system considers these populations to be "distinct and specific," by their ways of life, their language and cultures, and their social organizations and institutions. Second, the global sharing of information, on which Martínez Cobo's study was based and which has accelerated since the 1980s, has highlighted the communal nature of the discriminatory processes that these populations face. This has led to the UN anchoring its approach to these problems within the paradigm of fundamental rights.

It was during the negotiation of UNDRIP, which lasted 25 years from the beginning of the WGIP process until the adoption of this document by the UNGA,[14] that the emergence of the category "indigenous peoples" raised the issue of recognition of the right to self-determination of these entities. Article 3 states that:

> Indigenous peoples have the right to self-determination. By virtue of that right they freely determine their political status and freely pursue their economic, social and cultural development.

13 This guide is intended to interpret the Convention 169 in light of current international law. The text of the Convention is available at: https://www.ilo.org/dyn/normlex/fr/f?p=NORMLEXPUB:12100:0::NO::P12100_INSTRUMENT_ID:312314

14 143 states out of 191 voted in favor of UNDRIP, and only four voted against: Australia, Canada, United States and New Zealand rallied in 2009 and in 2010 (on the negotiation process see Charters and Stavenhagen 2009).

The participatory experience

The reflection on "the participation of indigenous peoples on issues affecting them," explicitly referred to in Article 41 of UNDRIP, is the fruit of this negotiation, which I have discussed elsewhere (Bellier 2011, 2012a, 2014; Bellier, Cloud, and Lacroix 2017), signaling the importance of the participation of indigenous delegates in the institutionalization of this political sphere.

Nigel Crawhall notes that this was the first time the beneficiaries of an instrument participated in its negotiation (Crawhall 2013), while Claire Charters, a Maori jurist, sees this participation as reinforcing the very legitimacy of UNDRIP[15] (Charters 2009). The program of action for the Second International Decade of the World's Indigenous People (2005–2014) itself highlighted the importance of ensuring their effective participation[16] in decision-making, and the Expert Mechanism on the Rights of Indigenous Peoples (EMRIP) studied this issue in 2010 (UN 2010). The expert report explicitly locates this question in the framework of international human rights (C.169, regional instruments) in light of the other problem raised by UNDRIP, namely the exercise of the right to self-determination and the right to free, prior and informed consent: "the principle is of fundamental importance for indigenous peoples' participation in decision-making" (paragraph 34). The EMRIP study is composed of 100 dense paragraphs that describe indigenous institutions and internal decision-making processes in a range of diverse situations: it notes the existence of indigenous parliaments and legal systems, tackles the issue of the place of women as well as transformations following "the intrusion of external and foreign factors, be it during colonization, later during nation-state building, or in the present day" (paragraph 61).

Ten years after the adoption of UNDRIP, indigenous leaders are still pressuring the UN system and, through it, the rest of the world, to respect the rights of indigenous peoples. Armed with an understanding of the vastness of the system, the incoherencies resulting from the specialization of UN bodies and the resistance of member states to recognize "in good faith" actions that affect them when they are not themselves stakeholders in all the relevant discussions, they want to go beyond discussion. They support their calls with the final sentence of Article 41 of UNDRIP, which indicates that "ways and means of ensuring participation of indigenous peoples on issues affecting them shall be established."

15 For Charters, a specialist in international law, the degree of legitimacy of an instrument depends on three factors which allow it to be measured: the quality of the process from which it issues – in terms of transparency, formality, coherence and predictability; the inherent justice of its content; and the extent of the engagement that international actors have with its implementation, whether they are individuals, civil societies, multinational companies, states or indigenous peoples (Charters 2009: 284–285).

16 One of the five objectives of the program, as adopted by the General Assembly in its resolution 59/174, was to promote the full and effective participation of indigenous peoples in decisions which directly or indirectly affect their lifestyles, traditional lands and territories, their cultural integrity as indigenous peoples with collective rights or any other aspects of their lives, considering the principle of free, prior and informed consent (A/60/270, paragraph 9 (ii)).

Several specialized UN organs welcome indigenous peoples as observers, listening to them and involving some of them as expert officials or secretariat members. This is the case for the two current organs, the PFII and the EMRIP. These bodies were established following two working groups that experimented with the first forms of participation by indigenous delegates and laid the foundations for their more permanent association with UN affairs. The Working Group on Indigenous Populations (WGIP, 1982–2006), established within the Human Rights Commission in order to examine discriminatory situations and draft legal provisions for remedying the marginalization of indigenous populations and preventing their extermination, widened the rules of participation. All indigenous organizations could participate, providing they held accreditation prior to each meeting but without necessarily needing to be international non-governmental organizations (NGOs) of the kind accepted by the rest of the world.[17] The Working Group on the Draft Declaration (WGDD, 1995–2006), established within the same Commission in order to negotiate the language and provisions of UNDRIP, also prompted the international movement to organize into regional and thematic groups, now known as *caucuses* (Bellier 2007).

Institutionalization of indigenous issues

I have described elsewhere an ethnographic perspective on the role of the UN in the creation of indigenous political actors (Bellier 2012b) and argued that, over the years, the international movement has been institutionalized according to unwritten rules. Indigenous organizations, of which only some (such as the International Indian Treaty Council, IITC), hold the most general accreditation from the Economic and Social Council (ECOSOC), are a driving force. Indigenous leading figures of various origins, whose declarations and strong capacity are recognized, have been involved for many years and are progressively co-opted by international agencies. Civil society organizations, such as the International Work Group for Indigenous Affairs (IWGIA), based in Copenhagen, and the Indigenous Peoples' Centre for Documentation, Research and Information (DOCIP), based in Geneva, also form part of the movement. IWGIA publishes annual reports on the situation of indigenous peoples in different countries and supports regional indigenous groups by helping them to organize themselves, facilitating dialogue with the UN and member states (particularly those described as "friendly" (Bellier 2011), and providing assistance to UN secretariats to facilitate delegate travel (Dahl 2009). Since 1978 DOCIP has been a technical secretariat for the movement, archiving its political declarations,[18] and collating all UN documents relating to indigenous

17 These criteria are defined by the Committee on Non-Governmental Organizations. For more on this topic see Daes (2008:31–32).

18 Docip has compiled a collection of statements made by indigenous organizations since 1978, classified by UNESCO as World Heritage. https://www.docip.org/en/our-services-solutions/news/single-news/article/the-speaking-of-indigenous-people-recognized-as-the-world-humanite-heritage/ (accessed 22 January 2019).

issues and international human rights. It also provides training to new delegates so that they can work effectively, draws up the agenda for all international meetings of interest to indigenous peoples available to them, and helps them with the practical aspects of UN working sessions.

It is not possible within the scope of this chapter to include the names of all those indigenous and non-indigenous organizations involved in the international movement, which come from all regions of the world. Meetings of the UNPFII in New York and the EMRIP in Geneva bring together 1,000 to 1,500 delegates every year, of which around 10% are subsidized by the Voluntary Fund for Indigenous Peoples.[19] About half of all the delegates are very regular participants (activists) and deeply invested. Among these, some work principally within UN mechanisms, for example, treaty organizations like the UNPFII and the EMRIP, while others specialize in areas that concern them but that are also relevant to international governance, such as sustainable development and climate change, to which I will return later. Rather than being exhaustive, I will highlight three elements that are important in understanding the "participation of indigenous peoples in issues affecting them."

The first is a bursary system, established by the High Commissioner for Human Rights in 1997, for training young indigenous people to understand the legal field and the workings of relevant UN bodies.[20] Every year, around 20 indigenous people complete this training, which lasts 3 to 6 months and is shared between an English-speaking university and a Spanish-speaking university, in conjunction with UN mechanisms.[21] This provides them with the skills and knowledge to take on the work of defending rights in their own countries.

The second is the regional organization of the international movement, which differs from the way in which member states are grouped at the UN.[22] In the area of human rights, member states fall into five regional groups (Africa; Asia; Eastern Europe; Latin America and the Caribbean; and Western Europe and Other States) that reflect geopolitical history. Indigenous representatives, on the other hand, have organized themselves into an alternative structure, accepted by the different UN departments and comprised of seven "socio-cultural" regions: Africa; Asia; Central and South America and the Caribbean; the Arctic; Central and Eastern Europe, the Russian Federation, Central Asia and Transcaucasia;

19 Established by the UNGA resolution to facilitate the participation of indigenous organizations and institutions, the Voluntary Fund is administered by a team of five people making up the Board of Trustees, who have relevant experience of different sociocultural regions of the indigenous world. For more information, see http://www.ohchr.org/EN/Issues/IPeoples/IPeoplesFund/Pages/IPeoplesFundIndex.aspx (accessed 12 January 2019).

20 See http://www.ohchr.org/EN/Issues/IPeoples/Pages/Fellowship.aspx (accessed 12 January 2019).

21 The training of French-speaking fellows was provided by the University of Burgundy in France until 2010.

22 Numerous other groups exist, such as the G8, G20, G77 (+China), "small island countries," and the European Union, which do not interact with indigenous peoples like the regional groups described here.

North America; and the Pacific. The principle of this regional grouping was developed within the WGDD during the negotiations leading to UNDRIP and it now defines the basis for choosing experts who, at the Permanent Forum, are on an equal footing with the representatives of member states (originating from the five regions outlined above). It represents a structural element of the global movement: the consultations (internal or external) leading to the formulation of a collective indigenous voice (Bellier 2007) are first held regionally, and during debates, the seven regions have the right to express themselves as such (under the names of "African caucus," "Asian caucus," etc.).

The third characteristic of the movement is the growing participation of indigenous women and young people, who introduce more focused issues into the general framework of "indigenous affairs." These two social categories are strongly supported by donors in the context of development policies that identify them as the most vulnerable groups of society. Although at the WGIP, in the 1980s, there was only one assembly bringing indigenous peoples together (named the "global caucus" in the early twenty-first century), today nine caucuses (seven regional and two thematic) are recognized as expressing shared positions and forming the collective indigenous voice.

The caucuses debate positions that will "officialize" this collective voice and prepare newcomers to gain an understanding of the UN, and of techniques for taking part in meetings. Indigenous peoples and NGOs take part on a voluntary basis, but UN secretariat officials and representatives of member states can only do so by express invitation (Bellier 2007). The caucuses are generally co-chaired by two indigenous people, from different language groups (English- and Spanish-speaking for the global caucus, English- and French-speaking for the African caucus) and with male-female parity except for the women's caucus (which does however accept the participation of men); these chairpersons change regularly. Work is mostly carried out remotely, but in person during UN sessions. Indigenous organizations and delegates thus form a unity in diversity, which is an asset in their negotiations with the international community and the representatives of member states.

Indigenous representatives, supported by the UN apparatus that established at its heart a space dedicated to the examination of their affairs, are strongly invested in the bodies described above, which include them as observers, and where they have the right to speak and to be recognized as spokespersons. They are making efforts to occupy an equivalent place in a series of spaces and events that "affect them," but that have a larger scope beyond their own concerns. I refer here to the UN Summits, which cover different areas of human rights.

The participation of indigenous peoples in global discussions

The Summits of heads of state and government are preceded by conferences that define new spaces of political interaction. In these meetings the participation of indigenous peoples, however central it may be, does not result in the same gains they have obtained in the space dedicated to discussion of their own issues. I carried out ethnographic research at two large conferences organized by UN secretariats, one on sustainable development (Rio, 2012) and the other about climate change (Paris, 2015). I observed that these global conferences do have other important effects that result from the inclusion of indigenous representatives in global discussions. At these summits, "indigenous peoples" formed one of the nine *Major Groups* of civil society, alongside: women, children and youth, non-governmental organizations, business and industry, workers and trade unions, farmers, the scientific and technological communities, and local authorities.

The formation of the major group "indigenous peoples"

The concept of the Major Groups, through which the participation of indigenous peoples is organized at this kind of event, emerged at the Earth Summit (1992). At Rio and Paris, as far as I could observe, action by the Major Group of "indigenous peoples" was organized at the core of the international indigenous movement, which depends on the matrix (as described above) in order to develop. But it also organizes itself outside this space in order to tackle the questions of preparatory discussions and the format of negotiations. A key difference is that, in the matrix, indigenous organizations were fully involved in the UNDRIP negotiations (and are still associated with subsequent developments), while in the global space only the representatives of member states are invited to the negotiating table. In the context of the two political domains of development and climate, indigenous peoples are focused on forging a shared position, identifying their areas of interest, mastering relevant terminology, and defining strategies for achieving results during the negotiations. Insofar as the indigenous Major Group is partly made up of the same actors across the two domains, and who can also be found in the indigenous matrix, I will outline the distinguishing features of their modes of participation.

The matrix space dedicated to the examination of strictly indigenous issues is clearly delineated, with annual meetings whose working methods are clear and understood, with funding mechanisms for ensuring the participation of a certain number of delegates, a system for communicating information that is regularly improved, and where expected rules apply for the hearing of observers and the drafting of session reports. None of this seems to work at the Global Summits. My participation-observation at the Global Summits reveals that the international procedures and protocols characterizing the framework of events – which the media and politicians tend to present as unique – are strengthened by repetition. However, these events also follow other rules that indigenous peoples have to learn to master in a very short period of time, and this drives them to develop new practices. Insofar as they make up only one of the parts of civil society consulted during these conferences, and their concerns are diluted within the set of issues that form the object of negotiations, the key issue for their Major Group is how it can exert a certain influence on the decisions to be agreed by the member states when its own approval is not a determining factor (Bellier 2015).

I do not analyze the decisions themselves here, but instead explore the ways in which the Group is organized, which reveals its recourse to forms of organization trialed in the matrix, despite the constraints enforced by the rules of participation of civil society that are in place at this kind of event. Indigenous peoples make their own way in these complex conferences, mastering the necessary codes of access, expression, and coordination. Nonetheless, although this Major Group is highly visible due to the appearance of its members and their spectacular hairstyles and clothing, it has fewer means at its disposal to prepare a negotiating position than other groups in civil society, due to the wide dispersal of its members and their relative poverty. Often, most of them do not know whether they will be able to attend the conference, or obtain the necessary visas, until the last moment.

The 2012 Conference, named Rio+20 as it took place 20 years after the first Earth Summit, seemed unique by virtue of its breadth – tens of thousands of participants were expected – and in the light of expectations generated in global civil society by a new approach to development (see also Foyer 2015). The document *The future we want* foregrounded the idea of the green economy, and discussed the need to find ways of confronting, at a global level, the imbalances between the three pillars of "sustainable development" (economic, environmental, and social), a concept that was successful at the first Rio conference in 1992. In the lead-up to the Rio+20 Summit, whose format differed completely from the annual meetings on indigenous issues in New York and Geneva, indigenous organizations prepared according to forms borrowed from familiar techniques: mobilization of the regional and global caucuses; passing up information to the global caucus, and producing shared messages.

Although similar in scope, the Paris Climate Change Conference was held in another temporality, which highlighted a different form of organization. A highly anticipated event, due to the major significance of climate change as an issue affecting all individuals, it was in fact one of a series of annual meetings called the "Conference of the Parties," or COP. The regularity of the conferences was due to the existence of the Framework Convention on Climate Change which was adopted at the first Rio Summit, in 1992. The Paris conference was the 21st in this series.

Although the first Earth Summit was exemplary in many ways, the adoption of two Conventions (on Biological Diversity and Climate Change) established a *de facto* framework of international action distinct from that conceived of for development. The framework for development followed a different international path, which led to the defining of the *Millennium Development Goals* in 2000, which were reformed in 2015 into the Post-2015 Agenda, framing the current definition of *Sustainable Development Goals.*

The Earth Summit: Rio de Janeiro, 1992–2012 – comparing indigenous participation

At the first Earth summit, in 1992, indigenous peoples played no part in the general conference. However, they did organize a global gathering in a village next to Rio de Janeiro, and produced the Kari-Oca Declaration. This declaration laid out the issue of the land for the survival of their societies, and it introduced the highly symbolic term *Mother Earth* (which has since become trivialized). The use of the possessive pronouns *we/our* testify to the emergence of this collective into the public space and its distinctiveness from the whole of the rest of humanity.

> We maintain our inalienable rights to our lands and territories, to all our resources – above and below – and to our waters. We assert our ongoing responsibility to pass these on to future generations. Nobody will make us leave our lands. We, the Indigenous peoples are connected by the circle of life to our lands and environments.[23]

This *we* is also found in the way in which indigenous peoples have appropriated UNDRIP, which for them represented the equivalent of the United Nations Charter, whose opening words are "We the Peoples" (Bellier and González 2015). In the matrix, the formula "We, the Indigenous Peoples" is regularly used, this *we* forming a counterpoint to the phrase "We, the Heads of State or Government" used in official UN declarations.

Twenty years later, the Major Group "indigenous peoples," fully integrated into conference proceedings, had deepened its criticism of development and sustainable development policies, supported both by self-reference to the ideological core of the rights of indigenous peoples, and their integration into the international system, as peoples constituting civil society. After regional preparations that enabled the formulation of positions in Africa, Central and South America and the Caribbean, North America, Asia, the Pacific, and the Arctic, several dozen delegates from all seven socio-cultural indigenous regions met at the Negotiations Centre (Rio Centro) to decide on a mode of working fit for the particular format of this conference and to fulfill the demands for participation. These were: to draft five key messages for heads of state and the rest of civil society; to identify in the 200-page final outcome document (the subject of the negotiations) the paragraphs concerning their interests and on which they might have an influence; to work on the topics to be discussed by "cluster groups," identify the member states that would preside over these groups and their positions in order to anticipate the arguments they might use; to share participation in these groups (where they did not have the right to speak) between them, together with the reporting of information; and to participate in dialogue sessions of various formats ("dialogue days," "interactive dialogues," and "round tables") where they had the right to speak for two minutes. They also organized Parallel Events based on the matrix model, through which they brought their topics to the attention of the wider public, as with, for example, an event on food security organized by the IITC. Finally, they produced a political declaration in the name of the Major Group, which they presented to the conference chair.

23 www.lacult.unesco.org/lacult_en/docc/Kari-Oca_1992.doc.

This process, which took place from June 13 to 23, 2012, was supported by a daily meeting of the Major Group at the Conference Centre, named Rio Centro, under the leadership of Tebtebba,[24] an indigenous organization specializing in development, which operates as a think-tank based in the Philippines and works in partnership with the Indigenous Environmental Network and the Indigenous Information Network. The methods of the caucus informed those used by the Major Group, at the Conference Centre, to make decisions and ensure the visibility of all parts of the indigenous world (Bellier 2015). However, indigenous participation, which included hundreds of people and was characterized by good will on the part of all actors, who were united by the goal of transmitting a common message and minimizing differences in viewpoints, took on a more complex form due to the involvement of different locations. Three political declarations came out of these processes, differing strongly from each other on three points, which are described below.

Three indigenous peoples' statements: unity in diversity

On the outskirts of Rio, the historic village of Kari-Oca (where the 1992 Kari-Oca Declaration was produced) was set up by the Federal Government of Brazil to hold indigenous cultural performances and sporting events under military protection. It was here that activists from indigenous and environmentalist networks gathered in 2012 and produced a radical critique of economic development. In the center of Rio, indigenous peoples were also very active at the People's Summit, a popular assembly on the margins of the official conference, where the entire social movement gathered in an immense debating forum that attracted a large public (cf. Chartier and Le Cronnec 2015). At the People's Summit, the Indian peoples (especially those from Amazonia) organized a series of thematic conferences; indigenous peoples were also highly visible in the large march that the summit organized across the city. The People's Summit produced a series of final declarations; one of these was written by indigenous peoples, and this one was collated with a third statement, which was produced by the Indigenous Major Group. All of these declarations were delivered to the Summit of Heads of State and of Government, which took place at the official conference site, called Rio Centro.

The three declarations produced at these simultaneous gatherings defined three aspects of a converging critical position, articulated at three levels. The first, produced in Kari-Oca, criticized public state policies, focusing particularly on Brazil but targeting all member states (national level). The second critique, articulated by the indigenous peoples active in the Peoples Summit, took up the issue of colonialism, denouncing "green capitalism" and illusory solutions (global level). The third critique, produced by the indigenous Major Group,

24 Better known under this name than under its official name, the Indigenous Peoples' International Centre for Policy Research and Education.

which was active at the center of the conference, focused on proposals for change, highlighting respect for rights, the responsibility of indigenous peoples, and the engagement of member states and industrial firms (level of practices).

In the final declaration issued by the Major Group active at Rio Centro, there was a particularly strong demand to respect the normative framework, as well as rights and participation ("actual" or "full and complete"). In this context, the reference seems to have the sole purpose of providing for the conditions of indigenous peoples' possible presence in other forums looming on the UN horizon – to be specific, the Post-2015 Agenda forum.

On the strategic level, the Rio+20 meeting raised several issues. The first was to implement use of the category "indigenous peoples," rejecting any substitution of phrases such as "traditional populations" or "local communities," and consolidating this terminology with reference to UNDRIP. The final text issuing from the Conference mentions "indigenous peoples" six times (in paragraphs 43, 49, 58, 109, 229, 238) but makes no reference to UNDRIP. The Major Group wanted to highlight the importance of indigenous peoples in achieving sustainable development goals and to concentrate on the institutional framework before specifying their participation, this "detail" being something for later discussion. Another objective was to oppose the concept of the green economy in order to demand the recognition of diversified economies and, on this basis, specify the meaning of the expressions used in the text of the member states. In particular, the inclusion of the notion of "traditional knowledge" was questioned in light of the limited place given to the concept of Free, Prior and Informed Consent – which indigenous peoples had asked for greater inclusion of. A final objective, which was not achieved, was to have *culture* recognized as the fourth pillar of sustainable development. Despite the usual congratulatory statements regarding the success of this mega-conference, in the end the concept of sustainable development in light of indigenous peoples' rights remains to be implemented, as the main outcomes of this global conference were to launch the Post-2015 Agenda and a new definition of the Sustainable Development Goals (SDG).

Indigenous peoples' participation in the Conference of the Parties on climate change (COP)

The contexts of climate change and the regularity of annual COP meetings on this issue led to a different way of organizing the indigenous movement. In 2010, during the COP16 held in Cancun, the indigenous organizations set up a regular structure, the International Indigenous Peoples' Forum on Climate Change (IIPFCC) based on the caucus formula trialed in the matrix. This proved to be necessary for ensuring coherent positions and better follow-up on elements in negotiation. As Francesco Martone, an expert who accompanies the indigenous movement in this domain, notes, this marked the beginning of a plea from indigenous peoples for participation in a more active and better informed manner, in order to access all the mechanisms, organs and procedures implemented within the framework of the fight against climate change (Martone 2011: 521). The issues of mitigation, adaptation, funding, and the mechanisms of monitoring, reporting and verification, and technology transfers, all required the establishment of a group of experts and the availability of funding for participation in meetings taking place in a range of cities, including Bonn, which is the seat of the Convention. In 2015, other mechanisms requiring similar follow-up emerged, requiring more indigenous participants who had acquired expertise.

As a non-specialist in this area, I was confronted at this time by a landscape of acronyms entirely opaque to a lay person, and the existence of a world with its own rules: subsidiary organs such as the SBSTA (Subsidiary Body for Scientific and Technological Advice) and the SBI (Subsidiary Body for Implementation), working groups set up after each COP ("post-Durban," "post-Kyoto," or "ALD," standing for Adaptation, Loss, and Damage). This world, defined by the framework of the Convention on Climate Change, is compounded by highly technical analyses that indigenous peoples, supported by experts, have themselves developed in areas affecting them most closely: for example, in the area of mitigation, in light of the REDD (Reducing Emissions from Deforestation and Forest Degradation) Programme, or for participation in the Green Climate Fund.

The participation of indigenous peoples in the COP (in a general sense) is based on the form of the caucus – stabilized from one COP to another and renamed the International Indigenous Peoples Forum on Climate Change (IIPFCC) – as a way of formulating collective positions and allocating work. It works through the mobilization of experts able to report back to the group on the state of the discussions held by the working groups, with the objective of identifying the points on which they can focus their efforts. In Paris, this took the form of events organized within an indigenous peoples' pavilion, based in an area accessible by the general public, where the members of the IIPFCC organized days presenting the impact of climate change in the seven regions of the indigenous world and distributed information on their ways of life, ecological practices and positive contributions. They received visits from heads of state, including the Prime Minister of Tuvalu who expressed his fears of the rising waters threatening to engulf the island, and the President of the French Republic, host of the conference, who during his fleeting visit demonstrated his interest in the role that indigenous peoples can play in the fight against climate change.

Rio 2012 – Paris 2015: negotiations take place without indigenous peoples but advocacy progresses ...

As at Rio+20, the conditions of access to different locations presented a problem. The "official" space, where the member states competed to present the most attractive pavilion and hold debates showing their engagement in the fight against global warming, was strictly reserved for persons with prior accreditation. Access to the negotiating rooms was limited to state representatives and just one or two observers with the highest accreditation, which applied only to a handful of indigenous persons, and was insufficient to accommodate all the negotiation groups. The IIPFCC Forum functioned as an ordinary caucus with parity chairs (French-speaking, Spanish-speaking, and by gender). As in Rio, it took place every morning at the conference center where negotiations would begin later that day, in order to share information and allocate activities. Unlike the Rio Conference, no declaration was written by the caucus during the Paris conference; the declaration announced at the very end of the meeting, at night to an almost empty room and an exhausted French Minister of Foreign Affairs, was produced by a handful of indigenous persons who had remained as the final process passed to the French presidency, the Conference having finished. The French presidency of the COP expended huge efforts on obtaining a consensus on the Paris Accords, through a series of consultations that included neither indigenous peoples nor the other Major Groups of civil society. The final indigenous declaration was, however, endorsed by the collective caucus participants, as demonstrated by the messages circulating on the IIPFCC's "public mailing" list.[25]

These two processes allow us to note the strong visibility of indigenous people, achieved both by the significant numbers of them who managed to attend this kind of conference (several hundred, despite the difficulty of finding information about accreditation and funding for travel and accommodation), and also by their unique appearance. Headgear, feather trimmings, face paints, and colorful garments distinct from Western clothing were all brought out in order to signal at these "high-level" meetings the cultural specificities and the status of indigenous representatives, some of whom being recognized authorities. Beyond this observation, it is notable that indigenous people had great difficulty accessing the actual negotiating space, and being recognized as sovereign entities (peoples with the right to self-determination); they also faced challenges to their efforts to include in the universal provisions outlined in the declarations of heads of state the terms that they considered to be indispensable for allowing them to exert this right in the context of global governance (in this instance, sustainable development and climate change). At stake was their status within these spaces, where they wanted not only to speak, as in the bodies dedicated to the examination of their issues, but also to be capable of influencing the decisions of heads of state and government that would affect the future. The following section will show that this constitutes the substance of current discussions on this subject organized by the General Assembly and in the dedicated UN organs.

The participation of indigenous peoples under scrutiny at the General Assembly

On December 21, 2010, the UNGA adopted a resolution (A/RES/65/198) on "indigenous issues," taking the decision to organize a world conference on indigenous peoples "in order to share perspectives and best practices on the realization of the rights of indigenous peoples." It invited the UNGA president

25 There are of course other email lists to which we do not necessarily have access.

to lead open-ended consultations with representatives of member states and indigenous peoples, the UNPFII and the EMRIP, in order to define the modalities for this conference and the participation of indigenous peoples. Another resolution (A/RES/66/142), adopted on December 19, 2011, called on the Secretary-General to organize a high-level event in preparation for the conference, to commemorate the fifth anniversary of the adoption of UNDRIP. On September 17, 2012, a new resolution (A/RES/66/296) defined the organization of a conference to be held in 2014, to conclude the second decade on indigenous peoples (2005–2014). Originally planned for mid-June it moved to mid-September due to various complications. The "High-Level Plenary Meeting, to be known as the World Conference on Indigenous Peoples (HLPM/WCIP)" took place in New York, on September 22 and 23, 2014, at the same time as another Summit for the heads of state and government on Climate. Frustrated not to be the main focus of the States' attention, indigenous peoples consoled themselves with the thought that this would guarantee the presence of heads of state and government at *their* conference, which was indeed the case, albeit to a lesser extent than they had counted on.

Two conflicting expectations

The participation of indigenous representatives at this major and highly symbolic event was complicated. Although the issue was the subject of internal reflection in the international movement, the UNGA enforced its own organizational methods, which introduced a series of tensions into preparations. Along with the question of what kind of participation would be accorded to indigenous people, a contentious issue was the themes to be discussed; these issues had an effect on the content of the resulting outcome document. In the preparatory phase, indigenous representatives were above all concerned with the modalities relating to their participation and strongly pressed for co-organization of the conference with the President of the General Assembly (PGA). Worried by the way in which their perspectives would be incorporated into the outcome document, indigenous peoples first held their own conference in Alta, Norway in June 2013, at the invitation of the Sámi Parliament in Norway, in order to agree on a text that would act as a kind of roadmap (the Alta Outcome Document, UN 2013). Within the UNGA, some member states openly supported indigenous positions, such as the plurinational state of Bolivia and Mexico; the latter also organized a preparatory conference. Other states were very reticent, such as the United Kingdom, which did not wish to reopen discussions on collective rights. There is not space to retrace here all the processes and exchanges leading to the organization of this conference, but I will highlight a few prominent points.

First, the hybrid nature of the conference was striking, as it combined two unlike things: a *High-Level Plenary Meeting* of the General Assembly, reserved for member states and presided over by the PGA, organized over 2 days, and a *World Conference*, which attracts thousands of delegates, requires special logistic arrangements (offices, an organizing committee, its own secretariat) and lasts for about ten days. In the end the HLPM/WCIP lasted for 2 days, ending on the third day with a Philanthropy Conference that was of great interest to indigenous organizations and networks, which are continuously in need of funding. An indigenous proposal that the meeting be co-chaired by a representative of the member states and of the indigenous peoples was refused outright by the PGA, which instead relied upon the work of four co-facilitators, two from the member states and two from indigenous peoples. This concession was a minimal condition imposed by the indigenous movement in order to retain the participation of one of the parties most involved in indigenous affairs since the beginning, the North America indigenous peoples' caucus, which was threatening to remove itself from the process.

A particular organization

To understand how the indigenous peoples' movement achieved the co-organization of the UN conference and set up such a precedent, we have to go back to the previous steps. In May 2011, indigenous peoples set up a Global Coordinating Committee (GCC) of 16 persons, comprised of two members chosen by the regional caucuses plus a representative of the "youth" caucus and one from the "women's" caucus. A first reflection document, produced by three indigenous organizations from Aotearoa-New Zealand, Asia (Asia Indigenous Peoples Pact, AIPP) and Scandinavia (the Sami Parliament of Norway), was circulated at the end of July 2011. In 2012 there was an intense consultation and lobbying process led by a partnership of the Mexican ambassador (former president of the Human Rights Council, who had gained the trust of indigenous peoples) and a representative of the Sami. Having no direct support from the PGA, this partnership was forced to resign, and for some time the preparatory process was in jeopardy. The subject was discussed by both the UNPFII and the EMRIP, while during the annual sessions of UN bodies the GCC organized parallel events in order to mobilize the movement, clarify the issues of this conference, and focus opinions. Between the end of 2012 and mid-2013, the regional and thematic caucuses each held a meeting on the HLPM/WCIP in their continents, and an indigenous drafting group started to work. During 2013, the UNPFII and the EMRIP again debated this project, which had been taken up at the Global Indigenous Preparatory Conference sponsored by the Sami parliament in Alta in June 2013. As preparations intensified and the participation of all the indigenous peoples at all these meetings posed a financial headache, new technologies were mobilized on a large scale in order to host full and relevant information on a website set up by the GCC, and made especially easy to use. The entire Alta conference was re-broadcast for remote access and the position documents were made available to all. This stood in sharp contrast to the opacity of the UN and the PGA.

The Alta conference defined four themes: indigenous peoples' lands, territories, resources, oceans and waters; action by the UN system for the implementation of rights; implementation of the rights of indigenous peoples; and indigenous peoples' priorities for development with free, prior and informed consent. Each of these contributed to the formulation of recommendations (43 in total) featuring in the Alta Outcome Document that resulted from this conference.[26] Once this work was complete, the challenge was to push the heads of state to recognize this document in order to identify the place it would occupy in the outcome document of the HLPM/WCIP. Prior knowledge of the UN system was required.

On September 10, 2013, the Alta Outcome Document was annexed to a letter to the UN Secretary General in order to make it an official document (A/67/994) that could be distributed as such. Shortly afterwards, the Human Rights Council adopted a resolution on this subject, then the Group of 77 and China[27] took position and the UNGA Third Committee[28] held two meetings on a resolution project. At the World Conference of Indigenous Women held in Lima, from October 28 to 30, 2013, a Political Position Document and a World Action Plan for Indigenous Women were adopted. On December 18, 2013, the UNGA adopted resolution A/RES/68/149. From January 2014, in the midst of some confusion, intense discussions were held on the question of indigenous co-facilitators, certain member states supporting this while others strongly opposed it on the grounds of preserving the intergovernmental nature of the UNGA. The function of indigenous facilitators was debated: indigenous organizations did not accept the limiting of their mission to the facilitation of discussions with them, while the GCC refused to hold separate consultations.

On March 5, 2014, the PGA appointed the permanent representatives of Costa Rica and Slovenia as member state co-facilitators, a little later defining a new framework for the consultations and negotiations. Indigenous lobbying of "friendly" member states (Bellier 2006) intensified and, at the UNPFII, the PGA envoy announced a new framework, which would apply to the work of the two member state co-facilitators mentioned above and the two indigenous co-facilitators proposed by the indigenous peoples: Myrna Cunningham Kain, a former president of the UNPFII, from Nicaragua; and Les Malezer, from Australia, who played a notable role as president of the global caucus during the adoption of UNDRIP. This date, 6 months before the conference, marked the start of negotiations on the final outcome document of the HLPM/WCIP.

For this purpose, a GCC team as well as the two indigenous co-facilitators decided to relocate to New York. The PGA organized a first round of informal consultations with the member states, indigenous peoples and the UN, on June 3, 2014, then "informal interactive hearings" on June 17 and 18, with the same bodies plus civil society groups. On July 8, the zero draft outcome document

26 http://www.un.org/esa/socdev/unpfii/documents/wc/AdoptedAlta_outcomedoc_%20FR.pdf (accessed 12 January 2019).

27 The Group of 77 (G-77) was established on 15 June 1964 by 77 developing countries signatories of the "Joint Declaration of the Seventy-Seven Developing Countries" issued at the end of the first session of the United Nations Conference on Trade and Development (UNCTAD) in Geneva. In the global summits I could attend, the G-77 was including China, thus G-77+China.

28 The Third Committee handles social, humanitarian affairs and human rights issues affecting peoples all over the world.

began circulating. On July 16 a second round of informal consultations was held and on August 8 the first draft was produced. The PGA then sent a letter regarding the organization of the HLPM/WCIP, including a program and the topics to be discussed. On August 18 and 19 the third and final round of informal consultation took place.

The somewhat tedious outline of this process, presented without detail, serves to highlight some of the inherent problems of participation in UN debates: their length, the challenges of protocol, and above all the problem of including very different actors in this kind of discussion. All the indigenous people of the international movement wanted to participate in the HLPM/WCIP, but the General Assembly Hall could not hold them all. Methods were required to limit the number (to 60 per region of the indigenous world), grant accreditations, and ensure the availability of overflow halls in order to accommodate those persons who could not be seated in the UNGA Hall. It was also necessary to decide on badge systems, ensure their correct distribution and to adapt UN security systems while a Global Climate Summit was being held simultaneously.[29]

But the HLPM/WCIP did take place on September 22 and 23, 2014, and is considered by the indigenous peoples to have set a precedent in the history of the UN. After an opening session in the General Assembly Hall, which followed an initial opening the evening before, reserved for indigenous peoples (and their supports), a series of official speakers was announced, including most notably, several words expressed in Maori and Malay by the Secretary-General Ban Ki-moon; a highly political speech from Evo Morales (the "indigenous" president of Bolivia); and alternating talks from representatives of member states in the name of their regional groups (Europe, Africa, and South America), indigenous representatives and representatives of the UN. Strong words were therefore heard, as a prelude to the unanimous adoption of the final outcome document by heads of state and government to the applause of the indigenous peoples and the NGOs supporting them (UN 2014). The Alta Outcome Document was annexed to this document and UNDRIP was at the heart of the proposal. Just after its final approval, the Holy See and Canada expressed reservations, the former on the question of sexual and reproductive health and the latter on the place given to the concept of free, prior, and informed consent. No negotiations took place during these days, at least not visibly.

Following formal adoption of the document, the conference itself took place, in the form of three round tables and an interactive panel, co-chaired by a member state ambassador and an indigenous representative put forward by the GCC. The first round table focused on a global system of action for the implementation of the rights of indigenous peoples; the second on the implementation of UNDRIP at a national and local level; and the third on the issue of lands, territories, and resources. The interactive panel had no defined topic, nor real substance: it served primarily to circulate information between the hall and the forum.

29 See Bellier 2012b on the subject of the handling of sacred objects brought with them by the indigenous peoples.

A result

Dedicated to means of implementing UNDRIP, and organized with the active participation of the international indigenous peoples' movement, this special meeting of the General Assembly allowed the adoption of many decisions. I will focus on only one, which features in paragraph 33[30] of the outcome document: the member states committed themselves to considering, at the 17th session of the UNGA, ways to enable indigenous peoples' representatives and institutions to participate in meetings of relevant UN bodies on issues affecting them.[31] A specific request regarding this is addressed to the Secretary-General in paragraph 40.[32] In the phraseology typical of the UN, the head of the organization is requested to report to the General Assembly on the implementation of UNDRIP, "taking into account the views expressed by indigenous peoples," and to submit recommendations on the use, modification and improvement of existing UN mechanisms for achieving the ends of UNDRIP. The Secretary-General is requested to identify ways of enhancing a "coherent, system-wide approach" and to present proposals for improving the participation of indigenous peoples' representatives and institutions. This mechanism, now known as the SWAP (System-Wide Action Plan, A/HRC/21/24), was presented at the 15th session of the UNPFII, in 2016. It was defined through three broad perspectives: the implementation of indigenous peoples' rights; in the context of the 2030 Agenda for Sustainable Development; and considering the directing lines adopted by UN agencies, international financial institutions, and the training needs of indigenous peoples.

The processes that I have described, the number of UN bodies involved in the handling of indigenous affairs, and the co-organization of a global conference, confirm the advances in participation achieved by indigenous organizations, and

30 "We commit ourselves to considering, at the seventieth session of the General Assembly, ways to enable the participation of indigenous peoples' representatives and institutions in meetings of relevant United Nations bodies on issues affecting them, including any specific proposals made by the Secretary-General in response to the request made in paragraph 40 below."

31 "We request the Secretary-General, in consultation with the Inter-Agency Support Group on Indigenous Peoples' Issues and Member States, taking into account the views expressed by indigenous peoples, to report to the General Assembly at its seventieth session on the implementation of the present outcome document, and to submit at the same session, through the Economic and Social Council, recommendations regarding how to use, modify and improve existing United Nations mechanisms to achieve the ends of the United Nations Declaration on the Rights of Indigenous Peoples, ways to enhance a coherent, system-wide approach to achieving the ends of the Declaration and specific proposals to enable the participation of indigenous peoples' representatives and institutions, building on the report of the Secretary-General on ways and means of promoting participation at the United Nations of indigenous peoples' representatives on the issues affecting them."

32 At the time of reviewing this chapter, the General Assembly has held its 71st session, and adopted a resolution on September 2017(A/RES/71/321) expressing satisfaction to the current process of consultations of states and indigenous peoples, and requesting the Secretary-General to report on achievements, analysis and propose concrete recommendations by the end of the 74th session. The process is likely to drag on.

invite consideration of their status within the UN. This issue has been at the heart of the discussions organized by the General Assembly, throughout 2016, all determined by a collection of decisions, resolutions, and discussions that I am unable to summarize here, but the elements of which are available on the UN site dedicated to this issue.[33]

What about today?

One important development took place in February 2016, when the PGA[34] appointed four councilors to assist its mission: two ambassadors – Kai Sauer, permanent representative of Finland, and Martha Ama Akyaa Pobee, permanent representative of Ghana – for the member states, and two leading indigenous figures. One of these was James Anaya (North America Region), a former Special Rapporteur on the rights of indigenous peoples of Purépecha ancestry, and a professor of international rights from Arizona and an expert on the UN system, and the other was Claire Winfield Ngamihi Charters (Pacific Region), a lawyer and jurist of Maori origin who notably produced a reflection on the legitimacy of UNDRIP inherent to the participation of actors (including indigenous peoples) in the negotiation of the instrument (Charters 2009). The councilors launched a wide consultation process, and analyzed the documents produced by the High Commissioner for Human Rights that have accompanied indigenous processes at the UN for decades, and by the Inter-Agency Support Group (IASG), which coordinated agency programs relating to indigenous affairs. They produced four compilation documents, and presented a report to the UNPFII and the EMRIP.

I attended one of the indigenous peoples' consultation meetings, which was held during 3 hours according to UNGA protocol, at the same time that the Permanent Forum held its annual session (in 2016), and in the same room. The meeting resembled one of the working sessions of the UNPFII, but the regular alternation between indigenous declarations, member state declarations and UN official declarations was noticeable, and a mechanism for the even distribution between the different categories of speeches was respected. My observations revealed that the issue was of interest to the member states, which sent their representatives, and it was an opportunity to hear their declarations. Simply reading the summary documents of such meetings is not sufficient to establish an understanding of what position is held by whom, as they do not include the names of member states or of indigenous organizations. Certain member states are, however, more active than others, just as certain indigenous organizations are more involved than others. In this area, more than in others, the search for a consensus from the total consultations, which will be the object of an UNGA resolution, is strengthened by the neutrality of rapporteurs.

33 https://www.un.org/development/desa/indigenouspeoples/participation-of-indigenous-peoples-at-the-united-nations.html.

34 The presidency of the General Assembly is renewed by annual election.

This example demonstrates the importance of participation in person for those who wish to influence the terms of the draft documents, and to identify the positions of member states: a key aspect of transparency. But do the international community, and the member states with the right to vote at the UN, actually want this transparency? The greatest resistance surrounds the nature of the status to be accorded to those "indigenous peoples" who have been dominated by the creation of modern states. Failing a change in the form of the member state, this status is likely to be solely consultative.

Concluding remarks

By way of conclusion, I will present a few reflections on the different ways of giving status to indigenous peoples. Since the early days of their appeal to the UN, in the 1970s, indigenous representatives have continued to assert their cultural specificities and the inadequacy of existing UN proceedings for ensuring their participation. Some arguments that have punctuated this debate still seem inherited from colonization methods, highlighting the forms of domination of indigenous peoples. The first such argument, used by indigenous leaders on the basis of the right to self-determination (Article 3 of UNDRIP), is that the modalities of their UN participation have had to be approved by representatives of member states whom they judge to be reluctant, if not altogether unwilling, to recognize the value of their own institutions. In their argument they are supported by "friendly" countries, notably those who have made efforts at a national level to hold dialogue with them. The second is a dual argument, brought to bear by several representatives of member states who defend the intergovernmentality of the system: that the heterogeneity of indigenous bodies does not allow for specific treatment nor should be distinct from that accorded to NGOs. The third argument related to the consultative status of the NGO contributes by the way to the categorization of the groups that they represent, not as peoples but as "non-state actors," a category which serves for many other entities who can participate in meetings at the invitation of UNGA, according to particular modalities. In this context, discussions seem to center on the question of what procedures should be adopted for recognizing the particularities of indigenous peoples in the areas affecting them – which entails clarifying *which* areas, as well as the spaces and organs concerned – while taking into account the monopoly of member states on decision-making at the UN.

The difficulty is the heterogeneity of governmental and non-governmental indigenous entities. Some peoples, notably but not exclusively those grouped under the "Native American" umbrella, have autonomous recognized governments – but their chiefs hold seats at the UNPFII as observers, as if they were merely NGOs. They feel this to be an injustice. But other peoples do not have the same representative figures, and their institutions may be ignored or disputed by their member states – an attitude that may extend to the NGOs they form in order to escape a subordinate position in which they are sometimes held in a highly policed manner (see Keating, this volume). In these cases, they are not recognized as *peoples* in the legal sense of the term. Many member states do not intend to grant them a specific place; in some cases, this refusal is presented in the name of non-discrimination, for example, by the African states (see Hays this volume).

The highly sensitive subject of political sovereignty and the territorial integrity of member states are at the center of the problem being discussed, but for indigenous organizations the rule of participation relating to them should now obey the rights defined by UNDRIP. This recognizes the right to self-determination, or the legal personality of indigenous peoples, in Article 3 and in the other articles on this subject (3, 4, 5, 18, 19, 20, 32, 33, 41 and 42). While the question of political organization is necessarily at the heart of reflection on international participation, little work has been done on indigenous institutions, even though the issue of their revitalization is at the heart of provisions in the Declaration, and they are mentioned in all the documents dealing with indigenous affairs.

Following the report of the Secretary-General, and the contributions from several UN bodies (including the IASG, HCHR, ILO, IFAD, WIPO, and UNIPP[35]) on their practices relating to indigenous participation, the discussion on indigenous participation on the issues affecting them has focused on four points: the procedures that would allow effective participation; the criteria for determining the eligibility of indigenous peoples for accreditation; the nature and composition of the body that would determine eligibility; and the details of the process and what would be requested from indigenous peoples for their accreditation. While the debates are not concluded, some member states support the creation of a special category for indigenous peoples, but others strongly oppose this, arousing fears from organizations whose desire is that, somehow, at the end of these discussions, the level of participation should not be inferior to that of the ECOSOC NGOs. We should recall that the Alta Outcome Document called for the status of permanent observer.

The regime of participation has many kinds of impact on the availability of information, including the number of delegates who can access the hall, the time allowed for speaking, and the way it should be allotted (for example, by indigenous regions? – but at this level, the peoples are very different and their organizational forms are very variable). On the issue of procedures, indigenous peoples highlight the importance of co-chairing official meetings, but also of choosing their representatives (Article 18 of UNDRIP) and, with regard to this, the question of criteria (which I posed in relation to the working definition of "indigenous peoples") is raised in relation to participation. While diversity still reigns, some elements are highlighted and referred to by the rapporteurs charged with compiling the views expressed: self-identification (important or essential); recognition by the member state (significant but not determining); the relation to lands, territories, and resources; cultural specificity; the exercise of

35 IASG - Inter-Agency Support Group; HCHR – High-Commissioner for Human Rights; ILO - International Labour Organization; IFDA - International Fund for Agricultural Development; WIPO – World Intellectual Property Organization; UNIPP – United Nations Indigenous Peoples Partnership.

collective rights; the practice of an autonomous government; and the existence of treaties, accords and other constructive arrangements.

At the time of writing, the conditions of indigenous peoples' participation have not changed, but the importance of the discussion that the representatives of member states, agencies, funds, and UN programs have held with indigenous peoples should be highlighted. It goes hand in hand with reflection on the definition of the mandates of the two bodies at the heart of what I have termed the matrix, UNPFII and EMRIP. It holds the promise of greater openness on the part of the international community. It remains to be seen in what way the member states will act on their own soils - will they adopt a more favorable status of representation for indigenous peoples who are not NGOs? Likewise, more detailed analysis is needed regarding the implementation of indigenous peoples' rights at the level of governance, in order to adjust the quality of their participation (including in terms of expertise) to the nature of the problems at hand. Despite the impression that progress has been made in the area of indigenous peoples' rights, my fear at this stage, based on the research I have carried out for over two decades, is that international normativity will be held back by member states' failure to recognize on the ground the principles and procedures that they support only at a level that does not really engage their responsibility locally.

Bibliography

Bellier, Irène. 2006. "Le projet de déclaration des droits des Peuples autochtones et les Etats américains: avancées et clivages." In *Etre indien dans les Amériques*, edited by Christian Gros and Marie-Claude Strigler, 27–41. Paris: Institut des Amériques.

Bellier, Irène. 2007. "Partenariat et participation des Peuples Autochtones aux Nations Unies: intérêt et limites d'une présence institutionnelle." In *Démocratie participative, cultures et pratiques*, edited by Catherine Neveu, 175–192. Paris: L'Harmattan.

Bellier, Irène. 2009a. "Autochtones." *Espace Temps.net*, revue en ligne. https://www.espacestemps.net/document7583.html (consulté le 12 janvier 2019).

Bellier, Irène. 2009b. "Usages et déclinaisons internationales de l'autochtonie dans le contexte des Nations Unies." In *Autochtones: vues de France et de Québec*, edited by Marie Salaün, Martin Thibault, and Natacha Gagné, 75–92. Québec: PUL.

Bellier, Irène. 2011. "De l'Indien aux Peuples Autochtones… À propos de l'engagement du sociologue et de l'anthropologue en Amérique latine." In *Le multiculturalisme au concret: Un modèle latino-américain?*, edited by Christian Gros and David Dumoulin, 105–116. Paris: Presses de la Sorbonne Nouvelle.

Bellier, Irène, 2012a. "Retour sur la négociation de la Déclaration des Droits des Autochtones: reconnaître le principe d'égalité pour avancer vers de pragmatiques interpretations." In *Le statut des autochtones à la croisée des saviors: Cahiers d'Anthropologie du Droit 2011–2012*, edited by Stéphane Pessina-Dassonville, 73–95. Paris: Karthala.

Bellier, Irène. 2012b. "Les peuples autochtones aux Nations Unies: la construction d'un sujet de droits/acteur collectif et la fabrique de normes internationales." *Critique internationale* 54: 61–80.

Bellier, Irène. 2014. "La *performativité* de la Déclaration des droits des peuples autochtones." In *Cultures-Kairós – Revue d'anthropologie des pratiques corporelles et des arts vivants*. http://revues.mshparisnord.org/cultureskairos/index.php?id=960 (accessed 12 January 2019).

Bellier, Irène. 2015. "L'avenir que veulent les peuples autochtones. Stratégies institutionnelles, mobilisations collectives et force de négociation, à Rio+20." In *Regards croisés sur Rio+20: La modernisation écologique à l'épreuve*, edited by Jean Foyer, 259–279. Paris: Éditions du CNRS.

Bellier, Irène, Leslie Cloud, and Laurent Lacroix. 2017. *Les droits des peuples autochtones. Des Nations unies aux sociétés locales*. Paris: L'Harmattan.

Bellier, Irène and Verónica González González. 2015. "Peuples autochtones: la fabrique d'une identité symbolique aux Nations Unies." *Revue Mots-langages du politique*, 108: 131–150.

Charters, Claire. 2009. "The Legitimacy of the UN Declaration on the Rights of Indigenous Peoples." In *Making the Declaration Work: The United Nations Declaration on the Rights of Indigenous Peoples*, edited by Claire Charters and Rodolfo Stavenhagen, 280–303. Copenhagen: IWGIA.

Charters, Claire, and Rodolfo Stavenhagen, eds. 2009. *Making the Declaration Work: The United Nations Declaration on the Rights of Indigenous Peoples*. Copenhagen: IWGIA.

Chartier, Denis, and Hervé Le Cronnec. 2015. "Acter la fin d'un monde pour activer l'alternative. ONG et acteurs de l'altermondialisme à Rio+20." In *Regards croisés sur Rio+20: La modernisation écologique à l'épreuve*, edited by Jean Foyer, 281–304. Paris: Éditions du CNRS.

Crawhall, Nigel. 2013. "L'Afrique et les droits des peuples autochtones: un bilan des réactions à la Déclaration des Nations unies." In *Peuples autochtones dans le monde: Les enjeux de la reconnaissance*, edited Irène Bellier, 183–208. Paris, L'Harmattan.

Dahl, Jens. 2009. *IWGIA: A History*. Copenhagen: IWGIA.

Daes, Erica-Irene A. 2004. *Indigenous Peoples' Permanent Sovereignty over Natural Resources* (E/CN.4/Sub.2/2004/30). https://documents-dds-ny.un.org/doc/UNDOC/GEN/G04/149/26/PDF/G0414926.pdf?OpenElement (accessed on 12 January 2019).

Daes, Erica-Irene A. 2008. *Indigenous Peoples: Keepers of Our Past – Custodians of Our Future*. Copenhagen: IWGIA.

Foyer, Jean, ed. 2015. *Regards croisés sur Rio+20: La modernisation écologique à l'épreuve*. Paris: Editions du CNRS.

Gonnella Frichner, Tonya. 2010. *Impact on Indigenous Peoples of the International Legal Construct Known as the Doctrine of Discovery, Which has Served as the Foundation of the Violation of their Human Rights* (E/C.19/2010/13). Available at: http://www.un.org/esa/socdev/unpfii/documents/E%20C.19%202010%2013.DOC (accessed 12 January 2019).

ILO (International Labor Organization). 2009. *Indigenous and Tribal Peoples' Rights in Practice: A Guide to Convention 169*. https://www.ilo.org/wcmsp5/groups/public/@ed_norm/@normes/documents/publication/wcms_116077.pdf (accessed 20 February 2019).

Martínez, Miguel Alfonso. 1999. *Study on Treaties, Agreements and Other Constructive Arrangements between States and Indigenous Populations* (E/CN.4/Sub.2/1999/20). Available at: http://undocs.org/E/CN.4/Sub.2/1999/20 (accessed 12 January 2019).

Martínez Cobo, José R. 1986. *Study of the Problem of Discrimination against Indigenous Populations* (E/CN.4/Sub.2/1986/7). Introduction (30 July 1981) E/CN.4/Sub.2/476; 10 August 1982E/CN.4/Sub.2/1982/2; 5 August 1983E/CN.4/Sub.2/1983/21.

Available at: https://www.un.org/development/desa/indigenouspeoples/publications/martinez-cobo-study.html (accessed 12 January 2019).

Martone, Francesco. 2011. "UN Framework Convention on Climate Change." In *The Indigenous World 2011*, edited by Kathrin Wessendorf, 519–525. Copenhagen: IWGIA.

UN (United Nations). 2013. *Alta Outcome Document*. UN Doc A/67/994. https://www.undocs.org/en/A/67/994 (accessed 24 February 2019).

UN (United Nations). 2014. *Outcome Document of the High-level Plenary Meeting of the General Assembly Known as the World Conference on Indigenous Peoples*. UN Doc A/69/L.1*. http://www.un.org/ga/search/view_doc.asp?symbol=A/69/L.1&Lang=E (accessed 24 February 2019).

UN (United Nations). 2010. *Progress Report on the Study on Indigenous Peoples and the Right to Participate in Decision-making*. UN Doc A/HRC/EMRIP/2010/2. https://documents-dds-ny.un.org/doc/UNDOC/GEN/G10/134/39/PDF/G1013439.pdf?OpenElement (accessed 24 February 2019).

2 Defining the terms of indigenous peoples' rights in Namibia

The role of the International Labor Organization

Jennifer Hays

Introduction

The International Labour Organization (ILO) was the home of the first international agreement specifically addressing the status of indigenous peoples, the Indigenous and Tribal Peoples Convention 107 (1957). In the early decades of the indigenous peoples' rights movement, updating this convention was a major focus of indigenous peoples' rights activists, and this international body became a central site for the movement. In 1989 a new version was adopted, the Indigenous and Tribal Peoples Convention 169 (C169). Although relatively few countries[1] have ratified the legally binding convention, the ILO continues to play a significant role in the promotion of indigenous peoples' rights globally. Over the years, depending on various factors including the availability of funding, ILO programs have identified specific countries in which to provide targeted promotion of indigenous peoples' rights. When funding for the promotion of C169 was committed from the Spanish government in 2007, Namibia was identified as a country that had the potential to move toward implementing policy ensuring indigenous peoples' rights in the country and promoting them in the region, and to ratify C169.

Through the lens of ILO efforts to promote indigenous peoples' rights in Namibia, this chapter examines the ways that various strategies and discourses regarding indigenous peoples' rights intertwine at national levels. Namibia is a multi-ethnic country in southern Africa, and home to a large number of the region's indigenous peoples, in particular former hunters and gatherers living primarily in the Kalahari desert – usually referred to as the *San*, as explained in the following section – and also small-scale pastoralists. The next sections will briefly introduce the indigenous peoples in Namibia, the ILO and their international work on indigenous peoples' rights, and the national context in Namibia.

1 As of 2018, 23 countries have ratified: México, Norway (1990), Bolivia, Colombia (1991), Costa Rica, Paraguay (1993), Peru (1994), Honduras (1995), Denmark, Guatemala (1996), Ecuador, Fiji, Netherlands (1998), Argentina (2000), Brazil, Dominica, Venezuela (2002), Nepal, Spain (2007), Chile (2008), Nicaragua, Central African Republic (2010), Luxemburg (2018). https://www.ilo.org/dyn/normlex/en/f?p=NORMLEXPUB:11300:0::NO::P11300_INSTRUMENT_ID:312314.

The ILO project *Promoting and Implementing the Rights of the San Peoples of the Republic of Namibia*, from 2008 to 2013, and the subsequent development of a "White Paper" outlining the government's policy on indigenous peoples provide windows through which to examine the particular challenges facing the implementation of indigenous peoples' rights in Namibia. In a southern African context, negotiations over terms reflect deeper divisions about the notion of indigenous peoples and their rights.

This chapter is based upon 20 years of work and research in Namibia, examining (among other things) the discourses and activities of indigenous peoples' rights in the region (Hays 2004, 2011, 2016). In 2011–2012, while working with the project SOGIP, I was based in Namibia for one year and worked closely with local non-government organizations (NGOs), and had the opportunity to collaborate with UN and government bodies that address various aspects of indigenous peoples' rights in the country.[2]

In 2012, I was a consultant for the evaluation of the ILO PRO169 project in Namibia (Hays and Kronik 2013); this was part of a larger evaluation of the Spanish-funded program led by Jakob Kronik (see Hays and Kronik forthcoming). In the intervening years, I have continued to follow the indigenous peoples' rights discourse in Namibia. This chapter is highly informed by the work that I undertook as a short-term consultant for the ILO and is grounded in long-term research and work experience on indigenous peoples' rights issues in Namibia.

The indigenous peoples of Namibia – focus on the San

There are three overarching groups generally considered to be indigenous peoples in Namibia. One group is referred to by the term *San* and is made up of a number of smaller language groups, all of whom are current or former hunters and gatherers, mainly residing in the Kalahari desert in the northeastern section of the country. The people in this category are almost universally agreed to be the "first peoples" of the region and are also the primary group in focus in this paper. The *Nama* and *Damara* are the descendants of small-scale pastoralists and speak a language closely related to those of the San.[3] These groups experienced severe marginalization in South Africa and were ultimately largely subsumed by other groups, but in Namibia the identities and their language have

2 This research was conducted for the European Research Council funded project Scales of Governance: The UN, the States, and Indigenous Peoples (SOGIP), led by Irène Bellier. During this period I worked with the Legal Assistance Centre (LAC) on a large survey of San livelihoods (Dieckmann et al. 2014); served on the board of the Nyae Nyae Development Foundation of Namibia (NNDFN); attended regular meetings of the San Support Organizations committee, which included the ILO representative in Namibia and the Division for San Development, along with a number of other NGOs; and organized a conference on indigenous education with UNICEF, the Ministry of Education, and other stakeholders.

3 The Khoi and San (also referred to as Khoisan) language family is composed of three distinct subgroups, each with a number of languages, all of which are characterized by their distinctive click sounds.

remained distinct, the language is spoken widely and used in schools, and they are not stigmatized. Although they are technically considered as indigenous peoples (and some Damara communities are also marginal), these groups are rarely the focus of specific programs to address marginalized groups in Namibia. The third set of peoples are usually referred to in general as the *Ovahimba*, or just *Himba*,[4] but also includes three other subgroups, usually called the *Ovazemba*, *Ovatjimba*, and *Ovatwa* (also written as *Ovatue*). These groups are primarily pastoralists raising sheep, goats, and cattle in the Kaokoveld region of Namibia, although the Ovatwa are historically hunters and gatherers and are particularly marginalized. All three groups speak dialects of the language Otjiherero, spoken by the Ovaherero (usually called Herero), one of the more dominant ethnic groups in Namibia.[5] All of the Himba groups are considered as both indigenous and marginalized within Namibia (though which specific groups are listed in documents varies).

Of these three major groups, it is the San that are the most marginalized and stigmatized on the basis of ethnicity in a way in which the other groups are not. This is generally recognized, and the name of the ILO project specifically refers to this group, as did the original name of the government body with whom the project partnered, the Division for *San* Development. This chapter will return to the issue of names and terms later, but as this particular set of ethnic groups was the main focus of the ILO project from the beginning, they are also the main focus of this chapter.

The category *San* includes several different language groups[6] residing across southern Africa, primarily in Namibia, Botswana, and South Africa, and also in Angola, Zimbabwe, and Zambia; a common estimate is that there are approximately 100,000 San in the region.[7] Recent estimates for the number of San residing in Namibia range between 32,000 and 38,000 (Dieckmann et al. 2014: 21). Formerly hunters and gatherers, San today practice mixed economies that include hunting (though this is limited by legal restrictions on hunting) and gathering (also often limited by the depletion of plant resources around settlements where they live), and other small-scale economic activities. Even for those who engage with other livelihood strategies, hunting and gathering remains a dominant feature of San identity; furthermore, the small-scale

4 The prefix *Ova-* is a noun class marker indicating the plural *people*, and appears before ethnic markers (*Omu-* is the singular used for one person). *Otji-* is the marker for language, as in *Otjiherero.* Often in English, however, just the radical is used when referring to ethnic groups and languages, this is especially common with "the Himba" and "the Herero."

5 The Herero were the victims of genocide at the hands of the German colonialists in the early 1900s, and although they are not the most dominant or numerous groups in the country, they are also not marginalized in the same way as the San or Ovahimba groups.

6 In Namibia these include the Ju|'hoansi, !Xun, Khwe, Hai||om, Naro, and !Xóõ; the special symbols indicate click sounds.

7 Exact numbers are difficult to come by, as most governments of these states do not collect statistics by ethnic group. Those that do, including Namibia, often use language as a proxy for identity marker, but some San groups speak other languages.

social organization associated with hunting and gathering, and other related cultural norms, values, and strategies, continue to characterize San communities (Barnard 2002; Dieckmann et al. 2014; Takada 2015; Ninkova 2017). Often, these norms, values, and strategies contrast sharply with those of more dominant groups and of social and political institutions of the countries they live in, making participation in these institutions difficult. In addition, the association with hunting and gathering is heavily stigmatized by dominant groups, who view it as backwards rather than as a legitimate subsistence strategy (Suzman 2001; Dieckmann et al. 2014; Hays 2016).

By all socio-economic measures the San are the most disadvantaged ethnic group in Namibia. One of the primary factors creating dependency and marginalization among the San of Namibia today is their widespread loss of land and access to natural resources, especially during the past century of colonial rule. Under the colonial apartheid administration of South West Africa (1919–1990)[8] while most other ethnic groups in the country were granted "homelands,"[9] most San found their land subsumed into commercial farming areas, the homelands of other ethnic groups, game reserves, or national parks. As their options diminished, San in many areas became progressively more dependent upon others for survival, primarily white farmers, military structures,[10] and later the patronage of communal area farmers after independence in 1990.

At the turn of the twenty-first century, the vast majority of San (about 90%) lived either in commercial farming areas or in communal areas in which they form small minority populations (Suzman 2001). The only area in which the San are granted "customary rights" to their land under existing law is in the Tsumkwe district, former "Bushmanland" (the one homeland granted to San groups during the apartheid area), but even this is only a fraction of their former territory (Biesele and Hitchcock 2011). A driving force for San loss of land historically and today is the perception that they do not "use" the land, because they do not practice intensive pastoralism or agriculture; their low-impact subsistence strategies make the land appear available for grazing or other intensive use. This perception makes them vulnerable to invasion and exploitation by cattle owners who see them as inferior people and cheap labor. The protection and expansion of land rights, and achieving land security in general, is thus a high priority of efforts to ensure human rights for Namibia's indigenous peoples.

8 The League of Nations gave Britain the mandate for the country, which was then placed under South African administrative rule.

9 These designated areas for separate ethnic groups, described by the Odendaal Commission in 1963, were based on the apartheid system of "separate development." One San homeland, ***Bushmanland***, was created in northeast Namibia, but this territory was a fraction of the territory of one specific San group, the Ju/'hoansi (Biesele and Hitchcock 2011).

10 In some areas San were incorporated as trackers into the South African military, who were fighting against the independence movement of the South West Africa People's Organization (SWAPO). Although they were not conscripted, the San had few economic options at that time and the military provided a salary, as well as material goods and food. See Lee (2006, 2013); and Hitchcock (2019) for discussions of the severe social and economic effects this had in Tsumkwe district.

Without access to land, livelihood options depend upon access to wage employment. However, low educational levels, stigmatization by other groups, residence in "remote" areas, and other factors combine to create conditions of high unemployment. The vast majority of those who are employed are working as farm workers in menial labor positions. Some are able to earn a little money gathering high-value export plants like "devil's claw."[11] Some are employed by NGOs and conservancies, by national parks as trackers and resource monitors, or by the government as police or teachers, but such positions are limited. For most San, access to cash is a major challenge. In many areas, San still rely upon "bush foods" for a part of their subsistence; however, opportunities to obtain these resources are very restricted everywhere (except within the Nyae Nyae Conservancy). The San thus have very limited subsistence options overall, and throughout Namibia they rely heavily upon Government food aid and old age pensions for their survival.

Their dispossession and marginalization has been thoroughly described elsewhere; in particular a recent large-scale socio-economic survey of San living conditions in Namibia,[12] entitled *Scraping the Pot*, shows that they continue to experience severe stigma, discrimination and exploitation, ongoing aggression by dominant groups, and marginalization from participation in mainstream economic social and political institutions (Dieckmann et al. 2014; see also Suzman 2001, ACHPR 2005). One of the foremost problems identified by the 2014 study was the lack of access to land. Very few San communities have access to land of their own or control over resources, and those that do find the boundaries continuously threatened by neighboring pastoralist or agriculturalist groups seeking land. After a visit in 2012, James Anaya, the Special Rapporteur on the rights of indigenous peoples also came to this conclusion, noting that although other Namibian groups had experienced "pervasive loss of land" during colonialism and apartheid:

> ... by all accounts, San groups in the country have experienced the greatest loss and resultant social, economic, and cultural disruption, the legacy of which has not been overcome since independence ... representatives of indigenous peoples with whom the Special Rapporteur met overwhelmingly expressed sentiments of exclusion from decision-making processes at both at the local and national levels because of their ethnic identities. (Anaya 2013: 7)

The exclusion noted by Anaya also matches a major problem identified by the 2014 report – limited political representation, participation, and consultation. Other major sets of problems identified include lack of access to productive assets, very low levels of education, and systematic discrimination (Dieckmann et al. 2014). All of these describe structural barriers that are common to indigenous peoples and

11 *Harpagophytum*, exported to Europe as an anti-arthritic medicine.

12 Sponsored by Land, Environment and Development Project (LEAD) of the the Legal Assistance Center (LAC).

that are rooted largely in different subsistence strategies and social organization. Such structural discrimination is deeply embedded in the institutions of a society, and changing it requires a variety of approaches. These can include the adoption of international principles that recognize and protect indigenous peoples' rights, and the development of national policies toward this goal. Also important are strategies designed to change the perception of such peoples in wider society, including in government bodies – these were important aims of the ILO PRO169 project in Namibia. Before returning to a discussion of Namibia, the next section will outline the role of the ILO in the global promotion of indigenous peoples' rights.

The ILO and indigenous peoples' rights

> Against the backdrop of the evolution of post-war international law, the emergence of the international regime on Indigenous peoples – in the modern sense – is inextricably connected to one international organization, the ILO … (Anaya and Rodríguez-Piñero 2018: 41)[13]

The International Labour Organization (ILO) was one of the first two intergovernmental organizations, created alongside the League of Nations in 1919 by the Treaty of Versailles. From its creation, the ILO has had a structure unique among such organizations. It is "tripartite" or made up of three equal partners: member states, employers, and workers, making it the only intergovernmental organization in which non-governmental representatives have equal weight to those of governments. As Swepston (2012) points out, this "gives a far better chance than in purely intergovernmental deliberation of allowing the voices of those who are affected by decisions to be heard" (2012: 354). Although indigenous peoples are not perfectly represented by workers unions, this general structure promoting dialogue among the three important sectors has allowed for some important opportunities addressing indigenous peoples' rights.

Swepston (2011) credits the ILO with calling into question the "moral underpinnings of colonialism" through a series of 1930 Conventions regulating working conditions in the colonies (referred collectively as the "Native Labor Code") and playing a significant role in the ultimate collapse of the colonial system (2011: 156). The ILO remained at the forefront of international standard-setting relating to indigenous peoples when the United Nations was founded after World War II. In an international context marked by increasing focus on the

13 The quote continues "… and to one region, the Americas" (Anaya and Rodríguez-Piñero 2018: 41). Latin America is the region in which a large majority of the ratifying countries of are located (this is also true of its predecessor, C107). Asia and Africa, also continents that have significant indigenous populations, have been far more reluctant to adopt C169, as have the major "settler states" of the US, Canada, New Zealand and Australia. Although the Scandinavian country of Norway was one of the first to ratify (with Denmark and the Netherlands a few years later), Europe has also been slow to adopt the convention – Spain's ratification in 2007 was thus also a significant addition.

development of such peoples, the ILO launched the Andean Indian Program in 1951, and in 1957 adopted the Indigenous and Tribal Populations Convention (Convention No. 107, or C107;[14] see also González-González, this volume).

C107 was progressive for its time and, as Swepston describes it, revealed "remarkable foresight and care in predicting the problems that would need to be dealt with" as decolonization continued (2011: 156). However, that Convention was grounded in a paternalistic and assimilative development model, which assumed the eventual resolution of the "problem" would happen automatically as indigenous identity disappeared and such groups assimilated into mainstream society.[15] Although still in force for those countries that ratified it (and that have not gone on to ratify its successor, Convention No. 169, described below), today C107 is mainly considered emblematic of the problematic emphasis on assimilation in early efforts to address what we know today as violations of indigenous peoples' rights. Nonetheless, as Anaya and Rodríguez-Piñero (2018) point out, the convention "consolidated a foothold for the "Indigenous" rubric within the international system and in particular within the burgeoning international machinery for the protection of human rights" (2018: 42).

Interest in indigenous issues globally dwindled in the late 1950s and 1960s, but with the establishment of the World Council of Indigenous Peoples in 1975 and the creation of the UN Working Group on Indigenous Populations (WGIP) in 1982, a new emphasis on the right to self-determination, rather than protection and assimilation, took hold. In this climate the ILO began to consider updating the Convention (Swepston 2012), and a meeting of experts was held in 1986; three years later the Indigenous and Tribal Peoples Convention No. 169 was adopted. Swepston, who was the ILO official responsible for indigenous peoples' issues at that time, says that the import of the new instrument was totally reversed, focusing on "consultation and participation, respect for the continued existence and ways of life of indigenous and tribal peoples, and continuation of their cultures" (2011: 157).

Despite this important turnaround, there was critique of the process of creating the convention, which did not specifically involve indigenous peoples' organizations (or others involved in the parallel UN processes); furthermore, the revision happened very quickly. The result, suggest Anaya and Rodríguez-Piñero (2018) was a slow acceptance among both indigenous peoples and the traditional ILO stakeholders. Nonetheless, as the highly inclusive process of creating the UN Declaration on the Rights of Indigenous Peoples (UNDRIP) dragged on for another 18 years before it was adopted by the General Assembly on 2007, for almost two decades ILO C169 was the only comprehensive indigenous peoples'

14 C107 was ratified by 27 countries, 14 of which were in Latin America. Of these, 17 did not ratify C169 and are thus still bound by C107, these include: Angola, Bangladesh, Belgium, Cuba, Dominican Republic, Egypt, El Salvador, Ghana, Guinea Bissau, Haiti, India, Iran, Malawi, Pakistan, Panama, Syria, and Tunisia.

15 This is signaled by its full name: the Convention for the *Protection and Integration* of Indigenous and Other Tribal and Semi-Tribal Populations in Independent Countries (my emphasis).

rights document. Anaya and Rodríguez-Piñero say that despite the initial reserved reaction, "Convention 169 proved to be ... absolutely crucial in the crystallization of baseline normative consensus that drove discussions toward the adoption of the UN Declaration" (Anaya and Rodríguez-Piñero 2018: 45).

Swepston describes the ILO as possibly "the most thorough and effective international mechanism for the protection of human rights," in large part because it "combines detailed standard setting and supervision, promotion and on-the-ground assistance in a way that no other institution of its kind does" (2012: 353). This assistance is referred to by the ILO as "technical cooperation" and programs with this focus are aimed at supporting governments in upholding the standards contained in its documents, through a variety of means including workshops and training, research, and publications, and by involving a variety of stakeholders from government and civil society. The ILO PRO169 was one such program.

ILO PRO169

In 1996 with funding from the Danish International Development Assistance (DANIDA), the ILO operated a technical cooperation program titled *Promotion and Application of Indigenous Peoples' Rights*, or PRO169. This program was designed to promote the application of the principles outlined in the ILO C169, mainly through technical assistance to representatives of the main stakeholders – including governments, employers, and employees – and indigenous peoples. Other donors over the years included the European Instrument for Democracy and Human Rights (EIDHR); the rest of the Scandinavian governments – Norway, Sweden, and Finland – and Spain (Hays and Kronik forthcoming).

Africa and Asia were originally identified as the priority global regions for PRO169. At the time no country had ratified in either continent,[16] and encouraging more ratifications in these regions was one focus of the program. The program was grounded in the recognition that promoting an effective policy environment – including ideally the ratification of C169 – requires translation of relevant terms and concepts into the local languages and cultures at various levels. The PRO169 program targeted these different levels – community, broader society, and government – to raise awareness, build capacity, and to develop policy regarding indigenous peoples' rights. To this end, the sponsoring of research on indigenous situations and the publication of informational materials was also a critical aspect of their strategy (Hays and Kronik forthcoming). It was under the PRO 169 program that the ILO published one of the most comprehensive tools on indigenous peoples' rights, *Indigenous and Tribal Peoples Rights in Practice: A Guide to ILO Convention No. 169*[17] (ILO 2009; see also ILO 2003).

16 Nepal ratified the Convention in 2007, and The Central African Republic in 2010.

17 Available at: http://www.ilo.org/wcmsp5/groups/public/@ed_norm/@normes/documents/publication/wcms_116077.pdf (accessed 20 February 2019).

In 2007, Spain became the 18th country to ratify C169 and the Spanish Agency for Development Cooperation (*Agencia Española de Cooperación Internacional para el Desarrollo*, AECID) committed funding to the PRO169 program, through the AECID-ILO partnership program (2008–2012).[18] This partnership consisted of three components: the *Latin American Program* (targeting 14 countries); the *Africa and Asia Regional Program* (primarily networking and training); and the only single-country component, *Promoting & Implementing the Rights of the San Peoples of the Republic of Namibia*. The program was initially conceived as a 5-year program (2008–2012) and was considered likely to be renewed for another 5-year period; however, following the global economic crisis of 2008, the country was not able to renew funding, and the program ended in 2013. The Spanish-funded program was evaluated in 2012.[19] At that time, the entire PRO169 program as such also ended, and the responsibility for technical support that the program had been providing was taken over by the new Department of Gender Equality and Diversity (see Hays and Kronik forthcoming for a more detailed discussion of the institutional changes and the implications).

Allotted about 16% of the Spanish budget from 2008 to 2012, the project in Namibia was the only one of the three components that had a single-country focus. Namibia provides an interesting case study with which to observe the specific interactions between international mechanisms and discourses, regional dynamics, national history, culture and politics, and the local situation on the ground – and the ways in which the premises upholding commitment to indigenous peoples' rights are continuously under negotiation. As in many countries, much of this negotiation at the national level takes place around the terms used to refer to indigenous peoples, and how to translate indigenous peoples' rights into the regional, national, and local "vernaculars." Understanding how these dynamics take shape in Namibia requires contextualization of the country within the continent of Africa, and the specific regional dynamics of southern Africa.

The ILO and indigenous peoples' rights in an African context

The concept of indigeneity is notoriously contested in Africa (see also Kenrick, this volume). The usefulness and appropriateness of the category and term has been the subject of lively debates among practitioners, social scientists and juridical scholars (see, for example, Saugestad 2001a, 2001b; Kuper 2003; Kenrick and Lewis 2004; Barnard 2006; Guenther et al. 2006; Bellier 2011), with the weight coming down on the side of recognition of indigenous peoples as a legitimate legal and social category in Africa, as elsewhere. An important aspect of the debate involves the definitional ambiguity of the term *indigenous*,

18 During its period of operation, the Spanish funding made up 37% of the total budget of the PRO169 program (Hays and Kronik forthcoming).

19 The two evaluations are available on the ILO website: https://www.ilo.org/ievaldiscovery/#b2iixln. These include an evaluation of the overall program, led by Jakob Kronik, and an evaluation of the Namibia project, led by Hays.

which is commonly understood as meaning simply "native" in relation to a colonizing population, in keeping with how the term is applied to plant and animal species. This is also the common understanding of the term *indigenous languages*, for example, which is understood to mean all African, as opposed to European, languages. In most African countries, the predominant political stance is that "all Africans are indigenous" in relation to European colonists and other immigrants. As such it is applied to all African citizens of a country, which effectively eliminates the usefulness of the term; I will return to a discussion of this point in the section on Namibia, below.

This understanding could be upheld by a simplistic reading of two criteria provided in the first point of Article 1 of C169, which characterizes the peoples to whom the Convention applies:

a tribal peoples in independent countries whose social, cultural, and economic conditions distinguish them from other sections of the national community, and whose status is regulated wholly or partially by their own customs or traditions or by special laws or regulations;

b peoples in independent countries who are regarded as indigenous on account of their descent from the populations which inhabited the country, or a geographical region to which the country belongs, at the time of conquest or colonization or the establishment of present state boundaries and who, irrespective of their legal status, retain some or all of their own social, economic, cultural and political institutions.

By itself, section (b) can be interpreted as referring to *all* Africans. However, such a reading disregards both the layers of internal colonization that took place over centuries in Africa, as well as the ongoing processes today. African governments and citizens do recognize that some groups of people were in the area before others. Crawhall (2011) cites the existence in Bantu languages[20] of special terms for aboriginal peoples, arguing that "the concept of indigenous, aboriginal or first peoples is deeply rooted in Africa" (2011: 6). This is certainly the case in southern Africa, where the San are almost universally acknowledged as first peoples in the region. However, this does not necessarily translate into the concept of indigenous peoples as a category of people meriting specific rights. To the contrary, it is usually seen as a condition to be overcome, as all citizens are brought into the mainstream economy. One form of resistance to the term and concept of *indigenous* is that it is a western concept that is being imposed upon Africans, and that serves to continue a romanticized vision what was previously called "primitive," and to prevent the integration of such populations into the mainstream society.

20 In southern Africa today, the dominant ethnic groups are Bantu speaking peoples descended from agro-pastoralists who migrated to and through the southern part of the continent between 300 and 800 A.D.

In a summary of its first research-based report on indigenous peoples in Africa, the African Commission on Human and Peoples Rights (ACHPR)[21] emphasizes the need to outline a set of "key characteristics" rather than a "clear cut definition" of indigenous peoples, and that such characteristics need to take into account regional variation (2006: 9). The report makes it clear that aboriginality, or "who came first" is not the defining characteristic of indigenous peoples in Africa (2006: 10). Instead, the ACHPR emphasizes the importance of *self-definition*. This element is also central to the ILO definition, and is stated in the second point of Article 1 (cited above), and the ILO definition is referenced in the ACHPR report. The report also refers to the "modern analytical form of the concept," which can be used "to draw attention to and alleviate the particular form of discrimination from which they suffer" (ibid: 12). This emphasis on the structural aspects of indigenous marginalization is critical. Equally importantly, this report also notes that repression did not end at colonialism in Africa, but that "dominant groups have also repressed marginalized groups since independence, and it is this sort of present-day internal repression within African states that the contemporary African indigenous movement seeks to address" (ibid: 10).

In 2009 the ILO and the ACHPR published the report of a joint study they conducted on *the Rights of Indigenous Peoples in 24 African Countries* (ILO-ACHPR 2009). The report notes that there is a widespread "reluctance to acknowledge the existence of indigenous peoples" and that although the specific reasons for this reluctance vary, they "almost uniformly" have to do with maintaining national unity (2009:vi). A concern often expressed by African governments is that indigenous peoples' rights are "special rights" that provide unfair advantage to (or potentially disadvantage) certain groups; this is also connected with protests that the term will promote "tribalism" or "ethnic tensions." In southern Africa this concern is often noted with reference to apartheid. Namibia was under South African administration from 1915-1990,[22] and apartheid laws were extended to its territory, including the creation of "native reserves." Its neighbor, Botswana, was a "front-line state," bordering both South Africa and Namibia, and deeply committed to resisting apartheid. In direct refutation of its neighbors' colonial ideology and policies that separated people and upheld separate access to resources on the basis of race and ethnicity, Botswana's constitution expressly forbids any kind of preference or exclusion on the grounds of ethnic identity. Today Botswana strongly rejects the term "indigenous" for any ethnic group,[23] preferring instead to use the term *Remote Area Communities* to

21 Conducted by its Working Group on Indigenous Populations/Communities.

22 The official mandate of the League of Nations was issued in 1920, and was terminated in 1961, after which time South Africa's rule in the territory was illegal.

23 At the UN Permanent Forum on Indigenous Issues in May 2017, Botswana minister Slumber Tsogwane made it clear that although Botswana supports UNDRIP, they do not "accept or subscribe to the labeling of any particular tribe or ethnic group as "indigenous peoples" and that "all tribes and ethnic groups are indigenous to Botswana." http://www.weekendpost.co.bw/wp-news-details-archive.php?nid=3808 (accessed 9 January 2019).

refer to those who live in small settlements outside of urban areas; a majority of these communities are San.[24]

The ACHPR (2006) found that this kind of refusal to recognize ethnic difference results in a situation in which the socially dominant groups force their own norms upon weaker groups, in the name of "unity"; this is certainly the case with Botswana (see Saugestad 2001a, 2011). Namibia does not have such policies and, as will be described below, is more open than its neighbor to the concept of indigenous peoples. Nonetheless, a wariness of both "special treatment" on the basis of ethnicity, and also of isolating particular ethnic groups, is often voiced by Namibian government officials. This particular form of resistance to indigenous peoples' rights is linked to continental colonial history, and also to specific regional dynamics rooted in southern African historical, political, and environmental climate (see Hays and Biesele 2011).

The current ACHPR website highlights the characteristics of indigenous communities in Africa, which include: cultural difference and cultures under threat; dependence on access to land and natural resources; discrimination; geographic isolation; experiences of domination and exploitation; and self-identification.[25] All of these characteristics describe the San populations in Namibia. The following section describes the ways in which these regional dynamics play out in that country – and the context into which the ILO project entered with its project to promote international indigenous peoples' rights norms.

Namibia as a site of PRO169

Upon becoming independent from South Africa in 1990, Namibia took a different approach to ethnicity than that of Botswana. Although the new nation rejected the apartheid system, it recognized that the racial inequalities inherent in it had left deep social imprints that could only be addressed through recognition of these same categories (see Hays 2019). This general perspective resulted in a policy environment that recognized and respected cultural diversity, and thus was potentially favorable to the acceptance of indigenous peoples' rights. An open and tolerant government also allowed for the development of civil society organizations promoting human rights in general. This general favorable environment was one of the motivations for identifying Namibia as a site for a targeted PRO169 project. A second important factor was the country's willingness to take a leading role in international discussions about indigenous peoples' rights. Interestingly, this was manifested most visibly in Namibia's role in the deferral of the adoption of the UNDRIP in 2006. Finally, and importantly, there was a newly-created government office devoted specifically to the development of the San; this provided a clear government body that the ILO could partner with

24 It is common knowledge in the country that most of the people in the *Remote Area Development Program* (RADP) are San, or Basarwa as they are called in Botswana. However, no official figures exist as the government does not record numbers of people by ethnicity (see Hays 2011).

25 http://www.achpr.org/mechanisms/indigenous-populations/about/ (accessed 9 January 2019).

to implement its program. A look at each of these characteristics provides insight into the necessity – and complexity – of translating international indigenous peoples' rights ideals into local contexts.

Namibian policy and organizations favorable to indigenous peoples' rights

The Namibian Constitution provides for affirmative action, and makes provisions for communal land. The *Traditional Authorities Act* (2000), under the Ministry of Regional and Local Government and Housing, allows a "traditional community"[26] to designate a traditional authority in accordance with customary law; this body includes a "chief or head," and traditional councilors. A traditional authority can make decisions about civil cases according to customary law, as long as it does not contradict the constitution of Namibia. There are five San traditional authorities in Namibia that are recognized by the government; the ILO worked with these leaders (among others) providing training on tools for upholding their rights as indigenous peoples.

The *Communal Land Reform Act* (2002) provides for the allocation of rights in respect to communal land and the establishment of *Communal Land Boards* under the Ministry of Lands and Resettlement. This Act also provides for the powers of chiefs and traditional authorities in relation to communal land Namibian policy and it includes an innovative program integrating conservation and development, known as *community-based natural resource management* (CBNRM). An integral part of Namibia's CBNRM program is the demarcating of *conservancies,* areas of communal land in which conservancy members are granted wildlife resource rights under Namibia's *Nature Conservation Amendment Act* of 1996. These Acts provide a potential avenue for indigenous communities to gain control of traditional lands; they also establish the legal association between ethnicity and land rights. However, in practice most San communities are landless, as described above; only two of the 72 registered conservancies in Namibia are San.[27]

There are several active civil society organizations focusing on indigenous issues in Namibia. The Working Group of Indigenous Minorities in Southern Africa (WIMSA), based in Windhoek was very active from 1996. Although it is currently dormant, WIMSA laid the groundwork for much of the current indigenous peoples' rights work in the country, including establishing the Namibian San Council – composed of 14 San representing the Traditional Authorities and Community Based Organizations (CBOs) of different language groups – which is

26 understood to be an entity sharing a common language, culture and heritage. To be a part of a community one has to (a) self-identify and (b) be accepted by the rest of the community.

27 These are N‡a Jaqna Conservancy in Tsumkwe District West and the Nyae Nyae Conservancy in Tsumkwe District East; Both the Nyae Nyae and N‡a Jaqna Conservancy face a number of problems including illegal occupation of their land by other ethnic groups. There are at least 15 conservancies in Kunene Region in north-western Namibia, where the Himba live.

still active today. The Nyae Nyae Development Foundation of Namibia (NNDFN) grew out of organizations that had been supporting San in the Tsumkwe District since the 1980s. The Legal Assistance Centre (LAC) has taken on legal cases, research, and activism regarding indigenous peoples' rights. The San Support Organization (SSO) board gathered all of these organizations, including the Namibian San Council, along with other organizations that work with San communities, in an effort to create a broader network and to more effectively lobby government on San issues.

San representative structures have struggled over the years to maintain the support that they need to flourish – both from their own communities and from the government. Nonetheless, the existence of both Traditional Authorities and the Namibian San Council meant that there were clear channels through which the PRO169 project could work to identify and include San representatives in their workshops and other processes. These individuals were important conduits of information to communities, as well as spokespeople for their communities.

Namibia and the UNDRIP process

A draft of the UN Declaration on the Rights of Indigenous Peoples (UNDRIP) was adopted by the UN Human Rights Council in June 2006, and was presented to the UN General Assembly in November the same year. During this process, Namibia led what was known as the "Africa Group" (or the "Group of African States") in a process of deferring the States' vote on the UNDRIP by one year (For a detailed description of the discourses and processes surrounding this delay see Crawhall 2011). Namibia outlined their concerns in a "Draft Aide Memoire" submitted to the General Assembly (Africa Group 2006) and 2 months later, the Assembly of the African Union voted in support of these efforts to ensure that African interests were "safeguarded" (African Union 2007). They agreed to work with other member states to address the concerns of African states, which they listed as: "(a) the definition of indigenous peoples; (b) self-determination; (c) ownership of land and resources; (d) establishment of distinct political and economic institutions; and (e) national and territorial integrity" (ibid.). These concerns are intertwined; for example, there were widely expressed fears that the concept of "self-determination" and distinct political and economic institutions could be misinterpreted to mean the right to secession would threaten the national and territorial integrity (Crawhall 2011). The lack of a clear definition of "indigenous peoples" further exacerbated such concerns.

These concerns were addressed, in part through small amendments to the UNDRIP and in part through consultations and dialogue with national representatives, and most African countries signed the UNDRIP in 2007. All of these points are also explicitly countered by the ACHPR on their website, and over the past decade, focused advocacy work has helped the governments to better understand the legal consequences of the adoption of UNDRIP. Nonetheless, the questions have not disappeared. African countries, including Namibia, have ongoing concerns with the concept of indigenous peoples' rights that must be addressed in order to persuade African governments, and civil society, to accept indigenous peoples' rights principles on both legal and philosophical grounds.

The San development program

During the same time that Namibia had taken a leading role in the deferral of the launch of the UNDRIP by spearheading the Africa Group in 2006, they had also taken concrete steps to address the situation of San people living in Namibia. Following discussion in parliament about a San man who had died of starvation, Dr. Libertina Amathila, early in her tenure as Deputy Prime Minister of Namibia (2005–2010), embarked on a research mission to determine the state of San communities in Namibia. Her findings matched those of other studies and of Namibian civil society organizations: San communities were extremely marginalized and faced severe shortages of food, basic shelter, and access to water and sanitation; the majority of San children were not in school, and the San were severely marginalized and exploited by neighboring groups – including cases which she pronounced as "criminal labour exploitation" (Shigwedha 2005). Highly concerned about this situation, Dr. Amathila decided to focus on the "development" of the San, and launched the *San Development Program* under the Office of the Prime Minister, directed specifically toward improving the situation of San communities.

Initially, the program was intended to focus almost entirely upon the San, as the name implies. However, from early in the program it was recognized that some of the Himba groups – specifically the Ovazemba, Ovatjimba, and Ovatwa also experienced marginalization in ways that were comparable to the San. The *San Development Website*[28] has not changed since the program was started, and contains photos of both San and Himba individuals and communities. However, until 2015 the name of the government branch referred specifically to *San* Development. Following a change of national government in 2010, the San Development Program was upgraded, and became the *Division of San Development*, still within the Office of the Prime Minister. In 2015, the name was changed again to the *Division for Marginalized Communities*, and placed in the Office of the Vice President. Also at this time, Kxao Royal |Ui|o|oo, a Ju|'hoan man, was appointed Deputy Minister for Marginalized Communities. Previously a member of parliament for many years, |Ui|o|oo is the highest ranking San person ever in the Namibian government structures, and currently the only San representative at the national level.

The text on the home page of the San Development Website, written a number of years ago, but still linked to the government office responsible for this program, provides insight into the country's official approach to indigenous peoples.

28 http://www.sandevelopment.gov.na/ (last accessed November 2018). Although the division is now called the Division for Marginalized Communities, the link for that office still connects to the Sa!n Development Website.

The text describes "Khoisan speakers"[29] and acknowledges that they were the "earliest inhabitants of Namibia," describing them as "a large group of hunters/gatherers who settled and led a nomadic life on the edges of the Kalahari and Namib deserts some thousands of years ago." The page goes on to say that:

> Due to the encroachment of the European settlers with their farming economies, the San people were dispossessed of their land and their traditional way of life has been severely destabilised. Consequently, they have been marginalised and started living in some of the most inhospitable terrains in the country, mainly surviving by hunting wild game and gathering roots and wild berries ... To curb the situation, the Namibia Cabinet directed the establishment of a focused and dedicated socio-economic San Development Programme under the Office of the Prime Minister in 2005. The main objective is to integrate marginalised communities into the mainstream of our economy and improve their livelihood.

This statement highlights a few important points relevant to current discussions on indigenous peoples' rights. First, it locates the source of their marginalization in the past, during European colonial settlement, without acknowledging ongoing encroachment onto San lands that is still happening today. Recognition of historical sources of marginalization is critical, but a development program founded in this perspective is less likely to consider ongoing cases of land grabbing, and current stigma and other structural problems, to be under their mandate. Second, hunting and gathering is presented as if it is an adaptation to losing their land, rather than a legitimate, and highly skilled element of a subsistence strategy based on deep connection to land over generations.[30] The portrayal of hunting and gathering as merely an adaptation to poverty devalues the sophistication of the skills that these strategies entail, as well as the central importance that they have in the cultures and economies of many San groups. The strategies are presented as something that must be overcome, rather than acknowledged and promoted. Finally, the main goal, clearly stated, is integration into the mainstream economy.

The focus of the Namibian government's San development activities has primarily been meeting the immediate physical needs of impoverished and marginalized groups through poverty alleviation projects such as small-scale income generation projects, and providing land in the form of resettlement farms for landless San, Ovatue and Ovatjimba communities. Although lack of land is undeniably one of the central factors in the marginalization of these groups, the national livelihood survey found that a lack of consultation with involved communities, or attention to specifics of land use patterns and social organization, have prevented San communities from fully benefitting from the interventions (Dieckman et al. 2014).

29 Further down in the quote they identify the San peoples as made up of "seven main traditional groupings."

30 Archaeological, genetic, linguistic and oral history all indicate that the San have been living in small groups, primarily as hunters and gatherers, since long before the colonial era.

In these ways, the program contrasts sharply with a "rights-based" approach, which (among other things) addresses structural causes of poverty and emphasizes consultation about what the "needs" are and the scope and nature of development interventions. One of the most important principles of indigenous peoples' rights is that addressing them today is not resolved by integrating people into existing social structures, but by recognizing their collective rights. A goal of the PRO169 project was to cultivate such a recognition within Namibia.

Promoting and implementing the rights of the San Peoples of the Republic of Namibia

During the period in which Namibia was simultaneously engaging in the UNDRIP process and establishing a government body specifically identifying the San as in need of support, the ILO's PRO169 Program was expanding, and wanted to increase its field presence in Africa. In an interview for the evaluation in 2012, Brigitte Feiring, who was Chief Technical Adviser of the PRO169 program during the initialization of the Spanish project, noted that although the ultimate goal was to promote ratification of the C169, this was a "big leap" for many African countries, and the program was designed to support a process within a country, rather than just encouraging ratification. The first field-based country program focusing on capacity building in indigenous peoples' rights was started in Cameroon in 2006.[31] A review on the PRO169 website in 2009 described a gradual increase of indigenous peoples in national processes in Cameroon, among other advances, as a result of the tools created by PRO169 – although the report notes that the challenges were also numerous.[32] The ultimate aim was also to use Cameroon as a kind of stepping stone to promote the application of C169 principles throughout the central African region.

When the Spanish funding was committed in 2007, Namibia was identified as the next African country in which to promote C169 principles and policy, with the idea that it would be a platform for indigenous peoples' rights in southern Africa. The ILO understood the seemingly contradictory actions of Namibia – questioning indigenous peoples' rights on the world stage of the UNDRIP negotiations, while simultaneously implementing a government program specifically dedicated to an indigenous minority in the country – as reflecting a general willingness to engage in international debates on indigenous issues, and as an entry point through which indigenous peoples' rights could be promoted. The ILO's Technical Cooperation agreement with Namibia was signed in 2008.[33]

31 The ILO PRO 169 programme was active in Cameroon from 2001, but prior to 2006 primarily focused on research and integration of indigenous issues into the poverty reduction strategy.

32 https://www.ilo.org/wcmsp5/groups/public/@ed_norm/@normes/documents/publication/wcms_117590.pdf.

33 AECID-ILO 2008. Document of Technical Cooperation: "Promoting & Implementing the Rights of the San Peoples of the Republic of Namibia" Namibia component of the Indigenous Peoples Programme under the AECID-ILO partnership programme 2008/12.

Activities of the PRO169 in Namibia

The main partners for the project were government ministries and departments, in particular the (then) Division for San Development, whose emphasis was on poverty reduction. According to the technical cooperation agreement, the project's immediate stated objective for Namibia was to contribute to the reduction of poverty, and to improvement the socio-economic situation of the San peoples; furthermore this was to be done through a rights-based approach. In the southern African climate described above, working on socioeconomic issues for the San was more acceptable to the government than focusing primarily on indigenous peoples' rights. Nonetheless the project document emphasizes that the approach is grounded in the application of indigenous peoples' rights, as outlined in C169. Specified in this agreement was the creation of a comprehensive regulatory policy framework that outlines the rights of the San as distinct peoples. This concrete goal became an important focus later in the project, as will be described below.

There was no project office in Windhoek during the first few years, and the Namibia program was run from the ILO office in Pretoria, in South Africa. This office commissioned three baseline studies, which were conducted by the Legal Assistance Centre in early 2010, on existing San development initiatives in Namibia (Dieckmann 2010); on the existing regulatory framework protecting San rights in Namibia (Jansen 2010a); and an assessment of the training needs of Namibian government ministries (Jansen 2010b). In September 2010, a National Project Coordinator (NPC) was recruited and the Windhoek project office was opened, and in October, the Sub-Regional Conference on the Rights of Marginalized/Indigenous Communities was held (ILO 2011). By the time of its mid-term review in 2011, the project was just getting started; the review report notes that "not much had been achieved" by that point (Arowolo 2011a: 4). Over the next two years, however, the PRO169 program engaged intensively with indigenous peoples' rights efforts in Namibia. Although the Division of San Development was its main partner, the program also engaged with other government representatives (most notably the Office of the Ombudsman, see below); with traditional San leaders; and with civil society organizations including the Namibian San Council, as well as NGOs supporting San projects and communities.

One of the most visible and noted activities of the PRO169 project in Namibia was a series of workshops arranged in Windhoek and Pretoria. Representatives of all of the stakeholders noted above participated in these workshops, and during the evaluation these were reported to be among the most effective activities of the project. The workshops specifically targeted relevant line ministries and other governmental bodies, civil society organizations, and San representative bodies. Some workshops were specifically designed for a particular group of stakeholders (i.e. government officials, or San representatives), and focused on their specific role in indigenous peoples' rights questions; some were larger workshops designed to facilitate dialogue. An important role of these workshops was to establish a common understanding of indigenous peoples, and their rights.

The Office of the Ombudsman

The Office of the Ombudsman is the government body responsible for ensuring that human rights are upheld in Namibia.[34] The office began dialogue with the ILO in late 2011, immediately recognized the relevance of indigenous peoples' rights to their overall mandate, and accepted ILO offers for further training on the issue. The engagement of this local institution in indigenous peoples' rights efforts was an important success of the PRO169 project. A key component of the ILO PRO169 project was the publication of materials designed to raise awareness of the principles of indigenous peoples' rights, and the project in Namibia supported the publication of the *Guide to Indigenous Peoples' Rights in Namibia*[35] (Office of the Ombudsman 2012). At the launch of this guide, Petrus Doëseb, then chair of the Namibian San Council, the representative body described above, made a statement that was widely cited in Namibia's media: "All we are asking is to be treated equal. It is our right, and we are not asking for charity" (Nunumbe 2010; see also Sasman 2010).

The quote is illustrative for many reasons. It provides a concise refutation of the "special rights" misperception, by a San man who is politically active and who has participated in training workshops on indigenous peoples' rights sponsored by the ILO. The fact that this quote was picked up by Namibian media outlets and circulated in the country is also notable, both because it presents a San activist speaking on behalf of his own community, and for the positive and accurate attention it brings to the concept of indigenous peoples' rights among the general public. This kind of public relations is crucial for creating positive attitudes toward indigenous peoples' rights within the country. The Ombudsman's office reported that, following the launch and the media attention, they received multiple requests for the booklet from various parties including government and non-government organizations, indicating an increased awareness among both government and relevant civil society organizations. This is an illustration of how the PRO169 project, although it was limited in time and scope, and (as described below) did not result in Namibia's ratification of the ILO C169, was nonetheless able to build upon the work that other organizations were already doing, and to cultivate critical awareness of the international understanding of *indigenous peoples' rights* within Namibia.

Ratification of ILO C169

Interviews with government officials, both for the ILO PRO169 evaluation and in recent years, indicate that the Namibian government is considering ratification of the ILO C169, although whether this will ultimately take place or not is far from clear. In its response to recommendations in the 2011 Universal Periodic

34 Accredited through the Global Alliance of National Human Rights Institutions (GANHRI).

35 Available at: https://www.ombudsman.org.na/wp-content/uploads/2016/11/Indigineous-peoples-rights.pdf.

Review (UPR) of the UNHRC that it should ratify several international conventions, the Namibian government notes that, before acceding to any international instrument, there must be a thorough study "to ensure that national laws are harmonized to meet the requirements of the international instruments" (UNHRC 2011b: 3). The government repeated this statement in its midterm UPR report. Although ILO C169 is not specifically listed, the report refers to "all outstanding international agreements to which it is not yet party" (GRN 2013: 28).

There has been, however, increasing focus on the creation of a "white paper" outlining the government's policy on indigenous peoples' rights; this is in effect the national policy framework that the PRO169 project was working toward, and is described in the following section. This process has involved a study of the international laws and national policy regarding indigenous peoples' rights.[36] Although it is far from clear that the Namibian government will ratify ILO C169, this study, and the drafting of a national policy document, are in line with the government's clearly stated process toward ratification of an international convention described in both reports of the Namibian government to the UPR.

The evaluation of the PRO169 project in Namibia was positive overall. However, a major concern was that the time span was far too short to allow for the principles of indigenous peoples' rights to fully take root within the country, creating the risk that the process would wither in the absence of a supportive international body. In fact, in the intervening years discussions around indigenous peoples' rights in Namibia have been ongoing, both within the government's own internal dialogues and with the critical support of other UN bodies, as described below. In these discussions, the Office of the Ombudsman has continued to insist upon the use of the term *indigenous* and to promote the international understanding of this term, while the Division specifically devoted to San development has increasingly moved toward the term *marginalized*. The following section will examine the different terms used to refer to Namibia's indigenous peoples, and the implications of these two different terms referring to the same groups of people.

Translating indigenous peoples' rights

In her closely observed discussion about how international human rights ideals are adopted in various local settings, the anthropologist Sally Engle Merry introduces the concept of *vernacularization*, the process by which transnational ideas are "extracted from the universal and adapted to national and local communities" (2006: 39). She makes clear that the terms *global* and *local* are more than just spatial designations and can be misleading – for example the global can also be a local site (see Bellier, this volume) and the word local often implies small scale and lack of mobility that is not necessarily accurate. Although the term

36 Begbie-Clench, Ben. 2016. *An Assessment of Namibian Legal, Policy and Institutional Frameworks Relevant to Indigenous Peoples*. Government of the Republic of Namibia (GRN) and United Nations Department of Economic and Social Affairs (UNDESA) – not for general distribution.

vernacular is often understood to refer to local languages and "non-standard" dialects, we can also think of a national discourse as a kind of "political vernacular" into which international human rights terms must be translated in order to have meaning and impact.

In the case of the ILO project in Namibia, this national discourse was the most salient, as the project was primarily working at the level of representatives of government and civil society organizations, based in the capital, Windhoek. The project agreement stipulated that it would work at the "macro" (national government) and "meso" (which they define as national and international organizations that have a mandate to work with San communities, including community-based organizations) levels. The strategy at the meso level was to facilitate effective dialogue between organizations working with San communities, and the government. Most of the awareness-raising and capacity-building was designed to influence national policy on indigenous issues, and the project had virtually no presence "on the ground" in communities. It was thus not the local San languages into which the concepts of indigenous peoples' rights were primarily being translated, but that of the national government.

This section will examine the use of terminology in discussions surrounding the creation of a national policy document regarding indigenous peoples' rights, referred to in Namibia as a "White Paper." In this context, the use of the terms *San*, *marginalized*, and *indigenous* to describe the same general group of people is not just a question of terminology; it is also a negotiation about the root causes and the appropriate approach to take to address the marginalization of these communities.

The White Paper

In January 2016, Namibia came up for its second review in the cycle of the Universal Periodic Review (UPR), of the UNHRC in Geneva; the first was in 2011. In both reviews, indigenous peoples' rights were noted, and Namibia was both commended for its work with San communities – in particular the existence of a special government office for this purpose – and also urged to go much further in committing to, and upholding, indigenous peoples' rights. In neither review is there a suggestion that Namibia should ratify the ILO C169, but both refer to a "white paper" that is in accordance with the convention, with the UNDRIP, and with other major relevant human rights instruments. The process around the creation of this document, including the dialogue between Namibia and the reviewing nations of the UPR, illustrates the complexity of translating the concept of *indigenous peoples' rights* into the political vernacular of the country.

When the policy framework on indigenous peoples' rights was discussed at an early ILO-sponsored workshop in October 2010, it was reported in *The Namibian*, the country's widely-read national English-language newspaper, in an article titled "Law on indigenous people's rights coming." This article describes the conference as bringing together "international and local stakeholders to discuss ideas, good practices, and norms for the formulation of a white paper that will prepare for the protection and promotion of indigenous and marginalized communities in Namibia" (Mongudhi 2010). The article refers both to *marginalized communities* and the need to integrate them into the economy, and to *indigenous peoples* and their rights, which it describes as "entailing the recognition of their cultural heritage, languages, customary laws and the need to accord them special protection." The article also makes a clear connection between economic development and a rights-based approach, noting that "by implementing such measures, the country will be able to address the marginalization and discrimination of indigenous people in the country." This was the message that the ILO was working to get across in Namibia, and the region.

In the January 2011 report of the UPR Working Group, a recommendation by Norway to formulate a white paper on indigenous peoples' rights is listed as "enjoying the support of Namibia" (UNHRC 2011a). In accepting the recommendation, Namibia strengthened the commitment outlined in the agreement with the ILO, to developing a statement of policy, and legislation on indigenous peoples' rights. The Office of the Prime Minister took the steps of commissioning a study on the living conditions of the San to identify the most important issues (Arowolo 2011b), as well as an evaluation of the Division for San Development, to determine what was already being done (Mayinoti 2011). The ILO provided financial and technical support for these studies.

At the request of the Office of the Ombudsman, the ILO also sponsored the Human Rights Training Workshop on the Rights of Indigenous Peoples, for staff of that office and for line ministries in July–August 2012. The need for a regulatory policy framework was strongly endorsed at this workshop, and discussions about this were ongoing at the time of the closing of the ILO PRO169 program in Namibia. Led by the Office of the Ombudsman, with support from the ILO office in Geneva, a *Draft White Paper on the Rights of Indigenous Peoples in Namibia* was circulated in late 2014. The forward to this draft directly acknowledges the UPR process and describes the White Paper in the exact terms that Norway used in its recommendation to the Human Rights Council (UNHRC 2011a: 16):

> In 2011 the Government of the Republic of Namibia, in collaboration with the United Nations Human Rights Council's Working Group on the Universal Periodic Review committed itself to formulate a White Paper in accordance with the United Nations Declaration on the Rights of Indigenous Peoples (UNDRIP) and, furthermore, that recommendations from the Committee on the Elimination of Racial Discrimination (CERD), the International Labour Organization (ILO) and the African Commission's Working Group on Indigenous Populations/Communities will be taken into consideration in the development of the White Paper.[37]

37 This document, which does not have a stated author, is available through the website of the Ombudsman: https://www.ombudsman.org.na/wp-content/uploads/2017/12/Draft_white_paper_IP_Rights.pdf.

Without support from the ILO after 2014, the process stalled, although the commitment was not forgotten. In the 2016 UPR Working Group report on Namibia, the "presentation of the state under review" refers to the draft, noting that "the Office of the Ombudsman had recently completed a draft White Paper on the *rights of marginalized communities*" (UNHRC 2016a: 4 emphasis added). In the same report, eight "comments and recommendations" (out of 219) are relating to "ethnic minorities," and four include the term "indigenous" (Recommendations 137.212-219). We also read in that report that Spain emphasized the inclusion of indigenous peoples in the dialogue, recommending that, in addition to providing indigenous minorities with access to basic social services, Namibia should proceed with the "rapid adoption and effective implementation of the 'White Paper on *Indigenous Peoples' Rights*' drafted by the Ombudsman Office" (Recommendation 137.214; emphasis added). Thus, in the same document, the existing draft White Paper is referred to by two different names.

In a final statement in the section recording the "interactive dialogue and responses by the State under review" it is noted that "the delegation of Namibia stated that Namibia had no national legislation directly related to indigenous peoples and that the term 'marginalized people' was used" (UNHRC 2016a: 14).[38] Namibia's formal response to the UPR was organized by category of the recommendations; one is "marginalized peoples" and its footnote lists the eight recommendations that refer to ethnic minorities in the UPR report. The entry says simply "enjoys the support of the state," indicating that all of these recommendations – including those that used the word "indigenous peoples" in the original report – had been accepted (UNHRC 2016b: 6). However, the term *indigenous* is not included anywhere in Namibia's response.

In 2016, the UN Department for Economic and Social Affairs (UNDESA) began to support the White paper process. At the time of writing, an updated draft is being finalized and the use of the terms "indigenous vs. marginalized" is still being debated. The next stage of the process is through the Ministry of Justice, and then the Cabinet, who will determine its ultimate acceptance – and the terminology used. The current version will be released for comments using the word *indigenous*, as in the original title, but the final decision will be made by the Cabinet.

The switch by the government to use the term *marginalized* is consistent with other changes. In March 2015 the Division for San Development was renamed the *Division for Marginalized Communities*, and moved to the Office of the Vice President, where it currently is based. Government officials connected with this office have consistently been reluctant to use the term *indigenous*, arguing that *all* Namibians of African descent are indigenous – and thus the use of the

38 The statement continues: "One of resolutions of the National Land Conference of 1991 had been that the land rights of disadvantaged communities should receive special protection, with the San and other marginalized communities receiving specific mention. The National Resettlement Policy of 2001 identified the San as a specific target group for resettlement, which was given conditional rights in terms of hunting concessions."

term would allow anyone to benefit from special programs that are intended for the *most* marginalized minorities. Because in Namibia (unlike Botswana, for example) identifying groups based on ethnic identity is specifically allowed, the various San language groups can be recognized as members of a broader category of people whose members are marginalized largely because of ethnicity. In practical use, in Namibia the term *marginalized minorities* (or *communities*) generally refers specifically to those who fit the category of *indigenous peoples*: the San, and the Ovahimba sub-groups.

Indigenous vs. marginalized?

This presents an interesting question for organizations such as the ILO that are seeking to translate international indigenous peoples' rights norms, values, and policies into the national political vernacular. Should they use the term *marginalized communities* – which for all practical purposes in Namibia refers to indigenous groups – and work from within this framework to achieve a practical recognition of indigenous peoples' rights? Or should they insist upon the use of the international term *indigenous peoples*, which includes in its definition recognition of the structural discrimination, specific relationships with the land, communal rights and free prior informed consent? As Merry points out, using terms that are already agreed upon within the country is one way to increase understanding when concepts developed and promoted at the international level are introduced into national and local dialogues, and to reduce friction with governments – which tend to be sensitive about how they address minority issues, and human rights questions in general. However as described above, the terms *marginalized* and *indigenous* signal different understandings of both the root causes and the appropriate avenues to address the specific marginalization faced by groups like the San (see also Saugestad 2001a, 2001b).

An important aspect of this terminological difference is highlighted by a brief examination of recent statements by Namibia's president Hage Geingob, who has expressed resistance to the term *marginalized*. Shortly after his election in May 2015, the President visited Tsumkwe, the main town in a district with the two San-owned conservancies mentioned above. Reporting on this visit, the newspaper *New Era* noted that Geingob had posted statements on social media indicating that the term *marginalized communities* as a designation is problematic, because ultimately the goal is for all Namibians to be treated equally. Therefore, the term *marginalized communities* "… must come to an end. Marginalization must not be permanent otherwise it becomes a state of mind." This perspective is also reflected in a statement published later that year on the website of the Office of the President: "The aim is to ensure that at some point, Namibia should not have communities that are peculiarly disadvantaged and unable to enjoy and take advantage of prospects available to all inhabitants."[39]

39 http://www.npc.gov.na/?p=823.

Here an important distinction becomes apparent between the terms *marginalized* and *indigenous*. The latter, as defined by the ACHPR, includes: cultural differences from the majority; subsistence strategies that depend upon access to land; and communal rights. These are not characteristics that indigenous peoples want to see "come to an end"; to the contrary, the point is to recognize them as legitimate *in order that* they may enjoy equal rights to the rest of the population, and *thus* end their marginalized status. This is an important point – the terms are not mutually exclusive. The experience of being indigenous today almost always includes an experience of marginalization – they are indeed *marginalized communities*. They also share the general experience of marginalization with other social categories. However, the global indigenous peoples' rights movement insists that ending their marginalization begins with recognition of their identities, and rights, as indigenous peoples – *not* through assimilation.

When they emphasize their use of the term marginalized communities *instead of* indigenous peoples – even if the terms refer technically to the same peoples – the government is in effect advocating an approach that sees this status as something impoverished to be overcome, largely through assimilation into the mainstream economy and institutions, rather than an identity to be recognized and accorded specific rights. This is the same approach that was seen in the previous ILO Convention on the Rights of Indigenous and Tribal Peoples, C107 – and that was expressly challenged by the global indigenous peoples' rights movement.

The San individuals that are in government almost uniformly express their preference for the term *indigenous* – even those working with the Division for Marginalized Communities. But what about other San community members? The next section will briefly examine this aspect of the promotion of indigenous peoples' rights in Namibia.

Promoting indigenous peoples' rights at the local level?

As noted above, the PRO169 project did not work with San communities on the ground. They did work actively with San community representatives, including the Namibian San Council and the Traditional Authorities, to raise awareness of indigenous peoples' rights, and to increase local leaders' capacity to actively engage with the government using international principles. Several local NGOs (including WIMSA, LAC, and NNDFN), and the regional organization Indigenous Peoples of Africa Coordinating Committee (IPACC),[40] had also been working with community representatives on indigenous peoples' rights issues for a number of years. San representatives have participated in the UN Permanent Forum on Indigenous Issues (UNPFII) on a number of occasions, sponsored in some cases by the Namibian government (through the Division dealing with San Development/ Marginalized Communities) and in others by international NGOs. Namibian San

40 https://www.ipacc.org.za/en/.

have also been sponsored to attend numerous international workshops and conferences where indigenous peoples' rights are at the forefront. As a result of all of these efforts with community leaders, awareness of indigenous peoples' rights at the local level has increased greatly in the last decade.

Local awareness and understanding is not enough to combat the violations of these rights, however. During the period of the ILO project in Namibia, several ongoing indigenous peoples' rights issues were playing out within the country. These include efforts by N≠a Jaqna Conservancy members to challenge the illegal fencing of territory by non-members of the conservancy; an invasion into the Nyae Nyae Conservancy by a neighboring pastoralist group; and land claims by the Hai||om in Etosha National Park that are being challenged by the Namibian government. None of these cases was specifically addressed by the ILO, which (since Namibia had not ratified C169) saw its role as to work toward the creation of a national policy environment that would allow these (and other) violations to be addressed as indigenous peoples' rights claims within national processes. This policy would facilitate the legal work on the cases by existing national organizations.

Local awareness of, and capacity regarding, human rights is a critical component of the indigenous peoples' rights movement, but it is not enough – especially when those who are violating these rights are more powerful politically, physically, economically, or numerically. Although leaders from all of the local San communities in the cases noted above have been sensitized about indigenous peoples' rights and use that discourse, none of these cases has been effectively resolved, and encroachment onto San land continues at the time of writing. Local indigenous communities and the organizations that work with them need support from national authorities, to protect their land and to secure other rights. This is why awareness and capacity at the national level, as well as a national policy framework, are so important. The ILO technical support for all of these at the "macro" and "meso" levels thus targeted a crucial space.

An ongoing process

As Merry (2006) points out, in addition to signaling differences in approach, resistance to human rights, and global terminology around it, can also reflect the interests of more powerful groups or of elites who stand to lose power, or to lose benefits that they gain when some groups can be easily exploited or dispossessed. These more powerful actors may be neighboring groups who aim to exploit natural resources for their own, more intensive, subsistence strategies or for financial gain; government officials that wish to consolidate their own position with their electoral base; or international companies that wish to engage in resource extraction on indigenous lands. Addressing the current situation of indigenous peoples as merely a form of marginalization leaves the door open for violations of indigenous peoples' rights. This can happen through the simple provision of land, resources, training, or other services without the required consultation of the communities; it can also happen when governments or international corporations offer indigenous communities money, low-wage jobs, or other compensation in exchange for access to the land and resources that they are depending upon, and have a right to.

If a government insists upon the concept of "marginalized communities" to refer to the same groups that are covered by the term "indigenous peoples," should an international organization like the ILO adopt this local vernacular, or insist upon the internationally recognized term? In the case of Namibia, the ILO chose the latter, and was able to support the growing awareness within another national institution, the Office of the Ombudsman, of the critical importance of the concept of *indigenous peoples' rights*. This office continues to promote national policy that uses the term, for example, in the policy framework outlined in the current version of the "Draft White Paper on the Rights of Indigenous Peoples in Namibia." This paper is now being circulated under the auspices of the Division for Marginalized Communities in the Office of the Vice President. It remains to be seen which term will ultimately be chosen. This choice will also be an indication of the government's commitment the recognition of a rights-based approach, or to one based on the assimilation of marginalized minorities into more dominant groups. Whatever the outcome in the near future, these issues are not going to be resolved by a single document, but require continuous pressure and ongoing negotiation.

Conclusion

It is tempting to see a kind of unilinear progress in the advancement of indigenous peoples' rights on the global stage, evidenced for example by the movement from an assimilative approach promoted by C107 to an emphasis on consultation in the ILO C169, and ultimately an approach based on self-determination outlined in the UNDRIP. A hopeful view is that, as progress continues, an increasing number of nations and their governments will accept the international definition of indigenous peoples, and recognize their collective rights. However, the very concept of indigenous peoples' rights challenges deeply embedded assumptions about the nature of human "progress" that sees the subsistence strategies of indigenous peoples as primitive and inferior. It also challenges the interests of more powerful actors, who wish to use the land currently occupied by indigenous peoples for other purposes. Furthermore, in various regions and nations, historical processes also influence acceptance of indigenous peoples' rights; the apartheid history of southern Africa continues to make government officials wary of identifying groups of people as "separate" from other groups in any way. This sensitivity interferes with a deep understanding of the concept of indigenous peoples and their collective rights.

By working with local institutions and building upon ongoing efforts, the Spanish-funded ILO PRO169 project played an important role in facilitating this understanding, and was successful in many ways. As described above the Office of the Ombudsman has adopted the term indigenous; and other government bodies appear to be opening up to the concept. Civil society organizations and local community leaders also became more aware of indigenous peoples' rights, through workshops and other training, and through literature produced on the topic. Nonetheless, negotiations around this topic are ongoing, and reflect deeper divisions within the country. The overall situation of the San in the country has not noticeably improved in the years since the project began, and the extremely slow pace of several current land rights cases for San individuals are indicative of the general lack of priority given to this issue in the country.

The ILO project in Namibia thus illustrates both the potential for international organizations to have an important effect on national discourses and to make progress on indigenous peoples' rights – and the limits of these efforts. The abrupt withdrawal of the ILO project from Namibia when funding was lost meant that processes that had just begun were stalled, until another international organization, UNDESA, was able to support them. The government did not have the capacity – or perhaps the will – to maintain the momentum by itself.

Indigenous peoples are everywhere among the most vulnerable people on the planet. In particular, such peoples in Africa are often at the bottom of a scale that includes many layers of marginalization, making it difficult for governments to recognize indigenous peoples as a category, or their collective rights. Indigenous peoples' rights also constitute a new field of human rights, and the terms are still being negotiated globally, in widely varied regional and national contexts. In Africa, especially in the post-apartheid context of southern Africa, this negotiation is especially sensitive and complex, and effective support for these processes requires time and a deep understanding of the contexts. There is a critical need for international support for indigenous peoples rights in Africa, and the ILO is well positioned to provide such support – but there is a need to prioritize and provide sustained funding for these ongoing negotiation processes at national and local levels.

References

ACHPR (African Commission on Human and Peoples' Rights). 2005. *Report of the African Commission's Working Group on Indigenous Populations/Communities: Mission to the Republic of Namibia, 26 July–5 August 2005*. ACHPR/IWGIA. https://www.iwgia.org/images/publications//ACHPR_Namibia_UK.pdf (accessed 20 February 2019).

ACHPR (African Commission on Human and Peoples' Rights). 2006. *Indigenous People in Africa: The Forgotten Peoples? The African Commissions Work on Indigenous Peoples in Africa*. ACHPR/IWGIA. http://www.achpr.org/files/special-mechanisms/indigenous-populations/achpr_wgip_report_summary_version_eng.pdf (accessed 20 February 2019).

Africa Group. 2006. "Aide Memoire: 'United Nations Declaration on the Rights of Indigenous Peoples.'" *New York*, 9 November 2006. https://www.ipacc.org.za/images/reports/human-rights/Africa_Group_Aide_Memoire_2006.pdf (accessed 20 February 2019).

African Union. 2007. *Decision on the United Nations Declaration on the Rights of Indigenous Peoples*. Assembly/AU/Dec.141 (VIII). http://archive.au.int/collect/auassemb/import/English/Assembly%20AU%20Dec%20141%20(VIII)%20_E.PDF (accessed 20 February 2019).

Anaya, James. 2013. *The Situation of Indigenous Peoples in Namibia*. Report of the UN Special Rapporteur on the Rights of Indigenous Peoples James Anaya (May). http://unsr.jamesanaya.org/docs/countries/2013-report-namibia-a-hrc-24-41-add1-en.pdf (accessed 10 January 2019).

Anaya, James, and Luis Rodríguez-Piñero. 2018. "The Making of the UNDRIP." In *The UN Declaration on the Rights of Indigenous Peoples: A Commentary*, edited by Jessie Hohmann and Marc Weller, 38–62. Oxford: Oxford University Press.

Arowolo, Oladele. 2011a. *Mid-term Self Review of the Project on 'Promoting and Implementing the Rights of the San Peoples of the Republic of Namibia'*. Geneva: International Labour Organization. Available at: https://www.ilo.org/ievaldiscovery/#b2iixln (accessed 24 February 2019)

Arowolo, Oladele. 2011b. "The San in Namibia: A Socio-economic Study." Prepared for the Office of the Prime Minister Division San Development, Windhoek, Namibia.

Barnard, Alan. 2002. "The Foraging Mode of Thought." In *Self- and Other-images of Hunter-gatherers*, edited by Henry Steward, Alan Barnard, and Keiichi Omura, 5–24. Osaka: National Museum of Ethnology (Senri Ethnological Studies 60).

Barnard, Alan. 2006. "Kalahari Revisionism, Vienna and the 'Indigenous Peoples' Debate." *Social Anthropology* 14 (1): 1–16.

Bellier, Irene 2011. "Misunderstanding of Autochthony vis-a-vis the Question of Indigenous Peoples." *Social Anthropology*. Special issue: *The Uses and Misuses of 'Indigeneity' and 'Autochthony,'* guest edited by Quentin Gausset, Justin Kenrick, and Robert Gibb. 19 (2): 204–212.

Biesele, Megan and Robert K. Hitchcock. 2011. *The Ju|'hoan San of Nyae Nyae and Namibian Independence: Development, Democracy and Indigenous Voices in Southern Africa*. New York: Berghan Books.

Crawhall, Nigel, 2011. "Africa and the UN Declaration on the Rights of Indigenous Peoples." *International Journal of Human Rights*. Special issue: *Indigenous Rights in Southern Africa*, guest edited by Jennifer Hays. 15 (1): 11–36.

Dieckmann, Ute. 2010. *Review Report on Ongoing San Development Initiatives in Namibia. Prepared for the ILO-ACEID Project on Promoting the Implementation of the Rights of San in Namibia*. Windhoek: Legal Assistance Centre (LAC), Land, Environment and Development (LEAD) Project.

Dieckmann, Ute, Maarit Thiem, Erik Dirkx, and Jennifer Hays, eds. 2014. *Scraping the Pot: San in Namibia Two Decades after Independence*. The Legal Assistance Center and Desert Research Foundation of Namibia. Windhoek: John Meinert Publishing.

GRN (Government of the Republic of Namibia). 2013. *Mid-term Progress Report on the Implementation of the Recommendations of the Human Rights Council Working Group on the Universal Periodic Review (UPR) Following Namibia's UPR on 31 January 2011*. https://www.upr-info.org/followup/assessments/session24/namibia/Namibia-State.pdf (accessed 20 February 2019).

Guenther, Mathias, Justin Kenrick, Adam Kuper, Evie Plaice, Trond Theun, Patrick Wolfe, Werner Zips, and Alan Barnard. 2006. "The Concept of Indigeneity." *Social Anthropology* 14 (1): 17–32.

Hays, Jennifer. 2004. "Indigenous Peoples' Rights in Education: The San of Southern Africa in Local and Global Contexts." In *Indigenous Peoples Rights in Southern Africa*, edited by Robert Hitchcock and Diana Vinding, 228–248. Copenhagen: IWGIA.

Hays, Jennifer. 2011. "Educational Rights for Indigenous Communities in Botswana and Namibia." *The International Journal of Human Rights*. Special issue: *Indigenous Rights in Southern Africa*, guest edited by Jennifer Hays. 15 (1): 127–153.

Hays, Jennifer. 2016. *Owners of Learning: The Nyae Nyae Village Schools over Twenty-five Years*. Basel Namibia Studies Series. Basel: Basler Afrika.

Hays, Jennifer. 2019. "Interpretations of San Ethnicity and Identity in Namibia: A Review of Two Ethnographic Accounts." *Journal of Southern African Studies* 45 (2): 433–449.

Hays, Jennifer, and Megan Biesele. 2011. "Indigenous Peoples' Rights in Southern Africa: International Mechanisms and Local Contexts." *The International Journal of Human Rights*. Introduction to the special issue: *Indigenous Rights in Southern Africa*, guest edited by Jennifer Hays. 15 (1): 1–10.

Hays, Jennifer, and Jakob Kronik. 2013. *Promoting and Implementing the Rights of the San Peoples of the Republic of Namibia. Single-country Evaluation for the AECID Funded ILO Programme PRO169*. Geneva: International Labour Organization. Available at: https://www.ilo.org/ievaldiscovery/#b2iixln (accessed 24 February 2019).

Hays, Jennifer, and Jakob Kronik. forthcoming. "The ILO PRO169 Programme: Learning from Technical Cooperation in Latin America and Southern Africa." *The International Journal of Human Rights*. Special issue: *ILO Convention 169 and indigenous rights: Critical Perspectives*, guest edited by Peter Bille Larsen and Jeremie Gilbert.

Hitchcock, Robert. 2019. "The Impacts of Conservation and Militarization on Indigenous Peoples: A Southern African San Perspective." *Human Nature*. Special issue *Warfare, Environment, and Social Inequality*, edited by Rick Chacon. 30 (2): 217–241.

ILO (International Labour Organization). 2003. *ILO Convention on Indigenous and Tribal Peoples, 1989 (No. 169): A Manual*. Geneva: International Labour Office. https://www.ilo.org/global/publications/ilo-bookstore/order-online/books/WCMS_PUBL_9221134679_EN/lang--en/index.htm (accessed 20 February 2019).

ILO (International Labour Organization). 2009. *Indigenous and Tribal Peoples Rights in Practice: A Guide to ILO Convention No. 169. Programme to Promote ILO Convention No. 169 (PRO 169)*. Geneva: International Labour Standards Department, International Labour Office.

ILO (International Labour Organization). 2011. *Report on the Sub-regional and National Conference on the Rights of Indigenous Peoples/Marginalised Communities, 11–13 October 2010*. Windhoek: Co-sponsored by: Namibian Office of the Prime Minister, African Commission on Human and Peoples' Rights, International Labour Organization.

ILO-ACHPR (International Labour Organization and the African Commission for Human and Peoples Rights). 2009. *Overview Report of the Research Project by the International Labour Organization and the African Commission on Human and Peoples' Rights on the Constitutional and Legislative Protection of the Rights of Indigenous Peoples in 24 African Countries*. Geneva: International Labour Office.

Jansen, Leslé, 2010a. *Review of the Existing Regulatory Framework for the Protection of San Rights in Namibia Prepared for the ILO-ACEID Project on Promoting the Implementation of the Rights of San in Namibia*. Windhoek: Legal Assistance Centre (LAC), Land, Environment and Development (LEAD) Project.

Jansen, Leslé. 2010b. *A Study on the Training Needs of 11 Namibian Government Ministries; Prepared for the ILO-ACEID Project on Promoting the Implementation of the Rights of San in Namibia*. Windhoek: Legal Assistance Centre (LAC), Land, Environment and Development (LEAD) Project.

Kenrick, Justin and Jerome Lewis. 2004. "Indigenous Peoples Rights and the Politics of the Term Indigenous." In *Anthropology Today*, 20(2): 4–9.

Kronik, Jakob, and Jennifer Hays. 2013. *Promoting and Implementing the Rights of Indigenous Peoples – External and Independent Global Evaluation for the ILO Programme*

PRO169. Geneva: International Labour Organization. Available at: https://www.ilo.org/ievaldiscovery/#b2iixln (accessed 24 February 2019).

Kuper, Adam. 2003. "The Return of the Native." *Current Anthropology* 44: 389–402.

Lee, Richard B. 2006. "The Ju|'hoansi at the Crossroads: Continuity and Change in the Time of AIDS." In *Globalization and Change in Fifteen Cultures: Born in One World, Living in Another*, edited by Spindler George and Stockard Janice, 144–171. Belmont: Thomson-Wadsworth.

Lee, Richard B. 2013. *The Dobe Ju|'hoansi*. 4th ed. Wadsworth: Cengage Learning.

Mayinoti, Sam. 2011. *Division for San Development Progress Assessment*. Widhoek: Division for San Development, Office of the Prime Minister.

Merry, Sally Engle. 2006. "Transnational Human Rights and Local Activism: Mapping the Middle." *American Anthropologist* 108 (1): 38–51.

Mongudhi, Tilen. 2010. "Law on Indigenous People's Rights Coming." *The Namibian*, 13 October 2010.

Ninkova, Velina. 2019. *"Now that we have development": Change, Resilience and Education for the Omaheke Juj'hoansi*. PhD thesis, Arctic University of Norway, University in Tromsø.

Nunumbe, Magreth. 2010. "Trapped on the Bottom Rung." *New Era*, 20 August 2010.

Office of the Ombudsman. 2012. *Guide to Indigenous Peoples' Rights in Namibia*. Windhoek: Ombudsmans Office.

PRO169 (Programme to Promote ILO Convention 169). 2009. *Indigenous and Tribal Peoples' Rights in Practice: A guide to ILO Convention No. 169*. Geneva: International Labour Organization.

Sasman, Catherine. 2010. "Indigenous Peoples' Rights Still not Secured in Namibia." *The Namibian*, 17 August 2010.

Saugestad, Sidsel. 2001a. *The Inconvenient Indigenous: Remote Area Development in Botswana, Donor Assistance and the First People of the Kalahari*. Uppsala: The Nordic Africa Institute.

Saugestad, Sidsel. 2001b. "Contested Images. First Peoples or Marginalised Minorities in Africa?" In *Africa's Indigenous Peoples: First Peoples or Marginalised Minorities?*, edited by Alan Barnard and Justin Kenrick, 299–322. Edinburgh: Centre of African Studies.

Saugestad, Sidsel. 2011. "The Impact of International Mechanisms on Indigenous Peoples' Rights in Botswana." *International Journal of Human Rights*. Special issue: *Indigenous Rights in Southern Africa*, guest edited by Jennifer Hays. 15 (1): 37–61.

Shigwedha, Absalom. 2005. "San Deserve their Own Land in Communal Areas: Amathila." *The Namibian*, 28 November 2005. https://www.namibian.com.na/index.php?id=17005&page=archive-read (accessed 24 February 2019).

Suzman, James. 2001. "An Assessment of the Status of the San in Namibia." *Regional Assessment of the Status of the San in Southern Africa*, Vol. 4. Windhoek, Legal Assistance Centre.

Swepston, Lee. 2011. "Good Governance and Indigenous and Tribal Peoples." *Yearbook of Polar Law* 3(1): 155–167.

Swepston, Lee. 2012. "The International Labour Organization and Human Rights." In *International Protection of Human Rights: A Textbook*, edited by Catarina Krause and Martin Scheinin, 353–371. Turku: Åbo Akademi University Institute for Human Rights.

Takada, Akira. 2015. *Narratives on San Ethnicity: The Cultural and Ecological Foundations of Lifeworld among the !Xun of North-central Namibia*. Kyoto: Kyoto University Press & Trans Pacific Press.

UNHRC (UN Human Rights Council). 2011a. *Report of the Working Group on the Universal Periodic Review: Namibia.* A/HRC/17/14. https://www.refworld.org/docid/50f3e57a2.html (accessed 20 February 2019).

UNHRC (UN Human Rights Council). 2011b. *Namibia Addendum: Views on Conclusions and/or Recommendations, Voluntary Commitments and Replies Presented by the State under Review.* (Report of the Working Group on the Universal Periodic Review: Namibia). A/HRC/17/14/Add.1. https://documents-dds-ny.un.org/doc/UNDOC/GEN/G11/137/02/PDF/G1113702.pdf?OpenElement (accessed 20 February 2019).

UNHRC (UN Human Rights Council). 2016a. *Report of the Working Group on the Universal Periodic Review: Namibia.* A/HRC/32/4. https://documents-dds-ny.un.org/doc/UNDOC/GEN/G16/078/53/PDF/G1607853.pdf?OpenElement (accessed 20 February 2019).

UNHRC (UN Human Rights Council). 2016b. *Views on Conclusions and/or Recommendations, Voluntary Commitments and Replies Presented by the State under Review.* A/HRC/32/4/Add.1. https://documents-dds-ny.un.org/doc/UNDOC/GEN/G16/121/10/PDF/G1612110.pdf?OpenElement (accessed 20 February 2019).

3 Indigenous peoples' rights and policies

The role of the UN in Mexico

Verónica González González

Introduction

Since its foundation in 1946, the activities that the United Nations (UN) has carried out in relation to indigenous peoples have been part of a global process that has determined the configuration of our current world polity. The UN has largely defined the political place occupied by indigenous peoples in the international system. The work of UN institutions around concepts such as *self-determination* has been crucial, for example, not just in shaping the political structure of the international system, but also in defining the place of non-State actors in it.[1] The UN has adopted normative instruments regarding indigenous peoples, including in particular the ILO Convention 107 concerning the Protection and Integration of Indigenous and Other Tribal and Semi-Tribal Populations in Independent Countries (ILO Convention 107); the ILO Convention 169 concerning Indigenous and Tribal Peoples in Independent Countries (ILO Convention 169); the United Nations Declaration on Indigenous Peoples' Rights (UNDRIP); and the outcome document of the High Level Plenary meeting known as the World Conference of Indigenous Peoples. These international standards have also played an important role in defining, sanctioning, or in some cases modifying, the relation that the State has established with indigenous populations, having important implications for the realization of their political projects.

An analysis of the role of the UN in defining the political place occupied by indigenous peoples requires consideration of initiatives carried out at the country-level. The UN was the first international organization to be present at the national level and to establish direct contact with local populations, instead of only with State representatives; this was in contrast to its predecessor, the League of Nations. This feature opened the possibility for the UN and its agencies to have a role in the development of a "governmentality" (Foucault 2004), and a recognition of the agency of indigenous peoples, an important aspect in the reproduction and normalization of the relationship between States and indigenous peoples.

1 In-depth studies on how the concept of self-determination relates to indigenous peoples include: Aikio and Schienin (2000), Anaya (2004), Pitty (2001), Thornberry (2002), Xanthaki (2007).

This chapter presents a chronological analysis of the activities of UN agencies in Mexico, a country with an important indigenous population,[2] in which the UN agenda in relation to indigenous peoples has been very active since the UN opened its first office in the country, in 1947. By engaging in complex dynamics with the national institutions that are competent in indigenous issues, and with indigenous populations, different UN agencies have contributed to the evolution of policy frameworks related to indigenous issues in Mexico.

The first part of this chapter analyzes the UN's multi-agency work in Mexico from the 1950s to the 1970s. During this period, the UN implemented an assimilationist policy, whose main basis was the Convention 107 concerning the Protection and Integration of Indigenous and Other Tribal and Semi-Tribal Populations in Independent Countries, adopted in 1957 by the International Labor Organization (ILO), the lead UN agency for colonial issues at that time.[3] The actions that the UN implemented in Latin America and in the field of "indigenous populations" (according to the UN language of that time) were aimed at supporting the modernization of the State. In a context in which the international system was recovering after the end of the Second World War and implementing a decolonization policy in a large part of the world, the UN promoted the consolidation of the State. This initiative reinforced the hegemony of the State as the sole political actor in national and international scenarios, which in turn reinforced the assimilationist policies that Mexico (and many other countries in which indigenous peoples live) were adopting at that time.

The second part of this chapter will look at the practices that the UN implemented in Mexico as part of its promotion of *multiculturalism*, which gradually replaced the assimilationist model as the dominant approach of UN bodies toward "indigenous populations." The application of this new policy model has been increasingly evident in Mexico since the end of the 1990s and reflects a paradigmatic shift in the way international organizations understand indigenous peoples' rights and issues. This new paradigm was encouraged by the adoption in 1989 of the ILO Convention 169. Under the leadership of the United Nations Development Program (UNDP), the implementation of multiculturalism in Mexico promoted the creation of a new relationship between the State and indigenous peoples, based on the recognition of collective rights. This section provides an analysis of the activities that the UN implemented to promote

2 Different official statistics exist regarding the number of indigenous peoples and indigenous persons in Mexico, depending on the criteria used by the different national institutions that elaborate the statistics, the most important of which are the Consejo nacional de población (CONAPO), the Instituto nacional de estadística y geografía (INEGI), and the Comisión nacional para el desarrollo de los pueblos indígenas (CDI). The most recent was the 2015 National Intercensal Population Survey, elaborated by CONAPO, which found that 21.5% out of the 121 million inhabitants of the country self-identified as "indigenous." They count 68 different linguistic groups in the country. See: Consejo nacional de población (CONAPO), 2016.

3 For a detailed analysis of the role of ILO in advancing indigenous peoples rights in the UN, see Rodríguez-Piñero Royo (2006).

multiculturalism in Mexico and argues that it aimed to create a social space whose main task was to enable the reproduction of that policy framework.

Finally, the third part of the chapter argues that, following the adoption by the UN General Assembly of UNDRIP in 2007, a new understanding of the political place of indigenous peoples at the national and at the international level is being promoted by the UN agencies in Mexico, particularly the Office of the High Commissioner on Human Rights (OHCHR). This approach promotes a global governance that sets indigenous peoples' right to self-determination as the basis for the articulation of matters concerning indigenous peoples to the State and to the international system. By analyzing the practices deployed by the UN to implement UNDRIP in Mexico, I will particularly focus on the opportunities for this model to reinforce indigenous peoples' political projects – and the ongoing challenges in doing so.

Reinforcing the State: the assimilationist action of the UN (1950s–1970s)

The actions that the recently founded UN undertook in relation to "indigenous populations" were largely determined by one of its main goals, the end of colonization. The discussions that led to the adoption of the UN Declaration on the Granting of Independence to Colonial Countries and Peoples by the UN General Assembly in 1960 influenced the policy applied to indigenous populations in the Post-War period. Various parties involved in the debates on decolonization raised the relevant question of whether or not to include the indigenous populations inhabiting the already independent States, including those in Latin America, in the UN decolonization agenda. This debate was finally solved by what is commonly referred to as the "Blue Waters Doctrine" or the "Salt Water Doctrine," which limited the scope of the decolonization process exclusively to the territories under UN trusteeship. This decision prevented indigenous peoples inhabiting independent countries from revindicating the right to self-determination. It also justified the implementation, especially in Latin America, of an assimilationist policy toward indigenous peoples, which did not threaten the sovereignty of those States. On the contrary, this assimilationist framework provided new support for their legitimacy, based in an understanding of self-determination at the *national* level, fitting with the international climate of decolonization. Left with no access to political resources from either the national or the international arenas, indigenous peoples often lacked enough power to implement their own political projects. Furthermore, this framework legitimized the State's claim to authority over all affairs concerning indigenous peoples. Indigenous affairs were considered to be under the exclusive jurisdiction of the State, which reserved the right to mediate between the international and local spheres.

In this context, when the UN was established, Mexico – a founding member – and other Latin American States lobbied for the adoption of an international agenda that could guide the State's action toward indigenous peoples.[4] According to them, assimilation was a fundamental component of such an agenda, and of the consolidation of modern nation-States. The "Indian problem," a term used by the Latin American States to capture the different challenges indigenous populations posed for the national project of "modernization" that the elites had in mind, became an important field within the UN agenda on development.

Along with the particular role that Latin America played in the debates related to decolonization, the continent also constituted a particularly important field for building UN expertise in the field of "indigenous populations." This became the first population sector targeted by the newly established intergovernmental organization, and the four specialized agencies that were part of the UN at that time: the ILO, the United Nations Educational, Scientific and Cultural Organization (UNESCO), the Food and Agriculture Organization (FAO), and the World Health Organization (WHO). In a multi-agency effort, those UN bodies collaborated at the country-level in what is known as the best example of the UN action in the field of indigenous populations at that time: the Andean Indian Program (AIP).

Set in indigenous communities in seven countries in Latin America, in the context of the UN Expanded Program of Technical Assistance (predecessor to the UNDP), the AIP was the most ambitious initiative that the UN carried out.[5] Conceived as a pilot project for UN activities in the field of "indigenous populations," the AIP implemented a series of capacity-building projects at the local level, in the fields of expertise of the UN agencies: vocational training, education, agriculture, health, etc. UN intervention at the country-level in Latin America enabled the intergovernmental structure to institutionalize the principles that would guide the State's action in the indigenous issues field. The experience acquired by the AIP led, in 1957, to the adoption of ILO Convention 107, a standard-setting document that acknowledges some collective rights of indigenous peoples – while still assuming the goal of their assimilation to the State. That instrument guided the policy-making and normative activities carried out by the UN in that area from the 1950s until the 1970s.

Through the implementation of development policies, capacity-building for indigenous populations at the local level, and the recognition that those populations were entitled to certain rights, both the AIP and the ILO Convention 107 positioned the UN to play a major role in promoting the agency of indigenous peoples – thus contributing directly to the formation of citizens in modern Latin

4 In particular, they pressured the ILO governing body to adopt an assimilationist agenda, supported at the regional meetings of the ILO State members in Mexico (1946) and in Montevideo (1949); this request was also taken to the Organization of American States (OAS). This approach was gradually adopted by ILO in the 1940s and extended to the work of other UN agencies (Rens 1961).

5 The program lasted 20 years (1953–1972). It was implemented in seven countries: Argentina Bolivia, Colombia, Chile, Ecuador, Peru, and Venezuela. It benefitted directly 250,000 people (Martínez Cobo 1982).

American nation-states. Those initiatives were a major inspiration for the objectives, and the methodologies that the UN agencies used to carry them out at the country level, even in countries such as Mexico and Guatemala, where the AIP had not been implemented.

The "indigenous populations" agenda: a space of knowledge-sharing between the UN and the Mexican State

Grounded in this assimilationist framework, the primary activities that the UN specialized agencies carried out in the local communities were designed to promote the idea of "community development." Relying on tools borrowed from applied anthropology, the efforts consisted mainly in the creation of "community centers." In Mexico, the Regional Centre for Adult Education in Latin America (*Centro de Cooperación regional para la educación de adultos en América Latina y el Caribe*, CREFAL), established in Patzcuaro in 1950 by UNESCO, was arguably the main institution implementing many of the assimilationist activities carried out by the UN.

Inspiration for these centers came from the model implemented by the Indigenist[6] Coordinating Centers (Centros coordinadores indigenistas) established from the 1950s by the Mexican National Indigenist Institute (*Instituto nacional indigenista*, INI), the national bureau in charge of implementing assimilation policies. Like the Indigenist Coordinating Centers, the "community development centers" created by the UN focused on the local implementation of national policies, and on programs promoting education, health, agriculture, and other services. Like its national counterparts, for its involvement in the local spheres, the UN relied on ideas provided by Mexican anthropology, a discipline that had a strong influence in fashioning the State policy regarding indigenous populations. Concepts like "refuge zones" (first coined by Aguirre Beltrán in 1967) inspired the action of those institutions in indigenous communities, and promoted the idea that they were essentially "local societies,"[7] isolated or not necessarily articulated with the national society; this in turn put them the role of passive recipients of the State's development model.

The implementation of an assimilationist agenda in Mexico by the UN agencies was further stimulated by the close collaboration of Mexican (non-indigenous) intellectuals in international policy-making processes. Anthropologists like Manuel Gamio and Juan Comas actively promoted the principles of *indigenismo*, and occupied positions as experts in some of the processes facilitated by the UN specialized

6 "Indigenist" is the direct translation of *indigenista*, a Spanish term that indicates the political approach to indigenous issues within the framework of assimilationist policies.

7 The INI identified corresponding social and geographic areas throughout the country. Between the 1950s and the 1970s, the INI created 80 coordinating and delegation centers; by 1998 it had created more than 100. Intervention was based on these centers, which in turn acquired a strategic importance for all governmental intervention at the local levels.

agencies that were relevant to indigenous populations.[8] Their involvement in key institutions in the Mexican, Latin-American (especially the Inter-American Indian Institute of the Organization of American States), and UN spheres strengthened the circulation of assimilationist ideas in the international institutions that had competence in indigenous populations issues at that time.

During the 1970s, the assimilationist model gradually ceded space to a multicultural model that gained influence both in the UN and in Mexico. As elaborated in the following section, multiculturalism was presented as a policy model capable of satisfying the growing claims of indigenous collectivities against the assimilationist model.

Toward enhancing diversity within the State: constructing a social space for multiculturalism (1990–2000)

From the 1970s onward, the UN System engaged in a process that eventually led to the elaboration of a new framework regarding indigenous peoples. In the 1980s, *multiculturalism* became the key word to describe a new approach, founded on acceptance of the legitimacy of diverse cultures and languages existing simultaneously within the country, in a state of ethnic pluralism. Corresponding approaches to public services such as education, health, and justice started with recognition of cultural and linguistic differences, and accommodated these in the implementation of such services. In Latin America, this term, and the processes it inspired, were in part a response to indigenous peoples' claims, including the right to *not* be assimilated by national societies. From 1982 to 2006, this process took place mainly in the Working Group on Indigenous Populations (WGIP, a subsidiary body of the UN Sub-Commission on the promotion and protection of Human Rights) but it had an important influence throughout the entire UN System. An important outcome of this process was the adoption in 1989 of the ILO Convention 169, which replaced the ILO Convention 107 as the major international framework on indigenous peoples' rights.[9] These processes set the framework for the evolution of indigenous peoples' policies at the international and national levels.

These normative developments opened a space to question key elements of the State's action in relation to indigenous peoples, including its function as an exclusive mediator between the international and the local spheres. This change was first illustrated by increasing and direct collaboration with indigenous activists and by the elaboration of standards in this field by the UN. The collaboration between the UN and indigenous peoples was not totally independent from the

8 Manuel Gamio was part of the FAO Committee on Rural Welfare (1948–1950), while Juan Comas collaborated in the elaboration of "The Race Question" by UNESCO, in 1949. They both were also involved in the Inter-American Indian Institute.

9 However, the ILO Convention 107 is still in force in 17 countries that ratified it but have not ratified the later Convention 169. These include Angola, Bangladesh, Belgium, Cuba, Dominican Republic, Egypt, El Salvador, Ghana, Guinea Bissau, Haiti, India, Iran, Malawi, Pakistan, Panama, Syria, and Tunisia.

UN member States, which maintained a major role throughout the negotiations on indigenous peoples. Nonetheless, during the negotiations that were taking place at the WGIP, and at other intergovernmental bodies that discussed matters related to these peoples, the collaboration of international institutions and local indigenous authorities in the elaboration of policies represented a rupture from the model on which the State hegemony had relied. The structure in which the State had an exclusive competence regarding indigenous affairs was progressively abandoned, first by a new affirmation of the legitimacy of intergovernmental action on this issue. Particularly in Mexico, this legitimacy was further confirmed by the delicate human rights situation that had existed in the country since the mid-nineties, particularly in relation to indigenous peoples; in 1997, UN experts on human rights addressed the Mexican government expressing these concerns.[10] Second, the inclusion and participation of indigenous peoples, among other groups such as the "civil society," in the framework of "global governance" gradually became one of the objectives of the UN.[11]

Facilitating the participation of indigenous peoples in the political arena was actually one of the main axes of the activities of the UNDP when this particular UN agency took the lead in the implementation of a multicultural agenda in Mexico in the 1990s. The engagement of the UNDP in this effort overtook the work done by other specialized agencies in the country, including those that were active in the indigenous peoples' agenda in Mexico in the 1970s. Notably, one of those was the ILO, which elaborated Convention 169, the most authoritative indigenous peoples' rights instrument existing at that time.

The commitment of the UNDP to indigenous peoples' issues in Mexico needs to be understood within the larger framework of its regional agenda to promote democracy and human rights in Latin America at the end of the twentieth century. Encouraged by the growing visibility that indigenous movements had gained during that decade, the UNDP elaborated a framework that aimed to respond to one of the demands of the indigenous peoples' movement: their inclusion in the national society and the political life of the State. The UNDP tried to facilitate the inclusion of indigenous peoples' issues as part of the State agenda, and promoted a governance approach according to which indigenous peoples, UN agencies, and State bodies all had to be involved in the elaboration of a national agenda regarding indigenous peoples.

Reproducing, reinforcing and widening a space in which different actors – experts, indigenous leaders, and civil servants, all claiming different identities

10 One of the most violent moments of this conflict was in 1997, when the Acteal massacre left around 300 dead persons. Asma Jahangir, the Special Envoy on extrajudicial executions, Mary Robinson, the High Commissioner on Human Rights, and Erica I. Daes, the chairperson and rapporteur of the UN Working Group on Indigenous Populations, expressed their concern for the situation.

11 The collaboration of the UN and indigenous peoples was actually highlighted in all the international observances that the UN dedicated to indigenous populations: "A new partnership," "Partnership in action," "Partnership for action and dignity" were respectively the themes of: the International Year of the World's Indigenous People (1993); the International Decade of the World's Indigenous People (1995–2004); and the Second International decade of the World' Indigenous People (2005–2014).

and coming from different backgrounds – could discuss the terms of a new governance thus became one of the main dynamics underlying the activities implemented by the UNDP-Mexico within its agenda on indigenous peoples. The UNDP became one of the main architects of a structure that was able to provide the social, political, and technical resources needed to implement multiculturalist policies in Mexico, and the principles established by ILO Convention 169. In order to achieve this objective, the proposed activities aimed to enable the engagement of both indigenous peoples' organizations and the State. To this end, they focused on capacity-building for indigenous organizations and leaders, and on the creation of new political and institutional resources that would facilitate the intervention of the State in that domain, based on the new framework. As the UNDP built these capacities, the contours of the scope of indigenous peoples' rights in that country were also being defined, and the dynamics that developed around UNDP initiatives helped determine key features of that structure. These features included, for example, a profile of indigenous leaders and organizations that were capable of, and interested in, being involved in such processes, as described in the following section. Other key aspects included the objectives that the State had to pursue in relation to the multicultural agenda (such as making new laws and new institutions), technical aspects that had to be discussed in the field, and the rhetoric that dominated the discussions; these will also be described in the sections below.

Capacity-building for indigenous peoples' organizations

The capacity-building activities undertaken by the UNDP allowed indigenous leaders from several regions of the Mexican republic to receive institutional support in order to create or reinforce the political and technical skills they needed to participate effectively in the political arena. The result of these activities has been an increase in the engagement of indigenous organizations and leaders in the public arena. However, the UNDP efforts also partly ***determined*** the characteristics of the indigenous movements in Mexico, which ultimately had an impact on the balance of power within the indigenous peoples' political field in that country.

An important aspect highlighted by the UNDP in its work with indigenous organizations consists of the reinforcement of indigenous identities as a legitimized political asset in the newly constructed political field of indigenous issues. The objectification of indigenous cultures fulfilled an important symbolic function in a political field dominated by multiculturalism. For example, the translation of relevant indigenous peoples' rights instruments into several Mexican indigenous languages[12] confirmed the will to affirm an indigenous identity, and

12 In 2009, in collaboration with the National Commission for the Development and the National Institute of Indigenous Languages (the CDI, and the INALI, according to its acronyms in Spanish), the UNDP translated UNDRIP into 11 Mexican indigenous languages: Nahuatl del Istmo, Totonaco de la Costa, Tojolabal, Chinanteco, Chol, Huasteco, Mazahua, Mazateco, Tzeltal, Tzotzil, and Zapoteco de la Costa.

invest it in the political-juridical arena. By enhancing capacities of indigenous peoples in order for them to contend in the political arena, and by highlighting that indigenous peoples were "different," the UNDP inspired a specific style of political action and influenced the "habitus" of the activists (Bourdieu 1980).

At the collective level, the activities undertaken by the UNDP have played an important role in defining the way indigenous organizations conceive and structure their political representation. By ensuring a wide diffusion of the international instruments related to indigenous peoples' rights, the UNDP reinforced the dominant profile among individual indigenous activists and organizations participating in the political arena. It indirectly strengthened the juridical capacities and the legally oriented vocation of indigenous activists engaged with it. The activities implemented by the UNDP empowered indigenous organizations for whom it would otherwise have been very difficult to contend for their political projects in these arenas.

The participation of indigenous peoples in UNDP activities also encouraged the formation of a particular model of political representation for indigenous movements, one that contributed to the emergence of non-government organizations (NGOs) as one of the most common organizational structures. Many Mexican indigenous organizations that have worked with the UNDP are now part of "umbrella organizations" that satisfy the need for indigenous participation at different levels of governance. As part of the process of building such NGOs, the UNDP has also highlighted the role of individuals, or "impact leaders"[13] – indigenous activists able to assure both indigenous participation at local, national, and international levels, and the articulation of the UN frameworks with the indigenous communities. This way of interfacing with the indigenous communities at the local level constitutes a major shift, especially compared to the presence that the UN agencies had in Mexican indigenous communities from the 1950s to the 1970s. Although there are still a number of UN agencies that have a local presence in cities that are close to indigenous territories, the liaison between the UN and indigenous societies is now ensured mainly by indigenous leaders or by consultants who are responsible for implementing projects or transferring expertise and information between the UN constituencies and the grass-root levels. This process relies on a more reduced and indirect contact with indigenous communities' realities, and involves a transfer of responsibility to individuals. This approach does not necessarily encourage the generation of sound institutional understandings of indigenous peoples' political aspirations, nor the adaptation of institutional tools to the situations faced by indigenous collectivities at the local level. Ultimately, this aspect compromises the support the UNDP can give to bottom-up empowerment, as well as the effective implementation of the alliance it has established with indigenous peoples at the national level.

13 This term, among others, was in the UNDP project *Strengthening Democratic Culture in the Indigenous Electoral Districts in Mexico*, implemented from 2008 to 2013, as well in other many projects implemented since the 1990s to empower indigenous women.

In fact, the experience of the UNDP-Mexico with indigenous political activists revealed the limits of a multicultural agenda to guarantee a broad interface with the indigenous peoples and their projects. The forms of engagement offered to indigenous peoples under the regime of multiculturalism encountered challenges, especially in the context of efforts to support important political projects. A particular example of such a project is the construction of autonomies sympathetic to the Zapatista Army of National Liberation (EZLN, after its Spanish initials); other indigenous initiatives have also proposed understandings of security, justice, and development models adapted to indigenous communities' particular problems, despite operating in an extremely tense situation characterized by the presence of paramilitary groups, and criminalization of indigenous leaders. For example, the Community Police of Guerrero and the indigenous Government of Cheran have proved to be successful in protecting communities from attacks perpetrated by armed groups of outsiders, from illegal plundering of natural resources, and in justice delivery.

More than 36 groups of citizens' defense models exist in the Mexican territory. The Community Police of Guerrero is a grass-root initiative rooted in ancestral community defense institutions. It proposes an alternative model of protection in a particularly exacerbated context of violence in which "entire regions of the country are controlled by non-State actors" (Campbell cited by Bartra 2014: 23).[14] In the territories in which the security services of the Community Police of Guerrero operate, "the rates of violence and crime are lower than in those protected by the various conventional police forces" (Aréstegui Ruiz 2014: 9), while "clandestine logging has drastically decreased" (Aragón 2017: 12) in the indigenous municipality of Cheran after they implemented their own justice systems to elect municipal authorities. As the indigenous initiative of government has been supported by some national institutions, the tensions these projects have with national hegemonic elites represent an important limitation to the implementation of the right to autonomy at the local level.

Despite the crucial symbolic importance that the UN normative frameworks on indigenous peoples represented for Mexican indigenous movements, not all indigenous communities felt equally supported by the UNDP. Important principles related to the construction of indigenous self-determination (such as adopting a "bottom-up" approach, and respect for development choices made by the communities) still need to be reinforced, to counter what the Zapatistas denunciated as an "epistemic hierarchy" regarding the UNDP development agenda in Chiapas (Andrews 2010). That criticism highlights the nature of the challenges that confronted some indigenous peoples in their efforts to find support for their political projects in the multicultural agenda of the UNDP.

14 Official figures published by the National Public Security System and the INEGI, declare that 234,996 homicides have been committed in Mexico between 2006, when the "War on Drugs" was declared by the Mexican government, and 2017. The same institution reports that 32,277 persons are missing. International institutions like the UK International Institute of Strategic Studies, consider the levels of violence existing in Mexico correspond to those of an armed conflict.

The UNDP and the development of a Mexican "ethno-bureaucracy"

An important objective for the UNDP consisted in working with the Mexican State to elaborate the policy frameworks, expertise, and structures that would enable it to be responsive to both the requirements of the multicultural model, and to indigenous peoples' human rights demands. This has not been an easy task. Following the EZLN uprising in 1994, the Mexican State became particularly cautious regarding the advancement of multiculturalism, unlike other Latin-American countries in which a multicultural agenda continued to advance.

At the beginning of the 2000s, the Mexican State carried out a reform in the field of indigenous peoples, the so-called *Ley indígena* (2001), a highly controversial initiative that consisted, in part, of the reform of several articles of the Federal Constitution. The changes made to the Constitution recognized a number of indigenous peoples' rights, including self-determination. However, the scope of the rights recognized is considered as insufficient to guarantee the implementation of indigenous peoples' rights in Mexico (López Bárcenas 2002). In addition, the reform involved building a national institutional machinery responsible for indigenous issues: this initiative included the creation of new bodies responsible for indigenous issues,[15] fulfilling a disposition contained in the UN normative framework that foresaw the need, at the national level, for the existence of "agencies or other appropriate mechanisms [...] to administer the programs affecting the peoples concerned" (ILO Convention 169: Article 33 (1)). The existence of a multi-level "ethno-bureaucratic field" (Boccara 2010) was a way of ensuring the interface between international organizations and the national level. It represented an opportunity to end the assimilationist approach that had been implemented by the State since the Mexican Revolution, and to better incorporate the development of expertise and the structural changes that the UN itself was undertaking at the international level through the creation of new UN bodies having a specific mandate on an agenda called "indigenous issues" – namely: the UN Permanent Forum on Indigenous Issues (UNPFII, established in 2000); the Special Rapporteur on the situation of human rights and fundamental freedoms of indigenous people (2001), now named the Special Rapporteur on the rights of indigenous peoples; and the Expert Mechanism on the Rights of Indigenous Peoples (EMRIP, created in 2008).

The UNDP also encouraged a number of measures to enhance the appropriation of a multicultural approach. These initiatives met differing degrees of success. The creation of indigenous jurisdictions by UNDP in 2004 was an initiative that involved the core of the national political electoral interests – but it did not have the impact expected – in fact, it was never implemented.

15 The reform included the dissolution of the INI (above mentioned) and created a new institution in charge of the agenda on indigenous peoples, the National Commission for the Development of Indigenous Peoples (CDI, in Spanish), as well as the creation of the National Indigenous Languages Institute, better known as INALI.

On the other hand, the UNDP programs that aimed at increasing indigenous peoples' visibility by elaborating a general socio-demographic profile of the indigenous populations were better accepted by the State. During the 1990s, the UNDP had collaborated with the State (through the INI and the National Institute of Statistics and Geography; *Instituto Nacional de Estadística y Geografía*, INEGI) in the elaboration of censuses that could better reflect the indigenous population in Mexico, and the collection of statistics indicating their well-being.[16] These measures in turn facilitated the adoption of international criteria regarding the identification of indigenous peoples in national censuses, for example, the criteria of self-identification; they were also key to adapting the numbers to a new understanding of indigeneity (Lavaud and Lestage 2009: 8).

The limitations of the multicultural approach to empowering indigenous peoples at the local level became evident not just in Mexico, but in the whole Latin American region. The construction of indigenous autonomies in Latin America faced major economic and political challenges that called into question the actual impact that a multiculturalist approach could have. This context encouraged indigenous movements to persuade the UN to adopt a more assertive position, intended to go beyond a basic understanding of multiculturalism. As multiculturalist measures are still promoted by national and international institutions, a new trend became gradually dominant in both national and international arenas, promoting, for example, a stronger emphasis on specific articles of the ILO Convention 169 such as the right of indigenous peoples to consultation, specified in Article 6. Even more important is the recognition of the indigenous peoples' right to self-determination, which was absent from the ILO Convention 169 but became central in 2007, when UNDRIP was adopted by the UN General Assembly. The recognition of collective rights, particularly that of self-determination in UNDRIP (explicitly recognized in Articles 3 and 4 and involving several other articles) constitutes a milestone in international law. The recognition by the UN of indigenous groups as peoples with the right to self-determination, a right that was thus far granted only to States, constitutes a critical step. It has the potential for enormous impact on the position of indigenous peoples – both within the State and in the international system, and the UN, in particular the OHCHR as the lead agency promoting that approach, has paid a particular attention to that right.

As UNDRIP gains influence in the context of global governance, the roles of the different actors involved in the field of indigenous peoples' issues in Mexico, including the State, are continuously evolving. The promotion of indigenous self-determination by some UN bodies in that country has opened new opportunities to implement a more ambitious project, upon which to found a new relationship between indigenous peoples and the State.

16 See, for example, the UNDP *Informe sobre desarrollo humano de los pueblos indígenas en México. El reto de la desigualdad de oportunidades*. Published in 2010.

A UN agenda based on the promotion of self-determination: opportunities and challenges for indigenous political projects (since 2007)

The overwhelming support in favor of adoption of UNDRIP[17] confirmed the States' recognition of indigenous peoples' rights as an important aspect of global governance, as well as the proactive role that the UN agencies should have in the implementation of that instrument.[18] In Mexico, one of the most active UN bodies in this area has been the OHCHR, which has promoted that instrument as the main reference to understand indigenous peoples' rights. As in other Latin American countries that recognize indigenous peoples' rights, a major challenge regarding an effective implementation of UNDRIP, including the right to self-determination, is the existence of different understandings of those rights – and major differences in their limits and scope. When observing the process of implementation of indigenous peoples' rights, the existence of such different perceptions has led to the prioritization of a set of "intangible minimal rights," leaving "overarching rights" as a pending issue (Yrigoyén Fajardo 2009). In an ambivalent neoliberal context, the advancement of indigenous peoples' rights has not necessarily prevented the States that supported UNDRIP, like Mexico, from adopting laws and policies that are not coherent with that Declaration. A strong interpretation of indigenous peoples' rights, like the one developed by the Inter-American Court of Human Rights,[19] is needed to ensure that the incorporation of indigenous peoples' rights into the national polity go beyond a merely symbolic adherence. As it has demonstrated, a superficial commitment to indigenous peoples' rights is a common position that hegemonic institutions have adopted in response to indigenous peoples demands for recognition of their rights (Speed 2008: 35). In light of this, ensuring interpretations and approaches faithful to the spirit of UNDRIP becomes of crucial importance.

The role of the OHCHR in advancing transformative conceptions of human rights

As an intergovernmental institution, the OHCHR has a good position to ensure the diffusion of UNDRIP within strategic sectors of the Mexican State, such as

17 UNDRIP was adopted by a majority of 143 States in favor, 4 votes against (Australia, Canada, New Zealand, and the United States) and 11 abstentions (Azerbaijan, Bangladesh, Bhutan, Burundi, Colombia, Georgia, Kenya, Nigeria, Russian Federation, Samoa, and Ukraine). Since 2007, the four countries that voted against the instrument have changed their decision and now support that normative framework.

18 The text of UNDRIP considers that UN bodies "shall contribute to the full realization of its provisions" (Article 41) and "shall promote respect for and full application of the provisions of this Declaration and follow up the effectiveness of this Declaration," including at the country level (Article 42).

19 On the role of the Inter-American Court of Human Rights in promoting a strong interpretation of indigenous peoples' rights in Latin America, see Bellier, Cloud, and Lacroix (2017).

the Federal Union Congress and the National Supreme Court of Justice. Lack of access to such institutions has been identified as one of the main challenges for the implementation of indigenous peoples rights (Stavenhagen 2003).[20] The access of the OHCHR thus enabled it to support the advancement of indigenous peoples' rights into the expertise of a state that was showing a particular openness to human rights in the current national conjuncture. In 2011, a milestone human rights reform was adopted in the country. Supported by a national network of human rights activists and the OHCHR, the reform recognizes the rights to which Mexico has subscribed at the international level to be on equal footing to the rights recognized in the Federal Constitution. The adoption of that reform, which includes the rights subscribed in the ILO Convention 169 and UNDRIP, confirmed a juridical and political trend toward opening important possibilities for the assertion of human and indigenous peoples' rights. Furthermore, by considering the rights contained in international instruments as intrinsic to the holders, and not derived from the State (as established by the prior national regime of human rights), the reform radically transforms the relation between the State and its citizens. From this new foundation, more space can be gained for indigenous peoples' rights like self-determination to be implemented.

As part of its strategy to support the incorporation of indigenous peoples' rights, the OHCHR also referenced its expertise in critical discussions, such as those regarding the Law on Consultation of indigenous peoples, held in the National Congress.[21] International experts have been invited by the OHCHR to speak in the legislative body about the international standards on consultation. Even if those discussions have not led to the adoption of the law, the OHCHR could position UNDRIP as a reference in the process of formation of a new State competence. This role was further strengthened by the publication and strategic diffusion of grey literature on key issues that could nourish the on-going national debates.[22]

The OHCHR also implemented an important capacity-building program for the judges of the Mexican Supreme Court of Justice, which facilitated the incorporation of indigenous peoples' rights standards in their decisions (Aragón 2013). Paradoxically, the normative framework related to indigenous peoples was not used by judges, even though the ILO Convention 169 was ratified by Mexico in 1990, and despite the recognition of the indigenous right of self-determination by the Indigenous Law in 2001. The OHCHR involvement in the Court of Justice

20 The capacity-building of State officials was also one of the recommendations that the then Special Rapporteur on the rights of indigenous peoples made to the Mexican government (Stavenhagen 2003).

21 The possibility to adopt a national law has been discussed in the Mexican Congress since 2008. In March 2011 a Panel on the Draft Law on Consultation to Indigenous Peoples and communities and International Law was organized. UN experts like Bartolomé Clavero Salvador, a member of the UNPFII and Jon Izaguirre García, a representative of the OHCHR, were invited to feed those discussions.

22 Those publications give general information on international instruments, mechanisms, reports, and recommendations on the rights of indigenous peoples, as well as specific topics such as consultation, indigenous normative systems, access to justice, and communication.

thus helped to overcome an important element of what the Special Rapporteur Rodolfo Stavenhagen called in his report about Mexico "the implementation gap" (Stavenhagen 2003), giving indigenous peoples' rights a new thrust. Since 2012, these rights have been recognized by historical decisions,[23] opening new opportunities for indigenous peoples to implement their political projects.

UN bodies' insights on indigenous self-determination: challenges to an increasingly complex bureaucracy

An important element shaping the political meaning of indigenous self-determination in Mexico is the way this key aspect of indigenous peoples' rights is perceived and promoted by the UN bodies having presence in Mexico City, and in the different Mexican federal states.[24] The UN system has a highly complex structure with a presence in different countries, whose own bodies pursue a wide range of mandates through different institutional cultures that they have developed throughout their existence. The adaptation of the UN to new challenges induces a further complexification of the bureaucratic field, through, for example, the creation of new bodies, ongoing reforms, and the implementation of new strategies. This complicated bureaucratic and political terrain encourages UN bodies to put forward their specialized mandate in particular subjects, as a way to acquire visibility and political weight. Having specialized expertise in a particular domain can be something desirable in policy making processes, but this feature can also have an undesired effect of transferring responsibility, which can undermine the promotion of the right to self-determination, as the Mexican case illustrates.

The new approach to indigenous issues based on the promotion of their right to self-determination has been driven in Mexico mainly by the OHCHR. Other UN bodies in Mexico have engaged in that approach to lesser degrees, largely because most of them consider issues pertaining to them as a field of human rights that goes beyond their expertise.[25] However, "indigenous issues" cut across a spectrum

23 A non-exhaustive list of those decisions are: *amparo* 753/2012, in favor of two Mayan communities in the State of Campeche, which opposed the concession to Monsanto genetically modified soy farming; *amparo* 631/2012, which revokes the authorization for the construction of the Aqueduct Independencia that deprived the Yaqui tribe of their water supply; the constitutional controversy 32/2012 promoted by the municipality of Cheran, that was resolved with the State recognition of the indigenous right to elect their authorities according to customary procedures; the *amparo* 1131/2013, in favor of the people of San Miguel del Progreso, Guerrero which recognizes the right of that people to decide over its territory, and suspends all mining concessions on it; the *amparo* 422/2014, which revokes the concession for the construction of an airport in the Tarahumara Sierra, in the state of Chihuahua).

24 Different UN bodies have established conventions with governmental dependencies or local governments in Mexico, in order to establish offices in some localities. This is the case of the UN Offices in Chiapas, or the UNDP Yucatan. Their presence in these localities relies on a conjunctural, temporary, agreement that involves specific objectives.

25 This concern was often mentioned in the interviews the author conducted with UN staff in Mexico during fieldwork from 2011 to 2014, in the research program SOGIP, funded by the European Research Council and coordinated by Irène Bellier.

of subjects, and include, for example, matters relating to education, health, and youth. The perception of indigenous peoples' issues as a specialized subject within the field of human rights presents a major challenge to the approach of "mainstreaming" them within the UN, because many people working for UN agencies in Mexico do not feel prepared to undertake an intervention based on the tools that have been produced by the organization itself to promote indigenous peoples' rights.[26] Existing policies and guidelines elaborated by the UN to orient the system's action regarding indigenous peoples' rights are often unknown to the UN offices based in Mexico City and in other states of the country; this is even the case in places in which indigenous issues have marked local history, such as Chiapas, where there is a strong indigenous population and the base of several social movements. Overall, the perception by UN bodies responsible for these areas that incorporating indigenous concerns into their agenda requires expertise that is outside of their competence results in an important loss of opportunities for the inclusion of indigenous views in the State, and for the promotion of indigenous peoples' rights.

These dynamics seriously challenge UN efforts to develop an integrated approach to indigenous peoples' rights. The non-systematic implementation of the UN human rights-based approach to indigenous issues hinders the engagement of UN agencies that are responsible for important aspects of UNDRIP. This kind of discontinuity in the UN structure is not particular to the indigenous peoples' rights agenda – it is inherent in the structure of an intergovernmental body. Nonetheless, this has rendered slow and uneven the diffusion of indigenous peoples' rights throughout the UN. Although several measures have been proposed by the UN and indigenous activists to address this deviance,[27] diverting "the biggest bureaucracy on Earth"[28] from the assimilationist approach that was the original model for its interventions regarding indigenous peoples has to overcome strong resistance of many kinds.

The implementation of human rights and the implementation of indigenous political projects: are they "false friends"?

The contribution made by the OHCHR to the implementation of UNDRIP in Mexico has been central to major specific achievements in the field of indigenous

26 Including the UN provisions regarding UN bodies and its country-level activities the "FAO Policy on Indigenous and Tribal Peoples" (2010), the "UNDP and Indigenous Peoples: A Policy of Engagement" (2001), the "IFAD Policy on Engagement with Indigenous Peoples" (2009), the "United Nations Development Group Guidelines on Indigenous Peoples' Issues" (2008). These resources should be reinforced by the System-wide Action Plan (2015). https://www.un.org/development/desa/indigenouspeoples/about-us/system-wide-action-plan.html (last accessed 11 January 11 2019).

27 Including the System-wide action plan, the ONE–UN program, and the Interagency Support Group on indigenous peoples' issues.

28 This phrase comes from a discussion with Dalee Sambo, a member of the Permanent Forum on Indigenous Issues, in the context of the conference "Enabling human rights-based development for indigenous and tribal peoples: Learning from 25 years' experience of ILO Convention No. 169," Geneva, 27–29 November 2014.

peoples' rights. Its work has helped to improve the status of human rights in Mexico, and it facilitated the recognition of self-determination as the basis for enhancing political projects grounded in indigenous institutions. However, these achievements can lose their meaning in the current international and national contexts. The security issues and institutional problems currently faced by the Mexican State create major challenges for the UN, further limiting possibilities for intervention.

A major challenge regards the fact that the Mexican State, the main counterpart for the UN as an intergovernmental institution, faces major obstacles in ensuring security and democracy. In part, this is because the hegemonic power that was previously centralized has become diffused across many groups of actors. This creates some major challenges – even as the legal-rational component of the Mexican State moves closer to international human rights' rhetoric. It is not clear, for example, how the UN's State-centered approach can deal with the power dynamics related to transnational crime actors and multinational companies. Complex underground networks of actors are increasingly gaining power (especially after the State declared the Drug War in 2006), a situation that has been described as the establishment of a "criminal liberalized State" built around the construction of "parallel sovereignties" (Aréstegui Ruiz 2014: 10). Multinational companies are also often outside the reach of the UN. These and other large-scale economic actors can severely impact indigenous peoples' livelihoods, wellbeing, and rights.

In this climate, it is vital that the UN continue its work in ensuring that a human rights agenda advances in Mexico. However, if the action undertaken by the UN does not affirm the inclusion of several stakeholders and partners, going beyond a State-centered framing, human rights work risks becoming a technical task. Such a situation would contribute to the "anti-politics" dynamic, where international organizations implement programs, but remain ineffective in improving the economic and social circumstances of the target population (Ferguson and Lohmann 1994). From that perspective, the goal of empowering indigenous peoples in the pursuit of their political projects needs to be conceived as going beyond the implementation of UNDRIP, to embrace a comprehensive approach capable of addressing the multiple barriers that indigenous peoples currently face to achieving self-determination.

Currently, the major challenges for the implementation and consolidation of indigenous peoples' rights are posed by dynamics brought in by transnational criminal actors and multinational companies. In this context, the UN has an opportunity to create new approaches that allow it to intervene in a scenario in which the distribution and the nature of power do not correspond exactly to the intergovernmental structure for which it was originally conceived. Just as, in the 1980s, the UN played a critical role in recognizing the damage that the assimilationist approach caused to indigenous peoples, and it supported, in the 2000s, the creation of policy frameworks that go beyond multiculturalism and reinforce indigenous peoples self-determination, the UN can elaborate innovative approaches to protect indigenous peoples rights, an issue in which it has been involved since its inception.

Conclusions

Through an analysis of the influence of UN agencies in Mexico since the 1950s in the field of indigenous peoples, this chapter shows that intergovernmental institutions are capable of influencing the power relations that exist between indigenous peoples and the State. This influence can reproduce and reaffirm those relations, or it can facilitate the creation of structures that have the potential to change them. The capacity of the UN to influence the role of indigenous peoples in the global political structures has mainly been examined through an analysis of actions at the international level. I argue that such analyses need to be complemented by analyses of the activities that the UN has implemented at the *national* level. The ability of the UN to carry out projects at the country-level allows the institution to interact in a systematic way with national structures, and with the national population. It is crucial to analyze the role that this feature of the institution has played in terms of governmentality, and in global dynamics. Understanding UN activities and strategies at the national level is central to a better understanding of the complex, multi-level dynamics in which the UN operates, and the opportunities and challenges these dynamics create for the implementation of international policies regarding indigenous peoples.

To this end, this chapter describes the evolution of the policies and norms that the UN has implemented in Mexico, since the beginning of its engagement with indigenous issues in the early 1950s. The guiding approach of the UN national offices in Mexico can be divided into three general periods. The first one corresponds to an assimilationist model that relied on a multi-agency model of action and reaffirmed the role of the State as the unique actor of the international scenario. Implemented in the early 1950s through the 1970s, this approach gradually lost influence as indigenous peoples proclaimed their desire to maintain their own cultures, languages, and structures. Since the 1990s, a multiculturalist model has been promoted, especially by the UNDP. By promoting some of the provisions of the ILO Convention 169, this model aimed to encourage: the official recognition of indigenous peoples as an important element of the State's cultural diversity; the right of indigenous peoples not to be assimilated; indigenous peoples' participation in the State and its institutions; and their inclusion as *peoples* in the national society. The multicultural model encountered practical limitations for empowering indigenous peoples, however, and as this became evident in the 1990s, a third approach to indigenous peoples' issues became dominant.

This approach was highlighted by the adoption of UNDRIP in 2007, and is currently being implemented in Mexico under the lead of the OHCHR. Although multiculturalist measures are still promoted by national and international institutions, the current trend promotes a wider understanding of indigenous peoples' rights, emphasizing the implementation of indigenous peoples right to self-determination in combination with other forms of recognition.

The analysis of the third period focuses on the challenges and opportunities that the UN faces today, as it promotes the implementation of UNDRIP in Mexico, in the framework of global governance. A major challenge is the need to reinforce a harmonization and a sense of coordination between the different UN bodies working in Mexico. Ruptures between the different specialized agendas can indeed neutralize the political potential that the right to self-determination has, by preventing the development of a coherent policy intervention that strengthens indigenous peoples' local political projects. A second major challenge involves critical problems that indigenous peoples face in the implementation of their political and autonomy projects – some of which are related to non-State actors, in particular transnational crime networks and multinational companies. Increasingly, those problems involve actors and dynamics that cannot be effectively addressed by the inter-governmental nature of the UN. If the promotion of human rights was a successful tool in creating opportunities to empower indigenous peoples' political projects, the UN now faces a new challenge to respond to those problems and ensure that what has already been achieved is not jeopardized in the context of the current global polity.

Bibliography

Aguirre Beltrán, Guillermo. 1991 (1967). *Regiones de refugio*. México: Fondo de Cultura Económica.

Aikio, Pekka and Martin Scheinin. 2000. *Operationalizing the Right of Indigenous Peoples to Self-determination*. Turku: Institute for Human Rights, Abo Akademi University.

Anaya, S. James. 2004. *Indigenous Peoples in International Law* (2nd edition). Oxford: Oxford University Press.

Andrews, Abigail. 2010. "Constructing Mutuality: The Zapatistas' Transformation of Transnational Activist Power Dynamics." *Latin American Politics and Society* 52 (1): 89–120.

Aragón, Orlando. 2013. "El derecho en insurrección. El uso contra-hegemónico del derecho en el movimiento purépecha de Cherán." *Revista de Estudos & pesquisas sobre as Américas* 7 (2): 37–69.

Aragón, Orlando. 2017. "Otra democracia es posible. Aprendizajes para una democracia radical en México desde la experiencia política de Cherán." In *Demodiversidad. Imaginar nuevas posibilidades democráticas*, edited by Boaventura de Sousa Santos and José Manuel Mendes, 475–499. Mexico: AKAL.

Aréstegui Ruiz, Rafael. 2014. "Preámbulo: Nunca más el silencio." In *La rebelión ciudadana y la justicia comunitaria en Guerrero*, edited by Marcos Matías Alonso, Rafael Aréstegui Ruiz, and Aurelio Vázquez Villanueva, 7–12. México: Instituto de Estudios Parlamentarios "Eduardo Neri" del Congreso del Estado de Guerrero, Centro de Estudios Sociales y de Opinión Pública de la Cámara de Diputados del Congreso de la Unión, Grupo Internacional de Trabajo sobre Asuntos Indígenas.

Bartra, Armando. 2014. "Armados." In *La rebelión ciudadana y la justicia comunitaria en Guerrero*, edited by Marcos Matías Alonso, Rafael Aréstegui Ruiz, and Aurelio Vázquez Villanueva, 23–28. México: Instituto de Estudios Parlamentarios "Eduardo Neri" del Congreso del Estado de Guerrero, Centro de Estudios Sociales y de Opinión Pública de la Cámara de Diputados del Congreso de la Unión, Grupo Internacional de Trabajo sobre Asuntos Indígenas.

Bellier, Irène, Leslie Cloud, and Laurent Lacroix. 2017. *Les droits des peuples autochtones. Des Nations unies aux sociétés locales.* Paris: L'Harmattan.

Boccara, Guillaume. 2010. "Cet obscur objet du désir… multiculturel (III): ethnogenèse, ethnicisation et ethnification." In *Nuevo Mundo Mundos Nuevos* [Online], Seminar materials, 2010, uploaded on 14 June 2010. http://nuevomundo.revues.org/59984 (last accessed 11 January 2019).

Bourdieu, Pierre. 1980. *Le sens pratique.* Paris: les Éditions de minuit.

CONAPO (Consejo nacional de población). 2016. *Infografía: Población indígena.* México: CONAPO.

Ferguson, James, and Larry Lohmann. 1994. "The Anti-politics Machine. "Development" and Bureaucratic Power in Lesotho." *The Ecologist* 24 (5), 176–181.

Foucault, Michel. 2004. *Sécurité, territoire, population. Cours au Collège de France, 1977–1978.* Paris: Gallimard and Le Seuil (coll. Hautes études).

Lavaud, Jean-Pierre, and Françoise Lestage. 2009. "Contar a los indígenas (Bolivia, México, Estados Unidos)." In *El regreso de lo indígena. Retos, problemas y perspectivas*, edited by Valérie Robin and Carmen Salazar Soler, 39–70. Lima: IFEA/CBC/CRPA.

López Bárcenas, Francisco. 2002. "Reforma constitucional y derechos indígenas en México: entre el consenso y la ilegitimidad." In *Los derechos indígenas y la reforma constitucional en México*, Francisco López Bárcenas, Guadalupe Espinoza Sauceda, Yuri Escalante Betancourt, Ximena Gallegos Toussaint, and Abigail Zúñiga Balderas, 7–37. Mexico: COAPI.

Martínez Cobo, José R. 1982. "Action Taken by the Specialized Agencies." In *Study of the Problem of Discrimination against Indigenous Populations.* UN Document, E/CN.4/Sub.2/1982/2/Add.1.

Pitty, Roderic. 2001. "Indigenous Peoples, Self-determination and International Law." *International Journal of Human Rights* 5 (4): 44–71.

Rens, Joseph Laurent. 1961. "Le Program Andin." *Revue internationale du travail* 84 (6): 463–505.

Rodríguez-Piñero Royo, Luis. 2006. *Indigenous Peoples, Postcolonialism and International Law: The ILO Regime (1919–1989).* Oxford: Oxford University Press.

Speed, Shannon. 2008. *Rights in Rebellion. Indigenous Struggle and Human Rights in Chiapas.* Stanford, CA: Stanford University Press.

Stavenhagen, Rodolfo. 2003. *Report of the Special Rapporteur on the Situation of Human Rights and Fundamental Freedoms of Indigenous People, Rodolfo Stavenhagen. Addendum Mission to Mexico.* Commission on Human Rights (E/CN.4/2004/80/Add.2). https://documents-dds-ny.un.org/doc/UNDOC/GEN/G03/172/95/PDF/G0317295.pdf?OpenElement (last accessed 11 January 2019).

Thornberry, Patrick. 2002. *Indigenous Peoples and Human Rights.* Manchester: Manchester University Press.

UNDP (United Nations Development Program). 2010. *Informe sobre desarrollo humano de los pueblos indígenas en México. El reto de la desigualdad de oportunidades.* Mexico. http://hdr.undp.org/sites/default/files/mexico_nhdr_2010.pdf (accessed 20 February 2019).

Xanthaki, Alexandra. 2007. *Indigenous Rights and United Nations Standards: Self-determination, Culture and Land.* Cambridge: Cambridge University Press.

Yrigoyén Fajardo, Raquel. 2009. "De la tutela a los derechos de libre determinación del desarrollo, participación, consulta y consentimiento. Fundamentos, balance y retos para su implementación." *Amazônica – Revista de Antropologia* 1 (2): 368–405. https://periodicos.ufpa.br/index.php/amazonica/article/view/294 (accessed 20 Feburary 2019).

4 Traversing the scales of rights

Interventions from indigenous peoples of Cambodia at the United Nations

Neal B. Keating

Introduction

Indigenous peoples' rights activists from Cambodia have in recent years broadened their strategies to include engagement with international human rights mechanisms and bodies that focus on indigenous peoples, such as the UN Permanent Forum on Indigenous Issues (UNPFII). In these actions, activists may aim to criticize the human rights violations of States and call for remedies, but through the physical process of making such interventions they must conform to temporal, spatial, and discursive limits set by UN culture – a culture that by definition is state-centric. Perhaps not surprisingly, the effects of their interventions can appear elusive to observers. Sometimes indigenous activists are further constrained by sponsoring non-government organizations (NGOs) that provide support for their transnational engagement on the one hand, but also assert control over their actions once they have arrived at the UN.

Drawing on fieldwork at UN headquarters in New York City and in Cambodia, this article argues that while participation at international human rights platforms can be frustrating for activists and result in little or no concrete change in states' behaviors, it can also generate resolve and empowerment of indigenous activists that in the cunning of history may change into new forms and assemblages of transnational politics that transcend the current State-restricted multilateralism of the international system.

The value of the UN intervention

During each spring season since 2002, between one and two thousand indigenous activists travel from around the world to the UN headquarters in NYC to deliver interventions at the UNPFII on behalf of their representative constituencies, and to talk back to States, international banks, and any number of UN agencies – but especially States. Their participation may appear to signify that indigenous peoples are now members of the UN, similar to Member-States with multilateral status. The indigenous intervention is a performative moment that seems to confirm this status. Many other things happen at the Forum, but the intervention is for many activists a key objective in participation.

It is a moment (actually 3 minutes usually) during which indigenous peoples may register their critiques of Member-States, similar in dramatic style to the critiques that Member-States make of each other in the UN General Assembly. But the sign of an inclusive neo-multilateralism is a bit of a ruse. The Permanent Forum on Indigenous Issues is a limited advisory board to the UN Economic and Social Council (ECOSOC), and all the Forum interventions and discussions ultimately are reduced to a list of recommendations the Permanent Forum provides to ECOSOC, which may or may not decide to bring to the General Assembly for its consideration, which in turn may take interest or decline. In the meanwhile, UN Member-States may continue to plunder the remaining resources of indigenous peoples in their countries. Indigenous peoples may be the most experienced people in the world when it comes to facing tricky Janus-faced State maneuvers of power, and there may be no greater example of this than the international system itself. But despite this – or because of it – each year activists return to deliver their intervention and speak their truth to power. What is it about this process that makes it meaningful to the actors involved? For many of them, getting to the UN is costly and time-consuming. Why do it?

Indigenous participants sometimes ask themselves this question. During my first participation in a UNPFII meeting, in 2007, I had an opportunity to interview Victor Kaiseipo (a long-time diasporic indigenous activist from West Papua who has since passed on). He described how people in West Papua expressed doubts about his participation in the UN system, and in particular, his practice of delivering interventions on the human rights situation of indigenous people in West Papua, which continues to be colonized by Indonesia as of 2018. According to Kaiseipo, West Papuans would ask him, "So what good is your intervention? What can we do with it? Can we eat it? Will it keep us warm?" Such local skepticism of international human rights processes appears to be valid. The form of the intervention, suggestive that indigenous peoples may now engage in effective multilateral discussions with States that have long oppressed them, is hard to reconcile against a lived experience of continuing dispossession by these same States. This conversation inspired me to examine more closely the value of intervention for indigenous groups.

The participation of indigenous peoples from Cambodia provides numerous examples of the ambivalence for indigenous individuals and communities of intervening at the UN. The first indigenous person from Cambodia to speak at the UNPFII, also in 2007, was a Kuy woman from Preah Vihear Province, accompanied by an NGO activist who provided translation. In her intervention, she denounced ongoing practices of land-grabbing and deforestation, and called on the Cambodian government to act. The problem of "illegal" logging is widespread throughout Cambodia, but has disproportionately impacted indigenous peoples since the mid-1990s. From 2007 through 2016, related denunciations have been included in interventions made by other indigenous delegates from other provinces in Cambodia, including Steung Treng, Rattanakiri, and Mondulkiri. Following requests from Cambodian communities and NGOs in 2010, over the years I have collaborated with Kuy, Tampuan, and Bunong activists in drafting and delivering interventions on deforestation in one of the last big forests in Cambodia, named Prey Lang,[1] a planned mega-development on largely Kuy lands involving iron ore extraction and processing,[2] the Lower Sesan II hydropower dam project,[3] and the Cambodian government's plan for rapid private land titling of collective indigenous territories.[4] The delegates that I worked with have not limited themselves to giving interventions – they also filed complaints with the Special Rapporteur on the rights of indigenous peoples, made side-trips to Washington DC to lobby the US House Foreign Affairs Committee, the US Agency for International Development (USAID), and granted interviews with Radio-Free Asia and the Voice of America. Despite all of these actions, the problems they sought to remedy have only grown (with the exception of the China North-South Railway project[5]). None of these "issues" have been addressed or remedied as a result of the interventions and other efforts of the delegates to the UNPFII.

The Cambodian indigenous delegates are from villages where poverty and oppression are severe. For example, in the Province of Mondulkiri where some of the Bunong delegates are from (and where the Bunong have until recently made up the majority of the population), the UN World Food Program reports extremely high rates of malnutrition, stunting and mortality rates for children under 5 years of age (WFP 2015). These poor health conditions are closely associated with the fact that many of the natural resources that Bunong peoples relied on previously for their livelihoods, health, and well-being, are no longer available to them. Primary among these were their upland forests. Once rich in biodiversity and important sources of food and medicines, most of these have been cut down in the last three decades and exported for plywood or furniture manufacture (Milne and Mahanty 2015). In many parts of Mondulkiri, the deforested lands have been converted to rubber plantations or gold mining operations. The transformation of Bunong lands has been carried out largely through commercial partnerships between private enterprises and the Cambodian state, which is not only a UN member state, but to a great extent is a "post-conflict"

1 "Prey Lang" is the Kuy name of a large forested region that straddles four provinces, and is considered the last remaining significant area of lowland evergreen forest on the Southeast Asia massif (Michaud 2012).

2 Known as the "Chinese North-South Railway Project" (cf. Equitable Cambodia and Focus on the Global South 2013).

3 At an estimated 400 MW, The Lower Sesan II will be Cambodia's largest dam when it is completed, and displace more than five-thousand indigenous Tampuan, Kreng and other people without their consent and with little or no compensation. It will impact tens of thousands more people downstream, in addition to causing irreversible damage to the ecosystem of the Mekong mainstream (Baird 2009).

4 Known as "Directive 01BB," this plan in many ways resembles the nineteenth and twentieth century "allotment" plans for Native American lands in the US (cf. Milne 2013; Rabe 2013).

5 The Chinese North-South Railway project has not gone forward, largely due to problems in China, regarding corruption and financing (Carteret 2014).

product of the UN.[6] Back "home" in Cambodia, when Bunong and other local people protest the acquisition of their lands and the destruction of their forests, the state often responds by arresting them, and occasionally assassinating them.[7] When they speak at the UN it is not at all clear that anyone with power to change their situation is listening any closer than they do at home. Among Cambodian activists and organizations involved with indigenous peoples' rights, the use of scarce resources to send delegations to the UN is contentious. Many feel it would be a better use of resources to organize physical blockades of the logging roads, patrol the forest, seize chainsaws and bulldozers, or otherwise engage at the local level. Yet, each year, subject to the approval of travel visas by the US Embassy in Phnom Penh, a delegation of indigenous peoples from Cambodia travels to the UNPFII, with the hope that maybe this year their words will have an effect. What keeps them coming back so consistently?

There are good grounds for immediate cynicism about human rights in general, and indigenous peoples' human rights in particular. But seen as a narrative form of "long-game," the UNPFII intervention is also a part of an ongoing and evolving politics of human life and social organization with regard to multilateralism, i.e., having a seat at the table. The extension of human rights to include indigenous peoples as *peoples* – in the international sense of the word – challenges the international system of states to evolve a new kind of expansive multilateral politics that includes *peoples* alongside *states*, which by most accounts states are not ready to do, and which the current multilateral system has an equally difficult time reconciling with its current structures.

Ethnography and human rights research

Since 2002, the UNPFII has provided a new platform upon which indigenous movements are able to develop their visibility and connect with transnational networks in ways that were previously unimaginable (see also Bellier, this volume). Its outstanding achievement to date is the General Assembly's adoption in 2007 of the Declaration on the Rights of Indigenous Peoples (UNDRIP), which provides a comprehensive and universal human rights framework with regard to indigenous peoples. Combined with the creation of the Expert Mechanism on the rights of indigenous peoples (EMRIP) in 2007 and the office of the

6 The postcolonial state of Cambodia was destroyed in the 1970s by the Khmer Rouge. The country was largely occupied by Vietnam during the 1980s. The UNTAC came in during the early 1990s and oversaw the transition to the "post-conflict" state it is today (Chandler 2008). Scare quotes are merited here on account of multiple indigenous elders in Cambodia informing me that the conflicts that have developed in the post-conflict period are far more destructive than the conflicts during the official conflict period, i.e., the postcolonial period.

7 The week before the UNPFII meeting in 2012, Chut Vutty, a well-known and outspoken environmental activist in Cambodia was shot dead. His murder was never fully investigated, and it appears that he was executed because of his work (Aun 2017). When the delegation of indigenous peoples from Cambodia showed up at the UNPFII that year, they wore t-shirts with Vutty's face, under which were the words, "we are all Chut Vutty."

Special Rapporteur on the rights of indigenous peoples (SRRIP) in 2001, the international system is now poised for mainstreaming indigenous peoples' rights globally.[8] Despite these developments, enormous obstacles stand in the way of the realization of indigenous peoples' human rights in actual lived reality, not the least of which is the structure of the international system itself, including the UN and the many NGOs that the system enables.

In 2007 I started participating in the annual UNPFII sessions as an academic observer-anthropologist, alongside indigenous activists and organizations who converged at UN Headquarters in New York City. Having some familiarity with indigenous activism through prior work with Haudenosaunee artists (Keating 2012a), I was interested in exploring how ethnography might contribute to a comparative understanding of the changing human rights situations of indigenous peoples, and the complex relations between indigeneity as articulated at the UN, and Indigeneity "at home" (with the understanding that "home" may mean different things, and may be rooted or mobile, diasporic, or annexed, and so on). My applied goals were to develop anthropological practice that contributes to the realization of indigenous peoples' rights. These goals, in turn, are shaped by my broader interests in problems of comparative freedom and cultural critique.

My first impressions at the UNPFII in 2007 led me to think that critical human rights-based ethnography could contribute to the work of the Special Rapporteur on the rights of indigenous peoples (SRRIP), to promote and protect indigenous peoples' rights (Keating 2007).[9] The mandate of the Special Rapporteur includes gathering information on human rights abuses from indigenous peoples and allied organizations, and officially confronting the governments of UN member states to answer to these complaints through formal channels of communication (cf. UN doc 2010). Along with many other ethnographers, including other authors in this book, I hoped that my work could contribute to such efforts. An ethnographer is not under the same constraints as a UN Special Rapporteur making what is called a "country visit." An apt ethnographer can get on the ground "behind the scenes" of human rights situations to make direct

8 The UNPFII is established within the UN Economic and Social Council (UN doc E/RES/2000/22). The UNDRIP was adopted by the GA by a 144-4 vote (officially 143-4, because Montenegro's vote did not get recorded due to a technical glitch), as resolution 61/295 (UN doc A/61/L.67). The SRRIP is established by the UN Human Rights Council (UN doc A/HRC/RES/15/14), which superseded a previous Indigenous Peoples' Rights Special Rapporteur position created in 2001 by resolution 2001/57 of the (then) UN Commission on Human Rights (cf. UN doc E/CN.4/2002/97). The EMRIP is established by the UN Human Rights Council Resolution 6/36 (cf. UN doc A/HRC/EMRIP/2008/1/Add.1). All of these are predated by many other actions at the UN, starting in the early 1980s, when the "Working Group on Indigenous Populations" was formed by Resolution 1982/34 of the UN Economic and Social Council (UN doc E/RES/1982/34).

9 I was influenced by learning the Special Rapporteur on the rights of indigenous peoples at that time was an anthropologist from Mexico, Rudolfo Stavenhagen, and I am indebted to him for encouraging me to pursue this work.

observations that could lend empirical depth to the fact-finding work of the SRRIP. Among the institutional constraints placed on the SRRIP is that she has to be officially invited by the government prior to visiting a country, and once there is subject to limited time, mobility and contact with indigenous peoples. While also subject to similar pressures, ethnographers face these with greater flexibility and options.

After several years of attending the UNPFII meetings and talking about this idea with indigenous activists from around the world, I received an invitation to run a pilot study. This came, not from a government, but from a number of Cambodian indigenous activists and an NGO worker who suggested I visit several Kuy communities and observe the human rights situations there, particularly with regard to state recognition of them as peoples with land and forest rights. I accepted the invitation and made these visits in 2010 and 2011 (Keating 2012b, 2013). Information from these visits was incorporated into reports and dialogues with the SRRIP during 2012 and 2013. Unfortunately, by this time the government of Cambodia was disengaged from returning correspondence to the SRRIP.

As my aim was collaborative and participatory research on the linkages between the UN and indigenous peoples, I followed up these ethnographic "country visits" by facilitating delegations of indigenous activists traveling from Cambodia to New York City to participate in the UNPFII, including Bunong, Tampuan, and Kreung people, in addition to Kuy.[10] The work of facilitation led my research into another direction of human rights practice – that of the local scale speaking back to the international scale. These activists represented indigenous organizations but were often accompanied by a delegate-chaperone from a Cambodian national NGO that was sponsoring their trip to the UN.[11] My facilitation work included making arrangements for the delegates' participation and registration, finding places for them to stay, and collaboratively learning with them how to compose and give interventions, prepare written information for dialogues with the SRRIP, network with other activists, and in general navigate the UN system (which for those unfamiliar with it can appear opaque and often intimidating). In 2013 this work took on another transnational aspect, as some of the activists I worked with began connecting with related diasporic indigenous Bunong communities that had immigrated to North America (via Cambodia) from across the border in the central highlands of Vietnam (Keating 2016). New diasporic Bunong activists soon began coming to the UNPFII, resulting in a new transnational assemblage that eventually proved generative of indigenous peoples' rights practice back home in Cambodia (through the formation of an indigenous peoples political party). Within this emergent assemblage of social actors, Bunong and other indigenous peoples are pursuing a difficult and dangerous

10 There are an estimated 24 different groups of indigenous peoples in Cambodia, making up about 2–4% of the national population overall (Keating and Pheap 2014).

11 The actual names of activists and NGOs discussed here are for the most part not disclosed.

politics of inclusion, driven by human rights-based aspirations of democracy. The risk comes from doing so within the ambit of authoritarian states, a status fairly ascribed to both contemporary Cambodia and Vietnam. As such, their actions and experiences are significant to a general understanding of nonviolent social change movements from below.

In this chapter, I offer a descriptive analysis of the dynamics at the UNPFII that I observed through my work facilitating the participation of the Cambodian delegations. Recounting some of our shared experiences at the UN, I highlight the paradoxical nature of the UNPFII, as a place where indigenous activists come to intervene in the interstate state system, but do so under conditions set by the Member States that constitute the UN, and also sometimes by the NGOs that sponsor the activists. There is thus an inherent ambivalence surrounding this participation. Nonetheless, I argue that, despite numerous and daunting obstacles to real multilateral engagements, the UNPFII becomes a critical platform for generating aspirations of *indigeneity*. It is this generative process that I focus on here, through an examination of the process of making and delivering interventions at the UN. While my arguments may have general relevance, what I am describing is framed within the regional Asian context, and more locally the countries of Cambodia and Vietnam. Throughout Asia, as in Africa, the concept of indigeneity is highly contested by States for reasons not found in settler States like the Americas, Australia, and New Zealand. As described in the following section, this regional dynamic shapes the participation of indigenous people in global processes.

The Asian "problematique" of Cambodian indigeneity

By most estimates, more than two-thirds of the world's indigenous peoples live in Asia.[12] Despite this – or perhaps because of this – the concept of indigenous peoples continues to be controversial throughout the diverse continent. The majority of Asian states maintain that the concept does not apply to them, as all of their citizens are indigenous (see also Hays, this volume for a discussion of how this argument takes shape in Africa). This controversy has a long history, dating back at least to the second UN Special Rapporteur tasked with addressing indigenous issues, Miguel Alfonso Martínez, who argued for an African-Asian "problematique" of Indigeneity that limited the concept's application to settler-states only:

> Africa and Asia autochthonous groups/minorities/ethnic groups/peoples who seek to exercise rights presumed to be or actually infringed by the existing autochthonous authorities in the States in which they live cannot … claim for themselves, unilaterally and exclusively, the "indigenous" status in the United Nations context. (Martínez 1999, para 88)

12 According to UN estimates the world population of indigenous people is 370 million, thus some 245 million indigenous people in Asia (UN DESA 2014).

Yet even before Martínez's *problematique* was published, an Asian indigenous peoples' movement was well underway, starting in the Philippines and Taiwan during the 1980s, and followed by new national policies of recognizing indigenous peoples – in 1997 (the Philippines), 2001 (Cambodia), 2005 (Taiwan), and 2007 (Nepal).[13] As noted for Australian Indigeneity (Povinelli 2002), policy practices of "recognition" in these Asian states do not automatically result in the physical protection and promotion of indigenous peoples' rights. For example, in Cambodia, the 2001 national policy granted limited recognition of indigenous peoples and their rights to communally held lands (Baird 2011; Keating 2013). The Cambodian Land Law was followed by subsequent legislation and policies that appear to reinforce this recognition, but were deficient in meeting the international standards set by the UNDRIP and ILO Convention 169 (Anaya 2010; Keating 2013).[14] My observations in Cambodia during 2010–2016 are that recognition has not resulted in structural changes in the way the state relates to indigenous peoples, but it has enhanced the conditions of possibility for the indigenous peoples movement in Cambodia to grow, which today includes several indigenous-led organizations, associations, networks, and a registered indigenous peoples political party (the Cambodian Indigenous Peoples Democracy Party). However, its development is complicated by its pseudo-patron/client relationships with non-indigenous NGOs that sometimes enable its development (Baird 2011) – or, as described below, sometimes constrain it.

These recognition policies notwithstanding, states throughout Asia continue to operate using various "minoritarian" frameworks of population management, in which a single dominant ethnic group commands state power over its multiple non-dominant groups.[15] In Cambodia, the dominant group is the Khmer; in Myanmar, the Bamar/Burmans; in Thailand the Thai; and in Vietnam, the Kinh/Vietnamese (Clarke 2001, Erni 2008; Winzeler 2011). In Laos, which has the highest degree of ethnic differences in the region (over 50% of the population), the pattern is similar; a single group (Lao Loem) controls state power (Baird 2015). In each of these countries there are substantial numbers of different peoples, many of whom are (or were until very recently) kinship-based forest dwellers and shifting cultivators in the uplands and mountains of the massif. Asian states' use of "ethnic minority" frameworks to configure these groups is a primary device for limiting the potential (or risks) of collective rights claimants to organize within the political boundaries of

13 In 1997, the Philippines government adopted the "Indigenous Peoples' Rights Act" (Republic Act 8371). In 2001, Cambodia included recognition of indigenous peoples in a new postconflict "National Land Law." In 2005, Taiwan adopted the "Basic Law of Indigenous Peoples" (Simon 2007). As the lone Asian signatory to ILO Convention 169 in 2007, Nepal can also be included in this list.

14 This critique was provided to the Cambodian government through official correspondence from the SRRIP, James Anaya. It went unanswered by the government.

15 Elizabeth Povinelli and others find that recognition does not automatically lead to substantive restructuring of state-indigenous relations, and may produce the opposite effect of reproducing conditions of domination (Povinelli 2002, Corntassel 2012).

the state. By states' definition, minorities have no collective human rights. Midway through the second decade of the twenty-first century, most Asian states continued to maintain that that the concept of indigenous people does not apply in their countries (AIPP 2014).

The Asian indigenous peoples' movement is also affected by the sheer force, speed, and violence with which the state and commercial interests are converting indigenous lands, forests, territories, and resources into capital and commodities, throughout much of Asia. I have argued elsewhere that it is not a coincidence that the indigenous peoples' rights movement in Cambodia is happening at the same time as the rapid and extensive expropriation of their lands and resources. Although not entirely determined by expropriation, the movement is driven by it (Keating 2013). It has become a matter of necessity and survival in a very desperate time. The extractive industries sector today drives much of the politics throughout Southeast Asia, and unless this changes very soon, the cultural diversity as well as the biological diversity of this planetary hotspot of life will be severely compromised, possibly beyond recovery. In this context, expending scarce resources to speak out about this at the UN is for some a sensible decision; it is a way to fight back. Nonetheless it comes with many frustrations and is draped with layers of ritualism.

Ritual aspects of the intervention at the UNPFII

To *intervene* is a multi-layered symbolic act of moving "in between." An interventionist steps into something: a situation occurring in a particular place and time. The ostensible purpose of the intervention is transformation of the situation. An intervention presumes the existence of at least two other entities, in order for there to be a between-space that can be entered. At the UNPFII these are usually UN Member-States and indigenous peoples.[16] To intervene at the UNPFII is to enter a ritualized place and time. The tacit goal of the interventionist may be that of transforming a situation, but the latent effects are often those of social reproduction, in this case the reproduction of the UN system and its regulative, ritual practices and structures, which have been observed in other human rights bodies besides the UNPFII.[17] This ambivalence puts the interventionist in a liminal situation. However, as Victor Turner pointed out long ago, the energy generated in ritual space can in some circumstances negate existing social orders (Turner 1969). In this ambivalent situation, the entities of states and peoples take on ritual forms that have been described as unmovable objects and irresistible forces (Barsh 1996). The symbolic stakes are high: legally binding multilateral relations with the formerly condemned. The physical implications are immense: re-worlding lands, territories, and resources.

16 The other entities include UN agencies.

17 For UN ritual regarding women's rights and CEDAW meetings, cf. Merry (2006). For related UN rituals of the Universal Periodic Review process, cf. Charlesworth and Larking (2015).

The usual expectation of many interventionists is that in the name of indigenous peoples they are stepping in between the discourse of international human rights on the one side, and the actual political and economic behaviors of UN Member-States on the other. In so doing they aim to reform state behaviors so that they come into greater alignment with newly established international human rights law. This in-between place is often referred to in spatial terms, as a "gap," as in "the human rights gap."[18] The positivist framing of this between-space as a gap implies a technical resolution: gaps can be closed through discussion and negotiation, and conscious application of appropriate policies and procedures. The commonly offered explanation for the existence of the gap regarding indigenous peoples' rights is that it is the result of states' "lack of political will."[19] While not altogether inaccurate, the explanation does not account for those countries that do recognize indigenous peoples, but do not protect and promote their rights. It might be more accurate to explain it as resulting from the presence of the unmovable object. The between-space here is not caused by an absence; rather it is a by-product of a cultural pattern at the UN since its inception in the 1940s, in which the majority of member-states maneuver the appearance of conformity with international standards of human rights conduct, without actually fostering them within their countries.

While indigenous peoples' interventions can be conceptualized spatially, they also typically involve temporal aspects that are lexical and performative. Interventions begin as writings, often produced, edited, and rewritten through a dialogic process of meetings and email chains that may involve many individuals and organizations in decisions about their formulation. This lexical preparatory phase establishes the substance of the intervention, what will be carried into the between-space. Although I have witnessed spontaneous interventions at the UNPFII, these are rare, and usually limited to the seasoned veterans of the indigenous peoples' rights movement who have long acquaintance with the UN protocols for speaking.[20] Most of the interventions delivered by indigenous speakers are carefully constructed in advance, and generally follow a similar, short format, limited to 3 minutes: first, congratulate the chair of the session; second, describe the substance or issue at hand; and third, offer recommendations to states and/or UN agencies. While variable in length of time, this format is common throughout much of the UN system, particularly its many human rights agencies. This crafted text does not enter the between-space until it is

18 The usage of the term "gap" in UN parlance is by no means exclusive to the human rights situations of indigenous peoples, but is also commonly used in association with the situations of women, children, minorities, people with disabilities, and refugees; all commonly referred to in human rights instruments as "vulnerable groups."

19 I have observed multiple UN officers offering this explanation, including former Chairs of the UNPFII.

20 UN Member-states have the right to spontaneous interventions, which usually result when a member-state objects to a preceding indigenous peoples' intervention that names and shames the member-state. States can do so at any time by raising their hand, an act usually not available to indigenous peoples. UN Protocols for speaking privilege Member-states; after all, it's their club.

performed as an act of speech on the floor of the UN – it must be said out loud. That is the moment of intervention.

Not all interventions are permitted, and the written form has a relatively short life (despite the distribution and archiving on the UN website). Copies may be distributed in the room and given to DOCIP[21] for their archive project,[22] and some parts of the text may be added to the recommendations database of the UNPFII, which many indigenous activists argue is ignored by the rest of the UN. The effect of such perlocutionary speech acts – in terms of causing change in the behavior of states or corporations – will largely be judged by indigenous activists in terms of their observable impacts, on a continuum ranging from valuable to worthless. But the spoken intervention may also produce significant effects beyond the UN arenas. An intervention may change the moods and motivations of the speaker and those closest to her, and this change can and does generate further political activism and social assemblage. In short, the intervention also has a type of secular ritual power. How does this occur? What is the value to speakers and their delegations of the interventions they make? What part rests in the hope generated by the possibility of speaking truth to power? To explore these questions, the next section offers a three-part vignette that describes the intervention process at the UNPFII, based on a collaboration with a group of indigenous people from Cambodia and Vietnam in which I was involved as a facilitator and activist researcher.

Part 1. Preparing the intervention

The night before the opening of the 14th annual session of the UNPFII in April 2015, found 14 of us (13 indigenous Bunong activists and one anthropologist) crammed into a tiny hotel room in a run-down part of Queens, in New York City, to talk about what they wanted to achieve at the Forum. Two of the bilingual youths served as translators. Most of the group spoke only Bunong, and the youngest Bunong person there (a high school student) spoke only English, as did I. Several of the people in the room had recently flown in from Cambodia, and were jet-lagged from the 30-hour flight. The others had driven ten hours on American roads to get here. There were two more people from Cambodia that were also supposed to be there, but their visa applications had been denied by the US Embassy in Phnom Penh. Despite exhaustion and disappointment about those who were missing, the room was filled not just with people, but also

21 Docip, Documentation Center for Indigenous Peoples, is an international NGO that provides a technical secretariat to indigenous people during the UNPFII (free computer, printing access, translation support). Since 1978, it also maintains an archive record of many past interventions. cf. www.docip.org.

22 On October 30th, 2017, UNESCO recognized 33 years of "Statements made by Indigenous Peoples at the United Nations 1982 to 2015" as a key element of World Heritage. https://www.docip.org/en/our-services-solutions/news/single-news/article/la-parole-des-peuples-autochtones-reconnue-comme-patrimoine-mondial-de-lhumanite/ (accessed 23 January 2019).

energy and anticipation. And unlike the previous UNPFII delegations I had worked with, this one was notable for its absence of any NGO presence.

Once we were settled in, I started facilitating by asking my colleagues about their aspirations at the UN. They unanimously expressed a strong desire to make an intervention. The dialogue then led into discussions of what issues should be included in the statement. The border was one of them. We started talking about the Association of Southeast Asian Nations (ASEAN), and its plans for launching a regional economic community in Southeast Asia at the end of 2015 (the ASEAN Economic Community, or AEC). Part of the AEC plan involves opening the borders of ASEAN countries to greater flows of capital, commodities, and labor, but not to indigenous peoples whose territories straddle states' borders. For example, Bunong territory straddles the Cambodia-Vietnam border. The border divides traditional Bunong lands and makes it difficult or physically impossible for Bunong people to interact with relatives on the other side. This became the first issue they wanted to include in their intervention, the so-called "normalizing" of the border.

The discussion then shifted as Pich,[23] one of the activists living in the US, started talking about the surveillance practices of the Vietnamese state. She said whenever she calls her sister in Dak Nong, her sister then receives a visit from the police, asking her who she was talking to in the US, and why. They warn her that "it is not good to talk to people on the outside." Others in the room expressed the conviction that the Vietnamese government maintains surveillance of Bunong people not just in Vietnam, but also in Cambodia and in the US. The theme of state aggression came up repeatedly, including land-grabbing of Bunong territories (both in Vietnam and Cambodia) as well as religious persecution and direct violence (more pronounced in Vietnam). Nong told me about family members in Vietnam who were poisoned by state agents.[24] He also talked about police beating Bunong people, and imprisoning them without cause. We compared the situations of Bunong in Vietnam to those in Cambodia, where the state is relatively weak, and as a result there is greater freedom of movement and communication. The Vietnamese state is much stronger, and thus able to exercise greater control over its population; in comparison to Cambodia's relatively laissez-faire regime, Vietnam appears almost paranoid. This plays out at the UNPFII with Vietnamese delegates maintaining constant vigil over the proceedings while Cambodia is rarely present.

Out of concern for their well-being, I suggested that for this intervention we stick with the border issue. This merits explanation. It was their first time speaking at the UN, and politically these Bunong are trying to distance themselves from the *Montagnard*/Degar groups that have previously taken an antagonistic

23 All of the individual names of people here are pseudonyms.

24 These are serious allegations, and based on what was described, impossible to prosecute. The poisonings were carried out so as to be untraceable, and filing charges with local police would bring new risks. Later I did secondary research that found some support for the political use of poison in post-colonial Vietnam, linked to Russia.

approach and delivered incendiary "naming and shaming" interventions about Vietnam at this and other international fora, as well as articulated aspirations of territorial secession (including the Central Highlands and the Mekong delta). These have had predictable results of enraging the state's representatives and have not led to any constructive change.[25] For the Bunong, including assertions of Vietnamese state violence, poisoning, and intensive surveillance in their first intervention might invite that very response from the Vietnamese government. I also suggested that since they were seeking an alternative approach to change based more on conciliation rather than antagonism, perhaps the first statement should evoke a corresponding register. After more discussion they grudgingly agreed.

But they were adamant that they wanted their statement to include acknowledgement that the Bunong people have a long interconnected history in the highlands of Cambodia and Vietnam, even if the world does not yet recognize that. In the end we crafted a 3-minute intervention that included affirmation of this long history, and offered four recommendations for states removing border-crossing restrictions for Bunong and other peoples, and for states to better recognize indigenous peoples' rights, especially freedom of religion.

The next step was to decide on which of the already-scheduled topics for the UNPFII session would be appropriate for making this intervention. Since 2015 was a "review year" for the UNPFII, many of the topics were geared toward a kind of institutional introspection. Given the session's "plan of work,"[26] the only scheduled topic where the Bunong intervention seemed to fit was topic 3(1), "Outcome of the high-level plenary meeting of the General Assembly known as the World Conference on Indigenous Peoples" (HLPM/WCIP). The inclusion of this topic was ostensibly to provide indigenous organizations with an opportunity to respond to the HLPM/WCIP and its "Outcome Document," a.k.a. the "OD" (UN doc A/69/L.1). In the OD, states vaguely promise to take action to implement indigenous peoples' rights, as established in the framework provided by the UNDRIP. Given that border-crossing rights are part of this framework (in particular, Article 36 in the UNDRIP), I suggested we sign up to deliver the intervention under topic 3(1), and they agreed.

Part 2. Entering UN headquarters

The next morning, we set out from Queens to make our way to the UN. It was cold, raining, and windy. Eventually we found the subway and made our way up to 42nd street, where we caught a cross-town bus to 1st avenue. Upon getting

25 Since 2007, I have observed at the UNPFII that almost every time an intervention is given by a representative of the Montagnard Foundation or the Degar Foundation, or the Kampuchea Krom Federation (a frequent ally of the Montagnard/Degar), it is followed by the Vietnamese State taking the floor to denounce it. On one occasion, the Vietnamese representative banged his shoe in protest while the intervention was being given.

26 UN doc E/C.19/2015/L.1. 2015. "Proposed Organization of Work." United Nations Permanent Forum on Indigenous Issues.

off the bus, the rain had increased. So had the wind. We bent into the wind and walked the four long blocks to the 46th street entrance. There at the gate stood some 100 students waiting to get in. The guard was surly toward us, and at first said we could not come in without an UNPFII escort. But there were no escorts anywhere to be seen. When we came back to the guard and told him this, he let a few of us in after we showed him our official letters of invitation from the UNPFII Secretariat. Then he changed his mind, and decided to let the now 100+ students go through first, leaving the remaining Bunong standing there in the rain. After that the guard decided that their letters were insufficient proof to allow them in. He had to see each person's ID as well. A rude start to be sure, but eventually everyone got in, albeit quite drenched. Once inside, the first stop was at the registration desk, where everyone handed over their soaking letters to obtain the coveted blue badges that grant entry into the UN conference rooms. Simply getting into the building was a challenging process – for indigenous activists, the logistics of participation in the Forum are themselves a series of obstacles to be overcome (see Bellier 2012).

After the opening ceremonies for the UNPFII, the delegation met the other members of the Asia Caucus and gathered endorsements of the Bunong intervention from five other organizations. After making multiple photocopies of the intervention in the Docip room (the Indigenous Peoples' Centre for Documentation, Research and Information), we signed up for the speakers' list, and found seats in the big conference room, and, waited to be invited to speak. But such was not to be the case. Neither our delegation, nor any of the other indigenous delegates who had signed up to give an intervention on topic 3(1), were invited to speak. Instead, states and "expert members" of the Forum,[27] along with UN agencies, consumed almost the entirety of the allotted 3 hours set aside to discuss the OD. Their main discussion was about creating a "system-wide" action plan. They spoke in a technical language about UN structures, systems, and bodies.

For example, one expert member discussed taking action in terms of a question about structure and task delegation. His question was: does "taking action" – at the system-wide scale – mean developing a new and special structure (a new "organ," or "body,"), or does it mean assigning already existing agencies and programs the task of integrating indigenous peoples' rights within their particular policies and practices? This kind of action is centrally focused on configuring the UN discourse machine, or reconfiguring it. It is about the institution, and not directly about concrete reality in the world. These rights, like all other human rights discourses, become matters of technical design at the "system-wide" level (Merry 2011). Another expert member raised the technical question about the action plan in terms of the "modalities for the follow-up document on

27 The UNPFII is comprised of 16 members, eight of whom are chosen by governments, and eight who are chosen by indigenous organizations from their region. They serve for a 3-year term. All of them are considered to be "experts" on indigenous issues (UNPFII 2015). For more discussion of UNPFII structures and indigenous caucuses, cf. Bellier, this volume).

the outcome document." Another Forum expert called for action-plans that "harmonize" with the different human rights instruments. A representative for the UN Economic and Social Council (ECOSOC) took up the largest chunk of time during the session, to suggest that the different UN bodies should become more "coherent" about indigenous peoples' rights. The expertise of the Permanent Forum members appears to lay in their grasp of the bureaucratic and technical frames within which rights are imagined at the UN.

After an hour of listening to this talk, my Bunong colleagues were visibly restless. According to the tentative schedule that had been taped to the wall, our intervention would be invited soon. But the schedule didn't conform with the sequence that followed, in which representatives of Colombia, the UN Environmental Program, and the Russian Federation took the floor.[28] The Colombia representative used almost ten minutes extolling the accomplishments of the Colombian state with regard to its indigenous peoples, including allocating them legislative seats, improved censuses, and creating special areas for political dialogue and policies. As with most of the statements made during this particular session, it was met with little applause from the indigenous delegates present in the large room.

The Russian state representative, with telling irony, stated that the HLPM/WCIP OD has "drawn a line" for states and the UN system to follow. Arguably the OD consists of multiple lines and shapes on paper, a script upon which to base other scripts. But the style in which the OD is written is one of vagueness, and the HLPM /WCIP follow-up session on the OD that we were observing seemed as vague and general as the OD itself. During the last 7 minutes of the session, a couple of IP caucuses were finally called on to speak, but they too were vague, and pointed toward the UN system itself, rather than the world the UN system is supposed to contribute to changing.

Are people really learning how to change the world when they come to the UN, or are they learning UN speech genres: how to talk, who gets to talk, what to say, how to say it, and how long to speak? The unspoken assumption in all this is that the activity, documents, and bodies of the UN will lead to a better life for indigenous peoples, therefore the investment in learning UN normativity is accepted as valuable. But for activists seeking real change to the situations of indigenous peoples in their countries and the world, it seems that nothing happens at the UNPFII. Action, such as a "system-wide action plan," consists of both discursive action and making bureaucratic rearrangements, but not much else. It appears evident that "realizing the ends of the Declaration" requires policy and practice action at the national and sub-national levels, particularly with regard to the rights of self-determination and land rights. But the OD action plans appear to be more like plans to take into consideration the idea of taking real action.

28 Bellier and González González (2015) describe the state power which gives them right to take precedence over indigenous voices.

Part 3. Struggling to speak

Activist-research involves immersion and participation in the creation of the data that is then analyzed. One cannot be a fly on the wall at the UNPFII and hope to gain an understanding of its dynamics – you would quickly fall asleep.[29] In my role as facilitator of indigenous delegations, I used my abilities with English language and dialogue to listen to activists' words, and build those into short interventions, or more detailed accounts for submission to the SRIP. At times my role would morph into teaching my colleagues how to navigate giant bureaucracy, plug into indigenous peoples caucus structures, find sponsors for your intervention, and sign up for the speakers list. While the chosen speaker of our intervention and I were standing in line to sign her up to speak, I struck up a conversation with a person behind me, who represented two indigenous NGOs. When I suggested that nothing happens at the UN, he responded by saying, "yeah it's all bullshit that happens here anymore. When the indigenous movement wasn't so institutionalized, when it was the Working Group (i.e., the Working Group on Indigenous Populations), there was a much different atmosphere than now."

By the end of the first day, our intervention had not been invited. The Chair of the session promised that the interventions on topic 3(1) that had registered speakers would be carried over into the next session on topic 3(2), and provided there was enough time would be invited tomorrow. But there was not enough time. Not was there the following day. By the end of the third day, the group had grown weary and started talking about going home. The person we had selected to read the intervention (a high school senior with good English skills) was starting to feel sick. I had to return home to teach classes the next morning. The anticipation and energy that was there on the eve of the UNPFII was gone.

As we exited Conference Room 4 at the end of the afternoon meeting on the third day, I thought we were going to leave the premises and head home. But then one of the Bunong activists, Leng, told us that the UNPFII reception and cultural performance was about to begin in the main lobby, and the group seemed interested in checking it out. As we wandered down the hall toward the reception, we passed an exhibit of photographs of traditional indigenous houses, many of them from Southeast Asia. I was walking with Nong, who started telling me about the traditional Bunong house they had built near their new communities in the USA. I asked him how many traditional houses remain in Dak Nong today. He smiled at me and shook his head, "no more."

The performers at the reception included the Ulali Project (Haudenosaunee), followed by a group of neo-Aztec dancers, whose performance was propelled by a very loud drum, the rhythms of which were pounding and repetitious. In the middle of their performance, the Bunong delegation withdrew from the crowd. I went to see what was wrong. Leng blurted out to me, "Dr. Neal, is it alright if

29 The first student I brought to the UNPFII tried this approach, and indeed often fell asleep.

we sit down here and pray?" He was concerned about getting ejected from the premises. After reassuring him that there was no restriction on praying at the UN (which I hoped but did not know), they found a quieter area of the lobby, just outside the "meditation room" where the big Matisse stained glass window used to be.[30]

I did not join in the prayer, but (in case my hope was wrong) offered to stand guard instead. I was caught off-guard by their sudden desire to pray and my first reaction was to try to facilitate this. At the same time, I was allowed to observe their actions. They first sat down on the floor in a circle, and Leng led them in a discussion for about 10–15 minutes. After this they remained in a circle but got onto their knees and all began chanting together, although each was vocalizing their own message. It is a form of individual public confession and aspiration, but performed within a collective group. While chanting, many of them shed tears. This lasted about ten minutes, after which they rose up, wiped their eyes, and walked over to where I was, ready to leave the premises. They appeared to be emotionally rejuvenated, and no longer tired and depressed like earlier in the day. They smiled and appeared much relieved. Their catharsis also took me by surprise. My interpretation was they had become tired by the psychic strain of the UNPFII and what to them must still be an opaque process. The prayer they engaged in at the UN released their stress. Although they are nominally Christian, the overall form of their ritual was more egalitarian and communal than any Western Christian rituals I have witnessed. I wondered if the Bunong "house churches" that the Vietnamese military burned down in 2001 were threatening to the state because they functioned like the ceremony I witnessed at the UN, as communal and collective catharsis that produces general revitalization.

On the way back to Queens, Leng explained to me that "we think we have trouble at the UN because something always happens when the Bunong try to speak. Something always goes wrong … God is testing the Bunong. We should have prayed at the beginning of the Forum. We have not been doing things right." They had so far failed to speak truth to power because they forgot about God.[31]

The next day, the Bunong delegation returned to the UNPFII for the fourth day, and in an impromptu extended meeting in a largely empty room, our appointed speaker was at last invited to read the intervention, and finally break the silence of the Bunong. I was on a train back to Rochester by then, but through a series of text-messages exchanged with one of the delegation after making the intervention, it was evident that they perceived this as connected to the ceremonial

30 Located on the main floor, just past the main entrance; my assumption that this space was okay was based on observation – no security guards nearby, with most or all peoples' attention drawn to the loud drumming down the hall.

31 Waves of variable Christian missionization have moved through the highlands of Vietnam and Cambodia on a fairly regular basis since the onset of French colonization, which have transformed but not entirely displaced prior spiritual knowledge. Many of the indigenous activists at the UNPFII are Christian in some way, yet also traditional in another.

prayer the day before. As a result, the delegation, including the Cambodian Bunong as well as the diasporic Bunong from Vietnam, left New York City feeling elated and empowered, and together drove the ten hours to the diasporic Bunong community where they made plans for strengthening the transnational network they are generating, including greater advocacy on human rights and freedom of religion. Later that year, the Cambodia Indigenous Peoples Democracy Party (CIPDP) officially registered with the government, and in 2017 ran its first candidates for public office. These events are not unconnected.

Analyzing indigenous peoples' rights-making: what are the stakes?

In her groundbreaking ethnography of human rights implementation and gender violence, Sally Engle Merry finds that international human rights law must be framed in local terms – the "cultural vernaculars" of a given place – if it is to be effective in the actual lives of people (Merry 2006). The human rights of indigenous peoples are now part of normative international law, but the difference between these norms and their realization on the ground is immense. Merry argues that framing human rights in local terms is work that is carried out by diverse social actors ("middlemen") who transport rights talk to localities, and then translate such talk into language that resonates with the cultural vernaculars of a given place. She stresses that such work is always fraught with uncertainty and risk of failure.

The people in the Bunong delegation to the UNPFII fit into the category of human rights transplanters and translators – Merry's "middlemen." Their aims in coming to the UNPFII are to better understand the human rights system so that they can explain it to other Bunong people, and to use their gained knowledge to bring human rights practices into their communities in Cambodia, Vietnam, and diaspora. Their actions take place in between the international scales at which human rights concepts and law are generated, the national scales at which states recognize or ignore human rights in policy and practice, and the local scales where the bearers of human rights – people – actually live. As activists, their work is aimed at the unlikely goal of bringing these three scales together, in harmony as it were. The UNPFII intervention ritual symbolizes the possibility of this goal: the indigenous interventionist represents the local scale, the UNPFII session chairs represent the international scale, and the states represent the national scale; all together in one room. While the intervention is being read aloud, it appears that the national and international representatives are listening to the local. But in the physical reality of Asia, where some 250 million indigenous people live, this symbolic appearance of inclusive multilateralism is difficult to maintain, given that almost all Asian states adamantly insist that indigenous peoples do not exist there. This condition of structural invisibility makes human rights activism particularly difficult. Imagine the women's rights movement being confronted with governments claiming that the concept of *woman* does not exist, and that there are no women as such in their countries. Such a claim would seem absurd and surreal. But this is the condition facing indigenous peoples in Asia, and in much of Africa. It is indeed a problematique, but not of the nature described by Alfonso Martínez; it is a problem of racist discrimination.

One example of this discrimination via invisibilization comes from the regional organization of Southeast Asian states known as ASEAN (Association of South East Asian Nations). ASEAN formed in 1967, and included five States only: Indonesia, Malaysia, the Philippines, Singapore, and Thailand. By the twenty-first century, ASEAN had grown to include Brunei Darussalam, Cambodia, Laos, Myanmar, and Vietnam. As a postcolonial intergovernmental regional body, its main platforms were economic development, regional cooperation, and peace. It took four decades before ASEAN would begin to engage with human rights. In 2007 ASEAN adopted a new Charter, in which human rights are for the first time explicitly affirmed by this regional body (ASEAN 2008). The new Charter also recognizes the existence of cultural diversity in the region, but does not connect that diversity to human rights. It called for the establishment of a regional human rights body, the ASEAN Intergovernmental Commission on Human Rights (AICHR), which was inaugurated in 2009 with the goal of promoting regional human rights cooperation (ASEAN 2009). Then in November 2012, ASEAN adopted a regional human rights declaration, the ASEAN Declaration on Human Rights (ADHR), (ASEAN 2012). All of this suggests that respect for human rights in the region is growing.

However, the ADHR was immediately denounced by international civil society as a seriously flawed document that undermines human rights rather than affirms them. In a joint statement from Human Rights Watch and 55 civil society organizations, the ADHR is described as "... a declaration of government powers disguised as a declaration of human rights" (HRW 2012). And if many civil society actors found fault in the ADHR for what it does say, indigenous peoples' organizations were disappointed by what it does not. It passes over in silence any recognition or anything else having to do with the human rights of indigenous peoples in the region.[32] As for the AICHR, at the time of publication, it has not adopted any guidelines for interacting with civil society organizations in general, or with indigenous peoples' organizations in particular (Tessire 2015). It is not clear when or if they will. In both the ADHR and the AICHR, indigenous peoples are not marginalized: they are ***invisibilized***. That is, they do not exist as legally recognized entities. To show up at the UNPFII with an intervention declaring that indigenous peoples exist in Asia is always already dangerous in itself.

Although the international system is founded on the premise that all peoples have the right to self-determination, in global practice this right is systematically denied to many peoples by governments through discursive strategies that attack subnational groups, and delegitimize their claims of peoplehood and land rights,

32 See the statement released in 2013 by the Asia Indigenous Peoples Pact (AIPP) and Indigenous Peoples Task Force on ASEAN (APTF), along with other indigenous peoples' organizations: *Indigenous Peoples Statement on the ASEAN Human Rights Declaration*. https://www.iwgia.org/images/newsarchivefiles/0740_IP_Statement_on_ASEAN_HR_Declaration_ENG.pdf.

as either subversive, dangerous, backwards, primitive, and/or otherwise standing in the way of progress. The rationale for this practice is based on other kinds of rights, those of States. These rights of national sovereignty, to protect "political unity" and maintain "territorial integrity," are exercised by States to override the rights of the peoples within their political territories (cf. Article 46 in the UNDRIP, and Article 2 in the Vienna Declaration, and Keating 2007). Culturally and ethnically, the region of Southeast Asia is highly diverse, with well over a thousand indigenous peoples (AIPP 2014) whose aspirations are grossly underrepresented by its eleven states. It is not that states deny the existence of these many different groups or the cultural diversity they represent. In some cases, like China and Vietnam, state-supported tourist industries have developed around this diversity. It is the political status of these groups that is at issue. What states deny is that these groups exist as *peoples*, with collective rights. Instead, these groups are constituted by states as "ethnic minorities" or "national minorities" whose fate is largely determined by the state. To paraphrase Hannah Arendt, the difference between a peoples (in the international sense of being included in a multilateral system as a "member") and a minority is having an opinion that really counts (Arendt 1973 [1951]). As a rule, minorities have no collective rights.

If designation as a minority is produced by the State, *peoplehood* is more a local grassroots process that derives from within individuals and groups as a result of their interactions with each other as well as with other groups. Most of the ethnic groups in Southeast Asia that already self-identify as indigenous peoples, or might in the future, have for multiple generations existed within states that designated them as ethnic minorities. This designation has been accompanied by highly discriminatory policies and practices that often denigrated them and characterized them as inferior sub-human savages whose modes of existence deserve to be eliminated. For the Bunong in Cambodia, there is a long list of pejorative characteristics that the dominant sectors of society have ascribed to them, such as that they have tails, or that they are cannibals, among others (Vater 2006). This sort of characterization is reproduced throughout much of the region, and elsewhere in the world.

For the Bunong and other indigenous activists from Asia as well as Africa, a primary structural aim of the indigenous peoples' rights movement is to overcome and supersede the designations of despised minority status with recognitions of viable peoplehood. Following Merry's analysis, this "middleman" work of human rights-making practice involves discursive flows in both directions between the international and the local. The UNPFII intervention is a key performative aspect of translating and transporting local indigenous human rights aspirations to the international scales of human rights law. It is a complex ritual element that is made ambivalent through states' entrenched immovability and the paradoxical tendency of the UNPFII intervention to reproduce UN culture more than it produces local change on the ground.

There is another aspect of human rights-making practice that feeds into the ambivalence with which interventionist-activists often contend, which is generated by the relations between indigenous activists and the non-indigenous organizations that provide them various support to come to the UNPFII and make their interventions. These include non-governmental organizations (NGOs) of many persuasions, along with donors and sometimes academics. While these various supporters may be considered as allies of indigenous peoples, my research suggests that this support may in practice not be as supportive as it may seem on the surface. In what follows I describe several observations of purported NGO allies acting to limit or control indigenous activists' discourses, and as a result causing state-like effects of obstruction. My point in discussing these is not to condemn the NGO sector in the way that authoritarian states tend to, but rather to examine the limits to which alliance may be subject. Whereas such states (Cambodia is a prime example) tend to view NGOs as pernicious "foreign interests" that cynically manipulate poor people toward "color revolutions" and the like, the brief examination here focuses around the pitfalls of NGOs when they turn into "anti-politics machines" (Ferguson 1994).

The NGO problematique

The relation of indigenous activists and non-indigenous allies in the international indigenous peoples' rights movement is highly variable and complex, ranging from what I call ***robust symbiosis*** to ***asymmetrical antagonism***. In varying form, alliance has been a key part of the indigenous peoples' movement from the start. The beginnings of this movement are often traced to the 1920s when the Haudenosaunee leader known as Deskaheh attempted to make a spoken intervention at the League of Nations, which would have been the first international indigenous intervention. Before, during, and after his travels to Geneva, Deskaheh worked closely with George Decker, a non-Native attorney from Western New York, to organize and carry out a plan to advocate for the admission of indigenous peoples into the League of Nations, as landholding peoples with multilateral status (George-Kanentiio 2000, Rickard 1984). In the end, Deskaheh and his ally/lawyer did not achieve their tacit goals, but they did inaugurate the international human rights aspirations of indigenous peoples and laid the foundation for the resurgence that began in the 1970s and has continued until the present. This is an example of robust symbiosis in the ally relations that are part of this rights movement. What is also distinctive in this example of collaboration is its focus on politics.

There are many more alliances between indigenous peoples and NGOs today, but not all these attend to the politics of Indigeneity in the explicit manner that Deskaheh and Decker did. Sometimes NGOs act as proxies of the state, in subtle and not so subtle ways. It is a mixed bag in post-conflict Cambodia. Some NGO actors have themselves played key roles as human rights middlemen, by introducing international indigenous peoples' rights discourses to communities unfamiliar with either "indigenous" or "rights" talk (cf. Baird 2011). However, through my work at the UNPFII, I encountered other Cambodia-based transnational NGOs acting more as proxies for state management of indigenous peoples, rather than as symbiotic collaborators in a common project. By this I mean that some NGOs would provide material resources to allow activists to participate in the UNPFII, but at the same time act to constrain the activities and interventions of the activists while at the Forum.

As an aid-dependent "post-conflict" country, many different sectors of Cambodian society became reliant on NGOs for resources and aid, starting in the 1990s. As disadvantaged culturally distinctive rural groups, indigenous communities have received a significant amount of NGO attention, and have grown dependent on the resources that NGOs can bring (Bourdier 2015). For their part, NGOs are donor-dependent and must comply with their missions, and are required by the Cambodian government to follow behavioral guidelines, including prohibitions against promoting any political activity. Thus, the aid that NGOs bring to indigenous communities may carry with it obligations of conformity to existing state structures. The visions of development that NGOs, donors and states maintain are often distant from the aspirations of indigenous communities, and the latter are often forced to comply in order to access the resources of the former. Like many of the local authorities in Cambodia, NGO workers here often have a weak grasp on the political and legal meanings of Indigeneity. This leaves indigenous activists in a precarious position of relative powerlessness that is difficult to overcome. While some NGO workers manage to provide support for the limited definitions of indigenous land rights that are allowed in Cambodia, most do not contribute to building the political capacity of indigenous peoples to claim their own peoplehood. Any NGO in Cambodia that openly advocates for indigenous peoples' rights to self-determination risks being closed down by their donor, or having its leaders deported and/or arrested by the state. NGOs may nevertheless sponsor indigenous activists to the UNPFII, but often seek to control the program to fit their agenda rather than that of the activists themselves.

As one example of this, during the 2012 UNPFII meetings the delegation from Cambodia arrived with an agenda that had largely been produced by a USAID-funded NGO, which constantly monitored their activities in NYC from Phnom Penh, via phone and email. I had agreed beforehand to facilitate the group, as it included several activists I had worked with previously. I did not realize that this role came with expectations from the NGO that I would keep the group "on task." The agenda had a single point of focus: preserving the Prey Lang forest via leveraging the Cambodian government to re-designate Prey Lang as a protected area. As indicated in footnote 1 above, Prey Lang is a very significant forest, and hundreds of indigenous Kuy village communities rely on it for their existence (Michaud 2012). The timber from the forest however, is a fast source of cash in a developing country, and Prey Lang has become the target of intensive logging operations, especially since 2006. While none of the indigenous delegates questioned the value of preserving Prey Lang (they had been funded by this particular NGO to advocate for this goal), once we started talking in New York, it became evident that some of them were dubious about the proposed solution of designating it as a protected area – they didn't think that would really work, given the government's poor track record of preserving its other "protected areas" (Keating 2013; Bourdier 2015). The delegates wanted to advocate for an alternate solution to preserving Prey Lang: that the Cambodian government should legally recognize the Kuy as indigenous peoples, including their rights to Prey Lang as indigenous Kuy territory. A further deviation was provided by one of the delegates, who was an indigenous Kreung person not from the Prey Lang area, but from a village designated for inundation due to the construction of the Lower Sesan II dam. He wanted to call for the cancellation of the entire dam project. I thought these were constructive elaborations on the agenda that the NGO would be pleased to hear of. So, when I informed the NGO in Phnom Penh of the delegates' expressed desires, I was surprised by the hostile reception I received. I was told in so many words, that we were to stay on-point and not deviate from the agenda, which in the end proved to be an NGO agenda, not an indigenous one.

In 2013 I observed a second example of NGO domination of the Cambodian indigenous peoples' movement. This time around, the delegation of Cambodian indigenous people that came to the UNPFII was accompanied by a Khmer chaperone from a large Cambodian NGO that was sponsoring their trip. Within minutes of meeting him, it became evident that he considered the whole endeavor of speaking at the UN to be a waste of time. The chaperone talked disparagingly of the leading regional indigenous peoples' rights organization, the Asia Indigenous Peoples Pact (AIPP), and as I tried to work with the delegates to draft interventions and organize a meeting with the SRRIP, he challenged almost all of the statements that the delegates made as being inaccurate and even disrespectful of the government. By the third day of the UNPFII he stopped participating in the sessions, and had discouraged two of the three indigenous delegates from participating as well. For the remainder of the meetings, I was left working with one delegate at the UNPFII, while the NGO chaperone and the other two delegates spent their time out in the city sightseeing and shopping.

As a final example, the reader may recall Part 1 of the vignette above, where I noted the absence of any NGO presence in the hotel room where we gathered the night before the 2015 UNPFII meetings began. But that was just in the hotel room. Another chaperone from the same Cambodian NGO had flown from Cambodia to NYC for the UNPFII, but arrived without anyone to chaperone. As I was informed, he was to chaperone the two Bunong people whose visas had been denied by the US Embassy. Even though they were unable to enter the country, the chaperone had come anyway. Upon learning this I asked Leng, "so why is he here then?" He looked at me wryly and said, "I cannot answer that question." We had no contact with the chaperone during our stay in New York, and no idea what he was doing. Furthermore, the indigenous activists were happy he stayed out of the way.

If NGO actors (such as the USAID organization director mentioned above) presume it normative to direct the words and movements of Cambodian indigenous people when they travel halfway around the world, my sources in the NGO sector in Cambodia tell me the situation is much worse within the country. The Bunong, Kuy, Kreung, Tampuan, and about 20 other distinct indigenous groups in Cambodia, collectively constitute one of the most vulnerable sectors of the Cambodian population today. Living in extreme poverty, poor health, with little or no education, they are easy targets for both developers who want to take their lands, and NGOs that want to "help" indigenous communities by making decisions for them, about things they are presumed to have little understanding of. The political effects of both approaches are similar: they silence indigenous aspirations. Arguably it is even more insidious with NGOs because they position themselves as helpers and deliverers of aid while suppressing the possibilities for indigenous people to help themselves. This is the pattern of asymmetrical antagonistic relations.

In suggesting this two-pattern typology, I am not trying to characterize the NGO sector in general, but to point to non-constructive tendencies that the structure of the NGO sector may enable, and to which a given NGO may be subject. The key difference between asymmetrical antagonism and robust symbiosis appears to be politics, and its relative exclusion and inclusion in the activism that occurs between NGOs and indigenous peoples. Those NGOs (or individual NGO workers whom buck the trend) that grasp the full meaning of indigenous peoples' rights and promote it – especially land rights and self-determination – are more likely to develop robust symbiosis. Perhaps not surprisingly, NGOs that are constituted by indigenous peoples tend to demonstrate greater symbiosis.

Conclusion

The indigenous peoples movement, if such a monolith can be said to exist, may be thought of as an evolutionary provocation to the next step of human *consociality*[33] in the Anthropocene, in which we come to grips with who we are as a species: physically, semiotically, and politically. The movement suggests we evolve the structures of market-based state society into something more conducive to social life. There is nothing backwards or primitive about indigenous peoples' rights movements. "Peoplehood" is an enduring pattern of variable collective consociality that persists within the frames of states and markets, despite centuries of efforts by the latter to eliminate or subdue it. Currently there exist almost 200 market-oriented Nation-States on Earth, but around 6,000 distinctive peoples (about 4,000 of whom may be considered or self-identify as indigenous peoples) living and contending within these states. Most peoples are facing challenges to their existence as a result of this political situation.

During the lead-up to WWII, Karl Polanyi analyzed the historical transformation of life that took hold as market-based forms of social organization replaced those of kinship and peoplehood (Polanyi 1957). He argued that the self-regulating

33 My use of the term "consociality" follows Ulf Hannerz, to focus on the ubiquity of co-presence in everyday life, and the potential of emergent forms of "togetherness" to shape the near-future of states, markets, and movements (Hannerz 2015). The indigenous peoples' rights movement and contemporary environmental science provide examples of emergent consociality that favors diversity of cultural and biological life.

market form of organizing society will, if left unchecked, destroy existing society and nature. His main examples were drawn from England (where it all began), and colonized peoples. Events since WWII, and especially since the Cold War ended, lend support to Polanyi's argument. Transforming states into market-oriented organizational forms has produced enormous wealth (which measured in terms of world GDP, currently hover around $78 trillion). This economic growth has resulted in rising global inequality, as the distribution of this wealth is increasingly concentrated in the hands of a few. The triumph of the market has also resulted in triggering wide-scale environmental disruption of the planets' ecosystems.

We are in the midst of market-driven socioenvironmental destruction today, and now possess the technology to more fully understand its impact on a planetary scale. Polanyi made another important observation: that society and nature will invariably resist being destroyed, and therefore attempt to limit the self-regulating market. These "protectionist" tendencies constitute the second movement in Polanyi's "double movement" theory of history in the age of capitalism. Unlike Hegel or Marx, Polanyi made no utopian predictions of how this double movement dialectic might eventually turn out. I follow Thomas Hall and James Fenelon in concluding that the activism of indigenous peoples in articulating and claiming human rights, including rights as peoples, is a part of this double movement (Hall and Fenelon 2009). Indigenous activism arose as a reaction to intensifying destruction of society and nature, but it does not end there.

Until quite recently, many of the groups that are now articulating their human rights as indigenous peoples were constituted by liberal and illiberal States alike as entities beyond the pale of the State, and outside of civil society. There are many examples of this, but one of the clearest is from that founding document of human rights, the 1776 US Declaration of Independence. In its second paragraph the Declaration proclaims that "We hold these truths to be self-evident, that all men are created equal, that they are endowed by their Creator with certain unalienable Rights, that among these are Life, Liberty and the pursuit of Happiness." Yet this same Declaration of inalienable human rights ends by excluding indigenous peoples from this family of man, because they are irrational "merciless Indian savages." Ironically, the Declaration charges these peoples with "undistinguished destruction of all ages, sexes and conditions," a kind of total destruction that Polanyi attributed to the imposition of self-regulating markets.

Despite the imposed conformity with UN ritualism that is required of indigenous delegates to the UNPFII, each time an indigenous activist delivers an intervention on the floor of the UN, they disrupt the deep-set duality of savage vs. civilized that the modern Market-State system is founded on. This is a ritual effect that in itself provokes no immediate change in the physical world. The duality holds firm – Barsh's "unmovable object" (1996). But there is something of value that is gained by indigenous activists from Cambodia and Vietnam when they engage with human rights mechanisms at the international scale – even though it may not be exactly what many from their communities back home wish for, such as an immediate change in the states policies and practices with regard to indigenous peoples.

During the 2013 UNPFII meeting I thought of indigenous Papuan critiques of UN interventions as I witnessed Leng deliver a joint intervention against the Lower Sesan II dam, in a Friday afternoon session called "Comprehensive dialogue with United Nations agencies and funds." Across the table facing him were representatives of five of the leading multilateral banks that have financed many similar mega-dam projects around the world. As Leng called for the cessation of the project and recommended to the banks that they rethink their whole approach to energy development, and do so in dialogue with indigenous peoples, I observed the representatives of the banks sit there in silence, with little visible expression or response. I am not sure if they were listening at all. In the following years construction on the Lower Sesan II proceeded, along with the predicted massive social and environmental destruction within some 40,000 ha of previously forested land, and the dam went online in 2017 (Keating 2018). One might reasonably conclude that his intervention was for naught. But after giving his intervention, Leng was positively charged with a strengthened intentionality and conviction that indigenous peoples' rights are possible, and he was ready to fight for them. Shortly after this session – and before returning home to Cambodia, he made a detour to the diasporic Bunong community, where he inspired them to organize around indigenous peoples' rights. Since then this community has organized a new association to begin providing aid and assistance to communities in Cambodia and Vietnam. What I observed in this lone delegate was the generative immanence of human rights aspirations – while he remained cynical about the UN ever doing anything, he found a new capacity for action within himself, and began generating new articulations of Indigeneity. Giving interventions may have no effect on their targeted subjects, but they do produce narrative effects for those who create and deliver them. Through diffusion, these effects can have powerful reverberations in time, and turn into an irresistible force.

Ultimately, the struggle for indigenous peoples' human rights requires hope and vision, particularly in countries like Cambodia and Vietnam where so many dreams were bombed out of existence or buried in killing fields. The concept of human rights retains its transformative power for radical social change despite the many problems of the international system of human rights. It is a tragic irony that in a time when it is becoming clear that the dominant socioeconomic forces are driving the planet to a global ecological disaster, that peoples whose world-making practices constitute truly sustainable life-systems, are considered by the powerful to be inferior and expendable. Given the huge odds against their success that are generated by the practices of states, commercial interests and the international system, the remarkable audacity of indigenous activists to struggle on is itself strong evidence of the human spirit and interest in freedom.

Ultimately, the indigenous peoples' rights movement is a political practice, engaged in by actors who do not hold the reigns of structural power, but yet may intervene and trigger the cunning – perhaps not of recognition, but of history (Turner 2007). When indigenous peoples in Cambodia realize that the UN and NGOs will not save them, they may opt for a more direct practice of politics. That is precisely what is emerging in Cambodia now, in the form of grassroots organization of an indigenous political party – which is a direct outgrowth of lessons learned at the UNPFII. Presuming it is not crushed by the current authoritarian regime, this political party offers a new possibility for the practice of making indigenous peoples' human rights in Asia, and the world. The evolutionary question is whether or not current world systems can accommodate a new inclusive form of multilateralism, in which peoples and nature are parties alongside states and corporations.

However improbable it may seem to a contemporary political realist that indigenous peoples may determine their own destinies, or that an indigenous political party in Cambodia will grow; it remains that a certain resiliency exists among indigenous activists to achieve the improbable. Perhaps this is best expressed by a comment by Tonya Gonella Frichner, a longtime Haudenosaunee activist in the indigenous peoples' rights movement since the 1970s, who has since passed. After a particularly frustrating meeting in 2010 with ILO representatives in Geneva, during which the ILO insisted that the solution to measuring indigenous peoples' self-determination was better State census-taking, I asked Tonya why she continued to struggle with the international system, given the enormous obstacles everywhere to the realization of indigenous peoples' rights, i.e., the object that won't move. By then, she had given more than three decades to service in this cause. She looked at me, and said with a smile, "because it's the only game in town." A couple of years later I asked the same question of Kenneth Deer, another long-time indigenous peoples' rights activist. His reply was, "the moment you stop struggling, you disappear."

Bibliography

AIPP (Asia Indigenous Peoples Pact). 2014. *Overview of the State of Indigenous Peoples in Asia*. Chiang Mai: Asia Indigenous Peoples Pact. https://aippnet.org/briefing-paper-overview-of-the-state-of-indigenous-peoples-in-asia/ (accessed 25 September 2018).

Anaya, James. 2010. *Report by the Special Rapporteur on the Situation of Human Rights and Fundamental Freedoms of Indigenous People, James Anaya. Addendum. Cases examined by the Special Rapporteur (June 2009–July 2010)*. United Nations General Assembly, Human Rights Council, Fifteenth Session, Agenda Item 3, Promotion and Protection of All Human Rights, Civil, Political, Economic, Social and Cultural Rights, Including the Right to Development. UN Doc. A/HRC/15/37/Add.1.

Arendt, Hannah. 1973 [1951]. *The Origins of Totalitarianism*. New York: Schocken Books. First published in 1951.

ASEAN (The Association of Southeast Asian Nations). 2008. *The ASEAN Charter*. The Association of Southeast Asian Nations. Jakarta: ASEAN Secretariat. https://www.asean.org/wp-content/uploads/2012/05/11.-October-2015-The-ASEAN-Charter-18th-Reprint-Amended-updated-on-05_-April-2016-IJP.pdf (accessed 9 December 2018).

ASEAN (The Association of Southeast Asian Nations). 2009 *Cham-am Hua Hin Declaration on the Intergovernmental Commission on Human Rights*. The Association of Southeast Asian Nations. http://hrlibrary.umn.edu/research/Philippines/Cha-Am%20Hua%20Hin%20Declaration%20of%20the%20AICHR.pdf (accessed 9 December 2018).

ASEAN (The Association of Southeast Asian Nations). 2012. *ASEAN Declaration on Human Rights* (ADHR). The Association of Southeast Asian Nations. https://asean.org/asean-human-rights-declaration/ (accessed 9 December 2018).

Aun, Chhengpor. 2017. "In Cambodia, 5 Years after Chut Wutty's Killing, Questions Remain." *Voice of America*, 19 April 2017. https://www.voanews.com/a/cambodia-chut-wutty-killing/3816512.html (accessed 9 December 2018).

Baird, Ian G. 2009. *Best Practices in Compensation and Resettlement for Large Dams: The Case of the Planned Lower Sesan 2 Hydropower Development in Northeastern Cambodia.* Phnom Penh: The Rivers Coalition in Cambodia.

Baird, Ian G. 2011. "The Construction of 'Indigenous Peoples' in Cambodia." In *Alterities in Asia: Reflections on Identity and Regionalism*, edited by Leong Yew. London: Routledge.

Baird, Ian G. 2015. "Translocal Assemblages and the Circulation of the Concept of 'Indigenous Peoples' in Laos." *Political Geography* 46: 54–64.

Barsh, Russell L. 1996. "Indigenous Peoples and the UN Commission on Human Rights: A Case of the Immovable Object and the Irresistible Force." *Human Rights Quarterly* 18 (4): 782–813.

Bellier, Irène. 2012. "Les peuples autochtones aux Nations Unies: la construction d'un sujet de droits / acteur collectif et la fabrique de normes internationals." *Critique internationale* 54: 61–80.

Bellier, Irène, and Verónica González González. 2015. "Peuples autochtones. La fabrique onusienne d'une identité symbolique." *Mots. Les langages du politique* 108: 131–150.

Bourdier, Frederic. 2015. *Cambodia: Indigenous Peoples in ASEAN.* Chiang Mai: Asian Indigenous Peoples Pact, and the International Working Group on Indigenous Affairs.

Carteret, Daniel de. 2014. "Lack of Funds Delays Railway." *Phnom Penh Post*, 22 April 2014. http://www.phnompenhpost.com/business/lack-funds-delays-railway (accessed 9 December 2018).

Chandler, David. 2008. *A History of Cambodia* (4th edition). Boulder, CO: Westview Press.

Charlesworth, Hillary, and Emma Larking, eds. 2015. *Human Rights and the Universal Periodic Review: Rituals and Ritualism.* Cambridge: Cambridge University Press.

Clarke, Gerard. 2001. "From Ethnocide to Ethnodevelopment? Ethnic Minorities and Indigenous Peoples in Southeast Asia." *Third World Quarterly* 22 (3): 413–436.

Corntassel, Jeff. 2012. "Re-envisioning Resurgence: Indigenous Pathways to Decolonization and Sustainable Self-determination." *Decolonization: Indigeneity, Education & Society* 1 (1): 86–101.

Erni, Christian, ed. 2008. *The Concept of Indigenous Peoples in Asia: A Resource Book.* Copenhagen: International Work Group for Indigenous Affairs.

Equitable Cambodia and Focus on the Global South. 2013. *Briefing Paper: The Chinese North-South Railway Project in Cambodia.* https://focusweb.org/content/briefing-paper-chinese-north-south-railway-project (accessed 30 June 2017).

Ferguson, James, with Larry Lohmann. 1994. "The Anti-politics Machine: 'Development' and Bureaucratic Power in Lesotho." *The Ecologist* 24 (5): 176–181.

George-Kanentiio, Doug (2000). Iroquois Culture & Commentary. Santa Fe: Clear Light Publishers.

Hall, Thomas D., and James V. Fenelon. 2009. *Indigenous Peoples and Globalization: Resistance and Revitalization*. Boulder, CO: Paradigm Press.

Hannerz, Ulf. 2015. "Writing Futures: An Anthropologist's View of Global Scenarios." *Current Anthropology* 56 (6): 797–818.

HRW (Human Rights Watch). 2012. "Civil Society Denounces Adoption of Flawed ASEAN Human Rights Declaration." *Human Rights Watch*. Joint Statement of HRW and 55 Other CSOs. https://www.hrw.org/news/2012/11/19/civil-society-denounces-adoption-flawed-asean-human-rights-declaration (accessed 9 December 2018).

Keating, Neal B. 2007. "UN General Assembly Adopts the Declaration on the Rights of Indigenous Peoples, 144-4." *Anthropology News* 48 (8): 22–23 and front cover.

Keating, Neal B. 2012a. *Iroquois Art, Power, and History*. Norman: University of Oklahoma Press.

Keating, Neal B. 2012b. "From Spirit Forest to Rubber Plantation: The Accelerating Disaster of Development in Cambodia." *ASIANetwork Exchange* 19 (2): 68–80.

Keating, Neal B. 2013. "Kuy Alterities: The Struggle to Conceptualize and Claim Indigenous Land Rights in Neoliberal Cambodia." *Asia Pacific Viewpoint* 54 (3): 309–322.

Keating, Neal B. 2016. "Kites in the Highlands: Articulating Bunong Indigeneity in Cambodia, Vietnam and Abroad." *Asian Ethnicity* 17 (4): 566–579.

Keating, Neal B. 2018. "Cambodia." In *Indigenous World 2018*, edited by Pamela Jaquelin-Andersen, 315–322. Copenhagen: International Work Group on Indigenous Affairs.

Keating, Neal B. and Sochea Pheap. 2014. "Cambodia." In *The Indigenous World – 2014*, edited by Cæcilie Mikkelsen, 290–298. Copenhagen: International Work Group on Indigenous Affairs.

Martínez, Miguel A. 1999. *Study on Treaties, Agreements and Other Constructive Arrangements between States and Indigenous Populations*. Final Report by the Special Rapporteur, Commission on Human Rights, Sub-commission on Prevention of Discrimination and Protection of Minorities. 55ème session. Doc NU E/CN.4/Sub.2/1999/20.

Merry, Sally E. 2006. *Human Rights and Gender Violence*. Chicago, IL: University of Chicago Press.

Merry, Sally E. 2011. "Measuring the World: Indicators, Human Rights and Global Governance." *Current Anthropology*. 52 (S3): S83–S95.

Michaud, Alan. 2012. *Prey Lang Development Case: Do People Benefit from Its Development?* Report and Film Prepared for the Cambodia NGO Forum. Not published.

Milne, Sarah. 2013. "Under the Leopard's Skin: Land Commodification and the Dilemmas of Indigenous Communal Title in Upland Cambodia." *Asia Pacific Viewpoint* 54 (3): 323–339.

Milne, Sarah, and Sango Mahanty, eds. 2015. *Conservation and Development in Cambodia: Exploring Frontiers of Change in Nature, State and Society*. London: Routledge.

Polanyi, Karl. 1957. *The Great Transformation: The Political and Economic Origins of Our Time*. Boston, MA: Beacon Press. First published in 1944.

Povinelli, Elizabeth. 2002. *The Cunning of Recognition: Indigenous Alterities and the Making of Australian Multiculturalism*. Durham, NC: Duke University Press.

Rabe, Alison. 2013. *Directive 01BB in Rattanakiri Province, Cambodia: Issues and Impacts of Private Land Titling in Indigenous Communities*. Chiang Mai: Asia Indigenous Peoples Pact.

Republic Act 8371. 1997. "An Act To Recognize, Protect and Promote the Rights of Indigenous Cultural Communities/Indigenous Peoples, Creating a National Commission on Indigenous Peoples, Establishing Implementing Mechanisms, Appropriating Funds Therefore, and for Other Purposes." *Republic of the Philippines.* http://www.officialgazette.gov.ph/1997/10/29/republic-act-no-8371/ (accessed 22 February 2019).

Rickard, Clinton (1984). Fighting Tuscarora: The Autobiography of Chief Clinton Rickard. Syracuse: Syracuse University Press.

Simon, Scott. 2007. "Paths to Autonomy: Aboriginality and the Nation in Taiwan," In *The Margins of Becoming: Identity and Culture in Taiwan*, edited by Carsten Storm and Mark Harrison, 221–240. Wiesbaden: Harrassowitz.

Tessire, Jade. 2015. *Indigenous Peoples and ASEAN Integration.* Chiang Mai: Asian Indigenous Peoples Pact (AIPP) Foundation. http://aippnet.org/wp-content/uploads/2015/12/iva.aippnet.org_wp-content_uploads_2015_12_Ips-and-ASEAN-Integration_Final-Small.pdf (accessed 22 February 2019).

Turner, Terence. 2007. "Indigenous Resurgence, Anthropological Theory, and the Cunning of History." *Focaal: European Journal of Anthropology* 49: 118–123.

Turner, Victor. 1969. *The Ritual Process: Structure and Anti-structure.* New Brunswick, NJ: AldineTransaction.

UN DESA. 2014. *Challenges Facing Indigenous Peoples of Asia Spotlighted as UN Forum Continues 2014 Session.* United Nations Department of Economic and Social Affairs. http://www.un.org/en/development/desa/news/social/indigenous-peoples-of-asia.html (accessed 22 February 2019).

UN doc A/61/L.67. 2007. "United Nations Declaration on the Rights of Indigenous Peoples." Sixty-first Session, United Nations General Assembly.

UN doc A/69/L.1. 2014. "Draft resolution Submitted by the President of the General Assembly: Outcome Document of the High-level Plenary Meeting of the General Assembly Known as the World Conference on Indigenous Peoples." Sixty-ninth Session, UN General Assembly.

UN doc A/HRC/EMRIP/2008/1/Add.1. 2008. "Annotations to the Provisional Agenda: Human Rights Council, Expert Mechanism on the Rights of Indigenous Peoples, 1st Session, 1–3 October 2008/Prepared by the Secretary-General." United Nations Human Rights Council.

UN doc A/HRC/RES/15/14. 2010. "Human Rights and Indigenous Peoples: Mandate of the Special Rapporteur on the Rights of Indigenous Peoples: Resolution/Adopted by the Human Rights Council." Fifteenth Session, United Nations Human Rights Council.

UN doc E/CN.4/2002/97. 2002. "Human Rights and Indigenous Issues: Report of the Special Rapporteur on the Situation of Human Rights and Fundamental Freedoms of Indigenous People, Rodolfo Stavenhagen, Submitted Pursuant to Commission Resolution 2001/57." Fifty-eighth Session, United Nations Commission on Human Rights.

UN doc E/RES/1982/34. 1982. "Study of the Problem of Discrimination against Indigenous Populations." Resolution 1982/34 of the UN Economic and Social Council.

UN doc E/RES/2000/22. 2000. "Establishment of a Permanent Forum." Resolution 2000/22 of the UN Economic and Social Council.

UNPFII. 2015. United Nations Permanent Forum on Indigenous Issues. https://www.un.org/development/desa/indigenouspeoples/unpfii-sessions-2/fourteenth-session.html (accessed on 23 January 2019).

Vater, Tom. 2006. *The Bunong: Caretakers of Cambodia's Sacred Forests.* Phnom Penh: USAID, European Union.

WFP (World Food Program). 2015. *The Food Security Atlas of Cambodia.* The United Nations World Food Program.

Winzeler, Robert. L. 2011. *The Peoples of Southeast Asia Today: Ethnography, Ethnology, and Change in a Complex Region.* Lanham, MD: Altamira Press.

Part II

Colonial legacies

5 Colonial legacy and public policy

From *primitive* to *indigenous* in French Guiana (1930–present)[1]

Stéphanie Guyon

French Guiana occupied a special place at the very heart of the former slave colonies of the Americas. Some particular characteristics of its colonization, and its decolonization process, make it stand out and serve to highlight key points regarding colonial categorizations of peoples, and the ongoing effects that these categories have on public policy and access to resources. This chapter sheds light on the production of a particular model of governing indigeneity as a figure of otherness as it took shape in French Guiana. It also examines the emergence of a new form of public policy to respond to indigenous demands, including a limited recognition of their specificity, and highlights the important role of ethnologists in this process.

Background

The colonial history of the Amazonian territory of Guiana was shaped by its centuries-long status as a French colony (1626–1946) including several years as penal labor colony (1795–1953[2]). In contrast to French colonies in other parts of the world, which went through decolonization processes in the 1950s through the 1970s, Guiana, along with the West Indian countries of Martinique and Guadeloupe, was decolonized in 1946. These American territories chose *départementalisation* – to become French departments rather than independent states[3] – making them unique in Latin America. This status was preferred by the elites in each territory (in Guiana the Creole elites, see below) because it meant for them equality in law – they would be French citizens.

Indeed, already from the start of the Third Republic in 1870, Guiana's political elites, like those of the French West Indies and the island of Réunion, demanded assimilation of their territory with Metropolitan France – in other words,

1 This chapter is a revised, updated and translated version of Guyon, Stéphanie. 2013. "Des "primitifs" aux "autochtones." Savoirs ethnologiques et politiques publiques en Guyane de 1946 à nos jours." *Genèses* 91: 51–70. Translated by Cadenza Academic Translations, revised by Jennifer Hays, and the author.

2 Although no new prisoners were sent there after 1936, officially the work prison closed in 1953.

3 Departments are at the second local level of French administrative and political areas.

a gradual alignment of the administrative, legal, and political institutions of these colonies with those of France. This was an ongoing process, which became more intense between the two world wars, when these political elites reaffirmed their choice to remain under French sovereignty with departmental status. At the time, this was considered the best means of attaining social and political equality with France. The law of 19 March 1946 saw the completion of this process, removing Guiana, along with Martinique, Guadeloupe, and Réunion, from the French colonial empire and turning them into overseas departments.

Although it shared departmentalization with the West Indian colonies, Guiana also had some characteristics that made it unique among them, in particular in terms of the status of its peoples. Two important population categories in Guiana both historically and today are the *Amerindian* and *Maroon* (in French, *Businenge*) peoples. *Amerindian* refers to the descendants of the populations present on the American territory at the time of the colonial conquest.[4] The *Maroons* are descendants of imported slaves who, in the eighteenth century, fled from the plantations of Dutch Guiana and took refuge in the forests.[5] The *Creole* population was, in accordance with the general usage of the term, composed of descendants of *all* imported populations.[6] However, although they shared the characteristic of being imported, the Maroons had a different status from the Creoles. This distinction, which will be elaborated in the section below, was in place throughout the colonial period and continued until the early decades of Guiana's departmentalization. Although they were descended from slaves, the Maroons, organized as an autonomous society within the Amazonian forest, lived outside of Creole colonial society.

In the second half of the nineteenth century, the Creoles became citizens and gained access to political rights and to general civil rights. The Amerindian and Maroon peoples, however, who lived in the forest far away from economic and administrative centers, were labeled as "primitives" and consequently excluded from citizenship. As in many colonial territories, conversion to "civilization" was the foundation of the hierarchy within Guianese colonial society and also

4 Three Amerindian groups are currently present on the coast of French Guiana: the Kali'na (formerly called Galibi by the colonizer, Lokono (formerly called Arawak) and Pahikwnene (formerly called Palikur). Three other groups are located within the territory, in the forest zone: the Wayana, the Wayampi and the Teko (formerly called Emerillons).

5 Different groups of maroons were formed, depending on the period and the area of marronage (Ndju'ka, Aluku, Paramaka, and so on). Some of these groups settled in French Guiana during the course of the eighteenth and nineteenth centuries.

6 The term *Creole* applies to the local descendants of any imported population living in a colonial framework. In Guiana, the white Creole population disappeared in the late nineteenth century because of the collapse of the plantation economy following the abolition of slavery. Those known as "Creoles" are therefore the descendants of black slaves and of the different nineteenth-century migrant groups. In the late nineteenth century and the first half of the twentieth century, the Creole population of Guiana in fact absorbed those Creole migrants following the gold trade (from St. Lucia, Martinique and Guadeloupe), together with colonial migrants (Chinese and, more marginally, Lebanese) and the few convicts who, having survived their sentence, had not been repatriated to France.

determined the boundaries between *subjects* and *citizens* (Saada 2005). Unlike all other colonized populations within the French empire, the Amerindians and Maroons were not identified as *native subjects* – a category of colonial law indicating French subjects deprived of the rights of French citizenship on the grounds that they have preserved a personal status, whether confessional or customary, that is distinct from the civil code (Blévis 2008). Thus, another specific feature of the French state in Guiana is that unlike other colonies (such as Mexico or Brazil, for example), it did not develop any policies designed for populations labelled "primitive" – at least not until the late colonial period, in particular during the post-colonial period.

The specific nature of Amazonian terrain – thick jungle – and the limited influence of colonization in Guiana allowed Amerindian and Maroon peoples to take refuge in areas where the French state had little control. However, following the creation in 1930 of the separate territory of Inini, an administrative area that covers the whole of Guiana with the exception of the coastal strip, the French state gradually penetrated the entire territory and began to govern these populations in earnest – this will be described in the section below. During this same period, ethnologists were beginning their early research on the Guianese Amerindians and Maroons, and they were able to play a part in developing specific policies. Ethnology was brought into play, first by the colonial states, and after decolonization by independent states, in order to both legitimize public action designed for the colonized peoples and to provide tools for carrying it out (De Souza Lima 2000; L'Estoile 2000).

The aim of this chapter is to shed light on the historical development of state management of the Amerindian and Maroon peoples of Guiana. I examine how ways of categorizing different groups – from "primitive populations" to "indigenous peoples" – originated, as well as the public policies devoted to the groups thus categorized. In particular, I examine the links between the ethnological construction of difference, the emergence of Amerindian and Maroon demands regarding identity, and the designing of a differentialist policy[7] by the French government. I also interrogate the ways in which categories and hierarchies that were forged between groups during colonial times were extended or contested in the postcolonial period.

This research aims to incorporate perspectives on these processes from a variety of sources, representing the various involved parties, including the administration, ethnologists, and Amerindians and Maroons. A variety of investigative techniques were used to gather this data. These include the analysis of a corpus of ethnological texts produced between 1946 and the present, and a study of archives of the sub-prefectures of the Inini and of St. Laurent du Maroni.[8] I also

7 *Differentialist politics* referred to administrative practices in which cultural difference was institutionalized, as opposed to universalist approaches that strive for inclusion and assimilation.

8 Since an inventory has not yet been made of the archives of the St. Laurent du Maroni sub-prefecture, the documents cited are not listed. In the rest of this article, I shall refer to them by the acronym ASP SLM.

carried out an interview survey with Guianese sub-prefects and prefects,[9] as well as with Amerindian and Maroon actors.[10]

From 1946 to the mid-1960s, the systems for governing the Amerindian and Maroon peoples were part of a conservation model that favored taking specific responsibility for "primitives," and acknowledged the central role of ethnologists. As I will describe in later sections of this chapter, it was only in the 1960s that France granted these groups mass citizenship as part of an assimilation policy, through which the state also included them in its education, training, and social support programs. This policy, however, was later contested by a new, mainly Amerindian elite, which labelled itself "indigenous," and through this demanded recognition and institutionalization of their culture difference. The categories in use today are rooted in categories of the colonial era – these categories and their significance are outlined in the following section (Figure 5.1).

Colonial categories of otherness and differentiated governance (1930–1969)

Colonial censuses from the late nineteenth century classify the residents of Guiana according to three categories. The "colonist population" includes the entire Creole population, whether they are the descendants of white settlers, black slaves emancipated at the time of abolition, or the former slaves known as *libres de couleur*, "free men of color." The "population other than colonists" includes both colonial "immigrants" (workers migrating from other colonies) and those who have been "freed" (former convicts incarcerated in the penal colony, who had been freed at the end of their sentence). Finally, there are the "aboriginal Indians," called so according to the state terminology of the time (Piantoni 2008: 193). The Maroons were not counted in the census. The categories in the census therefore intersect with differences in status between *citizens* (the "colonists" including some Afro-descendants) and subjects, who are *not citizens* ("immigrants" hired under contract, "penal elements" and "aboriginals"). In the early twentieth century, because the convoys transporting hired immigrants to Guiana had ended,[11] regulated immigration disappeared from the categories of colonial censuses. Because of their extreme marginality, Amerindians and Maroons were never encompassed by the colonial law and had never been subjected to native status ("indigénat"), a non-existent status in French Guiana. The variability of their denomination by the colonizer is another indication of

9 The prefects and sub-prefects are the highest representatives of the state in a department.

10 This research was carried out from 2010 to 2014; 30 interviews were realized (4 with prefects and sub-prefects, 2 with other high civil servants, 2 with ethnologists, 4 with local elected representatives, 18 with Amerindian and marron leaders and customary chiefs). This research is part of the SOGIP program, coordinated by Irene Bellier, and has received the financial support of the European Research Council under the Seventh Framework Programme of the Community (FP7/2007-2013 Grant Agreement no. 249236).

11 The last convoy took place in 1877.

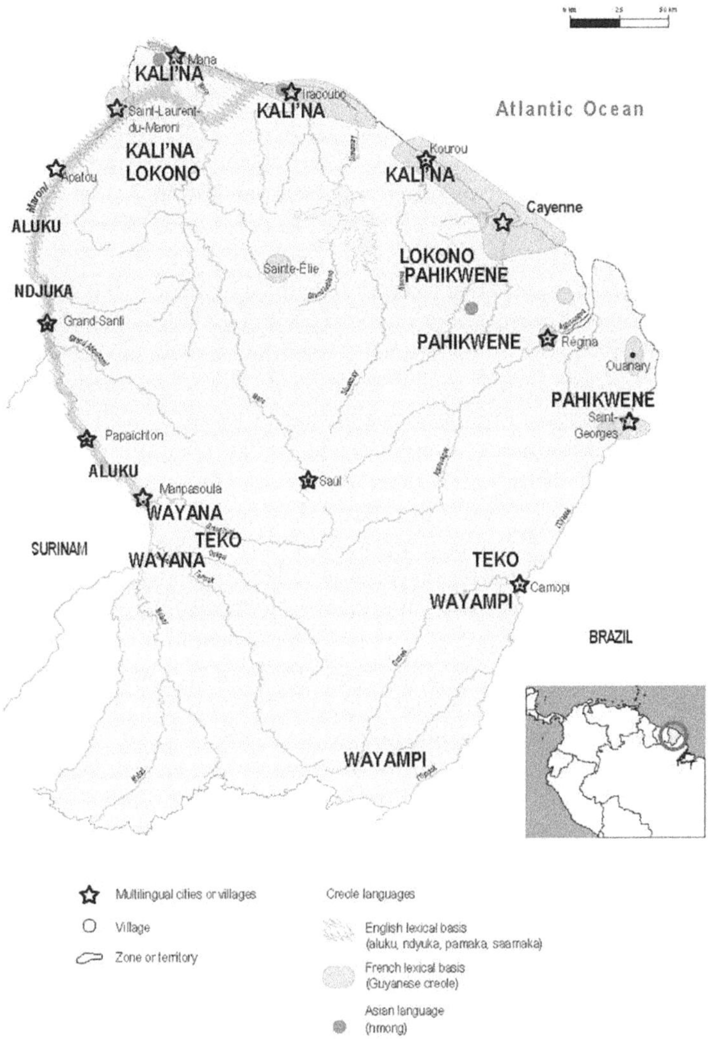

Figure 5.1 Languages of the Amerindians and Maroons of French Guiana.
Source: elaboration by the author based on original by Renault-Lescure and Goury, 2009.

their weak integration into the colonial state. On the other hand, the distinction between "civilian population," "Bosh [Maroon][12] tribes and native Indians" lasted until the 1961 census where a category called "primitive populations" still figured (Rallu 1998). This category of "primitives" is central, as it underpins specific devices for governing these populations.

12 The term Bosh is derived from the English word Bush meaning "men of the woods." It is a pejorative term to describe Maroon populations.

Colonial and postcolonial frontiers (1930–1969)

In Guiana, the distinction between "civilized" and "wild" noted above overlay contrasting views of living areas – the "civilized" coast versus the "wild forest" interior. The colonial frontiers of Guiana were very much based on the physical environment: colonial society was confined to the coast, which was developed as part of a plantation economy and then a penal settlement, in contrast to the forested interior, which was difficult to penetrate (Piantoni 2002). As we shall see, this colonial frontier continued after Guiana was incorporated as a French department.

The French state had only a limited presence in this forested interior until the creation, in 1930, of the separate territory of Inini, a new colonial entity with direct government that was independent of the coastal colony. From this date onward, Guianese territory therefore was governed according to two colonial regimes that were distinct from one another and were designed according to opposing models of colonial administration. The coastal colony, like other old French colonies such as the West Indies and Réunion, corresponded to the "assimilationist" model,[13] giving a central role to local institutions with elected officials (departmental council, municipality). The separate territory of Inini had a special system of government, following the model designed for the African possessions of the French empire (Thabouillot 2012). Under the influence of reformers connected to the Colonial School (for training colonial administrators), in the 1930s France's African colonization was directed toward a more "differentialist" model, in which the definition of indigenous policy had to be guided by respect for indigenous traditions (L'Estoile 2000). The split between the coastline and the interior of Guiana was therefore institutionalized in a ruling that established a specific kind of state management for the interior of Guiana and its inhabitants, outside the control of Guianese elected representatives on the coast. Indeed, the interior was – and is still – remote and, until the development of air transport, quite disconnected from the urban center of Cayenne, where state services and elected representatives were concentrated.

Those promoting the separate territory of Inini were for the most part senior colonial officials who had previous responsibilities in Africa. Their intention was to take over and valorize the Guianese interior by establishing a real and continuous governing presence (Thabouillot 2012: 128–135). Admittedly, government of the Amerindians and Maroons was not the main goal of this takeover. The principal desire of the colonial administration was to manage activities on the artisanal gold-mining sites, gain better control of the Creole population working on them, and set up frontiers in the south of Guiana. Nonetheless, it was within the separate territory of Inini that relations between the administration and the Amerindian and Maroon captains[14] became truly institutionalized, and that a

13 Assimilation was both a political model imposed by the colonizer and a political project entered into by the West Indian and Guianese elites in the name of universal Republican values (Mam Lam Fouck 2006).

14 Captains are the village chiefs officially recognized by the colonial state. They belong to the founding groups (or lineages) of villages, of which they are often the oldest representatives. However, they also draw their authority from their intermediate position in relation to the colonial administration (Collomb 1999).

policy of medical and material aid for these populations was initiated. The administrative personnel of Inini also developed better knowledge of these populations, which were starting to be registered in censuses and studied in a systematic way.

In 1946, the departmentalization of Guiana confirmed the completion of the administrative and political assimilation process for the territory and should have marked the end of the Inini territory. Thus, in 1947, the Council of State (*Conseil d État*[15]) released a statement making it clear that "the existence within a department of a territory having a legal personality and falling outside the jurisdiction of the departmental council is contrary to the law of August 10, 1871." However, the law of September 14, 1951 extended the life of Inini territory by turning it, within the same geographical limits, into the "district of Inini" (see the Figure 5.2 below).

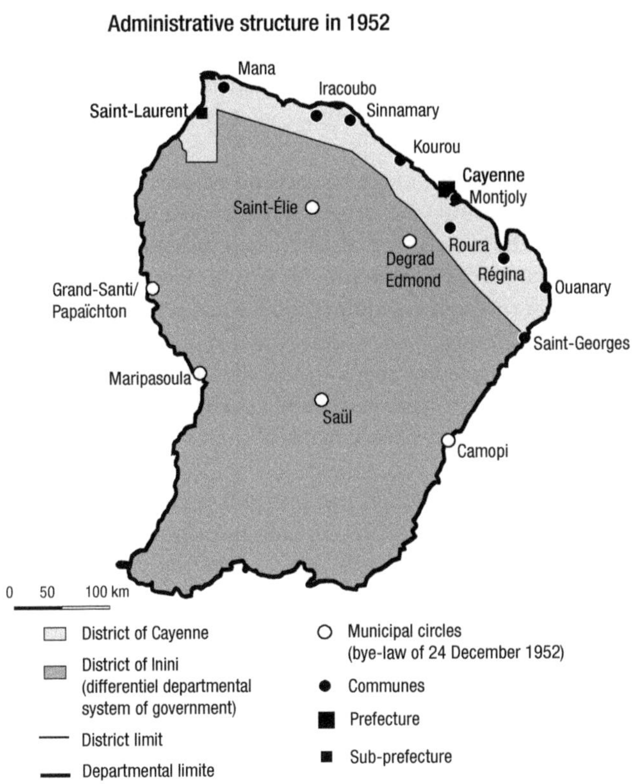

Figure 5.2 Administrative evolution of Guiana 1 / Administrative structure in 1952
Source: Piantoni (2009: 292).

15 The Council of State supervises the legality of legislative acts and executive regulations before they are adopted by Parliament and government, and implemented by public administration. It sanctions their violation and it operates as a Court for all activities engaging public administration with citizens.

Far from being merely an administrative frontier, the Inini district effectively extended the strictly colonial methods of governing the Guianese interior into the postcolonial period. In the absence of a "commune" (one of the basic units in the administrative and political hierarchy of the French state), responsibility for the "municipal circles" (a typically colonial administrative area) that had previously been overseen by the governor was transferred to the prefect and to the sub-prefect of Inini – political figures who were the principal representatives of the state on French Metropolitan or assimilated territory. The creation of the Office for Primitive Populations (*Service des populations primitives*, SPP), also known as the Office for African and Indian Populations (*Service des populations africaines et indiennes*), aimed to institutionalize and systematize the Amerindian and Maroon administration practices initiated in the 1930s (Thabouillot 2012: 185–214). I will return to this point below.

It was the first prefect of Guiana, Robert Vignon, who decided to create the SPP in 1949. The SPP project appeared to be largely informed by the indigenist policies developed in Brazil,[16] where Vignon spent his first foreign mission and where he visited the Office for the Protection of Brazilian Indians:

> The "Othering" of the primitive Indian and African populations in Guiana is too marked for an assimilation bringing real benefit to these populations to be accomplished in the near future. Rather than sudden assimilation, it is preferable to try and encourage – though this will be a long uphill task – adherence to our way of life through example [...] This can only be achieved if, from the start, unsuccessful contacts are avoided, and if protective legislation is drawn up. [...] For this, we need to create special aid organizations in the food, craft and medical fields and, insofar as possible, in the contacts that these Black and Indian people have with other elements of the Guianese population.[17]

Robert Vignon and Lucien Vochel, the first sub-prefect of the Inini district in 1951, defended the project for differentiated administration of the Amerindians and the Maroons, and were firmly opposed to any strategy for assimilation. Lucien Vochel managed to persuade the administrator of the Guianese Welfare Center (*Caisse générale de Sécurité sociale de Guyane*) to abandon a project for affiliating "primitives" to social security.[18] The SPP also had the task of providing minimal and "appropriate" education for children, as decreed when the office was created:

16 *Indigenism* refers to policies implemented by certain American states in order to govern their indigenous peoples with the assimilationist perspective of integrating them into the nation. Developed in Mexico in the early twentieth century, the indigenist principle was differently adopted by other states (Marroquin 1972).

17 ASP SLM. Letter sent from Robert Vignon to the directors of the offices for Algeria and the Overseas Departments, January 26, 1954.

18 ASP SLM. Letter from Sub-Prefect Vochel to the director of the Welfare Center, April 3, 1953.

> School attendance is very sporadic for the majority of Indians living on the coast, primary education being little suited to their needs. A boarding school for children will provide them with training in the different Indian techniques in accordance with their traditions, and the basic education will be supplemented by French and arithmetic, an elementary study of history, geography and the local environment, and vocational training.[19]

This indigenist vision was also expressed in the project to create an Indian law to recognize and protect lands and captains.[20] The envisaged statute displays the same logic as that shown by the Brazilian Department for Indian Protection (De Souza Lima 1995). The tutelary power of the state over Indians and Maroons aimed to save them, both from themselves (exemplified by a ban on the sale of alcohol to Indians) and from the rest of the Guianese population (through legal measures providing protection from exploitation or land seizures). The plan to create Indian reserves was part of this tutelary logic and of a population policy that favored "rational" management of these populations.

Ethnologists as the protectors and governors of "primitive peoples"

Although it was the prefect that dictated the main direction of Office for Primitive Populations, the state recruited ethnologists to develop and implement the prefect's policies with regard to Indians, and it was these ethnologists who determined the nature of the office. Guy Charpentier and Suzanne Vianès-Charpentier led the way. Their mission in St. Laurent du Maroni, from 1950 to 1955, consisted primarily of studying the Indian and Maroon populations (by means of censuses, examining their social organization and collecting craft items such as pottery and basketry). In addition to this ethnological dimension, a dispensary was set up in St. Laurent du Maroni for the protection of mothers and children, and to fight endemic diseases (such as parasitosis and malaria). They also established a co-operative for fishing and craftwork, which enabled trade between Amerindians, Maroons and Creoles to become more fair. In such cases, ethnologists were direct agents of the state, providing both specialist knowledge and services to manage the population. They developed an understanding of Indians and Maroons that highlighted the particularity of their social organization and craftsmanship – and justified specific policies for their protection and economic development:

> Here, as in other spheres of indigenist action, the importance of personal contacts with artisans needs to be stressed. The decorative themes and motifs need to be studied with them, along with the various styles that have succeeded one another and the meaning of the symbols. We need to awaken

19 Decree no. 809 setting up and organizing the office for primitive populations in Guiana, decree of November 22, 1952, ASP SLM.

20 ASP SLM. Notes from Guy Charpentier to the sub-prefect.

> their interest by showing that we ourselves are interested. In parallel with this aesthetic aspect of the problem, we need to examine the economic possibilities, make sure there is a flow of goods to sell and suggest products that might be traded. Research into the improvement of techniques is not forgotten. Earth samples have already been sent to the technical laboratory at the Musée de l'Homme [in Paris] and the experts will send their conclusions which will allow certain changes to be made.[21]

However, the emergence of an institution specialized in governing primitive populations came up against financial limitations. The funds allocated to the Guiana SPP were low; in addition to Guy Charpentier, who was paid as an ethnologist, and Suzanne Vianès-Charpentier, who received a nurse's salary, the office employed another nurse, a doctor, a mechanic and four representatives of the prefecture – who happened to be priests[22] appointed to the different municipal circles.[23] The education of children was also largely given over to priests. In fact, the SPP trained school assistants to teach in some Indian and Maroon village schools in the interior. On the coast, however, education was entrusted to religious congregations, and Indian children were gathered into single-sex boarding schools known as *Indian homes*.[24] Despite its claims, the SPP did not have a monopoly over the administration of populations in its charge.

The effects of indigenist policies in Guiana

The SPP played a decisive role in settling Indian and Maroon populations in the localities that they still occupy today, and also in establishing a permanent link with the state. Ethnologists, in fact, appear to have been the real mediators between the state and these populations. This was particularly the case for Suzanne Vianès-Charpentier, as testified by Léonida, an Amerindian woman who was born around 1930 and resides in the village of Balaté:

> It was Mme Charpentier who looked after us, and also the people from Maripasoula [*a commune of the interior*], the Djuk'a and the Saramaka [*two Maroon groups*], but she looked after the Amerindians more. That lady, she knew everything about the Amerindians, she worked in the hospital, her

21 ASP SLM. Guy Charpentier's note on the protection and development of popular arts in Guiana, February 25, 1954.

22 Although Guiana was a French territory when the law of separation between church and state was passed in 1905, this law was not applied because of the important role played by Catholic missions in colonial life. Guiana therefore remained under the concordat and after departmentalization priests received salaries from the prefecture.

23 ASP SLM, SPP Budget from 1950 to 1954.

24 In 1953, for example, the St. Laurent du Maroni orphanage run by the Franciscan Sisters of Mary was turned into an *Indian home*. Undated manuscript by Sister Paulette (Armanville 2012: 59).

> husband went to Maripasoula all the time, he went to see sick people and the wife stayed here with us. When we were ill, we went to see the wife. She gave milk for children, woven clothes, she gave everything, she looked after us well, she also gave cows that the state donated. One family, one cow. We let the cows loose but when the cows had calves, if they were female we kept them and if they were male the state took them. Mme Charpentier had a dispensary in her house that was just for the Amerindians. If we were about to give birth, she would send us to the hospital, but most people gave birth before arriving at the hospital and she, she would come, she would take the name of the child and send it to the hospital.[25]

The welfare services provided by this office were decisive in relocating and settling Amerindian groups from Surinam to different sites on the Guianese coast in the early 1950s. Nicolas Wyngaarde, born in 1930 and former captain of the village of Balaté in the commune of St. Laurent du Maroni, recounts how his village was created:

> There was a doctor who had passed through [*at Papatam, a Lokono village on the Surinamese bank of the Maroni*]. He said to us "You are poor and miserable, we're going to give you some land over there [*on the French bank of the Maroni*]." He was a French doctor. Afterwards another doctor came to try and find work for us. It was Mme Charpentier, Mme Suzy who took care of us.[26]

These settlements were part of the continuing population policy implemented by the prefecture, which, from 1947 onwards, organized the moving of Indian villages to different coastal localities like Yanou-Bellevue and Awala-Yalimapo, where they encouraged the Indians to occupy the sites of former penal colonies (Collomb and Tiouka 2000: 111). The directors of the Indian office always chose to settle these groups in villages close to, but outside of, Creole towns. This ensured their physical protection (in terms of health and food) while safeguarding the "authenticity" of their social organization (Bayart and Bertrand 2005: 25). For each village created, the SPP acknowledged a customary chief, who was appointed by a decree of the prefecture and received an allowance. This gave the prefecture substantial power to choose its representatives and intermediaries within these populations (Figure 5.3).

The implementation of this native policy at the start of Guiana's departmentalization process therefore resulted from a specific form of public action that involved the participation of two groups of players: ethnologists employed by the state and top-ranking civil servants – a prefect and a sub-prefect who developed an interest in the Amerindian and Maroon peoples.

25 Interview with Léonida, Balaté, January 2011.
26 Interview with Nicolas Wyngaarde, Balaté, March 2003.

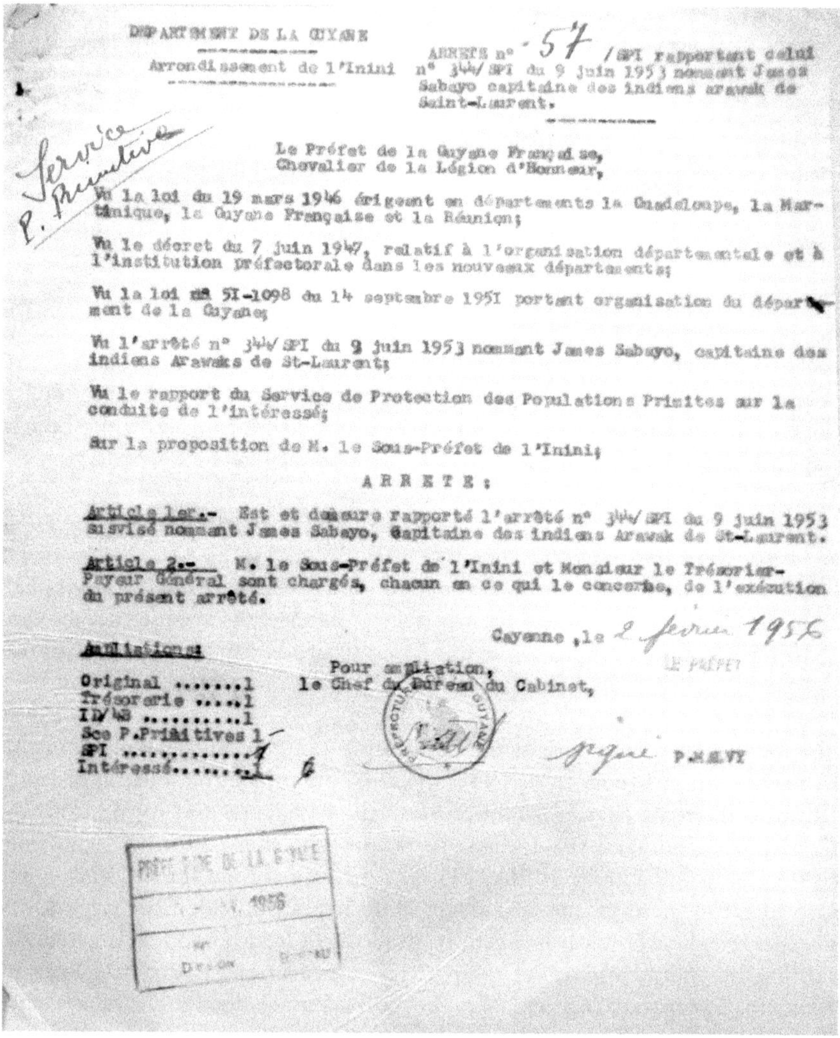

DÉPARTEMENT DE LA GUYANE

Arrondissement de l'Inini

ARRÊTÉ n° 57 /SPI rapportant celui n° 344/SPI du 9 juin 1953 nommant James Sabayo capitaine des indiens arawak de Saint-Laurent.

Le Préfet de la Guyane Française,
Chevalier de la Légion d'Honneur,

Vu la loi du 19 mars 1946 érigeant en départements la Guadeloupe, la Martinique, la Guyane Française et la Réunion;

Vu le décret du 7 juin 1947, relatif à l'organisation départementale et à l'institution préfectorale dans les nouveaux départements;

Vu la loi n° 51-1098 du 14 septembre 1951 portant organisation du département de la Guyane;

Vu l'arrêté n° 344/SPI du 9 juin 1953 nommant James Sabayo, capitaine des indiens Arawaks de St-Laurent;

Vu le rapport du Service de Protection des Populations Primitives sur la conduite de l'intéressé;

Sur la proposition de M. le Sous-Préfet de l'Inini;

ARRÊTE:

Article 1er.- Est et demeure rapporté l'arrêté n° 344/SPI du 9 juin 1953 susvisé nommant James Sabayo, Capitaine des indiens Arawak de St-Laurent.

Article 2.- M. le Sous-Préfet de l'Inini et Monsieur le Trésorier-Payeur Général sont chargés, chacun en ce qui le concerne, de l'exécution du présent arrêté.

Cayenne, le 2 février 1956

Ampliations:
Original 1
Trésorerie 1
ID/48 1
Sce P.Primitives 1
SPI 1
Intéressé.......1

Pour ampliation,
le Chef du Bureau du Cabinet,

P.MALVY

Figure 5.3 Decree appointing Captain Arawak of Paddock (St. Laurent du Maroni) and awarding him a monthly allowance of 3,000 francs.

Dated from May 15, 1950 (prefecture archives).

Administrative assimilation, "native" demands, and a new form of public action

Until the early 1950s, Indians and Maroons had been recognized as French subjects, but not individually registered – which meant that they were deprived of political rights. From 1956 to 1969, different campaigns to establish civil status together with an important administrative reform gradually put an end to this colonial exception. The decree marking the end of the Inini territory in 1969 also marked the end of the special collaboration between the prefecture and scientists as these latter were very critical of the assimilationist administration of Amerindians and Maroons that had been implemented in the 1960s and 1970s.

Political and civil assimilation of Amerindians and Maroons

The plan to give a specific status to primitive peoples had been devised by the SPP, but once this was abandoned the prefecture organized different campaigns to establish a Public Records Office in the Inini district, between 1956 and 1969 (Benoît 2016). The registering of "judgments establishing date of birth" enabled an overwhelming majority of Amerindians and Maroons to be accorded French nationality and citizenship. This process was accelerated in the 1960s as part of a national framework of normalization from the top for overseas departments. Central government reminded the prefecture that it should "make sure births and deaths were properly registered in the state population registers and make a census of persons born abroad who should be provided with the appropriate card."[27] It marked the start of what Jean Hurault denounced as the policy of "Francization" – which meant the eradication of Inini territory.

In 1969, a reform of commune boundaries merged Amerindian and Maroon populations into communal territories (see Figure 5.4). They would now be part of the same administrative organization as the one established in Metropolitan France. This meant that Amerindian and Maroon people acquired the right to vote – but they had to take the initiative of requesting that right. In 1965, the *gran man* aluku Tolinga (chief of the Maroon aluku customary chiefs) asked that "he and his family" be registered on the electoral lists.[28] However, the majority were not put on the electoral lists until the 1970s, when local political competition was intensifying and elected representatives of Creole origin were encouraged to seek – and register – new electors outside of their own group of origin (Guyon 2011).

The economic, cultural, and social effects of the "Francization" policy were immediate. Registration on the population register meant becoming eligible for social welfare and obtaining child benefits. The Indians and Maroons became increasingly involved in a market economy and settled close to schools and centers of government. All these processes had a profound effect on their social organization. For example, the people working for the child benefit office (*Caisse d'allocations familiales*) tended to substitute paternal filiation for the maternal filiation of the Maroons and Amerindians, as testified by a woman from the Lokono village of Balaté:

> Before, children took their mother's name. And then, the French started to acknowledge children through child benefits. My paternal grandmother was Sabayo, and my grandfather was Biswana. Until I was 13, I was known by my mother's name, Jubitana, and then my father recognized me. So now I'm called Sabayo.[29]

27 Departmental archives of Guiana. Ref. 1506 E. Letter no. 113 OA/0 from the Minister of Justice, June 5, 1965.
28 Departmental archives of Guiana. Ref. 1746 E. District Court. December 1, 1965.
29 Interview with Mme Sabayo, Balaté, February 2003.

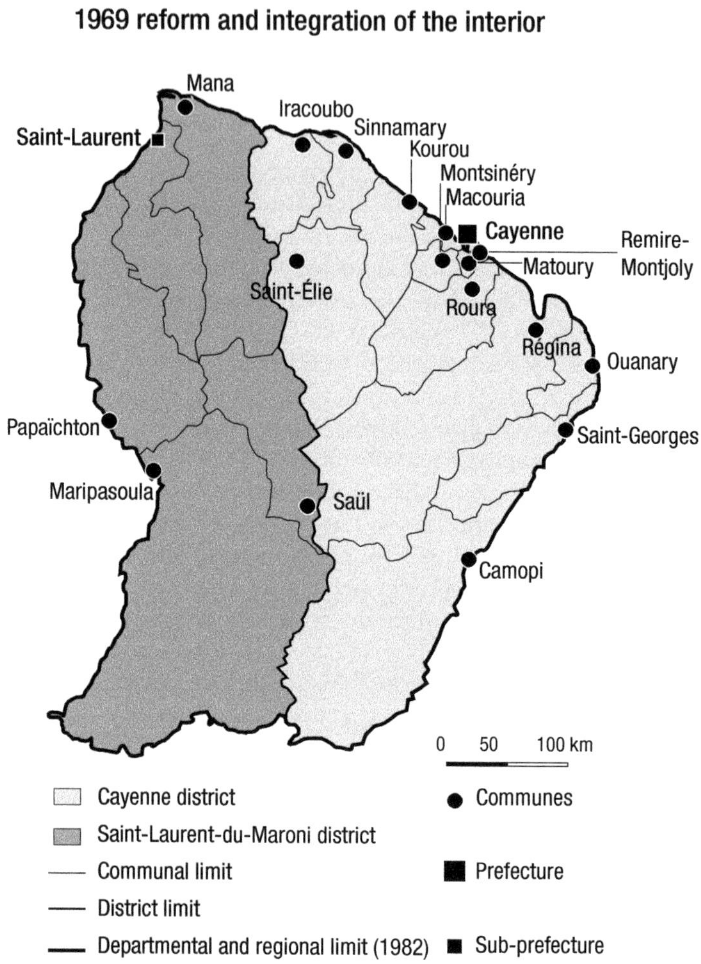

Figure 5.4 Administrative Evolution of Guiana 2 / Reforms of 1969 and the integration of the interior.

Source: Piantoni (2009: 292).

The registration of Amerindian and Maroon populations in general law did not, however, signal the end of all public policy specifically designed for them. When the Inini district was abolished, the "coordination of actions in favor of tribal populations" was entrusted to a committee presided over by the sub-prefect of St. Laurent du Maroni (decree of December 17, 1970). The prefecture administration only progressively abandoned its protection of Amerindians and

Maroons and the army intervened regularly to carry out maintenance or build amenities such as water towers in the coastal villages.[30] Nuns continued to provide education for Indian children in the *homes* – as so-called residential schools in French Guiana – until the late 1970s.

Once the Inini territory was abolished, collaboration between social science researchers who were Guiana specialists and the managerial staff of the prefecture underwent a marked deterioration. In 1962, Robert Jaulin, a young ethnologist (who later stood out for his stance against what he said was the "ethnocide" of the Amazonian Amerindians; Deshayes 1998), was made responsible for a mission in Guiana, at the end of which he declared himself to be against the abolition of Inini territory. Jean Hurault, until that time a valued collaborator of the Guiana prefecture, subsequently became a virulent critic of state action in Guiana. He strongly criticized the disappearance of Inini and the assimilation of the Indians into Guiana, calling it ethnocide, and proceeded to mobilize Americanist networks to the cause (Hurault 1970). On March 19, 1969, Henri Lehman, Claude Levi-Strauss, and Marcel Bataillon sent a letter of protest to the Overseas Secretary of State, which was published in the newspaper *Le Monde* a few months later.[31]

During the 1970s, a new generation of anthropologists descended upon Guianese territory. Among these, the Grenand husband and wife team stand out. In 1969, Pierre and Françoise Grenand each began a thesis in ethnoecology and ethnolinguistics (respectively), working with the Wayampi people of south-east Guiana and founding a school in the remote village of Trois-Sauts, where they lived. Following this they carried out work among the Wayana, the Palikurs (or Palik'wene) and, on a more minor scale, among the Arawak (Lokono). Continuing in the wake of Jean Hurault's endeavors, they pleaded in favor of legal protection for the Amerindians and the implementation of appropriate public policies (schooling, social welfare, and so on). In 1978 Pierre Grenand, Françoise Grenand and Simone Dreyfus-Gamelon published a report on the Palikurs of Guiana in which they demanded specific land rights for the Amerindians, stressing the collective ownership of land and the inalienability of rights. They found effective intermediaries within the Secretariat of State for Overseas Departments and Territories, particularly in the person of Jean Aribaud, its deputy director for social affairs. In May 1981, a ministerial report and a note by the Secretary of State, Paul Dijoud, advocated legal protection for Amerindian and Maroon territories, together with reactivation of the committee for "coordinating actions in favor of tribal populations" bringing together civil servants, elected representatives and scientists (Grenand and Grenand 2005; Filoche 2015).

30 Interview with Marinus MacIntosh, Village Espérance, St. Laurent du Maroni, January 2011.

31 Address on "the francization of indigenous districts in Guiana." *Le Monde*. July 8, 1969.

In the 1980s, criticism of French state policy was led by Amerindians themselves, demanding recognition of their peoples, their territories, and their own cultures. As described in the section below, the French state went on to satisfy some of these demands, although with certain limits.

Indigenous protests against public policies

The birth of an Amerindian movement in Guiana is part of a wider regional and international context of institutionalization of the indigenous cause, in Latin America (see also González-González, this volume), and in international organizations, particularly the United Nations (UN; Morin 2005). Although Maroon leaders of associations also emerged in Guianese municipalities in the 1980s, they failed to unite on a departmental level. The absence of a unitary movement and the low visibility of Maroon leaders in relation to Amerindian leaders can be explained by the inequality of educational resources allotted to these two groups, and also by the symbolic effectiveness of the claim to indigeneity, a concept that had been legitimized and institutionalized on the international stage (Guyon 2011).

The creation of Amerindian associations dates from the early 1980s, a period marked by the emergence of a new generation born of the "Francization policy" (Collomb and Tiouka 2000). The young men who played a part in it were the first Amerindians to have benefited from secondary education, and thus able to go to France for professional training. They developed links with the Grenand couple and with other anthropologists as well as with NGOs known to be supporting the rights of "indigenous peoples" (Survival France, Les Amis de la terre, CSIA-Nitassinan), and familiarizing themselves with the indigenous discourse developed in international institutions.[32] In 1981, they created the Amerindian Association of French Guiana (*Association des Amérindiens de Guyane française*, AAGF) and organized its first assembly on December 8 and 9, 1984. In their capacity as "first inhabitants," they demanded recognition of the Amerindian peoples of Guiana by the French state, as well as "sovereignty" over their territories, and cultural rights (Tiouka 1985). They wanted the French state to give them collective ownership of the lands they inhabited and which they used for farming, hunting, and gathering.

The supremacy accorded to the principle of collective land ownership was characteristic of the way in which the international indigenous movement, combined with Americanist anthropology, conceived of the specific nature of indigenous peoples in relation to Western societies. During the 1980s,

32 The Indians of North America were the first to identify themselves as *indigenous peoples* in the 1960s. International meetings between indigenous peoples were organized in the 1970s and the World Council of Indigenous Peoples was formed in 1975, but the international indigenous movement only became fully formed within the UN framework in the 1980s, with the creation in 1982 of the Working Group on Indigenous Populations (Morin 2005).

researchers actively communicated the demands of the AAGF both to the state authorities and to the French general public. In coordination with this, Pierre and Françoise Grenand published a special issue on the Amerindians of Guiana in the journal *Ethnies* (published by Survival International), including the speech by Félix Tiouka given during the 1984 assembly. In 1992, Félix Tiouka defended the decision to bring Guianese Amerindian demands to the attention of the UN and to strengthen links with Amazonian indigenous organizations (Collomb 2005). The UN thus became a pivotal resource for the movement to achieve local recognition and to put pressure on the French government.

From the moment of the AAGF's creation, the prefecture proved attentive to Amerindian demands. For example, the prefect, Bernard Courtois, went to the 1984 gathering together with his principal private secretary and the sub-prefect of St. Laurent du Maroni. On 9 December, Courtois gave a speech in which he recalled the "refusal to impose an unaccepted integration policy" and declared his intention to "propose a solution to this vitally important issue for the people he represented," namely "collective ownership of the lands they occupy."[33] This was when the administration stopped calling these populations by the pejorative terms of "tribes or forest peoples" and substituted the name *Amerindians*, which was used by the AAGF leaders themselves. The Committee for "coordinating action in favor of tribal populations," created in 1969, was renamed "Committee for coordinating action in favor of the Amerindians of French Guiana and the populations of the Maroni" and now included representatives from the AAGF.[34]

Because Guiana was a French department governed by Article 73 of the Constitution, it did not have special legislation. After the abolition of the Inini district, therefore, the adaptation of institutional and administrative systems to Guianese social reality was carried out in the margins of the law (Filoche 2011). Although France voted in favor of the UN Declaration on the Rights of Indigenous Peoples, since the 1980s it has maintained a limited understanding of indigenous peoples' rights. To the extent that the French state recognizes indigenous peoples' demands, they are seen as emanating from "populations" and not from "peoples" – the latter being a notion that runs counter to the principle of indivisibility of the Republic. At the same time, these demands must be linked to circumscribed and clearly delimited territories (Bellier 2009). Finally, the French constitution makes it impossible to recognize differentiated rights since it prohibits any positive or negative

33 ASP SLM. Note written by the Renseignements Généraux [Central Directorate of General Intelligence, a branch of the police ultimately answerable to the Ministry of the Interior. (Translator)], December 11, 1984.

34 ASP SLM. Note from the sub-prefect of St. Laurent du Maroni to the prefect, January 4, 1985.

discrimination between citizens.[35] At the international level, as in National Assembly debates, the French state consistently refuses all forms of minority rights (as evidenced, for example, by their refusal to ratify the ILO Convention 169, reservations on the declaration of rights of indigenous peoples, and their failure to ratify the European charter on minority and regional languages).

AAGF leaders, with the support of anthropologists and some senior civil servants from the Overseas Ministry, did, however, obtain some specific measures from the French state regarding land and education. The land issue was central to demands of the Amerindian movement. After it was brought to the attention of the Guiana prefecture and the Overseas Ministry by the Grenand couple, from 1984 the prefecture started looking for legal solutions that would allow rights of collective ownership to be accorded to the Amerindians.[36] The decree of April 14, 1987 gave to some communities the possibility of being granted "areas of special use rights" (*zones de droit d'usage collectif*, ZDUC)[37] and of state lands being collectively assigned or given over to them. This decree undoubtedly constituted a legal step forward: prior to this provision, concessions in Guiana only applied to individuals in their personal capacity and gave no advantage to Amerindian and Maroon communities who were organized according to the principle of collective ownership of the land. However, this measure only recognized rights for the indigenous Guianese populations in an indirect and implicit way. The circumlocution used to describe the populations concerned by the decree was "communities of inhabitants traditionally drawing their means of subsistence from the forest" – a telling illustration of the legislature's reluctance to recognize indigenous peoples' rights.

Furthermore, the implementation of the measure proved to be difficult. The procedures for allocating land gave a dominant role to the state representative, in order to avoid local pressures and obstacles. In fact, the veto of local elected representatives in the commission for land allocation was sufficient to block the process. Sixteen years after the decree was passed in 1987, only three out of about 30 Amerindian villages in Guiana had benefited from a transfer (Collomb and Guyon 2015). On the other hand, areas with the right of collective use, or ZDUC, were more widely granted; there are in fact 15 ZDUCs representing 8% of Guianese territory. Nevertheless, these land rights remain very vague,

35 Differentiated rights have indeed been granted in France, for example in the context of the Matignon and Nouméa accords concerning New Caledonia or again to ensure equal representation of men and women in policies (2000 law on parity). Voting through these laws did however necessitate prior revision of the constitution in favor of a political balance of power which Amerindians and Maroons would have difficulty in establishing.

36 ASP SLM. Note written by the Renseignements généraux, December 11, 1984.

37 The areas with right of collective use are situated in the forest, relatively close to the villages concerned. They are usually established around a water course which simultaneously facilitates access to the area as well as traditional uses; in it, the Amerindians can practice their slash-and-burn agriculture as well as hunting and fishing.

meaning that neither exclusive rights over these territories nor continuity of land rights are really guaranteed. Furthermore, the ZDUC are supposed to be devoted to traditional practices and to "subsistence"; yet these terms are not defined. This lack of definition potentially limits the use of these territories by the populations, and turns out to be poorly suited to an evolving way of life and to local practices (Filoche 2015).

Despite these limitations, the Amerindians have recently obtained important land retrocessions. At the end of the general strike movement in French Guiana in March–April 2017 (see Guyon 2017), on April 21, 2017, the government signed a memorandum with local elected officials and representatives of social movement organizations called the "Guiana Agreements." The memorandum provides for the free transfer by the State of 400,000 ha to the Amerindians and the creation of a Native Land Office to manage these lands. However, it is not yet known when and how (for example, their location and status) these lands will be divested.[38]

As noted above, language and education were another priority area for the AAGF, in which they also had some of their demands met. In the late 1990s, the French Ministry of Education implemented a strategy to adapt education to the specific needs and languages of different Guianese groups, mainly Amerindian and Maroon. Initiated by linguists at the IRD[39] in 1997, this strategy enabled the recruitment and training of cultural and bilingual mediators from these groups so that their mother tongue might play a role in classes for younger children (Goury et al. 2000).

The continuity of the different institutional and administrative strategies with the indigenous policy of the SPP in the early 1950s is striking. The fields in which the French state is now disposed to adapt its administrative strategies are effectively identical to the SPP's main sectors of intervention: protection of land areas devoted to settlement and traditional uses, and appropriate education. Although the role of anthropologists and other scientists in developing these public policies has undergone a marked change – they are no longer representatives of the prefecture – they continue to contribute to them through the new persona of the "expert" (Oliveira 2000). For example, from 1993, linguists from the IRD and researchers from the CNRS worked with politicians and leaders of the Kali'na association in a working group on the Kali'na culture and language. Their job (establishing the written form of Kali'na and compiling a dictionary) justified the demands for recognition of indigenous languages and cultures that the leaders of the Amerindian movement had been voicing.

Furthermore, the linguists, alongside the Amerindian leaders, played the role of mediators between the communities and the education authority regarding the provision of appropriate education. Once the education authority had adopted the principle, they called upon the linguists' expertise in order to develop the syllabus and design the tools. These scientists therefore

38 En janvier 2019, la mesure n'était pas encore mise en œuvre.
39 Institut de recherche sur le développement [Institute for Research on Development].

participated in the training of cultural and bilingual mediators (IRD Project Guiana-Education Authority of Guiana, 1998–2004) as well as developing learning tools. In this form of public action, ethnological knowledge appears to fulfil the dual role of legitimizing and orchestrating public policies (L'Estoile 2000). However, with the transformation of the Amerindian groups and their politicization through the shaping of an "indigenous" common cause, relations between ethnologists and the groups they study were profoundly changed. With the Amerindians' entry into politics and their increased ability to represent their own interests to the state, the mediation of ethnologists was no longer necessary. Scientists became one of several sorts of mediators working on the problem of how to bring about appropriate education and legitimize specific public policies.

Whether it concerns land rights or cultural rights, adapting French public policies to local social realities remains limited and fragile – the result, as can be seen, of a makeshift job designed to keep things within the Republican framework.

Political autonomy and indigenous institutions

Over and above territorial rights and appropriate public policies, since the early 1980s the Amerindians of Guiana have been demanding political autonomy and recognition of their own institutions such as customary chiefs, all in the name of indigeneity.

The creation of the Awala-Yalimapo commune in 1989, at the start of the Guianese indigenous movement, was for the state an indirect way of granting political autonomy and symbolic recognition to the Amerindians. Separated from the commune of Mana, which had a Creole majority, the two Kali'na villages of Awala and Yalimapo formed another territorial community, which is still unique today, and which enabled the Amerindians of Guiana to exist politically. Unlike the decree of 1987, researchers played little part in this cause, which was mainly led by representatives of the AAGF and by Claude Silberzhan, the prefect of Guiana from 1982 until 1984, who then became overseas adviser to Prime Minister Laurent Fabius until 1986:

> In 1982 it was a very difficult situation. I said to myself, this Creole claim to be the legitimate occupants of Guiana, well, I'm going to get the Amerindians to cramp their style. Really, I thought, to make the Amerindians appear I'll have to make them appear geographically. I'll start by giving them a territory, that way I'm giving them a political location with a mayor and a departmental councilor at the same time. And then they'll have to play the game and the others will have to accept them. That's the whole story of Awala-Yalimapo [...] At the time, you're the prefect in Guiana, you've got a lot of room for maneuver, you're a long way from the [French] Republic, nobody understands a thing about it and nobody could care less. The idea came just at that moment, it began to be discussed with Tiouka and his friends [...] Then there was a discussion with Paris. But after that I was at Matignon [French Prime Minister's

offices] and I was responsible for all the French overseas territories. So, the minister continued this operation and I helped it along and backed it.[40]

In the context of the early 1980s, when the cause for independence, carried along by a new generation of Creole elected representatives, was becoming institutionalized in Guiana, satisfying Amerindian demands was (as the prefect of the time recounts in the above quote) a means of counteracting the demands of the Creole elected representatives and fighters for independence. Nevertheless, the creation of this new community enabled the Kali'na leaders of Awala-Yalimapo to experience political autonomy, to build up elective and managerial experience and to implement an original model for linking the commune with customary authority. In fact, since a new team took over as head of the town in 2001, the commune has introduced a mixed commission combining the municipality with customary authorities, composed of five town councilors and ten members appointed by the two customary chiefs of Awala and Yalimapo. In this way, the customary authorities are systematically consulted on all the projects and deliberations of the town council.[41]

Although this mixed commission of the municipality and customary chiefs in Awala and Yalimapo is unique in Guiana, Amerindian and Maroon customary chiefs are recognized throughout the rest of Guianese territory. They are often special intermediaries between the state and local village communities and they receive a small allowance from the Departmental Council. Nevertheless, their prerogatives are not officially defined, and in fact the authority of these chiefs is gradually being challenged by that of elected representatives. Unlike New Caledonia, customary law is not institutionalized in Guiana, and the customary chiefs are not linked to the state justice system. Indeed, a mixed advisory council for the Amerindian and Maroon peoples (*Conseil consultatif des populations amérindiennes et bushinenge* (CCPAB), was created in 2009 at the instigation of Senator Georges Othily, without any real preliminary consultation on the role and organization of this council. A parliamentary report giving voice to certain Amerindian opinions questioned the appropriateness of a single authority for all these populations, arguing that because of their large numbers, the Maroons (or Businenge) would have other forms of representation in Guianese political institutions.[42] Furthermore, the CCPAB included 20 members, of whom 16 stood for associations that the French state considered "representative" of Amerindian and Maroon peoples. The list of these organizations was fixed by ministerial decree; it was therefore the French state that ruled on the composition, conditions of appointment and representativeness of CCPAB members.

40 Interview with Claude Silberzhan, prefect of Guiana from 1982 to 1984, Paris, 2013.

41 Interview with Jean-Paul Fereira, mayor of Awala-Yalimapo, Paris, October 14, 2001.

42 Archimbaud Aline and Marie-Anne Chapdelaine, "Suicides des jeunes Amérindiens en Guyane française: 37 propositions pour enrayer ces drames et créer les conditions d'un mieux-être." Overseas Ministry, Parliamentary Report. 2015: 68–69.

This in turn meant that it has the power to select and exert pressure on council members. A former member provided an example of how this happened:

> On the day we expressed an unfavorable opinion on the park charter, the prefect explained to us that the populations of the interior were in agreement with the charter, that we were not representative, we were cut off from the river, we were on the coast. They create this authority, they appoint us and then it's the same people who don't consider us to be representative when we oppose their point of view and interests. It was unbelievable.[43]

Finally, the function of the CCPAB was limited in that the council could not give out advisory notices on the decisions of Guianese communities. It was not systematically referred to by local communities, and it did not have power of authority for anything relating to the state. During its existence, the CCPAB had no human, financial or material means available to it, and therefore no independence in the way it worked. For example, advisory notices from the CCPAB were sent to the secretariat of the prefecture, and it was an official from the prefecture who published them or put them on line.[44]

In a very recent development, the CCPAB was replaced in February 2018 by the Grand Conseil coutumier des populations amérindiennes et bushinenges, which entailed a change of status, as well as a hope that indigenous peoples will be better heard and a fear that the new body would not be better subsidized that the previous one.[45] Although still an advisory body,[46] 16 of the 18 members are now elected by the Amerindian and Maroon communities themselves, and only two are appointed by the government – thus representation is in place, even though decision-making power is still limited.

Amerindian and Maroon representatives *are* present, however, in the decision-making bodies of the Guiana Amazonian Park.[47] The park's board of governors has five representatives of customary authorities, out of 44 members. Although the Amerindians and Maroons are certainly in a minority, in this body they have full voting rights, not merely an advisory role (Aubertin and Filoche 2008).

Since the late 1990s, the monopoly of the Federation of Indigenous Organizations of Guiana (*Fédération des Organisations Autochtones de Guyane* FOAG) speaking on behalf of Guianese Amerindians has been strongly contested, and new styles of representing Guianese Amerindians have been

43 Interview with a former member of the CCPAB, December 2015.

44 Interview with a former member of the CCPAB, December 2015

45 Decree n° 2018-273 of April 13, 2018 relative to the Grand Council of American and American populations https://www.legifrance.gouv.fr/eli/decret/2018/4/13/MOMO1807990D/jo/texte.

46 One of three consultative counsels in the territorial collective of Guiana.

47 The French state has created a natural national park covering a vast territory situated in the south of Guiana.

emerging alongside the demand for recognition of indigeneity. The crisis in the Amerindian movement of Guiana reflects the slow progress in this fight. But it is also due to internal tensions in the organization linked to the internationalization of its activities and the distance this produces between activists and leaders of the movement. Furthermore, the renewal of the Federation's structures in the mid-1990s has not changed the ways that it recruits its leaders, who essentially continue to be men from the Kali'na group. From the early 2000s, local leaders of associations and customary chiefs started to challenge this monopoly and demand a share of responsibility together with greater transparency in the governance of the FOAG. In 2001, for example, the association Guiana Villages was created, bringing together customary chiefs, including a certain number of female chiefs, who had never had a presence among the governing authorities of the FOAG. The principal leaders of Guiana Villages displayed a change of political strategy from the one the FOAG had been following: without completely rejecting the interest of international work, they intended to reverse the scales in favor of the villages:

> For the moment, we have priorities here, we are at a time when things are shifting a lot in Guiana; Guiana is in a critical phase, and we must be here on the ground. It won't be decided in the United Nations, we have to occupy the area here as well. The single assembly, it's here that it will be decided. If Guiana was to continue its usual routine, why not the United Nations, but now, the priority is here.[48]

Without completely breaking with the notion of indigeneity, what we are witnessing here is a transformation in the ways of expressing demands for Amerindian rights. Amerindian local elected representatives also distanced themselves from the FOAG's international strategy in favor of the participation of local and regional communities and an alliance with established political parties. The French program of decentralization and regionalization, which begun in 1982, transferred competence and authority to local departments and regions; Amerindians recognized that they could thus be more effective locally than in the UN arena, which was far from local concerns (Collomb 2005). In the current decade, mobilizations on behalf of indigenous peoples' rights have experienced a new dynamic with the creation in 2010 of ONAG (Organization of Indigenous Peoples of Guiana), and in 2017 of *Jeunesse Autochtone*, or indigenous youth. The latter organization has been particularly active, both during the 2017 general strike and in the current mobilization against Montagne d'Or, an industrial gold mine project located in the Guyanese forest south of Saint-Laurent du Maroni (supported by the Russo-Canadian consortium Columbus Gold/Nordgold and by the French government).

48 Interview no. 3 with Brigitte Wyngaarde, Balaté, December 2003.

Conclusion

From 1946 to the late 2000s, in the context of administrative reforms following the departmentalization of Guiana and intense social change within Amerindian and Maroon groups, the integration of these peoples into the state underwent considerable transformation. This occurred first under state tutelage as subjects of specific protection measures, and then, as French citizens coming under a shared status and administrative organization. Despite this increase in their rights as citizens, the demand for specific public policies in the name of cultural difference and indigeneity has not disappeared. Originally supported by ethnologists, it was continued by the leaders of the Amerindian movement.

In terms of responses from the state, however, the outcome of these four decades of indigenous activism appears limited. The reasons for this lukewarm result are of a demographic and institutional order. Although, according to the law of the French Republic, statistics on ethnic grouping are forbidden in Guiana, it is thought that Amerindians now represent about 4% of the Guianese population (about 10,000 individuals out of a total population of 275,000 inhabitants, in 2017), which marginalizes them on a long-term basis from the electoral and political point of view. The Maroon people represent more than 20% of the Guianese population, but they have never demanded rights as indigenous peoples.

Furthermore, as we have seen, its status as a department and overseas region as well as the new status as unique territorial collectivity, which was declared in 2015 (all ruled by Article 73 of the French Constitution) gives Guiana extremely reduced political autonomy with regard to the standards of Metropolitan France. Adapting institutional and administrative strategies to Amerindian and Maroon social realities has therefore resulted in a "legal hodge-podge" rather than real recognition of the rights belonging to Guiana's indigenous peoples. The French state's refusal to recognize all forms of minority rights – and therefore indigenous peoples' rights – and the internal conflicts of the FOAG have each been responsible for a decline in the Guianese indigenous movement; as a consequence, alternative strategies have emerged for ensuring participation in Guiana's local communities. Nonetheless, it seems a new dynamic is developing. Colonial and postcolonial categories that were ascribed by French authorities, and were the foundation of institutions and policies, have been re-appropriated by people themselves, as new institutions emerge and manifest greater autonomy. The creation of the *grand conseil* in early 2018, for example, is an indication that shifts and processes are ongoing, however, and is too soon to predict how these dynamics will play out in the near future.

Bibliography

Armanville, Françoise. 2012. "Les Homes Indiens en Guyane française, pensionnats catholiques pour enfants amérindiens, 1948–2012." Master's 2 disser., University of Aix-Marseille.

Aubertin, Catherine and Geoffroy Filoche. 2008. "La Création du parc amazonien de Guyane. Redistribution des pouvoirs, incarnations du 'local' et morcellement du territoire." In *Aires protégées, espaces durables?*, edited by Catherine Aubertin and Estienne Rodary, 163–185. Marseille: IRD Editions.

Bayart, Jean-François and Romain Bertrand. 2005. *La Problématique du legs colonial.* Paris: FASOPO Reports.

Bellier, Irène. 2009. "Usages et déclinaisons internationales de l''auchtonie' dans le contexte des Nations unies." In *Autochtonies vues de France et du Québec*, edited by Natacha Gagne, Martin Thibault, and Marie Salaün, 75–92. Quebec: Presses de l'Université Laval.

Benoît, Catherine. 2016. "'Pampila' et politique sur le Maroni. De l'état civil sur un fleuve frontière." In *Justice en Guyane. A l'ombre du droit*, edited by Sylvie Humbert and Yerri Urban. Paris: La Documentation française, coll. "Histoire de la Justice" 26: 237–259.

Blévis, Laure. 2008. "Des 'indigènes' en metropole? Catégories coloniales et catégories métropolitaines." In *1931. Les Étrangers au temps de l'Exposition coloniale*, edited by Laure Blévis, Hélène Lafont-Couturier, and Nanette Snoep. Paris: Gallimard.

Collomb, Gérard. 1999. "Du 'capitaine' au 'chef coutumier' chez les Kali'na." *Ethnologie Française* 4: 549–557.

Collomb, Gérard. 2005. "De la revendication à l'entrée en politique (1984–2004)." *Ethnies*, special edition "Guyane. Le renouveau amérindien." 31–32: 27.

Collomb, Gérard, and Stéphanie Guyon. 2015. "Droit à la terre, institutions coutumières et jeux politiques en Guyane. L'exemple des zones de droits d'usage collectifs." In *Terres, territoires, ressources. Politiques, pratiques et droits des peoples autochtones*, edited by Irène Bellier, 173–186. Paris: L'Harmattan, Collections horizons autochtones.

Collomb, Gérard and Félix Tiouka. 2000. *Na'na Kali'na, une histoire des Kali'na de Guyane.* Matoury, French Guiana: Ibis Rouge Editions.

Deshayes, Patrick. 1998. "Robert Jaulin. Un ethnologue engagé." *Journal de la Société des Américanistes* 84 (1): 289–291.

De Souza Lima, Antonio-Carlos. 1995. *Um grande cerco de paz. Poder tutelar, indianidade e formaçao do Estado no Brasil.* Petropolis: Vozes.

De Souza Lima, Antonio-Carlos. 2000. "L'Indigénisme au Brésil. Migration et réappropriations d'un savoir administratif." *Revue de synthèse* 121 (3–4): 381–410.

Filoche, Geoffroy. 2011. "Les Amérindiens de Guyane française, de reconnaissances disparates en bricolages juridiques. L'exemple des Kali'na d'Awala-Yalimapo." *Journal de la Société des Américanistes* 97 (2): 343–367.

Filoche, Geoffroy. 2015. "Objets déconnectés ou pièces d'un puzzle? Les droits fonciers des Amérindiens de Guyane." SOGIP seminar, EHESS, Paris, 9 April 2015.

Goury, Laurence, Michel Launey, Francisco Queixalos, and Odile Renault-Lescure. 2000. "Des Médiateurs bilingues en Guyane française." *Revue Française de Linguistique Appliquée* 1: 42–60.

Grenand, Françoise, and Pierre Grenand. 2005. "Trente ans de luttes amérindiennes." *Ethnies* 18 (31–32): 132–163.

Guyon, Stéphanie. 2011. "Politisation et hiérarchies coloniales. Amérindiens et Noirs-marrons à St-Paul (Guyane française, 1946–2000)." *Critique Internationale* 50: 21–37.

Guyon, Stéphanie. 2013. "Des 'primitifs' aux 'autochtones.' Savoirs ethnologiques et politiques publiques en Guyane de 1946 à nos jours." *Genèses* 91: 51–70.

Guyon, Stéphanie. 2017. "Mobilisations post-coloniales. Décryptage de la grève générale en Guyane." *Contretemps*, 18 avril 2017. https://www.contretemps.eu/mobilisations-post-coloniales-greve-generale-guyane/.

Hurault, Jean. 1970. "La 'francisation' des Indiens de Guyane." *Le Fait Public* 16: 1–8.

L'Estoile, Benoît de. 2000. "Science de l'homme et domination rationnelle. Savoir ethnologique et politique indigène en Afrique coloniale française." *Revue de synthèse* 121 (3–4): 291–323.

Mam Lam Fouck, Serge. 2006. *Histoire de l'assimilation. Des vieilles colonies françaises aux départements d'outre-mer. La culture politique de l'assimilation en Guyane et aux Antilles françaises (XIXe et XXe siècles)*. Matoury, French Guiana: Ibis Rouge Editions.

Marroquin, Alejandro. 1972. *Balance del indigenismo. Informe sobre la politica indigenista en América*. Mexico: Instituto indigenista interamericano.

Morin, Françoise. 2005. "L'ONU comme creuset de l'autochtonie." *Parcours anthropologique* 5: 35–42.

Oliveira, João-Pacheco de. 2000. "Sur l'expertise anthropologique territoires et identités au Brésil." *Revue de synthèse* 121 (3–4): 411–436.

Piantoni, Frédéric. 2002. "Pouvoir national et acteurs locaux. L'enjeu des mobilités dans un espace en marges. Le cas de la Guyane française." Doctoral thesis in Geography, University of Poitiers.

Piantoni, Frédéric. 2009. *L'Enjeu migratoire en Guyane. Une Géographie politique*. Matoury, French Guiana: Ibis Rouge, coll. Espace outre-mer.

Rallu, Jean-Louis. 1998. "Les categories statistiques utilisées dans les DOM-TOM depuis le début de la présence française." *Population* 53 (3): 589–608.

Saada, Emmanuelle. 2005. "Une Nationalité par degré. Civilité et citoyenneté en situation coloniale." In *L'Esclavage, la colonisation, et après…*, edited by Stéphane Dufoix and Patrick Weil, 193–227. Paris: PUF.

Thabouillot, Gérard. 2012. "Un Projet politique et administratif pour l'arrière-pays de la Guyane française. Le territoire de l'Inini (1930–1969)." Doctoral thesis in History, University of Paris IV.

Tiouka, Félix. 1985. "Adresse au gouvernement et au peuple français." *Ethnies* 1 (2): 7–10.

6 Decoloniality put to the test

The Plurinational State of Bolivia

Laurent Lacroix[1]

Introduction

> A civilization that proves incapable of solving the problems it creates is a decadent civilization.
> A civilization that chooses to close its eyes to its most crucial problems is a stricken civilization.
> A civilization that uses its principles for trickery and deceit is a dying civilization.[2]

For over a decade, Bolivia has been engaged in a new political cycle that appears, on first sight, to favor improvements in the living conditions of indigenous peoples and the consolidation of their international and constitutional rights. Two major events have contributed to this: the 2005 election of Evo Morales, whose campaign was supported by the country's main indigenous organizations, and the adoption in 2009 of a new constitution that incorporates all the provisions of the United Nations Declaration on the Rights of Indigenous Peoples (UNDRIP 2007). As a result of these events, the country now has a broad political, institutional, and legal framework that places it at the forefront of the recognition and normalization of the rights of indigenous peoples. These political trends have also laid the groundwork for a "plurinational" state, intended to comprehensively redefine relations with indigenous peoples. This is cast as part of a process of "re-founding" the country, which is outlined in the constitution and states explicitly that the Bolivian nation is composed of all Bolivians (male and female), indigenous nations and peoples, intercultural communities and those of afro-descent who "together" constitute the Bolivian people (Article 3).[3]

1 Translated by Cadenza Academic Translations, revised by Jennifer Hays, and the author.

2 Aimé Césaire, *Discourse on Colonialism*, 1955

3 *Artículo 3. La nación boliviana está conformada por la totalidad de las bolivianas y los bolivianos, las naciones y pueblos indígena originario campesinos, y las comunidades interculturales y afrobolivianas que en conjunto constituyen el pueblo boliviano.*

This plurinational state project is principally designed to "leave behind the colonial, republican and neoliberal state."[4] Integral to the project is a change of constitutional and political paradigm, breaking with the liberal multiculturalism adopted in the 1980s (see also González-González this volume). That model viewed indigenous peoples as cultural minorities who should be accorded a particular status, and for whom specific policies should be designed in the face of a hegemonic national culture (Gros and Dumoulin Kervran 2012). Plurinationalism, on the other hand, proposes to redefine historic social categories and abolish the distinction between cultural minorities and majorities through the adoption of a transversal approach to the indigenous question. In other words, in contrast to liberal multiculturalism, which seeks to mitigate the effects of inequality between the dominant and subordinate cultures, the plurinational state aims to place on an equal footing the principal norms, values and ways of life of different peoples and nations, whether indigenous or not, that make up the national society as a whole. It is founded on the implementation of a pluralist regime – political, economic, legal, cultural, and linguistic – that respects the unity of the state and redefines interculturalism as being founded on the principles of complementarity, equality, and equivalence.[5]

Unlike the majority of political regimes that have taken shape in Latin America since its colonization in the sixteenth century, the plurinational state seeks to institute its own societal model, which is neither imported nor adapted from exogenous models. By changing the political paradigm, the intention is to create a hybrid state that sits somewhere in between the nation state and multinational state models: a state that is both pluralist and unitary (Lacroix 2014). The plurinational state project in Bolivia has turned out to be closely linked to the indigenous question.[6] Since the country's independence in 1825, an "internal colonialism" had enforced the inferior position of certain sociocultural groups, in particular indigenous peoples and those of African descent (Casanova 1964). The plurinational project in Bolivia thus explicitly takes a ***decolonialist***[7] perspec-

4 "Dejamos en el pasado el Estado colonial, republicano y neoliberal" (Preamble to the Constitution).

5 In the Bolivian Constitution, the term [multiculturalism] is abandoned and does not appear. But the term [interculturality] is very present and so defined: "The instrument for the cohesion and the harmonious life between the peoples and the nations. It is a means to enforce the cultural differences and the equality of the living conditions" (Article 98). It is linked to the concept of plurinationality. The implementation of a plurinational state involves some conceptual changes currently in debate. For some observers, this state's form could redefine the neoliberal multiculturalism and then, the notion of interculturality linked to it (Lacroix 2011). For others, interculturality appears as a new central concept in the implementation of the plurinational state considering that interculturality has never existed before (Walsh 2008).

6 Unlike many multinational countries in which regional, religious and/or linguistic issues are discussed more generally.

7 Decolonial or "post-occidental" studies form a school of thought that is part of the line of postcolonial and subaltern studies. According to Capucine Boidin (2010), they are primarily distinguished by "demonstrating the permanence of the global coloniality of power, knowledge, and of being after decolonization." These scholars establish an insoluble link between coloniality

tive, and some see its current program of re-founding the state as a "decolonial option" (Mignolo 2007).

Decolonization of the state and its institutions was a key cohesive element in the political alliance that Evo Morales's political party formed with the country's principal indigenous organizations. It became, however, the subject of controversy from the moment of the plurinational state's foundation and initial development. Although the political constitution hardly uses the term *decolonization*,[8] the Evo Morales government made it one of the keywords of its indigenist rhetoric, even going so far as to create a Vice Minister (*Viceministerio*) of Decolonization in 2009. However, supporters of the historic indigenous peoples' movement were increasingly disappointed by the way the Morales government maintained control over the interpretation and implementation of the new constitution. These disagreements culminated in a break of the alliance in 2011. This chapter recounts some of the key moments that led to this rupture, and highlights the deep differences in objectives and political projects between the two main actors, represented by the Evo Morales government and the indigenous organizations. This gulf calls into question both the viability of the plurinational state in the current political climate, and received ideas relating to the goals of the Morales government with regard to indigenous peoples and their rights.

The genesis of the plurinational state

A political proposition of indigenous peoples organizations

The history of the Plurinational State of Bolivia is closely linked with that of the indigenous movement. The concept of such a state derived initially from *katarismo*,[9] an indigenous union movement[10] that arose in the Andean region during the 1970s. In the decades that followed, the vision of a plurinational state gradually worked its way through academic and activist circles to become one of the main demands of the country's indigenous organizations by the late 1990s.

and modernity, accord prime importance to the social and economic dimensions of coloniality, and rely primarily on Latino-American work (Mignolo and Escobar 2010).

8 Only two articles of the Bolivian Constitution use the term "decolonization": Article 9 on the ends and essential functions of the state, charged with "constructing a just and harmonious society, built on decolonization"; and Article 78, which states that "Education is unitary, public, universal, democratic, participatory, communitarian, decolonizing and of quality." It could be argued, however, that the decolonial perspective is implicit in the plurinational state project outlined in the same constitution.

9 Deriving from Tupac Katari, who led a large Indian rebellion on the Bolivian Altiplano in 1781. *Katarista* political ideas have been principally developed by urban elites.

10 The term "indianism" relates to the politicization of Indians who take a position on the issues concerning them; first used in the 1980s, it established an opposition with the "indigenism" of the state, which relates to a government policy or a tendency of peoples to treat indigenous matters in different ways, such as assimilationism, and without including the persons concerned in the development of policies or the evaluation of results.

In the agitated sociopolitical climate of the 2000s,[11] these organizations held several marches demanding respect for the rights of indigenous peoples, as recognized by the 1994 Constitution. These repeated mobilizations led to a unique rapprochement between organizations from the highlands (Andean Cordillera) and those from the lowlands (Amazonia). Strong in unity, this indigenous coalition called for the organization of a constituent assembly in order to end the country's tumultuous situation. From 2004 onwards, these indigenous organizations formed an alliance with the powerful peasant movement that constituted the electoral base of the *Movimiento al Socialismo* (MAS; the party of Evo Morales), to form the Pact of Unity. They actively participated in the future president's electoral campaign in the hope of seeing their vision of the plurinational state made reality as a result of the constituent assembly.

These events took place in a state of extreme political and social tension. Competing political projects and priorities prolonged the confusion of preceding years, which had been marked by mass social mobilizations, vandalism, confrontations, and violence (Lacroix 2006). Eventually, the proposal of the Pact of Unity served as the basis for the drafting of the constitutional text. It was the most successful and most detailed proposal and benefited from the support of the Evo Morales government (Garcès 2010). The text was discussed at length by the constituent assembly then discreetly negotiated with the political opposition, the *sine qua non* for the country's return to political stability.

During this period, the relationship between the Presidency and the indigenous movement seemed to be in good shape. In the constituent climate so vital to Bolivian political life, during his first mandate as elected president between 2005 and 2009, the government of Evo Morales offered a rhetoric that was highly favorable to the promotion of the rights of indigenous peoples. Some expected policies were indeed carried out. In 2006, the Communal Extension of the 1996 Agrarian Reform Law was promulgated, maintaining the recognition of indigenous territories – despite the misgivings of peasant organizations, who saw this right as an unfair privilege. In 2007, several decrees regulated socio-environmental control over petrol and gas activities carried out on the lands of indigenous peoples, and guaranteed the right to free, prior, and informed consent in relation to all extractive activities carried out on their lands and territories.

One of the most powerfully symbolic actions was the almost immediate elevation of the UNDRIP to the rank of law of the Republic in 2007. This constituted a significant act, charged with symbolic power in the eyes of both the international community and the country's indigenous peoples. It marked the beginning of Bolivian international diplomatic activism based on strong positions regarding the rights of indigenous peoples, the rights of Mother Earth, and the right to water – all of which would have major repercussions in terms of

11 Between 2000 and 2005, the country experienced a cycle of social and political instability. During this period, social unrest was so great that it led to three successive changes in the Presidency of the Republic (Gonzalo Sánchez de Lozada, Carlos Mesa Guisbert, Eduardo Veltzé, Evo Morales).

managing the country's natural resources, notably in justifying the nationalization of oil and gas reserves. As I discuss below, it also constituted an attempt to co-opt indigenous organizations that were calling for organizational and political autonomy from the state's power.

The constitution and the rights of indigenous peoples

It was in the context of the bubbling cauldron that I have just briefly described that the new Bolivian constitution was adopted and approved by popular referendum in January 2009. Innovative in many ways, it introduced a new envisioned future of "pluralist constitutionalism," in the view of some informed observers (de Sousa Santos 2009; Yrigoyen Fajardo 2010). Indigenous concerns occupied a major place in the constitution. Over 50 articles are dedicated to this topic, representing an eighth of its total content. The text recognizes 18 collective rights specific to indigenous peoples (Article 30.II). It guarantees the right to self-determination, to autonomy, to self-government, and to culture. Indigenous institutions, territories and systems of government are recognized in the respect of the unity of the state. This constitution incorporates every one of the 46 articles of the UNDRIP and surpasses existing international norms by providing for the institutionalization of indigenous territories in the new politico-administrative organization of the state (*cf. infra*). According to Article 1 of the Constitution, Bolivia is constituted as a "Unitary Social State of Pluri-National Communitarian Law."[12] However, the meaning and implications of this phrase in practice remained to be defined in the phase of implementation. The Bolivian Constitution otherwise proposes state control of some supposedly "indigenous" principles, such as Living Well (*Buen vivir*) or the Aymara moral code *Ama qhilla, ama llulla, ama suwa* ("neither be idle, nor lie, nor steal"). Some indigenous symbols became State symbols like the *wiphala*[13] (Article 6) which accompanies the Bolivian flag on the front of all state institutions. The Evo Morales government has supported this symbolic construction of the plurinational state by applying, in its own way and to reinforce its political power, the constitutional dispositions, as well as by incorporating new anniversaries into the national calendar[14] (Orduña 2015).

From a terminological point of view, the constitution uses a particular expression when referring to indigenous peoples. The text declares that "every human collective that shares a cultural identity, language, historic tradition, institutions, territory and world view, whose existence predates the Spanish colonial invasion" is considered to be in the category "nations and rural native indigenous peoples" ("*naciones*

12 Bolivian Constition of 2009: https://www.constituteproject.org/constitution/Bolivia_2009.

13 A flag with multiple significance, primarily borne by Bolivia's Aymara and Quecha organizations.

14 Plurinational State Foundation Day (22 January), Andean New Year (21 June), Military-Indigenous Parade Day (7 August, the day after national Independence Day), National Day of the Productive and Communitarian Agrarian Revolution (2 June, previously "Indian Day" from 1937 then "Peasant Day" from 1953), and Decolonization Day (12 October).

y pueblos indígena originaria campesinos," Article 30.I, my emphasis). The phrase derives from a conceptual innovation that aims to unify[15] through a selective grammatical agreement in Spanish, a range of historical and regional nominal categories, both social and identitarian: ***indígena*** ("indigenous") for the indigenous peoples of the lowlands, ***originaria*** ("native") for those of the highlands, and ***campesinos*** ("rural") for a diffuse ensemble of small cultivators claiming a certain Amerindianity.[16] This constitutional category of ***naciones y pueblos indígena originaria campesinos*** results from a series of semantic shifts linked to different periods of Bolivian history (Lacroix 2012). It was born in the very particular climate of the constituent assembly (2006–2008). However, its general meaning is that of "indigenous peoples," the expression used at an international level. In the Bolivian constitution, what unites ***indigenous, native***, and ***rural***, is their pre-colonial existence. It is in this context that specific collective rights are accorded to them in an effort to mitigate the principal consequences of the historic marginalization of colonized peoples, namely persistent racism, permanent discrimination, dispossession, assimilation, and acculturation. It is important to highlight here that the principal unifier proposed is an historical experience (colonization) and its effects (coloniality), and not the direct primordial spotlight of a sociocultural or civilizational difference.

The implementation of the new politico-institutional framework

These constitutional provisions translate into a collection of measures specific to indigenous peoples that are officially recognized by the Bolivian state. To ensure the political representation of the peoples who "constitute a minority population,"[17] the Evo Morales government implemented a system of reserved seats and posts in the main institutions of the plurinational state, in particular the legislative and legal bodies (*cf. infra*). With regard to political participation, the indigenous peoples' organizations holding legal status were recognized as representative political institutions, and thus able to participate in local and national elections along with political parties. Three forms of democratic expression are recognized by the law: representative democracy through the election of representatives by direct secret vote; direct and participatory democracy through referendum, citizen legislation, revocation of the mandate, the assembly (the *cabildo*[18]), and prior consultation; and communitarian democracy through the

15 According to Xavier Albó and Carlos Romero (2009), the singular used in the expression "native rural indigenous people" is intended to reinforce the idea of a shared unique category.

16 The terms "farmer" or "small agricultural producer" are reserved for other categories of smallholder.

17 The phrase "peoples [who] constitute a minority population" refers to thirty-one indigenous peoples from the lowlands and four peoples from the Andes. The Aymaras and the Quechuas are implicitly considered to be in the "majority."

18 A term inherited from the colonial period, which has no precise legal definition. The term has long been used to describe local and regional indigenous meetings but in the last few decades has been expanded to refer to other types of popular assembly.

election, designation and nomination of authorities and representatives according to the norms and procedures of each nation and indigenous people. The co-existence of these three types of democratic practice form what the Electoral Regime Law (2010) calls "intercultural democracy" (Articles 1 and 7).

On a linguistic level, the languages of 36 indigenous peoples and nations recognized by the state became official languages with the same status as Spanish.[19] This means that, in theory, from 2009 (date of the current Constitution), candidates for civil service positions will have to be able to speak at least two of the country's official languages, including at least one of the indigenous languages of the region in which they work. In this context, the Education Law (2010) provides for the study and use of mother tongues in the first years of schooling. Two official national languages and a foreign language must be taught at schools. It also states that the history, worldviews, and knowledge of indigenous peoples should be integrated into curricula in collaboration and cooperation with indigenous communities.

The reconstructed justice system now leans toward legal pluralism, and is based on four types of jurisdiction: ordinary, agro-environmental, special, and indigenous. This last jurisdiction is exercised by competent authorities, which are determined according to the norms and procedures of each indigenous people. There is no hierarchy between these four jurisdictions, meaning that indigenous justice holds the same status as the other official justice systems implemented in the country. Decisions arising from this jurisdiction are intended to regulate the internal conflicts of indigenous peoples and must not contradict constitutional rights nor international instruments concerning human rights. A Jurisdictional Demarcation Law (2010) attempted to define the fields of expertise of indigenous justice as well as the mechanisms for coordination and cooperation with other types of justice, in particular with ordinary justice.[20] A new legal arsenal accompanied this reorganization of the legal framework through the adoption of new types of collective and environmental rights. In 2007, UNDRIP was promulgated as national law. In 2012, Bolivia invested the Earth with rights, recognizing "nature" as a legal subject in its own right by promulgating the Framework Law of Mother Earth and Integral Development for Living Well (*Ley Marco de la Madre Tierra y desarollo integral para vivir bien*). However, legal vagueness persists regarding the very definition of Mother Earth, and certain

19 Article 5 of the Constitution: The languages are: Aymara, Araona, Baure, Bésiro, Canichana, Cavineño, Cayubaba, Chácobo, Chimán, Ese Ejja, Guaraní, Guarasu'we, Guarayu, Itonama, Leco, Machajuyai-kallawaya, Machineri, Maropa, Mojeñotrinitario, Mojeño-ignaciano, Moré, Mosetén, Movima, Pacawara, Puquina, Quechua, Sirionó, Tacana, Tapiete, Toromona, Uruchipaya, Weenhayek, Yaminawa, Yuki, Yuracaré, and Zamuco.

20 This attempt did not entirely succeed. The Jurisdictional Demarcation Law (*Ley de Deslinde jurisdiccional*) has been contested and criticized by indigenous organizations, who were not invited to participate in the drafting of this text. They judge the law to drastically limit the fields of expertise of indigenous justice. As far as we know, the rule has not been promulgated, due to a lack of consensus.

constitutional and legislative principles, like that of the non-commercialization of Mother Earth, remain subject to debate.

In the economic sphere, the constitution provides for the implementation of a plural economy, which recognizes and articulates four principal forms of economic organization: state, private, indigenous, and cooperative (Articles 306 to 310). The co-existence and interaction of these forms of economic organization is regulated by the state. The Evo Morales government proposed an "economic, social, communitarian, and productive" model in order to achieve this, but provided no further precision regarding its modalities, objectives, and perspectives, in particular regarding the businesses and initiatives led by indigenous peoples.

The implementation of these constitutional provisions, all designed to reestablish the legal foundations of the state, was a key element in political stability. Although the internal situation was calmed by the approval of the Constitution, new issues arose, creating new tensions (Lacroix and Le Gouill 2019). The current phase of political transition has sown discord between the principal indigenous organizations and the Evo Morales government. A series of disappointments has critically altered a relationship already marred by doubts and distrust on both sides, despite the fact that the political project was publicly presented as shared and historic. As the plurinational state developed, it became increasingly apparent that there were fundamental differences between the goals of MAS and of indigenous peoples with regard to numerous issues. The sections below will describe some of these.

The precarious territorial autonomy of indigenous peoples

One of the main innovations linked to the development of the plurinational state was the opportunity for indigenous peoples' legally recognized territories and municipalities to become territorial collectives, fully integrated into the new political and administrative organization of the country and recognized as territorial entities in their own right, in the same way as are non-indigenous departments, regions, and municipalities. These administrative divisions were granted autonomous powers, budgets and expertise similar to that of municipalities.[21] The state recognized a specific collection of rights as belonging to the inhabitants of these indigenous regions: collective and inalienable ownership of lands; prior consent over all projects within the area; priority over the usage and exploitation of renewable natural resources; and access to the benefits of the exploitation of non-renewable natural resources.

21 Notably the definition and application of a local development program (economic, cultural, and social), the development and maintenance of infrastructure, the management of health, the preservation of natural and cultural heritage, and relations with external institutions and organizations.

In parallel, a specific form of autonomy was granted exclusively to "indigenous nations and peoples." It granted their local (municipal, territorial, regional)[22] collectives additional powers, and most notably allowed them to adopt their own forms of government and their own institutions, to establish a more autonomous territorial policy, and to manage and administrate local renewable natural resources in accordance with national legislation. In addition, and independently of this specific autonomous regime, indigenous peoples were able to implement their own system of justice, which constituted an additional specific power. In order to adopt indigenous autonomy, the territorial entity must follow a precise procedure. This involves the organization of a local referendum and requires the backing of the Ministry for Autonomies, which accompanies the process throughout. Deliberative bodies are then elected by the population concerned, and are tasked with developing a "statute of autonomy," which must be approved by the Constitutional Tribunal. This statute must take non-indigenous minorities into account by guaranteeing them the rights established by the constitution, and must present a strategic vision for territorial development. Finally, the statute of autonomy must be submitted again to a local referendum and must be approved by two thirds of the population concerned in order to be validated. Once the statute of autonomy enters into force, indigenous governments can then form and wield the powers of legislation, deliberation, rule-making, and take up the other powers accorded to them.

Thus, determined by the constitution and the law, this "indigenous autonomy" is a response to the demands of the peoples concerned, who have called for decades for the recognition and institutionalization of their territories. Paradoxically, however, this kind of autonomy has not been met on the ground with the enthusiasm it provoked at the time of the constituent assembly. As of 2018, as far as we know, only 15 or so municipal governments (of the 337 municipalities making up the country) and a small number of indigenous territories were likely to adopt indigenous autonomy. The biggest movement was initiated in 2009 under the impulse of the state, when eleven municipalities were engaged in the application process. Since then, a few more declarations of intent have been recorded by the Ministry for Autonomies. In August 2016, Charagua (in the Santa Cruz department) was the first municipality to adopt indigenous autonomy. All the other territorial entities taking this route, whether they are municipalities or territories,[23] still have a long way to go. The need of consensus and local compromises often leads to deadlocks, considerably slowing the drafting of the statute of autonomy, and in many cases, existing power structures favor the *status quo*.

The number of procedures involved (around 15), and the bureaucracy of the processes imposed by ministerial administration, have also greatly slowed the advance of autonomization. The extreme control of the central state, and in particular of

22 For complex political and historical reasons, departments cannot adopt this regime of indigenous autonomy.

23 To date, no region has instigated the process for becoming an autonomous indigenous region. However, several parts of the country have begun to consider this scenario.

executive power, over the autonomization of territorial collectives has also slowed down some initiatives. A general sense of distrust has pervaded local territorial entities with regard to the state and the Morales government. They suspect Morales of wanting to take advantage of decentralization in order to finally establish his political hegemony through electoral control over the new autonomous territories, based on negotiations with local elected officials. In addition, since the issue of indigenous justice has not yet been resolved, these early experiences have affected local populations, who do not hold high expectations for the future.

For indigenous peoples, the great hope raised by the concept of "indigenous autonomies" has rapidly been replaced by frustration. On several occasions, their principal national organizations have mobilized to call for the easing and simplification of procedures, as well as guarantees regarding the pursuit of a policy of territorial tenure. This policy of land demarcation for indigenous peoples has been opposed by the peasant unions, who consider the indigenous territories as new forms of unproductive "large property."[24] The Unified Syndical Confederation of Rural Workers of Bolivia (CSUTCB) has, since 2013, pursued a project of Law on Lands that aims to implicitly suppress processes toward territorial tenure. Under pressure from the peasant unions – its main electoral base – the Evo Morales government itself is pursuing its support for the intensification and expansion of agricultural activity in order to guarantee the country food self-sufficiency by 2025. Although the available land surface remains large enough to achieve these plans, land pressure on indigenous territories is likely to strongly increase, leading to an escalation of tensions around the territorial issue and a slowing down, if not a suspension, of the process of indigenous autonomy.

Despite their progressive institutionalization, which represents an unprecedented legal and political advance, indigenous territories remain subject to the same vagaries as they were in the past, and are faced with persistent physical precariousness. In the lowlands, all territories without exception must contend with the imposed presence of extractive industries (forestry, petrol, mining), and/or infrastructure projects (arterial roads, dams, hydroelectric plants). In both cases, indigenous peoples have no real decision-making power over their territories and rarely derive benefits from their exploitation (Lacroix 2015). In other words, territorial autonomy, the cornerstone of the plurinational state, is far from becoming reality for indigenous peoples.

The trap of consultation

According to the main international norms[25] in force, indigenous peoples have the right to actively participate in the process of making decisions concerning them.

24 The notion of *gran propiedad* is a legacy of the pre-agrarian reforms period, when the possession of large pieces of land by white and creole landowners deprived indigenous peoples and peasants of lands to live on.

25 In particular, Convention 169 of the International Labour Organization (1989), and the United Nations Declaration on the Rights of Indigenous Peoples (2007).

They must be consulted by states and businesses with a view to obtaining their prior consent for any project carried out on indigenous territories or for all legislative and administrative issues that might affect their situation. Almost everywhere in Latin America, questions of *consultation* and *consent* are high on the political agenda (see also Cloud, Gonzalez, and Lacroix 2013) and have been at the heart of numerous socio-environmental conflicts. Both indigenous peoples and non-indigenous populations across the region are increasingly insisting upon free, prior, and informed consent, and Bolivia is no exception. Since the beginning of his second mandate in 2009, President Evo Morales has launched the country into an accelerated phase of modernization, which has involved the initiation of large-scale territorial improvement projects, the development of agriculture, and intensified exploitation of the country's main natural resources. The adoption of a "neo-extractivist" development model (Swampa 2011) has caused many socio-environmental conflicts, which in turn have provoked debate about respect for the rights of indigenous peoples in the Plurinational State of Bolivia.

One of the most representative cases is that of the Isiboro Sécure National Park and Indigenous Territory (*Territorio Indígena y Parque Nacional Isiboro Sécure – TIPNIS*). The proposal to build a highway traversing the Park has provoked a series of events that have marked Bolivian national political life in recent years.[26] These include two indigenous marches, in 2011 and 2012, that were largely supported by the Bolivian population; the first, in 2011, was violently broken up by the police. Two peasant counter-marches were orchestrated in quick succession by the government to counteract the indigenous mobilizations and legitimize the line taken by the executive. At the same time, two contradictory, and thus controversial, laws amplified an already confused situation. Law 180 (2011) declared the zone "intangible" while law 222 (2012) required consultation. This latter process, however, appeared to be too late for the indigenous peoples concerned, who considered it to be "post-consultative" since the project had already begun, and contracts had already been signed between the state and Brazilian companies. The consultation took place in a tense climate marked by a number of discouraging events, including the boycott of many indigenous villages, who refused to respond and to welcome representatives of the state; acts of violence toward these representatives, or between indigenous persons and peasants; and legal pursuit of the indigenous leaders who had organized the marches and acts of resistance.

The methods of consultation were strongly contested and opposing conclusions were drawn by the Evo Morales government on the one hand, and the institutions supporting the indigenous peoples of TIPNIS on the other (these included non-governmental organizations, the Catholic Church, and the Bolivian Public Ombudsman). Amid pressure to maintain the *status quo* and the threat of increased confrontations between indigenous persons and peasants, the project

26 Most of these events were widely covered by the national and international media, and have been the subject of numerous articles.

was suspended. The main effect of the TIPNIS conflict was to cast doubt upon, if not completely discredit, the indigenist rhetoric of the Evo Morales government. It sealed the quasi-definitive rupture of the political alliance between Evo Morales and the main indigenous historical organizations. Within a few years, TIPNIS had become the new symbol of indigenous struggle in Bolivia.

Ultimately consultation proved to be more problematic than constructive, and more conflictive than consensual. It had not met the objectives called for by international norms. This observation can be generally extended to many of the situations seen elsewhere in Bolivia, and leads us to consider the differences between *consultation* and *consent*. The first term refers to the process, while the second constitutes a purpose. The distinction is explicitly made in the United Nations Declaration on the Rights of Indigenous Peoples (UNDRIP), although that document establishes little exclusive correlation between these two principles of partnership recommended between states and indigenous peoples (Bellier, Cloud, and Lacroix 2017). A number of socio-environmental conflicts in Latin America have resulted from a divergence in interests and priorities between the parties; namely the states and indigenous peoples. The states, often under the pressure of indigenous movements and international organizations, deign to implement processes of prior consultation, while simultaneously insisting upon the non-binding nature of its results. The indigenous peoples, on the other hand, urgently call for their right to "free, prior and informed consent" according to the wording proposed by UNDRIP. This implies an automatic initial consultation process, which is irremediably binding in nature. While states focus on methods and procedures, indigenous peoples are calling for the right to participate in their own development, and demanding respect for local modes of decision-making, and their results.

At the root of this antagonistic difference is the lack of prior consensus on how to organize consultation, the explicit definition of its objectives, and the consequences for all the parties concerned. The most fundamental problem usually relates to the modes of consultation, which are generally unilaterally predefined by the states. This issue is both so crucial and so problematic that in Latin America, some indigenous peoples have organized their own consultation processes, which they have named "self-consultation," even before the state has begun proceedings, or as a way of contesting its methods and results.[27] For these

27 There has been no *a priori* comparative research into this kind of local initiative that would allow for an analysis of its contexts, reasons, conditions and effects. Self-consultations are generally organized in areas opposed to natural resource extraction, or infrastructure projects. These procedures are not recognized by the state, which considers them to be invalid (ILSA 2009; Berraondo 2013). The most notable self-consultations in recent years include: in Peru, those of the Achuar (2010) and Rukullacta (2011) peoples on the presence and installation of petrol industries, and those of the Cañaris peasant community on the concessions granted by the state to the Canadian mining company Candente Copper (2012); in Chile, that of the Mapuche in the Araucania region on hydroelectric projects (2014); in Guatemala, that of the Huehuetenango on a mining project (2015); in Honduras, that of the Pech people regarding the conversion of the Muäka Usku mountain (2013) and that of the Lencas peoples of La Paz on the construction of a hydroelectric plant (2016).

peoples, consultation organized by the state is seen as a trap that reduces their issues and focuses any controversy primarily on the running of the procedure and not its objective – which is consent. Whether this distortion of the process is voluntary or not, it is the source of mutual incomprehension and frustration. According to international norms, the right to consultation, in order to achieve free, prior, and informed consent, is presented as a process of negotiation between the parties concerned in an open, respectful, and multilateral dialogue. It should not be reduced to the state simply providing information to the indigenous peoples affected by the project, nor should it be approved by their vote without debate. The agreement should result from a negotiation conducted "in good faith," which leads to an obligatory or binding agreement for each party. Thus, consultation cannot be considered as a simple formality that the state must carry out, nor as the right of veto for indigenous peoples on state decisions. If these principles are not applied, the process of consultation perpetuates a relationship of subordination for indigenous peoples in relation to the state on which they depend. Consent appears to be presented by international norms as the right of indigenous peoples to make decisions for themselves and to their internal self-determination.

In Bolivia, the very principle of consultation seems to have been progressively abandoned by the Evo Morales government. A series of decrees in 2014 and 2015 repealed all provisions that had been included in the decrees of 2007 relating to prior consultation for petrol and gas activities on indigenous lands *(cf. supra)* (Tamburini 2016). The Mining Law of 2014 limited certain rights of indigenous peoples enshrined in the Constitution. For example, the right to free, prior, and informed consultation guaranteed to indigenous peoples by the state now *only* applies in the context of a new mining contract; prior to 2010 all mining operations on indigenous lands had been legalized without consultation (Tejada Soruco 2012). Furthermore, even this severely limited right applies only to open-cast mining projects; underground mining (which represents the majority of mines in Bolivia) is not explicitly mentioned. In addition, prospecting and exploratory operations are exempt from all prior consultation. In the context of territorial improvement projects, in particular the construction of hydroelectric dams, the consultation process has not been systematically proposed or implemented, leaving local populations poorly informed about projects and the size of their impact (CEADESC 2011). In cases where it has been put in place, consultation has often been superficial, lasting only for a few days. A national law regarding consultation had been under consideration since 2012, at the insistence of the United Nations High Commissioner – this law has been discreetly shelved. All these elements seem to confirm the perception that the Evo Morales government has made a U-turn in regard to its policies on indigenous peoples and their rights.

Truncated and limited political representation

In a self-proclaimed plurinational state as described above, we might expect that indigenous peoples would have stronger political representation in comparison to the past, or to other states, and that this would be guaranteed beyond the terms and vagaries of political life through specific structural, organizational, and institutional provisions. Yet it is difficult to make this claim in regard to Bolivia. The principle of plurinationalism constitutes a strong political and symbolic issue, and remains subject to interpretation, appropriation, and debate. The provisions defined by the law or the decisions of the Evo Morales government have rarely been in tune with the vision of the plurinational state held by indigenous organizations.

One of their principal frustrations concerns the representation of indigenous peoples in the Plurinational Legislative Assembly. Following negotiations between the governing party and the opposition, the Transitory Electoral Regime Law of 2008 reserves seven seats corresponding to the number of special districts to represent the 35 "peoples [who] constitute a minority population." Since then, indigenous organizations have called to have a seat for each one of the distinct indigenous peoples within this institution, to ensure fair representation. This request is in the name of the constitutional principle of plurinationality, but is also a strategy to lessen tensions between peoples, which arose during the process of designating representatives for the 2010, 2014 and 2015 elections. Differences in political habits and customs, competition between leaders and representative organizations, and relationships of power and domination between certain indigenous peoples made it difficult to achieve consensual representation within a single district. Although the current system tends to ensure a minimum indigenous presence in parliament, one effect has been to reinforce the marginalization of some peoples, who find it difficult to submit a candidate in this internal power game of special districts. The race to plurinational representation contributes to the weakening of the indigenous movement through multiple divisions and oppositions.

In addition, the official term of "peoples [who] constitute a minority population" has provoked growing skepticism among indigenous organizations regarding the ability of the plurinational state to abolish all minority situations. The status of demographic majorities implicitly accorded to the Aymara and Quechua peoples has also fostered controversy. These peoples have no reserved seats and must take part in the conventional party political system in order to ensure their representation in parliament. These two peoples are thus deprived of their own unitary representative organization[28] and they are often required to enter into unfavorable negotiations and compromises with political parties, and to have party projects, policies, and candidates imposed upon them. A presence within legislative assemblies, whether plurinational (at the level of the state) or

28 To date, there is no indigenous organization specifically representing the Quechua or Aymara peoples. The historical co-opting of conventional political parties as well as internal factionalism, regionalism, and localism are the main causes of this absence. However, the directions of the National Council of Ayllus and Markas of Qullasuyu (CONAMAQ), which represents the collective indigenous peoples of the Andes, are regularly taken up by Aymara representatives.

departmental[29] (at a local level) requires representative organizations to make definitive compromises with political parties. These are the source of internal tensions between candidate or elected leaders, and the indigenous organization bases, whom they are supposed represent to the legislative power. The development of the plurinational state has not, it seems, led to changes in these perverse effects of political representation, which have lingered for several decades (Albó 2002; Lacroix 2005; Van Cott 2005; Yashar 2005). The party system has endured and the partisan structure still predominates in state institutions, despite the provisions adopted in the name of the constitutional principle of plurinationality (Chávez 2012). Between 2005 and 2009, as the country was fiercely debating the new constitution, an indigenous parliamentary group managed to extend its support base beyond party ties. However, in the face of the persistent hegemony of the party system it has not been subsequently possible to repeat this, despite the existence of a new normative framework. Therefore, although certain modalities have changed regarding the political representation of indigenous peoples within the legislative power, these peoples, whether demographically in the "minority" or the "majority," are confronted on all sides by the same difficulties as in the past and struggle to escape their political marginalization.

Political and partisan issues also affect judicial power. The judicial personnel was largely renewed in October 2011 following the first judicial authority elections with universal suffrage outlined in the constitution. On this occasion, indigenous and female judges received an overwhelming share of the vote. Although posts were reserved for high court judges recognized to be indigenous,[30] four of the five candidates who received the most votes already self-identified as such.[31] However, despite a new structure and new personnel, Bolivian justice still suffers from the same flaws that it had under the previous government: complex bureaucracy, a lack of coordination between different jurisdictions, and the unethical activities of some judges, including proven corruption and questionable independence from the state's power. During the 2014 presidential campaign, Evo Morales laid much of the blame for these problems on a few

29 In Bolivia, each of the nine departments, as autonomous and decentralized entities, has its own legislative assembly. According to the constitution, norms regarding the representation of indigenous peoples are similar to those in force for the plurinational legislative assembly at the level of the state, the number of reserved seats varying according to each department's statute of autonomy.

30 According to the Constitution and legal texts, this should apply to two of the seven judges within the Constitutional Tribunal and the Supreme Plurinational Electoral Tribunal and one of five judges within the departmental electoral tribunals. In addition, following the first universal elections for the judiciary authorities organized in 2014, the Supreme Tribunal of Justice, the Agro-Environmental Tribunal and the Magistrates Council each had one member who publicly claimed indigenous identity.

31 Cristina Mamani was elected to the Magistrates Council with 457,399 votes, Bernardo Huarachi to the Agro-Environmental Tribunal with 290,556 votes, Gualberto Cusi and Efrén Choque to the Constitutional Tribunal with 273,081 and 184,284 votes. Within the Supreme Justice Tribunal, three high judges also claimed identity of an indigenous nation.

indigenous judicial authorities, claiming that their presence and acts had not had any effect.[32] In this way he discredited the few judges who had denounced executive meddling in important cases, including the internal affairs of tribunals, the nomination of presidents of grand tribunals and notable matters such as that of TIPNIS or the referendum on constitution reform – which opened the way for Evo Morales to stand for a fourth term as president. In 2015, three high court judges from the Constitutional Tribunal were suspended by Parliament for wrongfully accepting a recourse to unconstitutionality regarding a secondary law; the law was ultimately not promulgated. Those suspended included the indigenous judge Gualberto Cusi, whose keen eye for media attention had incurred the wrath of the government. During a showdown in which this judge was pitted against the executive power, he was the object of a campaign of discrimination destined to destabilize, humiliate, and discredit him. For example, the Minister for Health publicly revealed Cusi's HIV status during an audience before Parliament – in serious violation of legal protection for medical privacy.

The composition of the Evo Morales government was also the object of fierce criticism from the main indigenous organizations. They criticized the president's monopolization of symbolic Amerindianity for political ends, principally aimed at an international community fond of icons. They also condemned the absence of representatives at the heart of executive power, which included only a few high-ranking Aymara and Quechua officials – but these were representing peasant organizations, not indigenous ones. No member of the Evo Morales government self-identifies as indigenous. Only the chancellor David Choquehuanca was considered a legitimate representative by indigenous organizations, and his term ended with the TIPNIS conflict of 2011.

Hence, a battle for political legitimacy began between the Evo Morales government and indigenous organizations, focusing primarily on the manner of developing the plurinational state. The investment of public and political spaces, the staging of Indianism and the appropriation of constitutionalized identity categories became increasingly contested as the collective subjects of the plurinational state challenged the governing power. In keeping with a revolutionary and sovereign line of approach, the Bolivian government monopolized the discourse on indigenousness and plurinationality, forcing a "neo-indianism" (Galinier and Molinié 2006) into the service of power and the state. This was to the great chagrin of the main indigenous organizations, who desperately seek to have their voices heard before international authorities, in order to denounce their exclusion from the ongoing "re-founding of the country" and the violation of their constitutional and international rights. As a result, historical debates on racism, minoritization and discrimination are being prolonged, rather than resolved by the Evo Morales government as was hoped.

32 "We have incorporated the *ponchos* and *polleras* into Justice in vain" (*En vano incorporamos poncho y pollera en la justicia*): this derogatory speech, reducing the Indians to a typical dress (for the men, the cloak with a hole for the head, for women the thick woollen skirt) was partially reproduced by most of the national press.

Conclusion

The implementation of a plurinational state that aims to rebuild the country on a lasting post-colonial foundation still appears to be an enormous challenge, and has yet to become a reality. In the face of the numerous conflicts that have developed and issues that have been raised (some of which have been described in this paper), this grand project still seems fragile and under threat. Decolonial scholars have already begun to question the potential for this plurinational state to enact real societal change, evoking "an imaginary decolonization of a neocolonial state" (Mamani Ramirez 2013) and the emergence of an "avatar of a certain form of revisited colonialism" (Walsh 2008). In Bolivia, the constitutional category of "rural native indigenous people" is now being questioned by indigenous organizations who denounce the formation of a new majority, peasant rather than *mestizo*,[33] that is maintaining the status of indigenous peoples as cultural and political minorities within the vast project of building a plurinational state. The contradictions of the ongoing process have left some observers confused, evoking the specter of a new "monocultural state" (Mamani Ramirez 2013). The dichotomy proposed by Charles Hale between "authorized Indian" (*indio permitido*) and "undisciplined Indian" in his reflection on the framework of liberal multiculturalism (Hale 2004) appears to persist in the development of the plurinational state.

The social and economic situation of indigenous peoples has been significantly improved, partly due to the public policies implemented by the Evo Morales government. In contrast, the marginalization of many of these peoples from the process of developing the plurinational state presents a startling contradiction: the constitution promising a new kind of inclusive state – but practiced without the direct participation of its main constituents. For political, ideological, organizational, and geographic reasons, a great number of indigenous peoples have remained on the margin of this movement and remain cultural and political minorities. In light of this observation, the structural changes promised by "plurinationality" seem highly questionable. To return to the title of this chapter, the Plurinational State of Bolivia remains a political project, thus far unable to achieve the transformations it aims to implement. It is too early to predict that Bolivian society will become the civilization described by Césaire (1955) in the

33 The project of a plurinational state is clearly distinct from the historic Latin American model of a nation state, which was based on the biological, and later cultural, mixing of Amerindian populations for the purpose of assimilation. The republican models of the nineteenth and twentieth centuries envisioned a singular and mono-cultural nation, embodied in the "creole" or "metis" character – *mestizo* in Spanish. The plurinational state does not exclude any form of mixing, but it does firmly reject the figure of the *mestizo* as the unique and exclusive embodiment of the political project. In Bolivia, the word "*mestizo*" refers also to non-indigenous peoples; in the city it is used for non-indigenous Bolivians, and it is often used in the lowlands to name those people who arrived later on the river borders to settle and cultivate and who are of mixed origins (usually white and Indian but can also be other interethnic combinations). *Mestizo* is a social category constructed in opposition to Indigenous peoples (*originario*) and afro-descendants.

opening quote of this chapter, from his "Discourses on Colonialism". Currently, however, for the numerous reasons that this chapter has outlined, ***decoloniality*** remains yet an unfulfilled promise.

Bibliography

Albó, Xavier. 2002. *Pueblos Indios en la Política*. La Paz: CIPCA.

Albó, Xavier, and Carlos Romero. 2009. *Autonomías Indígenas en la Realidad Boliviana y su Nueva Constitución*. La Paz: Vicepresidencia del Estado Plurinacional de Bolivia/ PADEP-GTZ.

Bellier, Irène, Leslie Cloud, and Laurent Lacroix. 2017. *Les droits des peuples: Des Nations unies aux sociétés locales*. Paris: L'Harmattan.

Berraondo, Mikel. 2013. *El Derecho a la Consulta Previa en la Práctica: Desafíos y Oportunidades para los Actores en la Región Andina*. Cartagena: GIZ-AECID.

Boidin, Capucine. 2010. "Études décoloniales et postcoloniales dans les débats français." *Cahiers des Amériques Latines* 69: 129–140.

Casanova, Pablo González. 1964. "Société plurale, colonialisme interne et développement." *Tiers-Monde* 5 (18): 291–295.

CEADESC. 2011. *Atlas de Megaproyectos de Infraestructura en Bolivia*. Cochabamba: CEADESC.

Césaire, Aimé. 1955/2000. *Discourse on Colonialism*. Translated by Joan Pinkham. New York: Monthly Review Press.

Chávez, Patricia. 2012. *¿De la colorida minoría a una mayoría gris? Presencia indígena en el legislativo*. La Paz: Fundación Friederich Ebert, Editorial Gente Común.

Cloud, Leslie, Veronica Gonzalez, and Laurent Lacroix. 2013. "Catégories, nominations et droits liés à l'autochtonie en Amérique latine. Variations historiques et enjeux actuels." In *Peuples autochtones dans le Monde. Les enjeux de la reconnaissance*, edited by Irene Bellier, 41–74. Paris: L'Harmattan.

de Sousa Santos, Boaventura. 2009. "Las paradojas de nuestro tiempo y la Plurinacionalidad." In *Plurinacionalidad. Democracia en la diversidad*, edited by Alberto Acosta and Esperanza Martínez, 21–62. Quito: Abya Yala.

Galinier, Jacques, and Antoinette Molinié. 2006. *Les néo-Indiens. Une religion du 3ème millénaire*. Paris: Odile Jacob.

Garcès, Fernando, ed. 2010. *El Pacto de Unidad y el Proceso de construcción de una Propuesta de Constitución Política del Estado. Sistematización de la experiencia*. La Paz: Programa NINA.

Gros, Christian, and David Dumoulin Kervran, eds. 2012, *Le multiculturalisme "au concret". Un modèle latino-américain?*. Paris: Presses de la Sorbonne Nouvelle.

Hale, Charles. 2004. "Rethinking Indigenous Politics in the Era of the 'indio permitido.'" *NACLA Report on the Americas* 38 (2): 16–21.

ILSA (Instituto Latinoamericano de Servicios Legales Alternativos). 2009. *El derecho a la consulta previa en América Latina. Del reconocimiento formal a la exigibilidad de los derechos de los pueblos indígenas*. Bogotá: ILSA.

Lacroix, Laurent. 2005. "Indigènes et politique en Bolivie." Doctoral thesis, IHEAL – Université Paris 3, Sorbonne Nouvelle, Paris, France.

Lacroix, Laurent. 2006. "Bolivie: refondation du modèle politique national et tensions politiques." In *Amérique latine 2006*, edited by the Observatoire des Changements en Amérique Latine, 83–98. Paris: La Documentation Française.

Lacroix, Laurent. 2011. "Etat plurinational et redefinition du multiculturalisme en Bolivie." In *Le Multiculturalisme au concret, un model elation-americain?* Edited by Christian Gros and David Dumoulin Kervran, 135–145. Paris: Presses de la Sorbonne nouvelle.

Lacroix, Laurent. 2012. "Territorialité autochtone et agenda politique en Bolivie (1970–2010)." *QuAderns-e, Revista de l'Institut Català d'Antropologia* 17 (1): 60–77. http://www.antropologia.cat/quaderns-e-194 (accessed 12 January 2019).

Lacroix, Laurent. 2014. "Un multiculturalisme sans minorités? Quelques réflexions sur l'Etat plurinational en Bolivie et en Equateur." *Belgeo* 3. doi:10.4000/belgeo.11512, http://belgeo.revues.org/11512 (accessed 12 January 2019).

Lacroix, Laurent. 2015. "Le devenir incertain des territoires et des droits autochtones dans les Basses Terres de l'État plurinational de Bolivie." In *Les indiens d'Amazonie face au développement prédateur. Nouveaux projets d'exploitation et menaces sur les droits humains*, edited by Simone Dreyfus-Gamelon and Patrick Kulesza, 305–346. Paris: L'Harmattan.

Lacroix, Laurent, and Claude Le Gouill. 2019. *Le processus de changement en Bolivie. La politique d'Evo Morales.* Paris: IHEAL.

Mamani Ramirez, Pablo. 2013. "Estado Plurinacional: entre el nuevo proyecto y la factualidad neocolonial." *Bolivian Studies Journal* 19: 132–158.

Mignolo, Walter D. 2007. "The De-colonial Option and the Meaning of Identity in Politics." *Anales Nueva Época* 9–10: 43–72.

Mignolo, Walter D., and Arturo Escobar, eds. 2010. *Globalization and the Decolonial Option.* New York: Routledge.

Orduña Víctor. 2015. *Tan lejos, tan cerca del Estado plurinacional. Lecturas y reflexiones sobre la nación boliviana en tiempos del Estado plurinacional.* La Paz: PIEB.

Swampa, Maristella. 2011. "Néo-développementisme extractiviste, gouvernements et mouvements sociaux en Amérique latine." *Problèmes d'Amérique Latine* 81: 103–127.

Tamburini, Leonardo. 2016. "Bolivia." In *The Indigenous World 2016*, edited by Diana Vinding and Cæcilie Mikkelsen, 167–177. Copenhagen: IWGIA.

Tejada Soruco, Alicia. 2012. *Minería en las tierras bajas de Bolivia.* Cochabamba: CEDIB.

Van Cott, Dona Lee. 2005. *From Movements to Parties in Latin America: The Evolution of Ethnic Politics.* Cambridge: Cambridge University Press.

Walsh, Catherine. 2008. *Interculturalidad, Estado, Sociedad. Luchas (de)coloniales de nuestra época.* Quito: Abya Yala.

Yashar, Deborah. 2005. *Contesting Citizenship in Latin America: The Rise of Indigenous Movements and the Postliberal Challenge.* Cambridge: Cambridge University Press.

Yrigoyen Fajardo, Raquel. 2010. *Pueblos Indígenas: Constituciones y reformas políticas en Latinoaméric.* Lima: IIDS-INESC-ILSA.

7 Leveraging international power

Private property and the human rights of indigenous peoples in Canada

Brian Thom

Introduction

Private property presents a particularly challenging problem for indigenous peoples seeking recognition and accommodation of their land rights and ongoing cultural practices. Most states have privileged private lands, and in so doing placed them largely beyond the reach of indigenous peoples for purposes of land claims settlements, indigenous jurisdiction, or co-governance. This chapter explores how these dynamics take shape in Canada, tracing a case study of efforts by a coalition of indigenous peoples to have their rights recognized within large tract of land made private in an historic railway grant. My objective in tracing the contours of this case is to reveal the agency – and contingencies – involved in indigenous peoples' efforts to implement the potential power of international human rights. The path to leveraging international power in the Canadian context has not been straightforward. The case of the Hul'qumi'num Treaty Group – an organization representing six First Nations who share a language, culture, and territory – provides a critical vantage point from which to observe and evaluate the strategies and outcomes of an indigenous community's efforts to implement the soft law power of international human rights.

In this chapter, I describe Canada's failure to recognize and accommodate indigenous land rights where extensive fee-simple titles – which are the most complete, secure, transferable, property right recognized in Canadian law (Blomley 2014: 1295) – have been granted to private third parties in an historic railway grant. In this case, the Hul'qumi'num Treaty Group ("HTG") brought Canada before the Inter-American Commission of Human Rights ("IACHR") in order to receive a formal finding on the merits of their claim that refusing to recognize and respect indigenous peoples' rights on private lands is an ongoing human rights violation. The chapter details and evaluates four key strategies of the HTG leadership to implement the principles of international law on the ground in Canada, including: working to influence judges to draw international law principles into domestic common law; calling for recognition across multiple international human rights bodies and jurisdictions; drawing international law principles into public policy reform debates; and campaigning to influence markets and create corporate and public allies.

My analysis of this case reveals that, despite ten years of sustained effort to mobilize the principles of international human rights law in Canada, the HTG leadership's expectations – and indeed the potential of international human rights overall – have not been met. Several factors contributing to the stagnancy on this issue include the absence of a clear ruling on the merits of the HTG's claim by the IACHR; oblique references to the Inter-American jurisprudence by domestic courts; seemingly fixed state land claims policies; and profound public or corporate sector reluctance to push for reform or social justice relating to private lands. While First Nations in Canada whose territories are largely held as public lands (often referred to as Crown lands) have negotiated various forms of recognition and reconciliation agreements (for instance, the Nisga'a Final Agreement (Nisga'a 2000), the Haida Reconciliation Agreement (British Columbia 2009), and the Coastal First Nations Reconciliation Protocol (British Columbia 2011)), domestic solutions concerning private lands appear to be extremely limited (see also Egan 2013).

Human rights and private property

For indigenous peoples who seek recognition of their rights on private lands in Canada and elsewhere, the principle of free, prior, and informed consent articulated in the UN Declaration on the Rights of Indigenous Peoples (UNDRIP) has not been realized. Where private third-party owners have been the beneficiaries of large-scale land grants, the private lands status dramatically reduces opportunities for recognition and reconciliation of on-going indigenous land tenure. In Canada, while some limited willing-buyer-willing-seller arrangements have been implemented to provide indigenous communities small-area expansions to their land-bases (for instance, the Tla'amin [2014] and Tsawwassen [2010] Final Agreements in Canada), accompanying provisions limit or extinguish indigenous peoples' rights on private lands outside settlement lands (Rynard 2000; Alcantara 2009: 333; Blomley 2015: 172). This policy of extinguishment is a far cry from the standards emerging in international law.

Indeed, standards developing in international law do not in principle exclude privately held lands from claims settlements. The jurisprudence of the Inter-American Human Rights system suggests that in principle, indigenous titles must be recognized, demarcated, and delineated to their full extent (IACHR 2010). The norms of the Inter-American system hold that indigenous property rights are not automatically extinguished, and sufficient restitution must be provided to ensure indigenous peoples' "collective right to survival as an organized people, with control over their habitat as a necessary condition for the reproduction of their culture, for their own development, and to carry out their aspirations" (IACHR 2010: 50). The Inter-American jurisprudence stresses that private property interests need not always prevail over indigenous property rights. Where they do, compensation must be guided primarily by the meaning of the land for the indigenous peoples (IAHR 2010: 51). Indigenous communities appealing to international law principles to advance their cases at home do so in spite of significant challenges.

The Canadian government has signed both the *Charter of the Organization of American States*, and the *American Declaration of the Rights and Duties of Man* in 1948. However, it has never bound itself to the jurisdiction of the Inter-American Court, an autonomous body of the Organization of American States, which can enforce decisions if states voluntarily subject themselves to its jurisdiction. If disputes about Canada are raised regarding these human rights instruments, only the non-binding Inter-American Commission on Human Rights ("IACHR") can make findings of an advisory nature on asserted violations. While these findings are issued in periodic reports by the IACHR and in the adjudication of individual, group, and inter-state complaints, implementation requires domestic action and voluntary state compliance. Anthropologist Ronald Niezen sees mobilizing the potential power of the so-called "soft law" of the international community, which lacks formal enforcement or sanction mechanisms, as engaging popular opinion and activism to cultivate a sense of compassion, shame, or popular indignation (Niezen 2010: 2). In the Canadian context and elsewhere, such soft law mechanisms require political work by indigenous peoples and their partners to leverage the potential of international power at home.

The case of the Hul'qumi'num Treaty Group

The HTG is a political organization representing about 7,500 Coast Salish people from the Cowichan, Penelakut, Stz'uminus, Lyackson, Halalt, and Lake Cowichan First Nations in and around Vancouver Island (Canada) in comprehensive land and governance negotiations with the state. The six-member First Nation communities of the HTG have never signed a treaty, surrendered, nor ceded title to their ancestral lands. The HTG has engaged in over 20 years of comprehensive land and governance negotiations to "complete unfinished business with the federal and provincial governments" by negotiating a treaty that will "recognize and protect a way of life based on an economic and spiritual relationship between Hul'qumi'num First Nations and the environment" (HTG 1993). I have been privileged to bear witness to the remarkable campaign by the HTG to have ancestral land rights recognized in a territory that is now largely privately held. I have worked closely with the HTG leadership as an anthropologist and advisor since 2000 (Thom 2008, 2010), and have been, in an ethnographic sense, observing and participating in much of their international campaign and the work that followed (Thom 2014a, 2014b).

Seeking recognition from IACHR

For many local observers, modern-day treaty negotiation negotiations in British Columbia have all but failed. Central to the stalemate in treaty talks with the HTG member First Nations is the unwillingness of the Canadian Government to reconcile the near-complete privatization of indigenous territories on Vancouver Island by the 1884 E&N Railway Grant (see Figure 7.1). In the granting of over

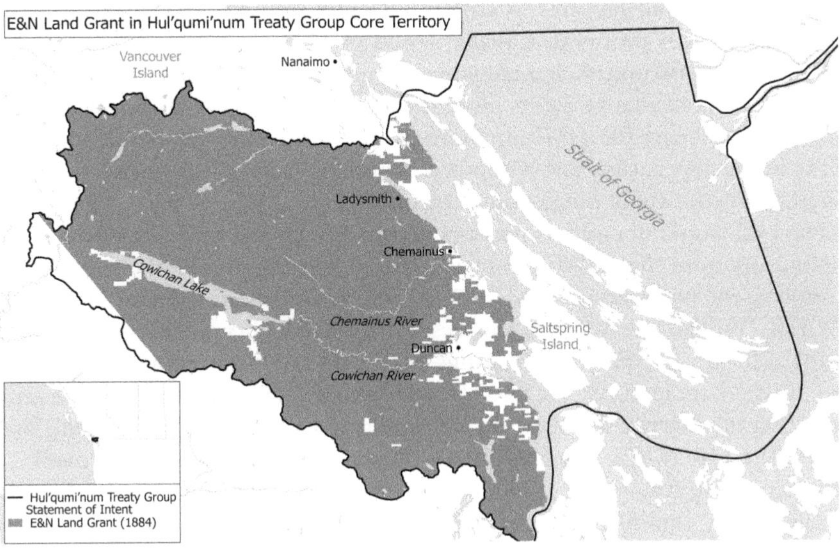

Figure 7.1 E&N Railway Grant within Hul'qumi'num Territories map courtesy of Hul'qumi'num Treaty Group.

800,000 ha of land, timber, and subsurface rights, almost the entire traditional land base of the HTG member First Nations became owned and occupied by coal and forest companies, private farmers, and townspeople. Today, three large logging and land development corporations own most of the watersheds of the Nanaimo, Chemainus, Cowichan, and Koksilah Rivers, with some of the highest-value lands outside major urban centers in Canada being developed as residential or commercial real-estate in the valleys, waterfronts, and Islands. Bare land values within these territories are in the billions of dollars.

During negotiations, the HTG sought to re-establish a territorial land base, looking to the state for some combination of land transfer or purchase, jurisdictional recognition, and where appropriate, shared decision-making authorities for cultural matters on lands not under indigenous jurisdiction. The state, apparently unamenable to pursuing these solutions, has unilaterally taken private land expropriation *and* compensation off the table for a negotiated settlement. Although small, scattered fragments of reverted Crown forest land are negotiable, for the HTG leadership these only partially meet the economic development aspirations of their communities – not their overall mandate to have their property or jurisdictional rights fully recognized into the future (HTG 2005). Formula-based cash settlement offers (carefully not called "compensation" in agreements, but rather "capital transfer") typically at play in Canadian comprehensive land claims negotiations, are monetarily insufficient (by an order of magnitude) to enable the HTG to regain lands in any significant quantity or at culturally central locations, on the open market. Instead, the state envisions transforming indigenous titles over ancestral lands into fee-simple ownership of several thousand hectares, with limited indigenous governance authorities. According to this proposal, Canada would provide small commercial forestry and fishing opportunities and recognize diminished, non-exclusive subsistence, cultural and consultative rights on remnant Crown lands. This position would profoundly alienate the Hul'qumi'num peoples from their ancestral lands. The HTG leadership is thus left without a negotiable solution to implement their vision for the future of indigenous territories.

The Hul'qumi'num leadership has sought intervention from the international community from this stalemate in negotiations, aiming to reset the frame of discussion at the negotiating table. In 2007, the HTG submitted a petition to the IACHR (Williams et al. 2007) protesting human rights violations (see Thom 2014a, 2014b). Admissibility hearings were held in Washington, D.C. in 2008 and 2009.[1] Late in 2009, the IACHR admitted the HTG's case given the argument that no effective domestic remedies exist in Canada to resolve private lands issues (IACHR 2009). The IACHR also based its strongly worded admissibility decision on the strength of *prima facie* evidence and legal arguments forwarded by the HTG, committing to examine and comment on alleged violations by Canada of Articles II (right to equality before the law), III (right to profess, manifest and practice a religious faith), XIII (right to culture) and XXII (right to property) of the *American Declaration of the Rights and Duties of Man.*

In late 2011, the HTG leadership argued the merits of their case in Washington, D.C.[2] Their presentation at the merits hearing focused on the continued detrimental impact of lands held privately by forest companies, municipalities, and small-land owners on the on-going, land-based cultural practices like hunting, fishing, gathering, and the practicing of spiritual and religious traditions. Elders shared testimony, having seen the impacts on their lives, such as Mr. Arvid Luschiim Charlie, who stated:

> We live in fear of [no trespassing] signs ... We live with the threat of being arrested. I try not to be afraid and go there to harvest plants. I have to. We need these plants for medicine and food. (transcript, 28 October 2011 hearings)

Amicus briefs from supportive First Nations and NGOs like Amnesty International (Amnesty 2011) and Lawyers' Rights Watch Canada (LRWC 2011)

1 The IACHR has archived audio recording of the 2008 and 2009 admissibility hearings. http://www.cidh.oas.org/Audiencias/133/B26HulquminumTreatyGroupCanada.mp3 (accessed 10 August 2015), and http://www.cidh.org/Audiencias/134/20.%20P%20592%2007%20y%20MC%20110%2007%20Hul%20qumi%20num%20Treaty%20Group%20Canada.mp3 (accessed 10 August 2015).

2 The Inter-American Commission on Human Rights hosts an online video of the merits hearing, "Case 12.734 – Hul'qumi'num Treaty Group, Canada." http://www.oas.org/es/cidh/audiencias/TopicsList.aspx?Lang=en&Topic=17 (accessed 24 January 2019).

backed up the HTG's claims, citing them as consistent with Canada's negotiating practices country-wide. Canada's response reiterated many of its arguments from previous hearings: that the case should be deemed inadmissible; that the existing negotiation process provides an adequate domestic remedy which other First Nations avail themselves of; and that the HTG could raise the issue in a Canadian court if confident of their claim's validity (transcript, 29 October 2011 hearings). Canada argued that it would be impossible for the IACHR to find rights violations if the First Nation has yet to prove *exclusive* Aboriginal title to the claimed lands, raising uncertainty about the validity of the HTG's assertions as 75% of their territory is also claimed by other First Nations – a significant point I have analyzed in detail elsewhere (Thom 2014a).

Incorporating Inter-American standards in Canada

At the time of writing in 2018, 7 years after the merits hearing, it has become clear that this complex case has challenged the ability of the IACHR to make a final determination, as no findings or further comments have been released. Irrespective of this unusually long delay, the HTG leadership has sought to implement the principles of the norms and jurisprudence of the Inter-American system, building on the strength of the IACHR's 2009 admissibility decision, and attempting to leverage the potential power of the international framework for recognizing indigenous land rights. Despite few financial resources, the HTG leadership has undertaken a multi-faceted strategy to make international legal principles relevant in Canada. The first strategy has involved bringing IACHR findings to the domestic courts by intervening in a critical land claims case at the Supreme Court of Canada (SCC). The second strategy is to share the HTG's story with other international human rights bodies, emphasizing IACHR's preliminary findings and attempting to focus the moral and political pressure of the international community on Canada to reform. The third strategy has been working with other First Nations to introduce the Inter-American system's principles into federal policy reform debates. The fourth strategy is to strategically engage media to influence the investment community to pressure governments to recognize indigenous peoples' rights in Canada. Through these strategies, which are described in the sections below, the HTG leadership has leveraged existing opportunities and processes to bring their story into public and political focus and has worked to draw the Canadian court's attention to the supportive principles of the Inter-American human rights system.

IACHR and the Tsilhqot'in *case*

Much of the law regarding Aboriginal rights and title has been developed through precedent-setting rulings of the SCC, rather than domestic legislation (McNeil 2008). The *Constitution Act* (1982) guarantees that "the existing aboriginal and treaty rights of the aboriginal peoples of Canada are hereby recognized and affirmed" (section 35.1), and the SCC has charted out legal principles that have established the distinctive Canadian framework for Aboriginal rights. In late 2014, the SCC considered arguments in the *Tsilhqot'in* case,[3] which eventually established the first on-the-ground finding of Aboriginal title in Canada. At stake in the appeal to the SCC were the legal tests for demarcating and delimiting recognized Aboriginal title lands. Canada and British Columbia have argued in the lower courts that Aboriginal property rights are most accurately envisioned with a "spot title" approach, where only local areas used exclusively and sufficiently intensively for traditional activities – such as at a fishing rock or a salt lick – would be eligible for Aboriginal title lands recognition. The Tsilhqot'in Nation argued that the full relationship of indigenous peoples to their lands must be taken into account: that Aboriginal title is *territorial* in nature. Following their merits hearing at the IACHR in 2011, the HTG petitioned to be an intervener in the final appeal of the *Tsilhqot'in* case. The SCC accepted their petition because the HTG could share unique perspectives from having engaged these issues at the IACHR. In their submissions (Morales 2014), the HTG's central argument was that domestic courts must incorporate international laws and standards, including the IACHR jurisprudence, in interpreting and implementing common law Aboriginal title and rights.

Specifically, in his testimony as intervener at the SCC, the HTG's legal counsel Robert Morales argued that the courts must carefully avoid limiting Aboriginal title to particular sites of sufficiently intensive use, but rather embrace the standards of the Inter-American jurisprudence, ensuring that Canadian law recognizes indigenous views of land tenure as territorial in nature (Morales 2014).[4] He also argued that those territories demarcated by the state must have sufficient geographical scope to enable those indigenous peoples' long-term survival and growth, and to preserve and develop their livelihood and cultures (Morales 2014). His argument challenged the principles set out in this case by a lower court, in which the judges had agreed with Canada that delineating areas for usufructuary rights (rights to use a property without the full beneficial interests in the land) was adequate for protecting Aboriginal interests without demarcating territorial-based titles.[5] Morales counter-argued that such logic diminished territorial property rights to small title areas with defined use rights, and is consequently incompatible with the norms of the Inter-American human rights system (Morales 2014) which insists that land titles (not merely use areas) must be delimited and demarcated to ensure the social, cultural, and economic survival and growth of indigenous peoples.

In the 2014 precedent-setting *Tsilhqot'in* ruling, the SCC did not directly cite the IACHR, but incorporated certain principles of Inter-American jurisprudence

3 *Tsilhqot'in Nation v. British Columbia* [2014] 2 SCR 256, 2014 SCC 44 (CanLII), http://canlii.ca/t/g7mt9 (accessed 3 August 2015)

4 The video of Robert Morales making these legal arguments at the Supreme Court of Canada seen online at: https://www.youtube.com/watch?v=DnMiPqWfmbA (accessed 3 August 2015).

5 *Tsilhqot'in Nation v. British Columbia*, 2006 BCCA 2 (CanLII), http://canlii.ca/t/1m8b7 (accessed 3 Aug 2015).

into Canadian common law. The SCC specifically recognized that Aboriginal perspectives must be weighed when considering evidence showing aboriginal peoples occupied their claimed territories. SCC justices emphasized that "the court must be careful not to lose or distort the Aboriginal perspective by forcing ancestral practices into the square boxes of common law concepts" (*Tsilhqot'in v. R*, [2014] 2 SCR 256, 32). In evaluating evidence for occupancy of claimed lands, the justices found that "... any number of other acts [beyond evidence of villages and enclosed fields] including cutting trees or grass, fishing in tracts of water, and even perambulation, may be relied upon" to establish occupation (*Tsilhqot'in v. R*, [2014] 2 SCR 256, 39). Overturning the spot-title theory of Aboriginal land use, the SCC established that "group size, manner of life, material resources, technological abilities, and character of the lands claimed" including the "carrying capacity of the land" must all be considered in demonstrating the sufficient occupation of lands to prove title (*Tsilhqot'in v. R*, [2014] 2 SCR 256, 37). This significant SCC recognition of the territorial nature of indigenous land rights in Canada ensures that Aboriginal title lands may be delineated to a size and extent sufficient for the survival, growth, and livelihood of the community.

While this is a critical development in Canada, how indigenous territorial ownership, jurisdiction, and use rights will be formally recognized in areas that are owned privately by third-parties areas is still unknown. The HTG argued in their IACHR admissibility hearings that a fundamental problem in Canada is the absence of domestic legal remedies; that no Aboriginal title claims in Canadian courts have resulted in titling and demarcation on private lands. The 2014 *Tsilhqot'in* ruling was silent on private lands, which were strategically excluded from the Tsilhqot'in claim area. In respect of privately held lands, the SCC decision includes measures suggesting that the government may be justified in infringing on Aboriginal title in circumstances where it has a "compelling and substantial purpose" (*Tsilhqot'in v. R*, [2014] 2 SCR 256, 18), that it has "discharged its procedural duty to consult and accommodate" (*Tsilhqot'in v. R*, [2014] 2 SCR 256, 77), and that government actions were "consistent with the Crown's fiduciary obligation to the group" (*Tsilhqot'in v. R*, [2014] 2 SCR 256, 77). This Canadian common law framework development raises serious concerns for Hul'qumi'num peoples, whose territorial lands may be subject to government infringement.

On the question of Aboriginal title infringement to create private land interests, the government would likely argue that original 1884 E&N Railway grant conditions – fee simple land title given to "private parties for settlement, farming, and the development of local industries" (Canada 2008: 14) – provide a compelling and substantial justification. In their comments to the IACHR on the HTG case, Canada has suggested that such land grants are justifiable, closely echoing the SCC's framework that "the development of agriculture, forestry, mining and hydroelectric power, [as well as] the building of infrastructure and the settlement of foreign populations" all satisfy the first element of the common law infringement justification criteria (*Delgamuukw v. R* [1997] 3 SCR 1010, 165).

However, Canada chose to be silent on the second element of the SCC's justification tests, which require that consultations take place prior to an infringement, and that the Crown uphold its fiduciary obligations with respect to indigenous peoples and their lands. In the HTG's case, the historical record is clear that no consultations with the Aboriginal title holders happened in the 1800s during or following the E&N land grant. Nearly the entire territorial land base of the Hul'qumi'num peoples was alienated, and the government's fiduciary duty has almost certainly not been discharged (Egan 2012, 2013). Indeed, the SCC elaborated on the justified infringement test in *Tsilhqot'in*, further incorporating the forward-looking principles of the Inter-American jurisprudence, which insist that "incursions on Aboriginal title cannot be justified if they would substantively deprive future generations of the benefit of the land" (*Tsilhqot'in v. R* 2014 para 86). In sum, while HTG's interventions at the Supreme Court did not conclusively resolve the predicament of recognizing indigenous territorial title in private lands, they have successfully drawn several principles of international human rights law into the Canadian common law framework.

Drawing the UN CERD's attention to Canada

The United Nations Committee on the Elimination of Racism and Discrimination (CERD) evaluates how states implement the *Convention on the Elimination of all Forms of Racial Discrimination*, an international treaty ratified by many nations including Canada. CERD regularly reports its observations and recommendations and has been critical of Canada's comprehensive claims policies (UN 2007). Following the 2011 IACHR hearings on the merits of their case, the HTG leadership felt that the 2012 CERD review of Canada would effectively highlight their case. Their goal was to draw CERD's attention to the IACHR's preliminary findings about the inadequacy of ligation and negotiation measures for resolving land disputes, and to show that Canada was non-compliant with international law principles around human rights.

In their testimony, the HTG requested that CERD urge Canada to reform its laws and policies to conform to international standards. The HTG's lawyers argued that Canada must establish effective remedies to recognize and protect indigenous title and rights; abandon policies that require extinguishing Aboriginal title in exchange for treaty; and affirm its duty to demarcate indigenous lands even if there are private interests or overlapping claims (Howard and Kinnison 2012). In respect of their particular circumstances, the HTG asked that CERD call on Canada to undertake a process to demarcate and title their territorial land base, or provide restitution as the replacement or payment of just compensation for those stolen lands (Howard and Kinnison 2012: 14). They further requested that CERD: recommend that Canada suspend sales, permits, licenses on E&N Railway Grant lands until Aboriginal title claims have been resolved; establish a plan to mitigate and repair environmental harm on HTG private lands; establish effective participation of Hul'qumi'num peoples in development, investment, exploration, and extraction plans; and ensure they receive reasonable benefits from such plans (Howard and Kinnison 2012: 14). These requests closely echo the arguments HTG previously made to the IACHR, drawing heavily on the language of Inter-American jurisprudence in engaging CERD committee members with the norms of international law rather than the Canadian common law language of Aboriginal title and rights.

In spite of the HTG's detailed submissions, CERD observations about Canada later that year only obliquely reflected on the HTG's concerns (UN 2012). CERD reported that Canada does not fully apply the rights to consultation or the principles of obtaining free, prior, and informed consent on projects and initiatives that affect Aboriginal peoples' lands or rights (UN 2012: 13). They also expressed concern that "aboriginal peoples incur heavy financial expenditures in litigation to resolve land disputes with the State party owing to rigidly adversarial positions taken by the State party" (UN 2012: 13). Canada was recommended to, in part, "continue to seek good faith agreements with Aboriginal peoples with regard to their lands and resources claims under culturally sensitive judicial procedures, [and] find means and ways to establish titles over their lands" (UN 2012: 14). Disappointingly for the HTG, CERD did not address the particular challenges in respect of private lands.

Canada followed up on CERD comments in their periodic report to the UN Human Rights Council, whose mandate is to promote and protect human rights and make recommendations on situations of human rights violence. The report evoked the language of market efficiency, claiming that Canada "is working closely with its Aboriginal partners to achieve more treaties in less time so that Aboriginal communities can begin to unlock economic opportunities" (Canada 2013a: 4). This "results-based" strategy is focused on investing time and energy at negotiation tables that are willing to accept existing federal mandates (see also BCAFN 2013: 10) and finding ways to divest settlement energy and resources from communities seeking alternate approaches (BC Treaty Commission 2013: 29).

Canada's optimism clashes with the observations of James Anaya, then the UN Special Rapporteur on the rights of indigenous peoples (also incidentally involved in drafting HTG's initial 2007 submission to IACHR). Anaya stated in his 2014 report on Canada that "many First Nations have all but given up on [treaty and other claims processes]. Worse yet, in many cases it appears that these processes have contributed to a deterioration rather than renewal of the relationship between indigenous peoples and the Canadian State" (Anaya 2014: 16). In negotiations Canada takes an adversarial position, "often insisting on the extinguishment or non-assertion of aboriginal rights and title, and favors monetary compensation over the right to, or return of, lands" (Anaya 2014: 16). Most recently, in the final observations by the UN Human Rights Council on Canada's sixth periodic report (UNHRC 2015), committee members reiterated that Canada resists alignment with international human rights norms with respect to indigenous lands and titles, saying:

> … the Committee is concerned about reports of the potential extinguishment of indigenous land rights and titles. It is concerned that land disputes

> between indigenous peoples and the State party which have gone on for years impose a heavy financial burden in litigation on the former. The Committee is also concerned about information that indigenous peoples are not always consulted, to ensure that they may exercise their right to free, prior and informed consent to projects and initiatives concerning them, including legislation, despite favourable rulings of the Supreme Court (Articles 2, 27). (UNHRC 2015: 6)

While neither the Special Rapporteur nor the UNHRC specifically raised HTG's particular concerns, their comments allude to the kinds of challenges HTG has faced in protracted and fruitless negotiations and the paucity of lands offered in claims settlements.

Hul'qumi'num leaders continue to hope that these highly public and influential UN bodies will be persuasive to both Canadian legislators reforming policies and judges interpreting international standards in domestic courts. The 1979 *Lovelace* case at the UN Human Rights Committee, which pressured Canada to amend egregiously discriminatory provisions of the *Indian Act* for Aboriginal women (*Lovelace v. Canada* [1983] 1 Can. Human Rights Yearbook 305), serves as inspiration. However, Canada remains seemingly impervious to critiques from international bodies, evidenced by the response of the Canadian Foreign Minister's office to a series of critical reviews of Canada's handling of human rights challenges in respect of Aboriginal peoples (Amnesty International 2012): "We find it strange that the United Nations Special Rapporteurs are devoting their scarce resources to countries like Canada, instead of countries like Iran and Syria where citizens do not enjoy rights and are subject to serious human rights violations at the hands of those regimes" (Cross 2012). Such a dismissive political response shrouds more substantial reverberations stemming from sustained international pressure on Canada to conform to international standards and norms. As I discuss below, an outcome of this pressure can be seen in the bureaucratic institutions beginning to work to revise long-standing federal land claims policies.

Joining voices to reform land claims policies in Canada

In discussions following their IACHR petition, the HTG leadership expected that Canada would resist adopting the language of the legal standards established by the Inter-American system in its land claims settlement approach, and instead continue to stall or stalemate challenging negotiation partners like HTG. The IACHR's concerns in 2009 about the absence of effective domestic remedies went unheard by Canada, evidenced by the 2013 *Consolidated Guide to the Government of Canada's Approach to Modern Treaty Negotiations* (Canada 2013b). Indigenous communities whose lands were extensively granted to private third parties as fee-simple property had little prospect for either the recognition of territorial integrity, or the provision of remuneration for such lands under this land claims policy (Canada 2013b). The HTG implemented a political strategy to unite First Nations in changing the political mandate that guides Canada's policy and negotiation approach.

In late 2012, precipitated by the historic Idle No More movement across Canada, the Assembly of First Nations (AFN) and the federal government collaborated to review and replace the Comprehensive Claims policy (along with several other joint initiatives) (BCAFN 2013). Informed by discussions with a broad base of First Nations leadership, including the HTG, the AFN advanced the *recognition* of preexisting indigenous title, rights, and governance as the central principle to base federal negotiation policy approaches (BCAFN 2013). This vision proposed a significant shift from existing government policy, where aboriginal title, rights and governance may be recognized as abstract legal principles, but not affirmed in any particular case until a treaty is ratified or there is a finding from the courts (BCAFN 2013: 4). The hope of the AFN leadership and bodies like the HTG who advised them, was that if Canada's policies were principled on territorial recognition, the conversation around land rights negotiations would change. They hoped such a revised policy would produce settlements with a sufficient land base or adequate compensation, and revenue sharing to support First Nations aspirations and lifeways into the future, rather than current arbitrary government approaches in determining land and resource quantum and capital transfer (BCAFN 2013: 19, 22–23). A forward-looking negotiated settlement would "ensure the sustainability of their economies, their culture, and way of life" (BCAFN 2013: 42). This vision of recognition reflects the norms of the Inter-American system, which holds that the geographic extent of indigenous lands property rights "extend in principle over all of those lands and resources that indigenous peoples currently use, and over those lands and resources that they possessed and of which they were deprived, with which they preserve their internationally protected special relationship" (IACHR 2010: 31) and are "of sufficient extent and quality of conserve and develop their ways of life" (IACHR 2010: 32).

The HTG sees the recognition principle as providing possibility for creative property and jurisdictional relationships, enabling Hul'qumi'num peoples to maintain important cultural connections throughout their ancestral territories beyond the limited, fragmented, and isolated areas of Indian Reserve and Crown land being considered for treaty settlement. As such, the HTG leadership understood that restitution of ancestral lands would demand novel and long-term techniques for incorporating privately held lands under their title or jurisdiction. Achieving this vision may include establishing a remuneration system for the long-term acquisition of lands alienated to private property holders, or incorporating shared planning and management jurisdictions for culturally significant places that are not included in treaty settlement (HTG 2005) – an approach consistent with IACHR norms, which state that "... restitution of lands is an essential right for cultural survival and to maintain community integrity" (IACHR 2010: 53). Restitution is the "preferential option even in relation to innocent third parties" like private land owners (IACHR 2010: 53) and persists as a right even if their use of the lands has diminished "due to causes that are beyond their will … until such causes disappear and the exercise of that right has been made possible" (IACHR 2010: 54).

Following high-level discussions with the AFN in early 2013, Canada announced its intent to re-draft its long-standing policy on comprehensive land claims and in the fall of 2014 their *Interim Policy* was launched (Canada 2014: 3). Despite feedback from HTG and others, the interim policy continued to exhibit striking differences from the norms of the Inter-American system and failed to meet the expectations of First Nations leadership. The policy stated that negotiated agreements "may recognize that the ownership of treaty settlement lands is linked to the Aboriginal party's historic presence within their asserted traditional territory" (Canada 2014: 12). Such language sidesteps the actual recognition of indigenous systems of land tenure, transforming indigenous title over treaty settlement land areas to a symbolic recognition of a "link" to an historic presence in an "asserted" territory. Blomley's analysis found that Canada sidelines indigenous conceptions of title in favor of the "*a priori*, singular, and definitive" (Blomley 2014: 1291) concept of property, fundamentally remaking indigenous space with profoundly colonial implications (Blomley 2015).

The *Interim Policy* states that "treaty settlement lands selected by Aboriginal parties for their continuing use should be asserted traditional lands that are currently used or occupied" (Canada 2014: 12). In mandating that lands demarcated for treaty settlement be currently used or occupied, the policy precludes the possibility of a territorial land base for indigenous peoples whose so-called "asserted traditional lands" are extensively privately held. This contrasts with the principle stated by the Inter-American Commission that "… indigenous peoples who have unwillingly lost possession of their lands, when those lands have been lawfully transferred to innocent third parties, are entitled to restitution thereof or to obtain other lands of equal extension and quality" (IACHR 2010: 51). Alternative lands can be provided "as a last resort" when it is not possible to return traditional lands (IACHR 2010: 59) or "where the peoples concerned express a preference for compensation in money or in kind, they shall be so compensated" (IACHR 2010: 60).

The *Interim Policy* acknowledges that "the monetary component of an agreement may comprise various forms of capital transfers, including cash, resource revenue sharing, or government bonds" (Canada 2014: 15). The neutral language of "capital transfer" circumvents applying a calculus of "compensation" to lost indigenous lands. While this "capital transfer" policy does not preclude providing funds for purchasing willing-seller lands, negotiators at several tables have told me that as Canada requires comprehensive land claims agreements to have comparable overall value across Canada. The policy thus precludes the possibility of restitution of large tracts of high-value land in Hul'qumi'num peoples' territories through buy-back from willing-sellers. The HTG calculated the amount for their territories in the billions of dollars for unimproved lands alone (Thom 2014a: 10), which would not fulfill the "comparability of value" requirement of the federal negotiating mandate, as the overall cost of modern-day land claim settlements is much lower.

Former federal chief negotiator Doug Eyford commented in a report commissioned by the Federal government that "although there is not a consistent Aboriginal perspective on all issues, there is a general consensus that Canada is inflexible in its approach to Aboriginal interests and endeavors to meet its minimum legal obligations, nothing more. Canada is seen as unresponsive to Aboriginal interests and rigid in its application of the comprehensive land claims policy. There is also a widely held view that federal policies lag behind legal developments" (Eyford 2015: 10). It is instructive, in light of the HTG case, to look in particular at how the principles of restitution profoundly differ between the norms of the IAHRC and Canada's new *Interim Policy.*

In the wake of the failure of the *Interim Policy* to meet expectations or align with international norms and jurisprudence, First Nations leaders continue to call on Canada to acknowledge the basis of relationships on the "recognition and implementation of the existence of indigenous peoples' inherent title and rights ... [the] acknowledgement that indigenous systems of governance and laws are essential to the regulation of lands ... [and] consent based decision-making and title-based fiscal relations" (FNLC 2014). The HTG leadership has called on other First Nations to bring recognition and implementation of international standards into view of federal policy reform and to their individual negotiation table discussions. While such a principle has offered powerful grist for speeches at indigenous political meetings, the negotiation community is justifiably skeptical that economically disadvantaged First Nations would unite to strategically withdraw from enticing "short-term benefit" and "interim measures" talks underway at many negotiating tables. While local economic needs have to date trumped taking a united, oppositional stance, HTG leaders still hope that a well-publicized ruling in their favor by the IACHR, CERD, or SCC could tap into the energies of movements like Idle No More, galvanizing political coalitions and collective action.

Bringing the message to the investment community

During the 2011 IACHR merits hearings, the HTG leadership discussed the likelihood that Canada, who so vigorously rejected their claims, would have to be pressured by corporations and citizens whose fiscal bottom-lines could be impacted, to change their position. Chief negotiator Robert Morales observed that "it will take the pressure of big business to change government minds" (fieldnotes, 2011). Discussions ensued as to how to activate ethical shareholders to press companies, whose activities are tangled in tarnished human rights records, to correct their dealings. The HTG hoped that lowering demand or creating land title uncertainty for large private timber or land development companies would depreciate stock values and compel companies' directors to be proactive with governments to resolve outstanding land title questions.

In May 2011, the HTG implemented a communications strategy to gain media visibility, to provide public information, and to target key stakeholder groups. Their objective was to underscore the links between the HTG's unsettled land claims and the private timberland holdings of TimberWest. The campaign had an immediate but short-lived impact. Once HTG's story was reported in the press, TimberWest shares traded in higher volumes and the stock price on the Toronto Stock Exchange went down (TWF.UN). Within days, however, the share price returned as shareholders regained confidence (Ebner 2011). The following month, TimberWest was delisted from the public stock exchange, as the BC Investment Management Corporation and the Public Sector Pension Investment Board acquired their shares (Lesprom Network 2011). This move compounded the sense of betrayal and indignation of the HTG leadership, as the provincial government's own investment and pension board became the major shareholder of the company that owned of the disputed lands. The HTG protested this conflict of interest to the BC Securities Commission (Siefken 2011), but with no impact to the $1.08 billion sale to the provincial government's own investment firm. Seeking the immediate intervention of the IACHR through a precautionary measures request, the HTG were met with no response. TimberWest remains a profitable timber corporation with an active private land sales division called "Couverdon," which develops high-value timberland into residential developments with seeming impunity in respect of outstanding indigenous title claims on those lands.

The HTG has taken a more circumspect approach to create potential allies from the 60,000+ private landowners whose homes, farms and businesses are located in their ancestral territory. When the HTG launched their IACHR case, they self-published and freely distributed the beautifully designed information book *The Great Land Grab* (Morales et al. 2007). The opening text declares the E&N Railway Grant as "an act of egregious piracy ... colonial theft, and remains to this day a largely invisible stain on BC history" (Morales et al. 2007: 1). The book – followed by lectures series and public speaking engagements by Robert Morales – uses engaging and straightforward language to explain to the public the history of granting Hul'qumi'num ancestral lands and the ongoing challenge to resolving this injustice. While the HTG is clearly trying to generate a sense of indignation with the general public (see Niezen 2010), evidently, any efforts to devalue private home prices or raise the specter of private land expropriation are non-starters in the public, and would likely provide political cover for the state to continue to deny and ignore indigenous peoples claims on private lands.[6]

Conclusions

These events illustrate that the HTG campaign for domestic implementation of international indigenous peoples' rights has had limited local impact. Despite more than 20 years of negotiations (funded by over $30 million in government loans

6 Indeed a 2002 public referendum held in British Columbia showed that 84.52% of voters agreed that private lands should be off the negotiating table (Elections BC 2002: 6; Egan 2011; Rossiter and Wood 2005). This referendum reinforced governments' position that private lands are unavailable for titling as indigenous lands, even if expropriation mechanisms which would compensate private land owners applied.

against potential future settlements) and nearly ten years of sustained petitions to the international community, no privately held lands have been titled, demarcated, compensated for, recognized for indigenous jurisdiction, or on which governments have sought the free, prior and informed consent of the Hul'qumi'num peoples. Robert Morales described Canada's approach as a "rope-a-dope" strategy, evoking the famous Muhammad Ali tactic of enduring hits until the opponent (in this case, the HTG) is exhausted, and then delivering the knock-out blow (breaking the fiscal and political will of the Hul'qumi'num peoples to carry on).

The HTG's case is distinctively challenging because the fiscal and economic stakes surrounding the surety of private land titles is too high for the state to divert from its current approach of non-recognition. The Crown and public are reticent to re-imagine their colonial relationship to these lands, and to see Hul'qumi'num peoples and other similarly situated indigenous communities as significant land owners or otherwise having any jurisdictions over their ancestral territories. Perhaps an eventual decision on the merits of the case by the IACHR – if it is forthcoming – will create new momentum in resolving these outstanding issues.

Perhaps there is some cause for optimism in Canada, as an indigenous woman was appointed Minister of Justice in the fall of 2015. Jody Wilson-Raybould is well aware of the HTG's petition to the IACHR, and in fact attended the 2011 merits hearings in support of the work of the HTG leadership. At a press conference following the hearing, Wilson-Raybould said:[7]

> Canada needs to be, and is here today, reminded of its responsibilities to Indigenous peoples. Canada cannot stand behind the Canadian justice system and the federal bureaucracy in terms of saying that "everything is ok". The justice system and the bureaucracy have become complacent, and are maintaining the status quo, for the most part, and thereby ensuring, or relegating, our First Nations to another generation of poverty. This must change.

While this statement points to potentially significant political will incorporate principles of international law, the machinery of government can be hard to change. Any optimism must be tempered by other voices, like that of the government of the Province of BC which vigorously opposed litigation launched by First Nations protesting a copper-gold mine, stating that "government must and will always defend, with conviction, the sanctity of private land and private land rights" (British Columbia 2016). This strongly worded legal position suggests that recognition and reconciliation of indigenous property rights on private lands will continue to be a source of human rights violations for the foreseeable future.

The situation in Canada has implications for other indigenous peoples looking to the international community for resolution and reconciliation. The HTG has

7 Jody Wilson-Raybould, BC AFN Regional Vice-Chief, speaking to the press at a press conference organized by the HTG following the merits hearing, 28 October 2011.

demonstrated that implementing the promise of indigenous peoples' rights requires a sustained, multifaceted campaign, with significant investment of funds, expertise, and long-term political commitment. Even with the best strategies implemented, there are still clearly huge risks and uncertain outcomes for indigenous communities that are appealing to the forums and processes of the international community. The vision of the HTG leadership reminds us that to implement contemporary indigenous territories in a way that is consistent with international human and indigenous peoples' rights, require creative persistence and a broad spectrum of support to instigate change. Without attending to these visions, the old colonial model of extinguishing indigenous titles to provide economic and political certainty to private interests will continues to dominate and disenfranchise indigenous peoples in Canada and other common law jurisdictions.

Bibliography

Alcantara, Christopher. 2009. "Old Wine in New Bottles: Instrumental Policy Learning and the Evoluion of the Certainty Provision in Comprehensive Land Claims Agreements." *Canadian Public Policy/Analyse de Politiques* 35(3): 325–341.

Amnesty International. 2011. *Amicus Curiae Case of the Hul'qumi'num Treaty Group V. Canada Submitted before the Inter-American Commission on Human Rights.* Ottawa: Amnesty International Canada. http://www.amnesty.ca/sites/default/files/2011-08-01amr200012011enamicuscuriae.pdf (accessed 30 November 2018).

Amnesty International. 2012. *Matching International Commitments with National Action: A Human Rights Agenda for Canada.* Ottawa: Amnesty International Canada. http://www.amnesty.ca/sites/default/files/canadaaihra19december12.pdf (accessed 30 November 2018).

Anaya, James. 2014. *Report of the Special Rapporteur on the Rights of Indigenous Peoples, James Anaya, Addendum: The Situation of Indigenous Peoples in Canada.* A/HRC/27/52/Add.2. New York: UN.

Blomley, Nicholas. 2014. "Making Space for Property." *Annals of the Association of American Geographers* 104 (6): 1291–1306.

Blomley, Nicholas. 2015. "The Ties that Blind: Making Fee Simple in the British Columbia Treaty Process." *Transactions of the Institute of British Geographers* 40: 168–179.

BCAFN (British Columbia Assembly of First Nations). 2013. *Communiqué, January 16, 2013.* http://www.afn.ca/uploads/files/13-01-16_afn_bulletin_fe.pdf (accessed 9 August 2015).

BC Treaty Commission. 2013. *Pathways to Change: BC Treaty Commission Annual Report, 2013.* Vancouver: BC Treaty Commission. http://www.bctreaty.ca/sites/default/files/BCTC-Annual-Report-2013.pdf (accessed 24 January 2019).

British Columbia. 2009. *Haida Kunst'aa guu – Kunts'aayah Reconciliation Protocol.* Victoria: Government of British Columbia. https://www2.gov.bc.ca/assets/gov/environment/natural-resource-stewardship/consulting-with-first-nations/agreements/haida_rp_fully_signed_and_dated_-_jan_22_2016.pdf (accessed 24 January 2019).

British Columbia. 2011. *Coastal First Nations Reconciliation Protocol.* Victoria: Government of British Columbia. https://www2.gov.bc.ca/assets/gov/zzzz-to-be-moved/9efbd86da302a0712e6559bdb2c7f9dd/9efbd86da302a0712e6559bdb2c7f9dd/agreements/reconciliation_coastal_haisla_amendment.pdf (accessed 24 January 2019).

British Columbia. 2016. "Province Files Response to First Nations Title Claim." *News Release*, 15 January2016. https://news.gov.bc.ca/releases/2016JAG0003-000043 (accessed 21 February 2019).

Canada. 2008. "Oral Submission of Canada to the Inter-American Commission on Human Rights on the Inadmissibility of the Petition of the Hul'qumi'num Treaty Group, Case No. P-592-07." 28 October 2008. http://www.cidh.oas.org/Audiencias/133/B26HulquminumTreatyGroupCanada.mp3 (accessed 23 January 2019).

Canada. 2013a. "National Report Submitted in Accordance with Paragraph 5 of the Annex to Human Rights Council Resolution 16/21." *Human Rights Council, Working Group on the Universal Periodic Review, Sixteenth Session, Geneva, 22 April–3 May 2013.* A/HRC/WG.6/16/CAN/1. Geneva: UN HCR.

Canada. 2013b. *Consolidated Guide to the Government of Canada's Approach to Modern Treaty Negotiations.* Ottawa: Aboriginal Affairs and Northern Development Canada.

Canada. 2014. *Renewing the Comprehensive Land Claims Policy: Towards a Framework for Addressing Section 35 Aboriginal Rights.* Ottawa: Aboriginal Affairs and Northern Development Canada.

Cross, Allison. 2012. "Canada Rejects UN Human Rights Criticism Detailed in Amnesty International Report." *National Post*, 19 December 2012. http://news.nationalpost.com/2012/12/19/canada-rejects-un-human-rights-criticism-detailed-in-amnesty-international-report (accessed 22 February 2019).

Ebner, David. 2011. "TimberWest Sale Faces First Nations Hurdle." *Globe and Mail*, 16 May 2011. http://www.theglobeandmail.com/report-on-business/timberwest-sale-faces-first-nations-hurdle/article4263216/ (accessed 23 January 2019).

Elections BC. 2002. *Report of the Chief Electoral Officer on the Treaty Negotiations Referendum.* http://www.elections.bc.ca/docs/refreportfinal.pdf (accessed 23 January 2019).

Egan, Brian. 2011. "Recognition Politics and Reconciliation Fantasies: Liberal Multiculturalism and the "Indian Land Question." In *Home and Native Land: Unsettling Multiculturalism in Canada*, edited by May Chazan, Lisa Helps, Anna Stanley, and Sonali Thakkar, 123–141. Toronto: Between the Lines Press.

Egan, Brian. 2012. "Sharing the Colonial Burden: Treaty-making and Reconciliation in Hul'qumi'num Territory." *The Canadian Geographer* 56(4): 398–418.

Egan, Brian. 2013. "Towards Shared Ownership: Property, Geography and Treaty Making in British Columbia." *Geografiska Annalser: Series B* 95 (1): 33–50.

Eyford, Douglas. 2015. *A New Direction, Advancing Aboriginal and Treaty Rights/Un nouvelle Orientation: Faire advancer les droits ancestraux et issus de traités des Autochtones.* Ottawa: Aboriginal Affairs and Northern Development Canada.

First Nations Leadership Council. 2014. "Statement: B.C. Government and First Nations Leaders Look to Future of Reconciliation," 11 September 2014. https://news.gov.bc.ca/stories/bc-government-and-first-nations-leaders-look-to-future-of-reconciliation (accessed 24 January 2019).

Howard, Seánna and Akilah Kinnison. 2012. *Submission to the U.N. Committee on the Elimination of Racial Discrimination by Hul'qumi'num Treaty Group in Relation to Canada's 19th and 20th Periodic Reports, 80th Session, 13 February–9 March, 2012.* http://tbinternet.ohchr.org/Treaties/CERD/Shared%20Documents/CAN/INT_CERD_NGO_CAN_80_8292_E.pdf (accessed 23 January 2019).

HTG (Hul'qumi'num Treaty Group). 1993. "Mission Statement." Unpublished document on Ceremonial Drum. Ladysmith: Hul'qumi'num Treaty Group. Text reprinted http://www.cowichantribes.com/tribes-governance/self-government-and-treaty/treaty-negotiations/ (accessed 23 January 2019).

HTG (Hul'qumi'num Treaty Group). 2005. *Getting to 100%.* Ladysmith: Hul'qumi'num Treaty Group. http://www.hulquminum.bc.ca/pubs/HTG%20Info%20Book6.pdf (accessed 23 January 2019).

IACHR (Inter-American Commission on Human Rights). 2009. *Admissibility Report, Hul'qumi'num Treaty Group (Canada).* Report No. 105/09, Petition 592-07. http://www.cidh.oas.org/annualrep/2009eng/Canada592.07eng.htm (accessed 8 August 2015).

IACHR (Inter-American Commission on Human Rights). 2010. *Indigenous and Tribal Peoples' Rights over their Ancestral Lands and Natural Resources: Norms and Jurisprudence of the Inter-American Human Rights System.* OEA/Ser.L/V/II. Doc 56/09. Washington, DC: Organization of American States Official Records.

LRWC (Lawyers' Rights Watch Canada). 2011. *To the Inter-American Commission on Human Rights on the Merits of the Petition of the Hul'qumi'num Treaty Group, Case No. 12.734, Brief of Lawyers' Rights Watch Canada as Amicus Curiae.* http://www.lrwc.org/ws/wp-content/uploads/2012/03/IACHR.Case_.12.734.LRWC_.Amicus.June_.3.11.pdf (accessed 23 January 2019).

Lesprom Network. 2011. *Acquisition of Timberwest by BCIMC and PSP Investments Completed*, 29 June 2011. http://www.lesprom.com/en/news/Acquisition_of_Timberwest_by_Bcimc_and_Psp_Investments_sompleted_48560/ (accessed 23 January 2019).

McNeil, Kent. 2008. Native Rights Case Law. In *Handbook of North American Indians, Volume 2, Indians in Contemporary Society*, edited by Garrick Bailey, 166–176. Washington, DC: Smithsonian Institution.

Morales, Robert (with Brian Egan and Brian Thom, eds.). 2007. *The Great Land Grab: Colonialism and the Esquimalt and Nanaimo Railway Land Grant in Hul'qumi'num Territory.* Ladysmith: Hul'qumi'num Treaty Group. http://www.hulquminum.bc.ca/pubs/HTGRailwayBookSpreads.pdf (accessed 9 August 2015).

Morales, Robert. 2014. *Factum of the Intervenor, the Hul'qumi'num Treaty Group.* File No. 34986, Supreme Court of Canada. http://www.scc-csc.gc.ca/WebDocuments-DocumentsWeb/34986/FM170_Intervener_Hul'qumi'num-Treaty-Group.pdf (accessed 23 January 2019).

Niezen, Ronald. 2010. *Public Justice and the Anthropology of Law.* London: Cambridge University Press.

Nisga'a Final Agreement. 2000. http://www.nnkn.ca/files/u28/nis-eng.pdf (accessed 23 January 2019).

Rossiter, David, and Patricia Wood. 2005. "Fantastic Topographies: Neo-liberal Responses to Aboriginal Land Claims in British Columbia. *The Canadian Geographer/Le Géographe canadien* 49 (4): 352–366.

Rynard, Paul. 2000. "'Welcome in, but Check Your Rights at the Door': The James Bay and Nisga'a Agreements in Canada." *Canadian Journal of Political Science/Revue canadienne de science politique* 33 (2): 211–243.

Siefken, Krista. 2011. "HTG Accelerates Protest of TimberWest Sale." *Cowichan News Leader Pictorial*, 14 June 14. https://infoweb.newsbank.com/apps/news/openurl?ctx_ver=z39.88-2004&rft_id=info%3Asid/infoweb.newsbank.com&svc_dat=AWNB&req_dat=0D0CB61A49773E6A&rft_val_format=info%3Aofi/fmt%3Akev%3Amtx%3Actx&rft_dat=document_id%3Anews%252F137E35E282E25B88 (accessed 24 January 2019).

Thom, Brian. 2008. "Dis-agreement in Principle: Negotiating the Right to Practice Coast Salish Culture in Treaty Talks on Vancouver Island, BC." *New Proposals: Journal of Marxism and Interdisciplinary Inquiry* 2(1): 23–30. http://ojs.library.ubc.ca/index.php/newproposals/article/view/170/0.

Thom, Brian. 2010. "The Anathema of Aggregation: Towards 21st Century Self-government in the Coast Salish World." *Anthropologica* 52 (1): 33–48.

Thom, Brian. 2014a." Reframing Indigenous Territories: Private Property, Human Rights and Overlapping Claims." *American Indian Culture and Research Journal* 38 (4): 3–28.

Thom, Brian. 2014b. "Confusion sur les territoires autochtones au Canada." In *Terres, territoires, ressources: Politiques, pratiques et droits des peuples autochtones*, edited by Irène Bellier, pp. 89–106. Paris: L'Harmattan.

Tla'amin Final Agreement. 2014. http://www.aadnc-aandc.gc.ca/eng/1397152724601/1397152939293 (accessed 23 January 2019).

Tsawwassen Final Agreement. 2010. https://www.aadnc-aandc.gc.ca/eng/1100100022706/1100100022717 (accessed 23 January 2019).

UN (United Nations). 2007. *Concluding Observations of the Committee on the Elimination of Racial Discrimination: Canada.* Seventieth Session, 19 February – 9 March 2007 CERD/C/CAN/CO/18. New York: UN. http://www2.ohchr.org/english/bodies/cerd/docs/CERD.C.CAN.CO.18.doc (accessed 10 August 2015).

UN (United Nations). 2012. *Report of the Committee on the Elimination of Racial Discrimination. Eightieth Session (13 February–9 March 2012). General Assembly, Official Records*, Sixty-seventh Session, Supplement No. 18 (A/67/18). New York: UN.

UNHRC (United Nations Human Rights Committee). 2015. *Concluding Observations on the Sixth Periodic Report of Canada*, 20 July 2015 (CCPR/C/SR 3192). Advance Unedited Version. http://tbinternet.ohchr.org/Treaties/CCPR/Shared%20Documents/CAN/CCPR_C_CAN_CO_6_21189_E.docx (accessed 23 January 2019).

Williams, Robert A. Jr., S. James Anaya, Angela C. Poliquin, and Jacklyn Hartley. 2007. *Petition to the Inter-American Commission on Human Rights Submitted by the Hul'qumi'num Treaty Group against Canada.* Ladysmith: Hul'qumi'num Treaty Group. https://law.arizona.edu/sites/default/files/Hul%E2%80%99qumi%E2%80%99num%20Treaty%20Group%20Petition.pdf (accessed 24 January 2019).

8 The logic of elimination in (post-)colonial law

Indigenous entanglements in the Kimberley region of Australia[1]

Martin Préaud

Introduction

Can peoples colonized by European powers be compensated for the wrongs that have been done to them? Is it possible for them to receive justice in a judicial framework that, if not unjust, is at least biased, since it was set up by the colonizing power? Many of the world's indigenous peoples face these kinds of questions, particularly in states that have developed out of "settler states," or states arising from settlement colonies, like Canada, the United States, New Zealand, and Australia. In these nation states, where nation means, above all, the community constituted by the settlers and their descendants, the state and society have effectively developed against or despite the presence of indigenous societies, cultures, and institutions. In these states, *invasion* is a "deep structure" rather than an historic event belonging to the past (Wolfe 1994). For indigenous peoples subsumed unwillingly into these states, post-colonial justice remains a pressing issue.

In Australia, the Mabo no. 2 decision of the High Court in 1992 represented a major change in the relationship between the state and the indigenous peoples.[2] It revoked the juridical doctrine of *terra nullius* which, until then, had provided legal justification for the settlement of the continent and the appropriation of political and territorial sovereignty by the British Crown and its local successors. The *Native Title Act 1993 (Cth[3])*, or NTA 93, the negotiated legislative translation of this decision, promised to recognize and bring into force the fundamental land rights of indigenous peoples – Aboriginal and Torres Strait Islanders. Today, a bit more than 20% of Australian national territory corresponds to the territorial rights and interests of indigenous peoples – which would seem to suggest a rebalancing of fundamental relationships with regard to land. But this figure is misleading. First, because it covers a large variety of rights and interests, from exclusive property deeds (especially in the Northern Territory), to simple long-term leases; and second, because the major lever of this rebalancing,

1 Translated by Cadenza Academic Translations, revised by Jennifer Hays, and the author.

2 The term "Indigenous Peoples" refers in Australia to Aborigines and to Torres Strait Islanders.

3 (Cth) signifies federal laws, under the Commonwealth.

the NTA 93, offers very little in terms of protection and guarantees to the indigenous peoples who get involved with these complex procedures.

The case study on which this article is based – the controversy surrounding the development of the largest gas project in Australia, on the Dampier peninsula to the North of Western Australia – will allow us to approach the limits of indigenous peoples' rights when the concept is put into practice by a settler state. After a brief presentation of the chronology of the controversy (2008–2013), and of the different stakeholders involved, this paper will come back to indigenous peoples' appeal to the law in their quest for justice and compensation. By demonstrating the limits of NTA 93 and analyzing the different legal systems mobilized by the different stakeholders during the controversy, this chapter argues that the rights of indigenous peoples, as promoted by the Australian state, constitute not so much a ruse (Povinelli 2002), as an impasse. Analysis of the dimensions structuring the field of indigenous politics reveals, on the side of Australian institutions, the functioning of a specific logic, a derogatory enactment of the law applying to indigenous peoples resembling in every respect the logic of the elimination of indigenous peoples which, according to Patrick Wolfe, is characteristic of settler states (Wolfe 2006, see also Veracini 2010, 2011).

This analysis casts doubt on the notion that Australia is a post-colonial society, in the sense that the most enduring colonial institutions – racial barriers, systematic discrimination, denial of indigenous societies – have been abolished. On the contrary, the Australian state and society are fully post-colonial in the critical sense of the term and, far from being abolished or eradicated, the colonial institutions continue to operate deep down, structuring social and power relations. In this framework, how can indigenous peoples hope to assert their rights and work toward the actual decolonization of their situation?

Rather than providing a response to this question, this chapter aims to shed light on the context in which it arises. The first section presents the chronology and stakeholders of the Walmadany controversy, followed by a clarification, in the second section, of the different ways in which these diverse stakeholders appealed to various legal systems (Aboriginal law, Australian law, international law). The paper ends by proposing an analytical cartography of the indigenous field as it has developed in Australia, identifying a variety of systems contributing to the construction of indigenous peoples as new legal subjects.

The Walmadany controversy: choiceless decisions

Walmadany/James Price Point

Walmadany, also known as James Price Point, is an area of the Dampier Peninsula, some 50 km north of the town of Broome in the state of Western Australia. Situated in Nyul Nyul country, it is a step on the mythological trail that runs along the northwest coast of Australia. A part of this trail, the Lurujarri Trail, was made known through the work of Paddy Roe, an important character in the history of Aboriginal-Australian relations; I will return to his story below. Every year Roe's descendants accompany groups of tourists to give them an idea of the local aboriginal cultures, histories, and traditions. This trail connects the town of Broome in Yawuru country to the One Arm Point community in Bardi country on the northern tip of the Dampier Peninsula, crossing the Yawuru, Junkin, Ngumbarl, and Jabirr Jabirr countries, which are collectively referred to by their Nyikina neighbors to the East as Goolarabooloo, "the lands of the setting sun" (Glowczewski 2004).

Between 2008 and 2013, Walmadany was the focal point of relations between indigenous peoples and the state in matters of development. The state of Western Australia had decided to exploit the gas deposits of the Browse Basin situated off the coast of the peninsula and had identified James Price Point as a site that could potentially accommodate a gas liquification factory and a deep-water port from which to export. This project, one of the largest in Australia in terms of investment, and put together by the Western Australian government in conjunction with a consortium of mining companies led by the Australian firm Woodside, met with fierce local opposition despite attempts at negotiation with Aboriginal traditional owners. This section describes the different stages of this controversy, which ended with the withdrawal of Woodside and its industrial partners in 2013, and the principal stakeholders.

From seeking consent to forced negotiation

Browse Basin's reserves of hydrocarbons, particularly its gas, have been known since the 1970s. The decision to exploit them was taken in 2008 by the government of Western Australia, in partnership with a consortium bringing together Shell and Chevron behind Woodside. The project involved building a gas liquefaction factory on the coast of the Dampier Peninsula and an industrial port for its exportation. The level of investment needed to realize the project made it one of the largest industrial projects of the last few decades in Australia.

The Kimberley region, the part of Western Australia situated to the north of the Great Sandy Desert, is Aboriginal country. Nearly half of the census population is indigenous, compared with 3.5% and 2.5% of the total population, at state and federal level, respectively. The settlement of the region only began in earnest in the 1880s, and the region continues to be seen by the authorities in the capital city of Perth, more than 2,000 km to the south, as a reserve for future development: mining having now supplanted extensive livestock farming.

Nearly 90% of the Kimberley's territory is claimed by Aboriginal claimant groups through the NTA93 framework – the only legal recourse by which indigenous peoples can claim their rights to land in this state. Today, more than 70% of registered claims have been decided in favor of their Aboriginal claimants, under settlements of exclusive or shared possession, representing nearly 70% of the region's territory.[4]

4 See https://www.klc.org.au/native-title-map/ (last accessed December 2018) and Jon Altman (2014).

At the start of the Walmadany gas project in 2008, the decision was made by the Western Australian government to discuss the choice of a project site with the Kimberley Land Council (KLC), the indigenous organization legally charged with representing Aboriginal claimant groups under the *NTA*. Given the scale of the project and the size of the potentially affected area, the KLC negotiated with the government for the establishment and financing of a Task Force (Traditional Owners Task Force, TOTF), which brought together representatives of the all the claimant groups potentially affected by the choice of site (based on an initial list of 45 sites suggested by the government and the consortium), as well as "special advisers" from the KLC who were respected Aboriginal figures from other parts of the region. The KLC obtained government funding for several years for the TOTF, providing the time and means for a delicate process of internal consultation. The intention of the approach was to secure consent, but there was no reference to the suitability of the project itself, only to the choice of a mutually acceptable site.

For the KLC, the anticipated returns of the project should benefit all the Aboriginal groups of the Kimberley, beyond the claimant group directly affected. This area of 400,000 km^2 is characterized by a great linguistic and cultural diversity and, paradoxically, a strong regional integration, born out by strong regional organizations. In addition to the KLC, which was initially an activist organization created in 1979 around a mining conflict (Hawke and Gallagher 1989), there is the Kimberley Aboriginal Law and Culture Centre (KALACC) and the Kimberley Language and Resource Center (KLRC), both created in 1984. All organizations bring together men and women representing the 30 or so Aboriginal groups of the region. These organizations, and the region's many communities and local organizations, face significant social, economic, and political challenges: the Kimberley is a region in Australia where the indigenous population is markedly underprivileged. The inequalities with the rest of the Australian population in terms of life expectancy, education, incarceration, income, and even suicide are very clear and continue to get worse, despite declarations of intent and federal and state policies (SCRGSP 2014; Martin 2015).

In this context, a project like the one envisaged for James Price Point was important for its potential impacts – social and economic as well as environmental – and the way in which it could empower indigenous organizations to manage such projects autonomously. This is why the KLC brought together a broad group in the TOTF and envisaged the creation of a regional Aboriginal fund, on the model of a sovereign fund, which would enable them to autonomously manage the financial returns of the project without getting entangled in Australian public policy.

The TOTF had hardly begun working and negotiating with its partners when the 2008 elections brought a new government to Western Australia. Colin Barnett's arrival in power meant a brutal reorientation of the negotiations. TOTF's financing was suspended and James Price Point designated as the only acceptable site. In addition, Colin Barnett's government mobilized the NTA 93 to accelerate the negotiation process and bring it to a close under 6 months, all under the threat of a unilateral acquisition of the site at James Price Point, which would have excluded the traditional owners from a share of the project's returns. According to the provisions of the NTA 93, the claimant groups whose claim has been registered with the National Native Title Tribunal (NNTT) acquire through this a right to negotiate on projects proposed on the territory in question; the project developer has 6 months to come to an agreement with the traditional owners before the matter gets referred to the NNTT, whose jurisprudence is particularly favorable to mining interests (O'Faircheallaigh 2013). Effectively a "negotiation at gunpoint" as Wayne Bergmann, the director of the KLC at the time, put it.

Aboriginal divisions and political mobilizations

The blunt approach of the Barnett government toward the Walmadany gas project led, in 2009, to the signing of a procedural agreement for the distribution of benefits between the Traditional Owners Negotiating Committee (TONC, set up by the KLC to replace the TOTF), the government of Western Australia, and the consortium led by Woodside. This agreement was one of the largest ever reached between an indigenous group and a mining group in Australia, covering 20 billion dollars over a 50-year period, the creation of infrastructure, jobs and training for indigenous groups in the region, and so on.

For the KLC, the signed procedural agreement was conditional on the recommendation of the Environmental Protection Authority of Western Australia, and the completion of a social and economic impact study. The signing of the agreement nevertheless led to acute tensions between the traditional owners of the affected area, and to the division of the Goolarabooloo's and Jabirr Jabirr's joint claim, first with Joseph Roe's removal from the list of named claimants on the joint claim,[5] and then with the creation of two separate groups each making a distinct claim: the Goolarabooloo, who strongly opposed the agreement and the choice of Walmadany as a site, and the Jabirr Jabirr who supported the location and the agreement negotiated by the KLC.

The term Goolarabooloo refers to a group of Paddy Roe's (c. 1912–2001) descendants. Roe was an extraordinary character, and a great mediator between the Aboriginal peoples of the Western Kimberley and Australians of all persuasions (see especially Roe, Stephen, and Kim Bentarrak 1984). Born in Nyikina country, Paddy Roe went to work as a stockman to the West of his country, first in Roebuck Bay and then on the Dampier Peninsula, where he lived for most of his life. He was initiated into local religious laws, and was ultimately entrusted with ritual responsibilities in the Nyul Nyul and Jabirr Jabirr countries, which he handed down to his descendants born in these lands. This transfer of responsibilities to a family from a different region, while not completely unheard of,

5 In the framework of the NTA 93, the named claimants are the legal representatives of the claimant group.

is nevertheless very unusual, and was directly linked to the violence of colonial implantation in the region, to the disappearance of whole groups and to the displacement and forced merging of populations in colonial institutions (missions, stations, and prisons; see, for example, Pedersen and Woorunmurra 1995).

The history of the Dampier Peninsula bears the scars of this violence. It was the first point of entry for settlers into the Kimberley region, especially pearlers who scoured the peninsula to forcibly enlist Aboriginal people to work for them.[6] It also housed several missions, notably Beagle Bay which, until the 1970s, cared for "stolen children" from across the region. Because of this, questions of territorial ownership and alliances between Aboriginal groups are particularly complicated, as can be seen from the disagreements between different groups claiming to be Walmadany's traditional owners, and authorized to make decisions bearing on this territory from the perspective of Aboriginal Law.

The Goolarabooloo, rallied around Paddy Roe's descendant Joseph Roe and his mother, led a campaign of systematic opposition to the Walmadany gas project in the name of Aboriginal Law. To do this, they recruited allies from the local community of Broome residents and, more broadly, from the networks of environmental activists and Aboriginal heritage protectors. This opposition took the form of systematic submissions to tribunals – against the process of unilateral acquisition of the Walmadany plot initiated by Colin Barnett, against Joseph Roe's eviction as a named claimant, against the Environment Authority's evaluation procedure – and a large-scale media campaign, at local and national level, particularly on social media networks (Muir 2012).

Victory, but whose?

The controversy came to an end in 2013 with the announcement of the withdrawal of Woodside and its industrial partners from the project, mostly for reasons of cost associated with the investment necessary for realizing the project,[7] which was even more significant since the price of gas on the global market was falling. In addition, there were alternative projects to Walmadany, such as using existing infrastructure in the neighboring Pilbara region, or the installation of a gas liquefaction factory on a floating platform. This retreat did not, however, discourage Colin Barnett's government, which remained determined to develop the North of the state through the exploitation of its natural resources: offshore gas, shale gas in the Fitzroy valley, minerals (iron, zinc, lead, uranium), and water.

6 The exploitation of Aboriginal people in the pearling industry in the Kimberley, led to a ban on their employment in the late 1890s and the influx of pearl workers from southeast Asia.

7 See in particular: http://www.miningaustralia.com.au/News/Woodside-scraps-James-Price-Point-development; http://www.sbs.com.au/news/article/2013/04/12/woodside-abandons-james-price-point-gas-hub; http://www.perthnow.com.au/news/western-australia/woodside-will-not-go-ahead-with-an-lng-processing-plant-at-james-price-point/story-fnhocxo3-1226618536271 (last accessed December 2018).

In 2012–2013, the mining industry represented 89% of Western Australia's exports (Government of Western Australia 2013).[8]

The Walmadany gas project seemed, for the moment, to have been set to one side, but it had produced some very significant divisions in the indigenous communities of the Kimberley region, and exposed political positions with respect to development that would be hard to reconcile. In addition, there was nothing to say that the gas project would not resurface, as a new front was opening with the desire to extract shale gas in the region. From this perspective, what seemed like a Goolarabooloo victory was neither total nor definitive. Furthermore, there was the major question of how to bring the indigenous groups and organizations of the region back together into a common movement.

This brief sketch of the Walmadany controversy highlights the diversity of the stakeholders involved in and impacted by the gas development project: the state of Western Australia and its industrial partners, the different Aboriginal groups, representative indigenous organizations, as well as the networks of activist organizations, particularly those defending the environment and groups of residents, both indigenous and non-indigenous. These different stakeholders positioned themselves in relation to the project according to their different perspectives, which varied depending on the scale considered – local, national, international – but which always involved some form of recourse to the law. It is this complex tangle of relationships centered on questions of law and social and environmental justice that the analysis of the second part of this article will seek to clarify.

The rights of indigenous peoples in the colonial situation

This broad-brushed description of the Walmadany controversy illustrates how Aboriginal people take up the defense of their rights at their own risk. In the Australian context, the dominant law providing actual content to the notion of indigenous peoples' rights as developed at the international level, particularly in the United Nations Declaration on the Rights of Indigenous Peoples (UNDRIP), remains one elaborated by non-indigenous members of Parliament and judges. Australia is a settler state. Within this frame of reference, the very idea of self-determination is nipped in the bud, and the "recognition" of indigenous peoples problematic (Préaud and Dousset 2014). This is one reason why part of the Walmadany controversy was played out through the contextualization, mobilization, and implementation of different juridical systems; while the law is encountered everywhere in the unfolding and outcome of the controversy, the stakeholders marshaled very different references to it. In this second section, I will analyze how the different juridical systems mobilized enable the construction of *indigeneity* as a field (Bourdieu 1994: 55) in which the indigenous peoples are not necessarily at an advantage from a juridical point of view.

8 This figure has remained fairly stable; in 2009–2010 it was 90%, and in 2017–2018 85% of the exports of Western Australia (Government of Western Australia 2010, 2018).

The appeal to law in the gas project

The controversy around the gas project brought different groups of stakeholders into play, including: the Goolarabooloo and their allies (political and ecological activists, residents of Broome, political and media personalities); the KLC and the groups trusting them in their mission to represent their rights and interests to land; the governments of Western Australia and the federal government; and finally, the consortium of businesses with Woodside at its head.

These groups of stakeholders, which have only been sketched out here, had particular ways of appealing to the law and distinct legal references, and an analysis of this sheds light on the juridical and political terrain characterizing indigeneity as it is negotiated at the local level. While the Goolarabooloo and their allies mobilized Aboriginal Law and the international rights of indigenous peoples to legitimate their resistance to the project, the other stakeholders appealed for the most part to the framework of the NTA 93 as they organized their negotiation and attempted to settle their differences. More broadly, however, all the stakeholders relied on common law, at the state and federal level (notably for the environmental impact study) – something that would ultimately prove decisive for the indigenous peoples involved.

Aboriginal Law refers, in the first instance, to the ritual sphere and to the initiation processes followed by individuals based on their territorial and societal position. For the Goolarabooloo, this reference to the Law is essential as it is the induction of Paddy Roe (born in Nyikina country) into the ritual sphere of the Jabirr Jabirr, which confers on him and his descendants, who have followed a similar initiation process, a legal and moral legitimacy to speak for Jabirr Jabirr country. In this case, it also gives them the right – and responsibility – to fight tooth and claw to defend it from the gas project. As a Federal Court judgment stated "the claim by the Goolarabooloo to hold native title… depends on the incorporation of [the Roe] family, through Paddy Roe, into Jabirr Jabirr society" (cited by Burnside 2013). The reference to Aboriginal Law not only allowed the Roe family to be integrated into the Native Title procedures, but also to benefit from the special aura which comes from the supposed authenticity deriving from this ritual law.

Furthermore, the Roe family and its allies also mobilized the international law of indigenous peoples, in particular the UNDRIP. Although the Australian government had been late in supporting this Declaration, their ultimate support was nevertheless official, committing the state to certain responsibilities. The Goolarabooloo were the only ones in this debate to make explicit and direct reference to the Declaration, particularly the articles concerning the free, prior, and informed consent of indigenous peoples in decisions and projects by which they are directly affected. Like Aboriginal Law, the Declaration has no explicit (or direct) application in Australian Law, but it does confer a certain moral and political legitimacy, which explains in part the Roe family's ability to gather a large group of supporters in opposition to the project. For the other stakeholders in the controversy, the law of the Australian state should prevail in the negotiations, meaning the laws specifically established for the indigenous peoples of the continent, particularly the NTA 93. In Western Australia, these laws are the main mechanism for regulating land issues between indigenous peoples, the state, and third parties with interests in development projects affecting territories covered by a claim registered with the National Native Title Tribunal. The NTA is the KLC's *raison d'être* – it is a statutory organization in accordance with the NTA 93 – and for the state of Western Australia and Woodside, the NTA 93 was the framework offering them the greatest legal security.

The limits of native law in Australia: the NTA 93

It is the juridical framework of the NTA 93 that sets up the conundrum structuring this article: is it possible to receive justice in a legal framework that, if not unjust, is at least severely biased? Indeed, the limits of NTA 93 – a law that was negotiated between the Australian parliament and representatives of indigenous peoples in light of the Mabo no. 2 judgment – are many and well-known (Sutton 2003; Strelein 2009; Préaud 2011). This section will pick up on the main aspects of these limitations, which are due less to the law adopted in 1993 than to the amendments brought to it in 1998 (which were condemned at the international level),[9] and to the effects of the jurisprudence.

The first of these limitations is that Native Title is not, as its name would suggest, a property title, but only a set of more or less coherent rights and interests that the claimant groups must demonstrate individually. In addition, this demonstration requires that claimant groups conform to an image of Aboriginal society and its laws that relies on an anthropological model (Radcliffe-Brown's) which ethnography has long since shown to be abstract and obsolete (Dousset and Glaskin 2007). It is in this sense that Patrick Wolfe (1994) speaks about Native Title in terms of "repressive authenticity" and Elizabeth Povinelli (2002) of a "ruse of recognition" – both refer to the observation that for Aboriginal societies seeking native title, a large portion of recent history must be eradicated, or at least obscured, because any disparity with the model risks voiding the claim. In a place like the Dampier Peninsula, which received stolen children and refugees from all over Kimberley, and where new alliances and relations have been formed (as we saw with the induction of the Roe family into the local ritual system) it is an eminently problematic situation.

A second political limitation comes from the fact that, although the Aboriginal claimants must take upon themselves the burden of proof of demonstrating the existence of a precolonial society with continuous cultural and territorial

9 In March 1999, the Committee for the Elimination of Racial Discrimination established that, with respect to the International Convention on the Elimination of All Forms of Racial Discrimination, the amendments of the NTA 93 by the Australian government contravened Australia's international obligations: UN Doc CERD/C/54/Misc.40/Rev.2, Committee on the Elimination of Racial Discrimination, *Decision (2)54 on Australia – Concluding observations/comments*, 18 March 1999.

relations through to the present day, this society does not obtain any formal recognition following a legal victory (Wyatt 2014). The claimant group is not considered a society in political terms but simply changes into a corporation responsible for managing the rights and interests that have been painfully obtained at the end of a long and costly process.

Finally, at a more operational level, while the registration of a claim with the National Native Title Tribunal – whose conditions were made much stricter by the 1998 amendments – opens a right to negotiate for the claimant group, it does not in any instance allow for a veto against the project. It is precisely to this point that the government of Western Australia appealed to speed up the negotiations, as they threatened to refer the question to the NNTT at the end of the 6 months allowed by the law – the NNTT whose jurisprudence is very favorable to industrial interests. In other words, the NTA 93 does not in any way guarantee a procedure which measures up to the *minimum* standard established by the UNDRIP – free, prior, and informed consent on the part of the indigenous peoples. Furthermore, it provides a framework in which the government of Western Australia was able to impose a negotiation with a metaphorical gun to the head of the KLC, making the position of the latter untenable and imposing on them a choiceless decision.

The NTA 93 replaced the doctrine of *terra nullius*, which had enabled the *a posteriori* justification in law of the acquisition of sovereignty by the British Crown, with a doctrine that the Parliament can, with valid actions, legitimately extinguish native title. This title is not a title of ownership, it offers no form of political recognition to the societies which have nonetheless had to prove their existence, and it constitutes a negotiating framework through which to force the hand of clearly disadvantaged groups.

In these conditions, it is not surprising that the gas project's opponents should have drawn on all the legal means at their disposal in their media and political mobilization: internal submissions against the relevant procedures of the NTA 93 (like Joseph Roe's eviction from the list of named claimants) appeals to common law (to challenge the unilateral acquisition procedure for the plot by the government and the impact study carried out by the federal Environment Protection Authority), or the assertion of local sovereignty (opening a tent embassy at Walmadany).[10] It was not, therefore, the alternative legal references they mobilized – Aboriginal Law and the UNDRIP – which led to the abandonment of the project, but the use of legal appeals to slow down the conclusion of the decision-making process, combined with the change in the price of gas on the international markets.

10 The tent embassy of Canberra was erected in 1972 and is a lasting symbol of the self-determination of Aboriginal peoples and the islanders of the Torres Strait. It has spread in recent years to different towns and regions of Australia in the context of renewed indigenous activism. For more information, see the site http://www.nationalunitygovernment.org (last accessed October 2016).

Dimensions of indigeneity

This overview of the ways in which the different groups concerned appealed to the law allows us to suggest an analytical cartography of the political field covered by the notion of indigeneity in Australia – sketched out in Figure 8.1. This relational diagram identifies different institutions – the state, indigenous communities, international institutions – each of which refers to specific communities, geographical levels, and systems (political and representative); it also describes the different ways in which these institutions organize the representation of those who are primarily concerned by indigeneity. So, in this analytical frame, the term "indigenous peoples" constitutes a central reference, whose definition is at stake; in contrast, the notion of "community" refers more directly to the relation between the state and the variously constituted indigenous communities (communities, organizations, networks, etc.).

In addition, the analysis of the interplay of stakeholders around the Walmadany gas project makes it necessary to distinguish different systems – both relating to the sphere of representations, as well as to the political practice connected with it. In this framework, it is important to isolate a "native system" underpinning the behavior of the settler state with respect to the indigenous peoples; here, this refers to distinct judicial systems (like the NTA 93) as well as to specific public policies based on representations that make them acceptable

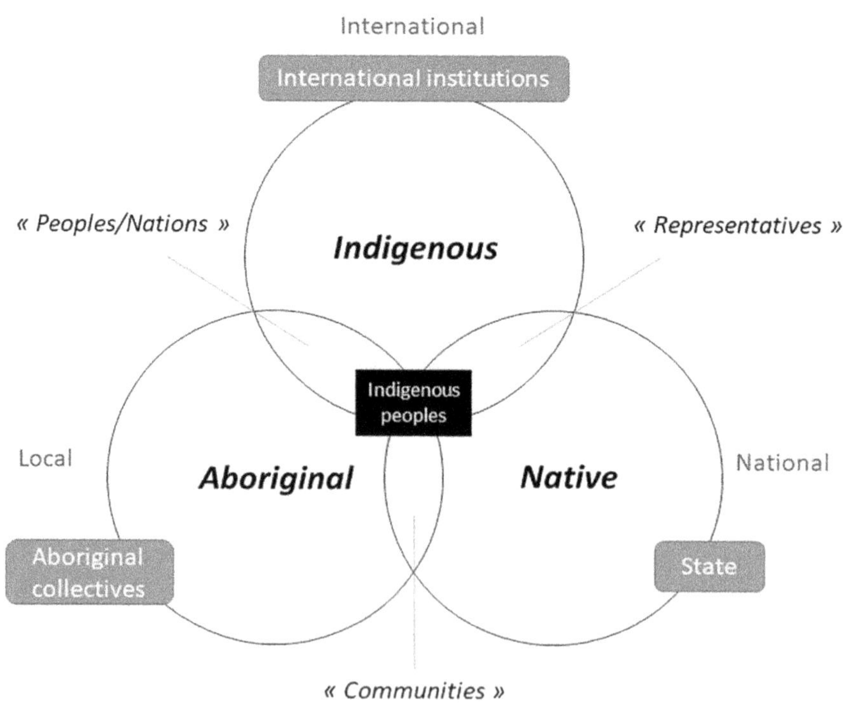

Figure 8.1 Indigeneity: comprehensive analytical framework.

to the Australian population. This system of the *indigénat* (to reference French colonial practice and underline its racial foundation, embodied by the Federal Constitution of 1901), operates within larger systems – the Australian state (its development policies or common law, for example), and the global geopolitical system (its raw-materials markets and its migratory flows, for example). In other words, the native system is only one component of the whole Australian legal system. I will return to this in the conclusion.

It is important to note that this "native system" is distinct from the system of international institutions addressing indigenous peoples' rights. Australian governments, especially that of Tony Abbott (elected in 2013), have maintained highly ambivalent relations with international human rights institutions in general (see, for example, the recent convictions in accordance with the United Nations Convention against Torture) – a stance that continues today. Through these international institutions, indigenous peoples have been constituted as legal subjects – especially through the UNDRIP, and in the understanding of the dedicated organs of the United Nations (The Permanent Forum on Indigenous Questions, The Expert Mechanism on the Rights of Indigenous Peoples) – thus setting up a system which itself proceeds according to representations, negotiations and specific political practices. These are quite removed from the territories that brought them into being, where the daily realities, along with the challenges encountered and the forms of organization mobilized in response, are more obviously rooted in the histories and practices of indigenous societies (ritual, kinship, subaltern history: for an example of an Aboriginal system see Doring and Nyawarra 2014).

The notion of *indigeneity*, therefore, far from describing a set of characteristics belonging to certain people or groups, actually covers a differentiated political field, a relational field polarized by the actual meaning attributed to the sovereignty or self-determination of infra-state communities separated by history and practical politics from the national communities around them.

Conclusion: justice and settlement colonization

This chapter has described the controversy around an industrial project on Aboriginal country at Walmadany/James Price Point. The unfolding of this dispute between 2008 and 2013 generated a set of stakeholders that broke with the reductive dichotomy of "state vs. indigenous people." This was not simply because the state, especially the federal state, is not a homogenous institution, but also because the very concept of *indigenous peoples* includes varied forms of collective organization (representative organizations, groups of claimants, activist networks, etc.) with distinct interests, objectives, and strategies. The highlighting of the juridical references and forms of action adopted by these different stakeholders shows the importance of common law as the ultimate recourse for indigenous peoples, rather than the native laws that specifically define the rights accorded to "native peoples." The functioning of the latter, particularly the NTA, demonstrates how what is presented by the state as the right of indigenous peoples can become the means of their continued repression, following the cultural logic of elimination characteristic of settler states. This analysis led me to suggest an analytical cartography of the political field of indigeneity in Australia. This model clearly distinguishes the different systems, actors and institutions contributing to the debate on the current situation and the future of "indigenous peoples." The aim is to bring to light the mechanisms by which the recognition of indigenous peoples, when it is undertaken by a settler state, can lead to the continuation of the *status quo* of inequalities – or to the worsening of their situation.

The system of the *indigénat* prevails in a federal state whose history is the history of settlement colonies aiming for political autonomy. In this framework, even the recourse to common law can be no guarantee for indigenous peoples who, while they have won certain victories as citizens, are always brought back to their native condition, the more so since there is no charter of fundamental rights in Australia.[11] In 2014 Colin Barnett announced the closing down of hundreds of communities in Australia, through the removal of water and electricity services, mostly in the Kimberley with several others on the Dampier Peninsula. This had an explosive effect in indigenous circles, with its forced displacements, its breaking of territorial bonds, and its serious social implications – but it was not altogether surprising in this context. Such moves are a consequence of the return of legal authority to the states of the federation from the federal state. They are also integral to the logic of state governments (in Southern Australia as well as Western Australia) which, while garnering the benefits of the growth in mining activities, are very happy to condemn the exorbitant costs of minimal public services for indigenous communities, even as they continue to finance similar infrastructure for non-indigenous people. This is part of an ongoing story in the Australian system, which has only very rarely produced significant progress for the Aborigines and Torres Straits Islanders – it is proof that a settler system persists in Australia. The backlash may be a new impetus in the creation of a more unified front, and a more fully engaged indigenous mobilization.

References

Altman, Jon. 2014. "Economie et écologie politique des droits sur la terre des autochtones en Australie" In *Terres, territoires, ressources: politiques, pratiques et droits des peuples autochtones*, eduted by Irène Bellier, 47–68. Paris: L'Harmattan, collection Horizons autochtones.

11 A constitutional reform proposition seeking the recognition of indigenous peoples in the Australian Constitution was announced in 2013 and has given rise to a significant media campaign under the slogan "Recognize." Different forms have been debated, from simply mentioning the prior presence of indigenous peoples in the Preamble, to the actual registration of their rights in the main body of the Constitution, with other suggestions in between. Fearing a purely symbolic gesture, many indigenous organizations are opposed to this reform and are reviving the call for an actual treaty between Australia and its indigenous peoples.

Bourdieu, Pierre. 1994. *Raisons pratiques: sur la théorie de l'action*. Paris: Seuil.

Burnside, Sarah. 2013. "James Price Point: Victory or Loss?" *Arena Magazine*. http://arena.org.au/james-price-point-victory-or-loss/ (last accessed 20 February 2018).

Doring, Jeff, and Paddy Nyawarra. 2014. "Gwion Artists and Wunan Law: The Origin of Society in Australia." *Rock Art Research* 31 (1): 3–13.

Dousset, Laurent, and Katie Glaskin. 2007. "Western Desert and Native Title: How Models Become Myths." *Anthropological Forum* 17 (2): 127–148.

Glowczewski, Barbara. 2004. *Rêves en Colère. Alliances aborigènes dans le Nord-Ouest australien*. Paris: Plon (Terre Humaine).

Government of Western Australia, Department of Mines and Petroleum. 2010. *Western Australian Mineral and Petroleum Digest 2009*. Perth: Government of Western Australia. http://www.dmp.wa.gov.au/Documents/About-Us-Careers/AboutUs-StatisticsDigest_2009.pdf (accessed 20 February 2019).

Government of Western Australia, Department of Mines and Petroleum. 2013. *Western Australian Mineral and Petroleum Digest 2012–2013*. Perth: Government of Western Australia. http://www.dmp.wa.gov.au/Documents/About-Us-Careers/AboutUs-StatisticsDigest_2012-13.pdf (accessed 20 February 2019).

Government of Western Australia, Department of Mines and Petroleum. 2018. *Western Australian Mineral and Petroleum Digest 2017–2018*. Perth: Government of Western Australia. http://www.dmp.wa.gov.au/Documents/About-Us-Careers/Stats_Digest_2017-18.pdf (accessed 20 February 2019).

Hawke, Stephen, and Michael Gallagher. 1989. *Noonkanbah: Whose Land, Whose Law*. Fremantle: Fremantle Arts Centre Press.

Martin, Wayne. 2015. "Indigenous Incarceration Rates: Strategies for Much Needed Reform." Speech, Perth, Supreme Court of Western Australia. http://www.supremecourt.wa.gov.au/_files/Speeches_Indigenous_Incarceration_Rates.pdf (accessed 19 December 2018).

Muir, Kathie. 2012. "Politics, Protest and Performativity: The Broome Community's 'No Gas on the Kimberley Coast' Campaign." *Australian Humanities Review* 53: 1–17. http://australianhumanitiesreview.org/2012/11/01/politics-protest-and-performativity-the-broome-communitys-no-gas-on-the-kimberley-coast-campaign/ (accessed 19 December 2018).

O'Faircheallaigh, Ciaran. 2013. "Registered Native Title Bodies Corporate and Mining Agreements: Capacities and Structures." In *Living with Native Title: The Experiences of Registered Native Title Corporations*, edited by Toni Bauman, Lisa Strelein, and Jessica Weir, 275–291. Canberra: Australian Institute of Aboriginal and Torres Strait Islander Studies.

Pedersen, Howard, and Banjo Woorunmurra. 1995. *Jandamarra and the Bunuba Resistance*. Broome, WA: Magabala Books.

Povinelli, Elizabeth. 2002. *The Cunning of Recognition: Indigenous Alterities and the Making of Australian Multiculturalism*. Durham, NC: Duke University Press.

Préaud, Martin. 2011. "La terre à plusieurs: territorialités autochtones et déterminations juridiques australiennes." *Multitudes* 41: 82–90.

Préaud, Martin, and Laurent Dousset. 2014. "Reconnaissance? Une critique anthropologique du cas australien," In *Les sciences humaines et sociales dans le Pacifique sud: Terrains, Questions, Methods*, edited by Laurent Dousset, Barbara Glowczewski, and Marie Salaün, 333–357. Marseille: PCP.

Roe, Paddy, Muecke Stephen, and Kim Bentarrak. 1984. *Reading the Country: Introduction to Nomadology*. Fremantle: Fremantle Arts Centre Press.

SCRGSP (Steering Committee for the Review of Government Service Provision). 2014. *Overcoming Indigenous Disadvantage: Key Indicators 2014*. Canberra: Productivity Commission. https://www.pc.gov.au/research/ongoing/overcoming-indigenous-disadvantage/2014 (accessed 20 January 2019).

Strelein, Lisa. 2009. *Compromised Jurisprudence: Native Title Cases Since Mabo* (2nd edition). Canberra: Aboriginal Studies Press.

Sutton, Peter, 2003. *Native Title in Australia: An Ethnographic Perspective*. Cambridge: Cambridge University Press.

Veracini, Lorenzo. 2010. *Settler Colonialism: A Theoretical Overview*. London, New York: Palgrave Macmillan.

Veracini, Lorenzo. 2011. "Introducing Settler Colonial Studies." *Settler Colonial Studies* 1 (1): 1–12.

Wolfe, Patrick. 1994. "Nation and MiscegeNation: Discursive Continuity in the Post-Mabo Era." *Social Analysis* 36: 93–152.

Wolfe, Patrick. 2006. "Settler Colonialism and the Elimination of the Native." *Journal of Genocide Research* 8 (4): 387–409.

Wyatt, Brian. 2014. "Protéger les droits, la culture et la tradition au sein d'une économie en croissance." In *Terres, territoires, ressources: politiques, pratiques et droits des peuples autochtones*, edited by Irène Bellier, 323–336. Paris: L'Harmattan, coll. Horizons autochtones.

Part III

Resisting processes of invisibilization

9 Criminalization and judicialization of indigenous peoples' rights in Chile

Current dynamics[1]

Leslie Cloud and Fabien Le Bonniec

Introduction

As they transitioned to democracy in the 1980s, most Latin American countries adopted a pluralist-minded constitutionalism. Although this approach aims to protect the rights of indigenous peoples to ancestral lands and territories, the number of environmental and territorial conflicts caused by development or extractive industries on the continent continues to multiply. This new scenario has led to the emergence of two new contemporary phenomena in which judges play an essential role, involving both the criminalization of indigenous persons mobilized to protect their lands, and the increased judicialization of these conflicts by the affected indigenous communities. Chile, though deeply affected by this dynamic, is an exception in the constitutional landscape of Latin America. As the leading neoliberal economy in the region, the country has not yet incorporated the rights of indigenous peoples into its constitution. This Chilean particularity exacerbates the lack of synchronization within the Chilean legal system – torn between the constitutionalized neoliberal economic model in place since the military dictatorship of Augusto Pinochet, and the rights of indigenous peoples recently recognized and weakly protected at an infra-constitutional level. To fully understand this dynamic, the Chilean exception in dealing with indigenous peoples' rights needs to be viewed in the context of the unique historical perspective of the Chilean state's founding.

As Chile moved toward independence, the southern territories, which were Mapuche lands, remained free under the treaties signed between the Spanish Crown and representatives of the Chilean government. In the twentieth century, neighboring countries such as Argentina, which was dedicated to liberalism, denied all rights to indigenous peoples based on the principle of equality. Meanwhile, the Mapuche lands in Chile, which were gradually granted individual land deeds, came under special schemes that fell outside of ordinary law. Finally, even though Chile was one of the last states in the region to ratify Convention 169 of the International Labour Organization concerning the rights of indigenous and tribal peoples (C169) in 2008, it was also among the first to adopt laws on the

1 Translated by Cadenza Academic Translations, revised by Jennifer Hays, and the authors.

principle of consultation and free, prior, and informed consent, and as a result, also one of the first to have legally ruled on this issue. These Chilean paradoxes make the country today a laboratory for the instrumentalization of the international rights of indigenous peoples by the state, and by the indigenous peoples themselves.

In this context, the emergence of the Mapuche movement over the last 20 years onto the public and media scene in Chile, by way of their land and political claims, has had a range of repercussions. Indeed, this period has also been characterized by multiple initiatives put forth by a succession of different democratic governments that recognized the multicultural nature of the country and its "historic debt" to the indigenous peoples, especially the Mapuche. As Michael Barbut (Barbut 2015) indicates, the Mapuche have represented a twofold challenge for "Chilean-style democratization." This challenge has first been economic; the Mapuche population was among the poorest in Chile, and it also needed to benefit from the "Miracle of Chile." Second, it was a moral challenge, since every modern democracy is obligated to recognize human rights – especially those of indigenous peoples.

The policy of purchasing land was presented as addressing these challenges. However, at the same time, various programs and legal measures were implemented that would lead to the "proper development" of these indigenous populations and their territory, and as a result, to their better integration into the country's economy. Public policies shifted between the paradigms of interculturalism and multiculturalism, primarily in the areas of health care, development, and education, but without successfully meeting the political demands of a Mapuche social movement that grew during the 2000s (see also González González, this volume). The neoliberal nature of these indigenous policies did not allow for addressing issues as fundamental as the reproduction of the socio-racial asymmetries and inequalities they masked, the autonomy and self-determination of the Mapuche people, or the protection of their territories occupied or threatened by extractive companies (Cuadra Montoya 2014).

The differentialism enacted by neoliberal multiculturalism (Bolados and Boccara 2014) becomes visible, not only in the effect of essentialization – evident in the oppositions established between the *authentic* and the *inauthentic*, or the *indigenous* and the *non-indigenous* – but also within the indigenous social world itself. Media and political leaders have thus spoken of the existence of a "Mapuche conflict," making a distinction between cooperative Mapuche populations participating in public policies and those who are more reticent to do so – the so-called "rebel Indians" who oppose development methods unilaterally decided on by the state. This mistrust can be explained in part by the history of relations between the Mapuche, larger society, and the Chilean state (Correa and Mella 2010), a history that has been marred by various forms of physical and symbolic violence that continue today. The most striking of these are the unequal distribution of wealth suffered by the indigenous populations, the reproduction of various asymmetries within Chilean society (Salas and Le Bonniec 2015), and the persistence of latent racism, especially in the justice system.

Such a symbolic division of the social indigenous world has had effects on the treatment and dominant representations of two fictional categories of the population, constituted on the one hand by the *indio permitido* (permitted Indian) or "project Indian," and, on the other hand, by the "terrorist Indian" (Hale and Millamán 2006). Within the same macro-regional space in southern Chile, indigenous territories have been created in parallel, some of which are to be "ethno-developed" and others to be pacified.[2] In a geopolitical context marked by public indigenous mobilization leading to an increasing number of violent encounters between communities inhabitants,[3] forest rangers, and large property owners, the state has drawn upon the law and its actors in order to deal with conflicts that are more political than legal.

In order to understand the current dynamics of criminalization and the judicialization of indigenous peoples' rights, the section below will first examine the way in which the Mapuche have responded to the territorial dispossession they have experienced since the nineteenth century, a response mainly involving a repertoire of legal and political actions. We will then present the range of public policies that were implemented to try to compensate for this dispossession, but which provoked various controversies leading to different forms of judicialization. This has both manifested itself in the criminalization of Mapuche territorial demands, and been reflected in the increasingly frequent appeal by indigenous peoples to the courts with the goal of protecting their lands and gaining recognition for their normativity. The effects of both the criminalization of the Mapuche, and their own use of the judicial system, represent a challenge for Chilean law, and call on it to consider, and recognize, indigenous peoples, their territoriality, and their ways of life.

Indigenous lands: from dispossession to the recognition of rights to lands and territories

Although set in motion from the time of Independence (1810–1818), the main dispossession of Mapuche lands did not take place until indigenous territories were conquered militarily in the second half of the nineteenth century. From this period on, the granting of ownership deeds to European or Chilean settlers for Mapuche lands sanctioned the usurpation of the majority of historical territories. It would take another century, until the end of the military dictatorship in 1980,

2 The idea of the "pacification" of the Mapuche land and its inhabitants was a key feature of the military campaign conducted at the end of the nineteenth century (1868–1883), called the "Pacification of the Araucania," which was the precursor for putting indigenous lands into reserves (*reducciones*).

3 The indigenous community is defined by Article 9 of law No. 19.253 of 1993 as "any group of persons belonging to the same indigenous ethnic group and that find themselves in at least one of the following situations: they are from the same family branch (a); they recognize a traditional chief (b); they possess or did possess share indigenous land (c); they come from the same ancient settlement area (d)." Translation by the authors.

before the rights to reclaim these lands were recognized through indigenous law No. 19.253 of 1993, and especially C169, ratified in 2008.

History of the dispossession of Mapuche lands

Several studies (Bengoa 2000; Comisión Verdad Histórica y Nuevo Trato con los Pueblos Indígenas 2008; Correa, Molina, and Yañez 2005) have given an account of the relatively recent history of the Mapuche experience of territorial plundering. This dispossession was primarily carried out through three successive and corollary events. During the first half of the nineteenth century, "the infiltration of the *frontera*" (Leiva 1984: 42–53) allowed colonists and the mestizo to illegally capture the lands situated in Mapuche territory. This was followed by a military conquest, ironically named the "Pacification of the Araucania" (1868–1883). Finally, toward the end of the nineteenth century, the Chilean state granted collective property deeds, called *Titulos de Merced* ("titles of favor"), a gesture that can be considered as foundational for contemporary legal Mapuche communities. The policy of subjugating persons and land reservation resulted in a 90% to 95% reduction of the historical Mapuche territory.[4] In many cases, the granting of communal deeds by a special commission simply ratified and legalized illicit appropriations. Even worse, as Victor Toledo has indicated (Toledo 2006), in the early twentieth century, the creation of large colonizing companies responsible for populating these vast territories with European populations was encouraged in order to make the land "productive," to the detriment of indigenous populations. Furthermore, during the twentieth century, land recognized as communal and indigenous, and thus supposed to be inviolable, passed in a more or less fraudulent way into the hands of *latifundista*, large land owners.

From that point on, just three decades after their military defeat and forced assimilation into the Chilean population, educated Mapuche living in the city organized themselves and established their first organizations such as the Sociedad Caupolican (1910) and the Federación Araucana (1916), which shared the mission to fight against the various forms of territorial plundering their people had experienced. These organizations denounced the destructuring caused by the establishment of collective property deeds and by the bureaucratization of intra- and inter-community social ties that followed. Paradoxically, this was because the legal recognition of these communal titles ultimately subjected the Mapuche populations to the regime of private property, a notion that until that point had been foreign to them, as was communitarianism (Míguez Núnez 2013). The large number of complaints and denunciations indicating abuses and misappropriations involving the selling of indigenous land was the

4 This corresponds to the distribution of around 3,000 community property deeds for a total surface area of 475,194 hectares (Comisión Verdad Histórica y Nuevo Trato con los Pueblos Indígenas 2008).

subject of various reports, and many debates within the Chilean parliament – where Mapuche organizations had succeeded in obtaining political representation (Foerster and Montecino 1988). In the 1930s, this enabled the passing of laws and decrees that were supposed to strengthen the protection of Mapuche land and offer legal provisions for reclaiming land that had been usurped. The main function of the five *Juzgados de Indios* (1930–1972 "Indian Courts") – established in this new context and dedicated to the division of communities and the resolution of issues involving succession, possession, and land inheritance – was to resolve problems caused by putting land in reserve, and in particular land conflicts with individuals. In fact, they only succeeded in increasing the frustration of many community inhabitants and their feelings of injustice. While some of the complaints were ignored, on others action was taken in favor of those who had invaded the indigenous land. It is estimated that 100,000 ha of reserved lands passed into the hand of non-indigenous individuals during this period (Ormeño and Osses 1972).

The enthusiasm of many communities for the agrarian reform undertaken in Chile during the 1960s can thus be understood. The inhabitants saw it as an opportunity to access the land that had belonged to them – although their motivation was quite different from that of Chilean farmers, who were claiming the land for "those who farmed it" (Correa, Molina, and Yañez 2005; Le Bonniec 2014a). This reform, undertaken by three different governments (1962–1972), sought to change the so-called feudal agrarian structures of the country by tackling inequality in the matter of land ownership through redistribution and collectivization, to the benefit of farmers and agricultural workers. Taken to its highest point by the Popular Unity government (1970–1973), agrarian reform led to various farmer mobilizations supported by far-left movements; the most well-known of these are the *tomas*, actions that involved occupying large properties with the aim of accelerating expropriation procedures. Numerous communities participated in these *tomas* while also deploying their own mobilization modalities, as evidenced by the *corridas de cercos* ("moving fences") with the goal of re-establishing the boundaries of the original community deeds (Bastias 2009). This important process of redefining agrarian structures and distributing land ownership became connected to the historical demands of the Mapuche communities, which resulted in the recovery of approximately 200,000 ha of land (Correa, Molina, and Yañez 2005). These illegal rural occupations were not exempt from violence, whether it was committed by the occupants of the *latifundios* or by the militias prompted by their owners to disrupt the *tomas*. These occupations were labeled "land takeovers" and subjected to an ongoing smear campaign by the national and regional press that called, with a united voice and in support of the unions of agricultural owners and conservative parties, for the rule of law to be re-established. The mobilizations, however, enjoyed a level of tolerance by the Popular Unity government, which often preferred a political resolution to conflicts rather than police or legal repression. This stands in stark contrast to the crackdown that took place across the entire country from

September 11, 1973:[5] of the 220,000 ha recovered between 1962 and 1973, 90% of the land was returned to its previous owner or ceded to the state, which sold it off to lumber companies.

This historical overview reveals the roots of current legal or political community struggles for the land that was taken from them during the twentieth century. This fight, with few successes and numerous setbacks, affected several generations, especially those who had to migrate to the city. The dictatorship imposed a "respite" in this struggle for communal lands, forcing a withdrawal that allowed for a renewal in the anti-establishment repertoire both at the level of praxis and discourse, and signaled a movement from the issue of the *land* to that of *territory* and *autonomy*, in large part due to the internationalization of the Mapuche movement (Guevara and Le Bonniec 2008). At the end of the dictatorship in 1990, it was therefore not surprising to see the re-emergence of a Mapuche movement that had not given up on recovering their ancient communal lands, and had integrated their claim into the political issues affecting democratic states at that time. As a result, the state and Chilean society had to re-examine their relations with the Mapuche, a very difficult task given that the country's elites and structures had been characterized by their authoritarianism and monoculturalism.

From indigenous Law No. 19.253 to the ratification of Convention No. 169 of the ILO: a fragile recognition of land rights

The end of the Chilean dictatorship coincided with the period during which the rights of indigenous peoples came to the fore at international and regional levels, energized by the adoption of C169 in 1989. This convention was ratified by the majority of countries in the region and was accompanied by pluralist-minded constitutional reforms. This period had a minor impact on Chile through the Nueva Imperial Agreement of December 1, 1989. This agreement between Patricio Aylwin, the candidate for the chairmanship of the Concertación parties,[6] and representatives of the Aymara, Rapanui, and Mapuche peoples, committed them to supporting the future Concertación government. In return, the parties promised to constitutionally recognize indigenous peoples, ratify C169, create a national commission for indigenous development (the future Corporación Nacional de Desarrollo Indígena–CONADI) responsible for indigenous public policy, and establish a special commission for indigenous peoples, in order

5 A recent report (Curiñir Lincoqueo 2016) written by historian Hernan Curiñir Lincoqueo with the help of Pablo Silva Carrasco and Conrado Zumelzu Zumelzu for the Institut National des Droits de l'Homme (INDH) indicates that there were at least 170 disappeared prisoners of Mapuche origin, most of them having fallen victim to the repression in a rural environment during the first weeks of the dictatorship.

6 The "Concertación de Partidos por la Democracia," known as the "Concertación," is a coalition of socio-liberal political parties, composed of the Socialist Party (PS), Radical Social-Democrat Party (PRSD) and the Christian-Democrat Party (PDC).

to study ways to incorporate proposals by indigenous organizations party to the future government's program.

However, two decades later, only the latter two commitments have been accomplished, and these only partially. A neo-indigenist law, known as indigenous law No. 19.253 (*ley sobre fomento, protección y desarrollo de los indígenas*) was adopted in 1993. It covers a range of issues intended to promote the social, economic, and cultural development of the "ethnic groups of Chile," including land ownership, health care, and education; and the organization of indigenous peoples into associations or communities. In particular, it provides for the recognition of Chilean "ethnic groups" and of indigenous "communities," and a scheme for the protection of indigenous lands as well as specific provisions for access to land and water. The law strategically avoids referring to the concept of "indigenous territory" and natural resources, by limiting itself to the recognition of indigenous peoples' rights to land and, under certain conditions, to water. The discussions preceding the adoption of the law in question introduced the possibility for an indigenous territory separate from the national territory; however, during the debates between indigenous organizations, legislators, and government representatives, the concept of indigenous territory was erased, and in the end disappeared from the final version. As a result, in law No. 19.253, the only references to territory strictly concern the national territory.

The law implemented a Fund for Indigenous Land and Water, administered by CONADI, which established mechanisms intended for the purchase of ancestral lands in the public domain or that today belong to non-indigenous third parties (Articles 20 to 21). These provisions were subject to much criticism. Their implementation often led to the division and relocation of beneficiary indigenous communities (Cloud and Le Bonniec 2012: 31). Approximately 137,000 ha were returned to Mapuche through these mechanisms,[7] but they were insufficient to meet the demand that covered all of the ancestral indigenous lands. Although to a certain degree these provisions have made it possible to increase the surface area of indigenous land, they do not cover all of the property claims that fall outside the scope of the law's provisions, which has led to actions for territorial recovery being violently repressed (Cloud and Le Bonniec 2012: 31).

Finally, this *ley indígena* has been criticized for its inability to ensure the legal and environmental protection of indigenous lands. Only a few years after it came into effect, law No. 19.253 revealed its limitations in dealing with the Ralco hydroelectric plant, on which work began in 1994. While the law speaks of a "special interest" as the foundation for the protection of indigenous lands, in this case, the judges determined that "the national interest" in the production of

7 According to a 2015 report by the International Work Group for Indigenous Affairs (IWGIA), between 1994 and 2014, 17,527 hectares were acquired by the Fund for Indigenous Land and Water (Article 20a) to be granted by lots attributed, for the most part, to Mapuche people. In addition, in accordance with the mechanism for the restitution of land from usurped land (Article 20b), 120,322 hectares have been returned, of which 119,886 has gone to Mapuche people (IWGIA 2015, 210).

electricity was superior to any "special interest," thereby justifying the flooding of indigenous lands with water from the dam. This scenario showed how far the rights protected by law No. 19.253 were from the standards established by international law for indigenous peoples at the time (including C169 and case law of the Commission and the Inter-American Court for Human Rights, IACHR). Over the last few years, in applying the Chilean neoliberal economic model that is outlined in the Constitution and framed by a series of codes and constitutional organic laws adopted under the military dictatorship of Pinochet,[8] there has been a marked increase of development, infrastructure, and extractive projects on indigenous lands, with or without property deeds. Protected by these norms, the country's strong economic development during this period has primarily involved mining resources in the north, especially copper, as well as the timber industry and fisheries in the south. These various activities all depend on the exploitation of natural resources that extend into Mapuche territory. The mining industry requires a significant amount of electricity[9] which is mostly produced by hydroelectric plants situated in the south of the country, where there are also a large number of forest properties and fish farms.

In this context, the provisions of the law urgently needed to be strengthened in order to fight against the impact that economic provisions, which were constitutional, would have on indigenous lands. This strengthening came 20 years after the end of the dictatorship with the ratification of C169 in 2009,[10] which introduced into Chilean law a series of collective rights such as the right to participation, the right to consultation and "free, prior, and informed consent" (FPIC), and rights to the lands and territories traditionally used and occupied. These two latter rights in particular provided an essential contribution in the context of Chilean land ownership. Articles 13 to 15 of C169 provided for property and possession rights on the lands traditionally occupied by indigenous peoples the protection of rights to natural resources, and the right of indigenous peoples to participate in the management of the natural resources on their land. Article 6, the basis of the judicialization of the rights of indigenous peoples in Chile, included the obligation for governments to "consult the peoples concerned, through appropriate procedures and in particular through their representative institutions, whenever consideration is being given to legislative or administrative measures which may affect them directly" further noting that "the consultations carried out in application of this Convention shall be

8 In particular the Water Code of 1981 (reformed in 2005) the Mining Code of 1983, and the general law on electrical services of 1982 (reformed in 2006).

9 According to the National Statistics Institute (INE 2011), the copper mining industry has, since the 1990s, required more and more electricity, and now represents 34.9% of consumption nationally. This increase in electrical consumption corresponds to an energy crisis that has spread throughout the country during this same period. In response to this crisis, power stations have been built in the southern part of the country.

10 The authorities had long opposed the ratification of C169, by blocking its adoption or by trying to neutralize its scope. On this point, see the analysis by Observatorio Ciudadano (2010).

undertaken, in good faith and in a form appropriate to the circumstances, with the objective of achieving agreement or consent to the proposed measures."

It was necessary for these new provisions to be implemented and respected by the Chilean state. Yet only Article 6 of the Convention, related to consultation and to FPIC, has been recognized by regulatory measures, contrary to international standards on the rights of indigenous peoples. In these circumstances, in which the executive and legislative authorities refused to take into account all the consequences involved in the recognition of the rights of indigenous peoples, the resolution of conflicts related to indigenous lands was handed over to the courts. This action gave rise to the increased judicialization of the rights of indigenous peoples, legal procedures in which indigenous peoples are either plaintiffs or defendants.

Increased judicialization of environmental and territorial conflicts: between criminalization and the search for protection

The absence of the recognition of ancestral rights to the land – which would enable Mapuche communities to confront the threats presented by extractive, development, and infrastructure industries on ancestral lands – is the source of the judicialization of these land ownership conflicts. It should be remembered that "indigenous law" only allows for the recovery of lands previously granted under the form of a *Merced* or Commissioner deed,[11] which excludes the majority of lands belonging historically to the Mapuche. This situation conflicts with international law relating to indigenous peoples and the case law of the Inter-American Court of Human Rights, which recognizes, for example, the rights of indigenous peoples to traditionally occupied land (that has since been dispossessed or confiscated) when they maintain a cultural link with the land. These conflicts related to land ownership have led to the judicialization of territorial conflicts and the rights of indigenous peoples from two perspectives. On the one hand, indigenous peoples have sought remedies in the courts by presenting *recurso de amparo* (a writ of protection)[12] to demand the voiding of illegal or arbitrary acts or omissions that allowed for the implementation of a development, infrastructure, or extractive project on their ancestral lands, in violation of their right to consultation and FPIC sanctioned in C169. On the other hand, indigenous people have been accused of criminal or terrorist actions for mobilizations organized

11 Commissioner deeds refer here to property deeds granted to the Huilliche Mapuche between 1824 and 1848, primarily in the towns of La Unión, Remehue, Pilmaiquen, Lago Ranco, and San Juan de la Costa (Comisión Verdad Histórica y Nuevo Trato con los Pueblos Indígenas 2008, 449).

12 In Chilean law, in accordance with Article 20 of the Constitution, an appeal for protection – which in Latin America falls under the category of appeals for *amparo* – is a constitutional action that enables seeking in the courts the immediate cessation of the violation of a fundamental right protected by Article 19 of the constitution, and which would be altered or threatened by an arbitrary or illegal act or omission.

with a view to the recovery or protection of their historical lands. Insofar as these actions go against the economic order protected by the constitution, the indigenous peoples, now criminalized, have become "enemies of the law."[13]

The criminalization of Mapuche territorial claims

At the beginning of the 2000s, while Chile was reforming penal procedures in the pilot region of Araucania, the issue concerning the criminalization of Mapuche territorial demands arose in the public discourse of Mapuche organizations (Le Bonniec 2003). These organizations highlighted "martyrs" and "Mapuche political prisoners" who were victims of the repression. While there is no doubt that the state's repressive action came in response to a new praxis by a part of the Mapuche movement, which used violence not only in their discourse but also in their practices (Pairican 2014), this criminalization was disproportionate, and often blind and ineffective. Indeed, it reinforced the feelings of injustice and inequity before the law in the persons who were subjected to this repression as well as in the entire Mapuche collectivity (Le Bonniec 2014b).

The denunciation of the criminalization of Mapuche territorial demands was based first on the inappropriate application of security laws such as the internal state security law and especially law No. 18.314 on terrorist conduct. Through the application of this law alone, fifteen cases were tried between 2000 and 2013, a dozen of which involved the Mapuche and their claims.[14] Critics have primarily focused on the violations of the fundamental guarantees of the Mapuche defendants made possible through the use of exceptional procedures, such as the appearance of anonymous witnesses or not respecting the principle of presumed innocence. While the very notion of "terrorist conduct" (Vial 2013) can be debated, by questioning the relevance of associating it with a social movement such as the one led by the Mapuche communities, the controversy gradually spread to the Chilean social world. The stigma and prejudices concerning the Mapuche that were conveyed by the media and political authorities on a daily basis legitimized the use of the antiterrorist law and the symbolic and physical violence that went along with it. As demonstrated in the critical

13 Cloud, Leslie. 2015. "Entre homogénéité, monisme et pluralisme, enjeux et résistances du 'Mapuche permis' au Chili." Paper presented at the "Séminaire SOGIP: perspectives comparatives sur les droits de peuples autochtones 2014–2015," in session 3, "Les peuples autochtones face aux institutions: problématiques de subjectivation autour de 'l'Indien autorisé,'", Paris, France, January 8.

14 This estimate is based on various sources of information, especially those supplied by the public ministry for the Inter-American Court of Human Rights (IACHR 2014), those that appeared in the 2013 edition of the annual report on human rights by the University Diego Portales (UDP 2013) as well as the Chile mission report by the Special Rapporteur on the promotion of human rights and fundamental freedoms in the anti-terrorist fight, Ben Emmerson (UNHRC 2014), which indicates that the anti-terrorist law was applied on 19 occasions to 108 persons, who were, in the majority, related to Mapuche protests.

discourse analysis by Carlos del Valle (Del Valle 2014) and confirmed by the IACHR,[15] these prejudices were present in the convictions handed down.

More recent studies have focused on other aspects of criminalization that go well beyond the use of special laws, such as the disproportionate and unjustified use of violence during community police operations, violence against children (Faundes Peñafiel 2013), or the extensive time spent in custody by defendants who are often acquitted after a year in pre-trial detention. These studies reveal a differentiated legal treatment for residents of communities that mobilize to reclaim their dispossessed lands, either by occupying and using them, or by conducting public protests. Faced with this repressive policy, the Mapuche have used various "registers of resilience" such as an individual or collective "practical reservoir" (Offerlé 2008: 197) in order to deal with the courts and prison (Le Bonniec 2014b). Among these repertoires of action, ceremonies before the courts and in prisons, the use of the *mapudungun* language and appeals to anthropological experts during trials, as well as obtaining special treatment for political prisoners in prisons, are a few of the common practices used over the last fifteen years, notwithstanding difficulties and resistance on the part of the public authorities.

However, due to the increasing number of imprisonments in the context of territorial claims as well as a growing number of legal actions and grievances (especially in international forums, denouncing the absence of protections for Mapuche persons brought before the courts), some of these concerns have been reflected in public policies. In 2001, a special defense unit was created, the Mapuche Public Penal Defense, in order to provide legal assistance and the means to a fair trial, thanks in particular to the availability of "intercultural facilitators" (Le Bonniec 2015). Every year, lawyers from this specialized unit defend around 2,000 Mapuche persons in the Araucania region, with only a small percentage corresponding to infractions related to territorial claims. Among the initiatives taken to introduce interculturality into the courts and thus enable a more equitable trial, we can also point to the use of intercultural facilitators by the public

15 In its decision of May 29, 2014, case *Caso Norin Catriman y otros (dirigentes, miembros y activista del pueblo indígena mapuche) vs. Chile*, the IACHR ruled on an appeal presented by a group of seven Mapuche and one sympathizer with the Mapuche cause, who had been sentenced to between five and ten years in prison after having been found guilty of "terrorist threats of arson," "terrorist arson," and "terrorist conduct." In this case, the Court agreed that the Chilean state had violated the principles of legality, the right to the presumption of innocence, the right to a defense, the right to individual freedom, the freedom of thought and expression, political rights, and the protection of the family. Furthermore, the Court considered that only using arguments based on stereotypes and prejudice as the basis for sentencing demonstrated a violation of the principle of fairness and non-discrimination. Most notably, it ordered that the rulings be annulled as well as penalties involving the deprivation of liberty and supplementary penalties, and that the victims who were still subject to conditional liberty be freed. Similarly, the state had to eliminate the legal, administrative, penal, or police case histories that existed against the eight victims in the case, as well as their registration on any kind of national or international list that linked them to acts of a terrorist nature.

prosecutor in cases in which he is seeking to apply security laws against Mapuche persons. A special hearing room for cases involving the Mapuche has also been set up at the Court of Guarantee of Temuco.

During the bicentennial celebration of Chilean independence in 2010, 15 Mapuche political prisoners staged a hunger strike. This strike succeeded in its demands: to have the anti-terrorist law changed so that it no longer applied to minors, to move cases from military tribunals when the defendants were civilians, and to reduce the penalty for arson from a terrorist nature. This hunger strike created a measure of political consensus concerning the limits of anti-terrorist laws as the only way to resolve conflicts, noting that in such cases the conflicts had a tendency to multiply and become more radical. In spite of this consensus, successive governments have continued to invoke anti-terrorist laws against Mapuche persons accused of infractions related to the Mapuche conflict. Even if the term "terrorist" and the mention of anti-terrorist laws are dropped by the prosecution in the course of judicial proceedings, the accused continue to be stigmatized and can be sentenced for a common infraction using evidence gathered under anti-terrorist laws.

This persistence of criminalization can be explained structurally. It corresponds to a transformation of the penal model that has moved from the paradigm of *protections* to so-called *citizen security* (Lillo 2015), an observable trend throughout the country. In the southern regions, in a context close to a state of emergency, this evolution is visible in the repressive techniques characterized by the increase of a heavily armed police contingent tasked with protecting the forest and *latifundist* properties. This militarization, which was initially considered by neighboring communities as provocation and harassment, has finally become part of their landscape and daily life. The paradigm of an "internal enemy" and terrorism has been replaced by that of "rural violence," an expression currently used more and more by the media and the authorities to trivialize and naturalize various tensions caused by the regional conflicts and thus justify the state of exception and the militarization of the Mapuche communities.

At the same time as this criminalization, there has also been another form of judicialization before other Chilean courts, one undertaken by the indigenous peoples and the organizations that support them: the weaponization of the law as a way of resisting the socio-environmental threats weighing on their lands.

Advances, setbacks, and limits to the legal protection of indigenous lands[16]

As a legal strategy developed by indigenous communities to protect their lands, the judicialization of indigenous peoples' rights in territorial and environmental conflicts began with the approval of C169. Once the constitutional court

16 In this section dedicated to the analysis of case law adopted in the scope of the use of the justice system related to the protection of indigenous lands, we will examine all of the decisions related to indigenous lands, both Mapuche and non-Mapuche, since the case law on the matter reflects a general trend in the Courts in dealing with indigenous peoples' rights.

ruled in 2000 and 2008[17] in favor of the directly enforceable nature of Article 6 of the Convention related to consultation and FPIC, the defense attorneys for indigenous peoples went to court for any project involving the development, infrastructure, or extraction of natural resources on indigenous land that was not subject to any consultation with the indigenous populations concerned. They thus sought the cancellation of administrative or legislative measures related to these projects. In 2015, 6 years after C169 came into effect, the Supreme Court ruled 23 times on the right to consultation and FPIC (Fuenzalida Bascuñan 2015, 151). What assessment can today be made concerning the massive judicialization of the rights of indigenous peoples in Chile? It is worth analyzing the results from both a quantitative (number of legal actions won) and qualitative (type, nature, legal value of the right recognized, and intercultural interpretation of human rights) perspective.

The strategy to judicialize C169 began to achieve some success in the Courts of Appeal in 2010, a year after C169 came into effect in Chile.[18] However, three years of indecisive case law[19] passed before the Supreme Court ruled that there been an absence of consultation and FPIC in accordance with the standards of international law for indigenous peoples. These decisions, adopted in 2012–2013, made it possible to put several large projects on hold due to violations of Article 6 of C169.[20]

This situation was overshadowed, however, by a decision by the constitutional court, dated January 21, 2013[21] in which the judges confirmed the infra-constitutional and supra legal value of C169 and considered that the obligation for consultation was limited to situations specifically affecting indigenous interests. In this way, situations in which the indigenous peoples were not the sole

17 Decisions by the constitutional court of August 4, 2000 (roll No. 309-2000) and April 3, 2008 (roll No. 1050-2008). However, in its decision of 2008 (roll No. 1050), the constitutional court incorrectly interpreted Article 6 by indicating "that the purpose of the consultations is to arrive at an agreement concerning the measures proposed" but that it does not "imply an obligatory negotiation, but represents only a way to acquire their opinion, which is not restrictive and does not affect the private powers of the authorities which the Political Constitution of the Republic establishes" (Preamble 14). Translation by the authors.

18 We can cite the decision by the Court of Appeals (CA) in Concepción of August 6, 2010, *Presidente de comunidad de Chilcoco contra la Municipalidad de Arauco*; the decision by the CA in Temuco of January 21, 2010, *Puelman Ñanco Mariano y otro con Corema, IX Region*; the decision by the CA in Valdivia of August 4, 2010, *Manquepillan Faumeliza con Conama de la Región de los Ríos*; the decision by the CA of Puerto Montt of July 27, 2010, *Vera Millaquén y otro con Empresa Pesquera Los Fiordos Ltda*; the decision of the CA of Temuco of January 21, 2011, *Asociación indígena Tragun Mapu Maile Allipen contra* Comisión Evaluadora Ambiental, Región de la Araucanía; the decision by the CA in Antofagasta of February 17, 2012, *Comunidad Agrícola Los Huasco Altinos.*

19 See, for example, as a typical decision of this period, roll No. 4078-2010 [2009].

20 Roll No. 10.090-2011 [2012], *Parque Eólico Chiloé*; roll No. 11.040-2011 [2012] *Sondaje de Prospección Paguanta*; roll No. 2211-2012, *Estudio de Impacto Ambiental Proyecto el Morro*; roll No. 11.040-2011 [2012], *Sondaje de Prospección Paguanta*; roll No. 495-2013 [2013], *Newen*; roll No. 9526-2012 [2013], *Sollipulli*; roll No. 3010-2013 [2013], *Cementerio Topater.*

21 Decision by the Constitutional Court of January 23, 2013, roll No. 2387-13 [2013].

victims of damages caused were excluded from the application of FPIC. In spite of case law favorable to indigenous peoples in the *El Morro* judgment,[22] two new case law approaches by the Supreme Court would threaten compliance with the right to consultation and FPIC. On the one hand, the Court considered the conformity of the consultation and FPIC process to decree 124 (2009), on the "regulation of the participation and consultation of indigenous peoples," even though it had been widely criticized a few years earlier and replaced by the new law of consultation.[23] On the other hand, in 2012, the creation of three environmental courts in Arica, Santiago, and Valdivia seems to have provided the Court with a new pretext to avoid ruling on indigenous affairs; in numerous cases, in fact, it delegated knowledge of respecting consultation concerning environmental matters to the environmental courts, to the detriment of standardizing case law on this issue.[24]

Finally, if we consider the coming into effect of decree No. 40 (of the Ministry of the Environment, which regulates the environmental evaluation system and provides for a special consultation mechanism) and of decree No. 66 (which regulates the indigenous consultation procedure), in 2013 and 2014, respectively, we can see that these norms violate the standards of international law relating to indigenous peoples and that the consultation proceedings that conform to their regulations should suffice to carry the support of the courts (Cloud 2017). While overall results have been negative in terms of the effective judicialization of violations of indigenous lands, there have been collateral beneficial effects, caused by the increased invocation and protection of the rights of indigenous peoples in court.

Despite the absence of favorable case law regarding rights to indigenous territory and to consultation, the quality of the interpretation of indigenous peoples' rights, and the human rights of indigenous peoples in general, has slightly improved. During these years of judicialization, the interpretation of human rights has improved, particularly through association with the violations highlighted by indigenous peoples. We are thus seeing an extension of the range of fundamental rights considered to be violated during territorial conflicts. While at the beginning, violations of the right to the environment, and then equality before the law, were timidly invoked (because C169 of the ILO was not applied), other violations of rights in the constitution were gradually put forward, especially concerning the right to life, the freedom of worship and of property, and the right to economic activity.[25] An analysis of a sampling of decisions illustrates the gradual invocation and implementation of a variety of indigenous peoples rights (based on various articles of the Convention and the United Nations Declaration

22 Decision of October 7, 2014, roll No. 11.299.

23 Roll No. 1515-2014, *Proyecto de Agua Potable Rural Ko Winkul Pocura.*

24 Decision by the SC of April 22, 2014, *Proyecto de Agua Potable Rural Ko Winkul Pocura*, roll No. 1515-2014, and decision by the SC of August 12, 2014, *el proyecto de Manganeso Los Pumas*, roll No. 1712-2013.

25 From Cloud, Leslie. 2013. "Balance de la judicialización de los derechos de los pueblos indígenas en Chile desde la ratificación del Convenio 169 de la O.I.T. sobre los pueblos indígenas y tribales." Paper presented at the *Congreso ALAS*, Santiago de Chile, Chile, September 29–October 4.

on the rights of indigenous peoples-UNDRIP, as well as IACHR case law), unlike early appeals which were limited to invoking a violation of the right to consultation and FPIC. The specificity of the issues presented to the judges has led to the more frequent use of anthropological expertise. This expertise is not submitted as evidence in the decisions made, but it helps judges become familiar with another interpretation of human rights.

In spite of these positive observations, it must be emphasized that in several decisions, the Supreme Court has avoided the creation of case law in indigenous matters; in some cases, even as it ruled favorably for the indigenous cause, it insisted on erasing all of the recitals from the Courts of Appeal related to indigenous peoples rights.[26] Some decisions reveal the existence of a dialogue between the human rights recognized by the constitution and indigenous conceptions of the law based on the case of the Mapuche in the *Az Mapu*.[27] However, in most cases, this dialogue has not resulted in a recognition of the violations of the Mapuche's property rights; the same goes for the freedom of worship. However, based on a dynamic and evolutionary interpretation of the Convention of San José[28] in light of Convention 169 of the ILO and the Declaration, the case law of the Inter-American Court of Human Rights underscored the special and spiritual relationship of the indigenous peoples to the land and the inter-connection between rights to the lands, territories, and natural resources, property rights, the right to life, and the right to cultural integrity. In support of this, the Inter-American Court of Human Rights has adopted an evolutionary and dynamic interpretation of human rights in light of the international law relating to indigenous peoples, by using the theory of homeomorphic functional equivalencies by Raimon Panikkar (1984). This approach involves searching through human rights instruments for equivalent concepts belonging to indigenous juridical statutes and, at the same time, searching the indigenous juridical statutes for the concept or concepts that fulfill a similar function to that of human rights.

Final considerations

The work done before the courts by the indigenous peoples and their defense attorneys since the ratification of ILO C169 has changed the history of relations between the indigenous peoples and the Chilean justice system by, for the first time, making it possible to submit to the courts the existence of a law of indigenous peoples as well as indigenous juridical statutes. Several advances can

26 Most notably, the decision by the SC of November 30, 2009, *Linconao Huircapan con Sociedad Palermo Ltda*; and the decision by the SC of January 4, 2011 (*comunidad Puquiñe C. Corema*).

27 *Az*, "nature, way of being"; *mapu* "land." According to Mapuche cosmo-philosophy, the *Az Mapu* corresponds to the shapes and dynamics of the cosmos, that is, to cosmic law. On the *Az Mapu* and Mapuche conceptions of law, see Cloud (2009–2010), COTAM (2003), Antona Bustos (2014).

28 American Convention on Human Rights, adopted in San José, Costa Rica, on November 22, 1969.

be observed at the level of the Courts of Appeal, as well as preliminary considerations of the need to better understand the rights of indigenous peoples, in light of their interpretation internationally and from the point of view of fundamental rights. These premises for a dialogue between various legal cultures, which was initiated by the indigenous peoples themselves, facilitated the emergence and implementation of intercultural practices. We can cite here the introduction of anthropological expertise, the application of a model of indigenous penal defense, the intervention of intercultural facilitators at the penal level, and certain exceptional procedures authorizing the carrying out of indigenous ceremonies within prisons.

However, these new practices involving the recognition of an "indigenous culture" still have no impact on the recognition of an "indigenous territoriality." Furthermore, this new dialogue includes hidden shadows that may undermine it. In some cases, indigenous juridical statutes and C169 have been instrumentalized and stereotyped, as evidenced by the use of compensatory agreements in places where common law excluded it in matters of intra-familial violence or by the use of public apology as a form of traditional resolution of intra-community conflicts. Finally, in order to understand and measure the harm suffered, indigenous plaintiffs and defense attorneys have been obliged to present to judges their knowledge concerning the dynamics of the *Az Mapu* (cosmic law), which until then had been preserved by the holders of traditional knowledge, with the goal of preserving their cultural integrity and the balance of their environment; they worry today that this knowledge will be exploited against them, by jeopardizing, for example, their traditional authority, certain medicinal plants, and ceremonial spaces. The successes achieved by the dialogue between cultures and standards taking place before the courts are hindered by the cultural characteristics of the judicial body itself.

It should be recalled that Chilean judicial authority is characterized by an extremely legalistic position that is resistant to the recognition of collective rights. Until the creation of the *recurso de amparo*, the Supreme Court refused to control the acts of the three other authorities by sheltering itself behind the role of an administrator of justice. In so doing, it positioned itself at the opposite end of a strong judiciary authority within which judges assume roles that have political impact. In Chile, there is also no suitable method for interpreting the constitution: it continues to be read through the interpretative approach provided by the Civil Code, thereby hindering any dynamic interpretation that would be favorable toward fundamental law in agreement with Convention 169 of the ILO and any binding international developments of the rights of indigenous peoples. The highly centralized nature of Chilean justice also does not encourage dialogue on rights, given that the Supreme Court in Santiago is located several hundred kilometers away from ancestral indigenous territories. It seems that the understanding of indigenous peoples' rights is proportional to the distance that separates indigenous territories from the Supreme Court.

The current panorama of judicialization involving the territorial rights of indigenous peoples has illustrated the limits of such a strategy, due primarily to the significant lack of synchronization within the Chilean legal system. A review of territorial and environmental conflicts leads to the conclusion that the neoliberal economic model that dominates the current era not only blocks the incorporation of the rights of indigenous peoples – as illustrated by the impossibility of prosecuting violations of indigenous land property rights – but also contributes to the criminalization of those who oppose it. The impasse in the judicialization of territorial and environmental conflicts to protect indigenous lands, combined with the judicial and police persecution of those who resist the neoliberal economic model, illustrates the deficiencies of the rule of law with regard to the indigenous peoples in Chile. We need only examine the simple material criterion of this concept, involving the respect of human rights, to arrive at such a conclusion.

The fact is that the Chilean Constitution of 1980 has undergone no major reforms relating to the protection of human rights. It still does not incorporate the rights of indigenous peoples and only includes a very limited list of human rights. Since the constitutional court claimed that C169 of the ILO had no constitutional value, the respect of human rights concerning indigenous peoples supposes at a minimum the application of human rights as defined generally; but it also requires judges to make a hermeneutic effort so that the interpretation of fundamental rights truly allows for protecting the fundamental rights of indigenous peoples. Based on this approach, a dynamic interpretation of the right to life would not only enable the protection of individual and collective conceptions of the right to life but could link it, for example, to the right to territory, natural resources, or spiritual activities.

Nonetheless, the human rights of the indigenous populations of Chile are in permanent violation, and have been since Chile's independence. This can be seen in the criminalization and repression of the Mapuche population fighting for the protection of its rights; this criminalization has been condemned by international and regional organizations for the protection of human rights. It is also demonstrated by the results of legal actions conducted to protect Mapuche lands. The primary challenge today involves the general respect of human rights by the Chilean state; the second, closely tied to the first, requires the adoption of a new Constitution, one that protects human rights in general, and the rights of indigenous peoples.

Bibliography

Antona Bustos, Jesus. 2015. *Los derechos humanos de los pueblos indígenas. El az mapu y el caso mapuche*. Temuco: Ediciones UCT. http://repositoriodigital.uct.cl/handle/10925/1804 (consulté le 12 janvier 2019).

Barbut, Michael. 2015. "Penser le 'néolibéralisme multiculturel.' La démocratisation chilienne à l'épreuve des Mapuche." *Nuevo Mundo Mundos Nuevos*. http://nuevomundo.revues.org/68226 (accessed 12 January 2019).

Bastias, Julián. 2009. *Memorias de la lucha campesina. Cristiano-Mestizo y Tomador de fundo*. Santiago: Editorial LOM, Coleccion Memorias.

Bengoa, José. 2000. *Historia del pueblo mapuche* (siglo XIX y XX). Santiago de Chile: Editorial LOM.

Bolados, García, and Paolo Guillaume Boccara. 2014. "Du néolibéralisme multiculturel aux mobilisations post-multiculturelles." *Actuel Marx* 56 (2): 74–84.

Cloud, Leslie. 2009–2010. "Az Mapu, derecho del invisible o derecho mapuche." *THULE. Rivista Italiana di Studi Americanistici* 26–29: 491–531.

Cloud, Leslie. 2017. "Los tribunales chilenos y la protección de los territorios indígenas: los desafíos de una resolución jurisprudencial de la discronía entre el modelo económico neoliberal chileno y la efectivación de los derechos indígenas." In *Autodeterminação, autonomia territorial e acesso à justiça: povos indígenas em movimento na América Latina*, edited by Ricardo Verdum et Edviges M. Ioris, 99–125. Rio de Janeiro: Associação Brasileira de Antropologia.

Cloud, Leslie, and Fabien Le Bonniec. 2012. "Entre logiques d'État et autochtonie: Dynamiques de la territorialité mapuche à l'heure du droit à l'autodétermination des Peuples Autochtones." *Revista Quaderns-e* 17 (1): 25–43.

Comisión Verdad Histórica y Nuevo Trato con los Pueblos Indígenas. 2008. *Informe de la Comisión Verdad Histórica y Nuevo Trato con los Pueblos Indígenas.* Santiago: Comisionado Presidencial para Asuntos Indígenas. http://www.corteidh.or.cr/tablas/27374.pdf (accessed 12 January 2019).

Correa, Martín, and Eduardo Mella. 2010. *Las razones de illkun/enojo: Memoria, despojo y criminalización en el territorio mapuche de Malleco.* Santiago: LOM Ediciones, Observatorio de Derechos de los Pueblos Indígenas.

Correa, Martín, Raúl Molina, and Nancy Yañez. 2005. *La Reforma Agraria y las tierras mapuches. Chile 1962–1975.* Santiago: LOM.

COTAM (Comisión de Trabajo Autónomo Mapuche). 2003. *Mapu Küpal Azkunun Zugu. Fundamentos y Manifestaciones del derecho propio mapuche.* Informe final de la Comisión de Trabajo Autónomo Mapuche a la Comisión Verdad Histórica y Nuevo Trato con los Pueblos Indígenas. http://www.memoriachilena.cl/602/articles-122901_recurso_7.pdf (accessed 12 January 2019).

Cuadra Montoya, Ximena. 2014. "Nuevas estrategias de los movimientos indígenas contra el extractivismo en Chile." *Revista CIDOB d'Afers Internacionals* 105: 141–163.

Curiñir Lincoqueo, Hernan, Pablo Silva, and Conrado Zumelzu. 2016. *Informe Final trabajo de investigación, de ejecutados y desaparecidos, 1973–1990, pertenecientes a la Nación Mapuche.* Temuco: Asociación de Investigación y Desarrollo Mapuche – INDH Instituto Nacional de Derechos Humanos. http://www.mapuche.info/wps_pdf/curinir_et_all_2016.pdf (accessed 12 January 2019).

Del Valle, Carlos. 2014. "La presencia de estereotipos, prejuicios y discriminación étnica en los tribunales de la Región de La Araucanía en Chile: peritaje analítico-discursivo." In *Lenguas, Literatura y Comunicación. 20 años de investigación en la Universidad de La Frontera*, edited by Alonso Azócar Avendaño, Luis Nitrihual Valdebenito, and Aldo Olate Vinet, 189–206. Temuco: Ediciones Universidad de la Frontera.

Faundes Peñafiel, Juan Jorge. 2013. "Integración regional, reformas a la justicia y respeto del estándar internacional de derechos humanos en los procesos penales seguidos contra indígenas movilizados socialmente." In Derechos Individuales e Integración Regional, edited by Mario Alvarez and Roberto Cippitani. Rome/Perugia/Mexico: Istituto per gli Studi Economici e Giuridici.

Foerster, Rolf, and Sonia Montecino. 1988. *Organizaciones, Lideres y Contiendas Mapuches, 1900–1970.* Santiago: Ediciones CEM.

Fuenzalida Bascuñan, Sergio. 2015. "Desarrollo de la jurisprudencia en Chile sobre la consulta indígena: los casos del tribunal constitucional y la corte suprema." *Revue Quebecoise de Droit International.* Special Issue: 149–197. http://www.sqdi.org/wp-content/uploads/RQDI_HS201503_8_B.pdf (accessed 12 January 2019).

Guevara, Ana, and Fabien Le Bonniec. 2008. "Wallmapu, terre de conflits et de réunification du peuple mapuche." *Journal de la Société des Américanistes* 94 (2): 205–228.

Hale, Charles, and Rosamel Millamán. 2006. "Cultural Agency and Political Struggle in the Era of the Indio Permitido." In *Cultural Agency in the Americas*, edited by Doris Sommer, 281–304. Durham, NC: Duke University Press.

IACHR (Inter-American Court of Human Rights). 2014. *Sentencia caso Norin Catriman y otros contra el estado de Chile*, 29 May 2014. http://www.corteidh.or.cr/docs/casos/articulos/seriec_279_esp.pdf (accessed 12 January 2019).

INE (Instituto Nacional de Estadísticas). 2011. *Análisis del comportamiento del consumo eléctrico y la actividad minera.* Santiago: INE.

IWGIA (International Work Group for Indigenous Affairs). 2015. *El Mundo Indígena 2015.* Copenhagen. http://www.iwgia.org/iwgia_files_publications_files/0717_EL_MUNDO_INDIGENA_2015_eb.pdf (accessed 12 January 2019).

Le Bonniec, Fabien. 2003. "Etat de droit et droits indigènes dans le contexte d'une post-dictature: Portrait de la criminalisation du mouvement mapuche dans un Chili démocratique." *Web-Revue Amnis* 3. Brest: Université de Bretagne Occidentale.

Le Bonniec, Fabien. 2014a. "La participación de las comunidades mapuche-huilliche en el proceso de la Reforma Agraria en la Provincia de Valdivia - 1970–1973." *Revista Austral de Ciencias Sociales* 23: 27–49.

Le Bonniec, Fabien. 2014b. "Las Cárceles De La Etnicidad: Experiencias Y Prácticas De Resistencia De Los Mapuche Sometidos a La Violencia Política En La Era Del Multiculturalismo (2000–2010)." *Oñati Socio-Legal Series* 4 (1): 104–121.

Le Bonniec, Fabien. 2015. "La culture mapuche à la barre. Pouvoir et médiation linguistico-culturels des facilitateurs interculturels dans les tribunaux pénaux du sud du Chili." *Autrepart. Revue des Sciences Sociales au Sud* 73 (1): 55–71.

Leiva, Arturo. 1984 *El Primer Avance a la Araucanía, Angol, 1862.* Temuco: Ediciones Universidad de La Frontera.

Lillo, Rodrigo. 2015. "Justicia penal y derechos indígenas: El largo camino del reconocimiento de la diversidad." *Revista Austral de Ciencias Sociales* 28: 99–115.

Míguez Núnez, Rodrigo. 2013. "Estado chileno y tierras mapuche entre propiedades y territorialidad." In *Derecho y Pueblo Mapuche: Aportes Para la Discusión*, edited by Helena Olea, 21–50. Santiago: Centro de Derechos Humanos UDP.

Observatorio Ciudadano. 2010. *Las implicancias de la ratificación del Convenio N° 169 de la OIT en Chile*, Documento de Trabajo N° 10. https://observatorio.cl/1283-2/ (accessed 22 February 2019).

Offerlé, Michel. 2008. "Retour critique sur les répertoires de l'action collective (XVIIIe–XXIe siècles)." *Politix* 81 (1): 181–202.

Ormeño, Hugo, and Jorge Osses. 1972. "Nueva legislación sobre indígenas en Chile." *Cuadernos de la Realidad Nacional* 14: 15–45.

Pairican, Fernando. 2014. *Malon. La Rebelión del Movimiento Mapuche 1990–2013.* Santiago: Ed. Pehuen. https://tienda.pehuen.cl/products/malon-la-rebelion-del-movimiento-mapuche-1990-2013 (accessed 12 January 2019).

Panikkar, Raimon. 1984. "La notion des droits de l'homme est-elle un concept occidental?" *Interculture* 17 (1): 3–27.

Salas, Ricardo, and Fabien Le Bonniec, eds. 2015. "Prologue." *Les Mapuche à la mode*, 7–16. Paris: Editions l'Harmattan.

Toledo, Victor. 2006. *Pueblo Mapuche, Derechos colectivos y territorio: Desafíos para la sustentabilidad democrática*. Santiago: Ed. LOM.

UDP (Universidad Diego Portales). 2013. *Informe Anual sobre Derechos Humanos en Chile 2013*. Santiago: Universidad Diego Portales. http://www.derechoshumanos.udp.cl/derechoshumanos/index.php/informe-ddhh-2015/7-news/176-informe-anual-sobre-derechos-humanos-en-chile-2013 (accessed 12 January 2019).

UNHRC (Human Rights Council). 2014. *Report of the Special Rapporteur on the Promotion and Protection of Human Rights and Fundamental Freedoms While Countering Terrorism. Addendum: Visit to Chile, March 10, 2014*. http://www.refworld.org/docid/534e712b4.html (accessed 12 January 2019).

Vial, Paula. 2013. "Juicios a mapuches desnuda las deudas de la justicia." In *Rebelión en Wallmapu. Resistencia del Pueblo Nación Mapuche*, edited by José Bengoa, 37–41. Santiago de Chile: Aún Creemos en los Sueños.

10 Burning a home that "doesn't exist," arresting people who "aren't there"

A critique of eviction-based conservation and the Sengwer of Embobut forest, Kenya

Justin Kenrick

Introduction

Since January of 2014, the Sengwer of Embobut Forest in the Cherangany Hills, Western Kenya, have experienced the full force of the state as Kenya Forest Service (KFS) armed guards force them off their lands and burn their homes to the ground. This has continued despite an injunctive order in place in the High Court since March 2013 forbidding this practice (Forest Peoples Programme, FPP 2016). The justification of the KFS and the (then) Ministry of Environment and Natural Resources[1] for the evictions of these forest peoples from their ancestral lands is that their forested hills provide vital watersheds that need to be protected and regenerated for the nation as a whole. Despite scientific evidence indicating that protecting resources – including water – is best achieved through protecting indigenous peoples' land rights, and clear support from Kenya's 2010 constitution, evictions have continued.

This chapter examines the evictions of the Sengwer from their forests at Embobut between Independence and 2016. While describing the immediate role of the KFS in these evictions, this paper pays particular attention to the larger roles played by the Kenyan Government, the Finnish Government, and the World Bank. It then analyzes how such exclusion and control over the Sengwer is exerted, including through policies and institutions that present themselves as "participatory." Finally, this case is examined in the broader perspective of the global framework driving "development" and "conservation." Forest peoples have their own proposals for how to reconcile the supposedly "irreconcilable" conflict between human rights and environmental protection, and this chapter places a strong emphasis on the perspectives of the Sengwer

1 This ministry was renamed the Ministry of Environment and Forestry in 2017, following the national elections. In this paper I use the name for the ministry at the time of the events being described.

themselves, through quotes from testimonials gathered in 2016 to support a Sengwer court case.[2]

The rights of indigenous peoples to their lands is highly problematic in Africa, and the term *indigenous* is contested throughout the continent, even where it is acknowledged legally within states. Although the term *indigenous peoples* is not used in the 2010 Constitution of Kenya, Article 2.5 notes that "The general rules of international law shall form part of the law of Kenya," and Article 260 defines a *marginalized community* as a community that fulfills any one of a range of criteria, including the following:

a a community that, because of its relatively small population or for any other reason, has been unable to fully participate in the integrated social and economic life of Kenya as a whole;
b a traditional community that, out of a need or desire to preserve its unique culture and identity from assimilation, has remained outside the integrated social and economic life of Kenya as a whole; and
c an indigenous community that has retained and maintained a traditional lifestyle and livelihood based on a hunter or gatherer economy.

Thus, in practice the Constitution recognizes indigenous peoples, and in relation to land, recognizes that the "ancestral lands and lands traditionally occupied by hunter-gatherer communities" are community lands (Article 63.2.d.ii). The 2016 Community Land Act makes this recognition possible in practice for these forest-dependent indigenous peoples. Despite these protections, and international pressure and attention, the rights of the Sengwer to their traditional lands continues to be violated. This paper considers how these issues might be addressed more effectively in Kenya and elsewhere.

The dispossession of the Sengwer

The Sengwer are an indigenous people living along the slopes of the Cherangany Hills in three administrative districts of Kenya: Trans-Nzoia, West Pokot, and Elgeyo-Marakwet. Their traditional economies were based on hunting and gathering, herbal medicine, and bee keeping. The current population of this ethnic minority, who are considered to be one of the most marginalized peoples in Kenya, is estimated to be 33,000 (2009 Census Report, cited in Chepkorir Kuto 2016: 5). They are organized according to sub-tribes and clans; there are 21 Sengwer clans in Embobut. The numerically far larger Marakwet ethnic group, who identify as agriculturalists, dominate the Sengwer around Embobut. One way

2 These testimonials were collected by Justin Kenrick and Tom Lomax of the Forest Peoples Programme in 2015 and 2016. The languages used were English, Swahili and Sengwer, with translation from Swahili and Sengwer provided by Yator Kiptum of the Sengwer Indigenous Peoples Programme. The case is number 3 of 2018 in the Environment and Land Court, Eldoret, brought by Elias Kimaiyo and others, acting as representatives of the Sengwer of Embobut.

that they do this is through holding key political positions in Elgeyo-Marakwet County; in a similar way the Pokot ethnic group dominate the Sengwer in neighboring West Pokot.

The Sengwer livelihood, health system and culture have depended on natural resources found in the forests. Their subsistence strategy today includes some keeping of cattle and planting family gardens in the glades in the forest. The forests support their cultural practices and provide spiritual anchorage. Thomas Kirotich, a 55-year-old Sengwer man,[3] describes his memories of this mixed economy, and their relationship with the forest; he also describes how things have changed in recent years:

> I remember clearly the initiation in 1974 … All of this area was for us. We had cows, sheep and goats, and were depending on bee keeping. We were not tilling any land. We took honey and animal products to market on the eastern side to exchange for millet and other food stuffs … Forest was very important to us, we were not allowed to cut a single tree and the forest was subdivided into clans … Someone was not allowed to just get fruits and other things from others clans' land … For firewood we collected wood from fallen trees, just as we are doing now. Forest has decreased greatly because we are not allowed to conserve as we used to. Before there were areas which were deep for initiation, and we were very careful not to make fire. KFS came and disrupted our governance, allowing other people to come and encroach, so the forest is much degraded. (Embobut, 8th March 2015)

History of Sengwer evictions

The Sengwer were initially forcibly displaced from the lower reaches of their territories in the late nineteenth century by the British colonial administration (these lower areas were considered richer lands for agricultural purposes), but were permitted to occupy the less agriculturally fertile highland forest and moorland areas of the Cherangany Hills. Subsequently, under British colonial rule, ten large forest blocks of these higher areas in the Cherangany Hills (including Embobut forest) were gazetted as government forests, and then a further two blocks under the post-independence government,[4] prohibiting anyone from residing in the forest or carrying out activities without the Government's authority. All of these happened without the community's endorsement.

When Kenya gained independence in 1963, the Sengwer expected to get back their land. Instead their land was gazetted as forest reserve or given to other

3 Thomas Kirotich is a member of the Kaptoyoi clan. His grandmother was from the Marakwet, the dominant cultivators who neighbour the Sengwer of Embobut, but he and everyone else in his group was a Sengwer

4 Listed in the 3rd Schedule (77a) of the 2016 Forest and Conservation Management Act as gazetted in 1941: Kapolet, Kaisungurr, Toropket, Chemurokoi, Kipkunurr, Cheboit, Sogotio, Kapchemutwa; in 1954: Embobut, Kerrer; in 1958: Lelan; and in 1967: Kapkanyar, Kiptaberr.

more dominant tribes. The forest highland areas – formerly held by the County Council as Trust Lands – were declared national forest reserves in 1964. Since that time, forest legislation in Kenya has excluded communities from living in protected areas. This approach, often referred to as "fortress conservation," effectively outlaws Sengwer occupation of their ancestral lands, and disregards not only their customary ownership rights, but also effective approaches to forest conservation.

Starting in the 1970s, the eviction of Sengwer from their lands has involved the burning of their houses. In interviews (some of which are presented here), and in their meetings with the National Land Commission and others investigating their situation, the Sengwer clearly articulated both the injustice, and the inefficiency, of this strategy. Lukas Kiraton, a 57-year-old Sengwer elder in Embobut, describes it this way:

> The first eviction I remember was 1978. They didn't tell me why they were burning our houses. During that time they came and built [guard] houses, after a month they came back and burnt again. They were burning in a humane style, allowing you to take your property out. In the 1980s they started burning everything, taking everything including our cows to Iten,[5] and then we got them back. KFS said they marked this forest in 1968 and said it was theirs and they didn't want anyone living in it. It is the Sengwer's forest, and we Sengwer own it together. KFS say the wild animals and forest are disappearing, but the forest has degraded faster as KFS burnt our homes pushing us deeper into the forest, and as they have allowed other people to come and degrade our forest.
>
> If the NLC [National Land Commission] allows us to live freely in our forest we can protect along with KFS and any other stakeholders, using our traditional bylaws to protect the forest. An example of our unwritten bylaws is that you are forbidden to take anything from our sacred forest areas, which are just for rituals. If you are found to have cut a tree without permission then you will be arrested and fined by the community. (Embobut, 8th March 2015)

Usurping the Sengwer from their forest lands led to a dramatic loss of forest cover and to the destruction of large forest ecosystems. Kirotich described the efforts of the community to report this destruction:

> We were scrambling with the other tribes for land. They were clearing our forest, setting fire to bamboo mangroves, and making big areas [for] cultivation. When we complained about them to the assistant chief's office, they told us: "Be the first people to move out to set an example, and then we'll move everyone out." (Embobut, 8th March 2015)

5 Iten is a local administrative town outside the forest. It is where forest guards are based.

Throughout the 1980s evictions increased, and this process accelerated in 1992 when the KFS excised thousands of hectares of land through illegal alterations of forest boundaries and irregular allocation of the land to non-Sengwer (especially Marakwet). This seriously impacted on water resources by reducing the flow regime of major rivers feeding Lake Victoria and Lake Turkana, a trend threatening the stability of the lakes' ecosystem (Kiprop et al. 2017)

The situation worsened when a World Bank funded project began in 2007. The forced evictions and displacements of the Sengwer from their ancestral land increased. Other violations of their rights as indigenous minorities include policies intended to assimilate them into dominant society, violation of their rights to live in their ancestral homes (their forests), and the settling of other communities on Sengwer land. It is worth noting that such policies and actions are built upon clear expressions of British colonial attitudes.[6] The following section will describe the World Bank project, and the evictions related to this.

Impact of the World Bank funded Natural Resource Management Project

The Natural Resource Management Project (NRMP), funded by the World Bank and implemented primarily by the Kenya Forest Service, had the stated aim of securing the Embobut forest and water catchment, as part of securing the forests of the Cherangany Hills, of which Embobut is one part. Running from 2007 to 2013, it received around $68.5 million from the World Bank. Other donors provided additional funding and support, including the Finnish Government through a project designed to support forest reform (described in more detail below). Because the World Bank has an indigenous peoples' policy,[7] the Bank was obliged to develop an Indigenous Peoples Planning Framework (IPPF) in

6 For example, in 1934, Chief Native Commissioner Watkins wrote about the "Dorobo" (the derogatory word for forest dwelling peoples such as the Sengwer): "The word Dorobo is one of wide application. It connotes any native who is neither agricultural nor pastoral, ancient primitive stock reinforced by outlaws or rebels from the later Bantu and Nilotic invasions, who live by the produce of the chase and on honey barrels in the forest, formerly often in caves or in stone-lined roofed-in pits of prehistoric type. These people under the Pax Britannica have come out of their fastness, and either tried to become pastoral, or to attach themselves to agricultural or pastoral tribes. This is the right future for them. They cannot exist in the modern world as forest dwellers without danger to forest and so to water, already a scarcening commodity in Eastern Africa" (Cavanagh 2016: 11). This colonial attitude itself continued dominant ethnic groups pre-existing attitudes, for example the 1934 Carter Commission stated that "the Dorobo so fell into an inferior position and either left [Kikuyu] country or sought adoption by the Kikuyu. In some cases, it seems from the evidence that they were forced into the adoption ceremony by the fear that their lives would not be safe otherwise" (Government of Kenya, 1934, Kenya Land Commission Report (also known as the "Carter Land Commission": 92).

7 The World Bank's Indigenous Peoples Policy OD 4.20 is a safeguard policy which is currently being reviewed and in danger of being weakened: http://www.forestpeoples.org/topics/safeguard-accountablility-issues/news/2016/10/world-bank-undermines-decades-progress-building.

consultation with the affected indigenous peoples (Schmidt-Soltau 2006). The Sengwer initially welcomed the NRMP, because it promised to ensure that their rights to their lands would finally be recognized, through implementing the IPPF.

Despite this initial optimism, the focus of the project turned out to be primarily on strengthening the KFS. When the NRMP was evaluated by the World Bank in 2011, it was determined to be an ineffective project. From the perspective of the Sengwer, this ineffectiveness was largely due to the project's focus on the KFS, and also from its unwillingness to secure forest peoples' rights to their customary lands. However, instead of addressing these critical issues, the project was restructured, and the focus on land rights was dropped, without the agreement of the Sengwer. The Sengwer submitted a complaint to the World Bank Inspection Panel in January 2013 about the harm the project was causing, and asked the Inspection Panel to investigate whether the project was contravening its own safeguards.[8]

The Inspection Panel's findings were damning. The executive summary states that it found non-compliance with OP 4.10 [Indigenous Peoples Safeguard Policy] "because the proper steps to address the potential loss of customary rights were not taken as provided by the policy" (WBIP 2014: ix, paragraph 19). In addition to the many policy violations committed by the NRMP (detailed in the report) was a finding that the World Bank itself was non-compliant with its own safeguard policies. They found that the project sustained the conditions for further evictions by failing to adequately identify, address or mitigate the fact that the institution it was funding, KFS, was (and remains) committed to eviction "before, during and after the conclusion of the NRMP" (WBIP 2014: 58, paragraph 236).

The Inspection Panel made clear that, although it could not prove a direct link between World Bank funding and the forced evictions, the NRMP had failed to assess the institution it was working with – namely the KFS. Furthermore, it had failed to understand that pouring money into capacity building for an institution whose ideology and leadership was (and continues to be) dedicated to enforcement, exclusion and evictions, would simply aid that institution in entrenching the flawed approach to forest conservation that the project was supposedly intended to transform. This was largely recognized by the meeting of the Board of Executive Directors of the World Bank under president Jim Yong Kim, on 30 September 2014. Despite some differences of opinion, the Board sided with the Inspection Panel in recognizing the Bank's responsibility to support the different parties' capacity to address the underlying issue of land tenure.[9]

8 The World Bank describes the Inspection Panel as "an independent complaints mechanism for people and communities who believe that they have been, or are likely to be, adversely affected by a World Bank-funded project." http://ewebapps.worldbank.org/apps/ip/Pages/AboutUs.aspx.

9 See the World bank news release *Joint Statement from World Bank Management and Inspection Panel: World Bank Board Discusses Inspection Panel Cases in India and Kenya*, October 2, 2014/143/ECR, available at https://inspectionpanel.org/sites/inspectionpanel.org/files/ip/PanelCases/81%20-%20Press%20Release%20on%20Board%20Discussion%20%28English%29.pdf (both sites last accessed 10 February 2019).

Current evictions, negotiations, and stalemate

After World Bank funding for the NRMP ended in November 2013, the new Government decided unilaterally to "solve" the problem by insisting that they would dispense some money as compensation to the Sengwer, and declared that this meant the Sengwer no longer had any right to their lands at Embobut (the amount was 400,000 Kenyan shillings per household, equivalent to $4,585 at the time). In recent interviews with Amnesty International, members of the Embobut task force[10] said that this "was based on the figure that victims of post-election violence got. It led to a negative social impact. It reduced the [forest residents] to poverty levels – it removed them from their homes" (Amnesty International 2018: 7).

From the Sengwer perspective, no amount of money could compensate them for their ancestral home. This deep connection with place, at the core of their identity and experience, is something that can be hard to grasp for those who are used to moving between cities and even countries in response to work opportunities and demands. An Ogiek elder, Fred Matei, from the nearby Ogiek forest peoples' community of Chepkitale explained to me: "To be forced to leave our homes and made to settle somewhere else is, for us, what it would be like for you if you were forced to leave your wife and children and made to take another wife and other children elsewhere." As Elias Kimaiyo, a young Sengwer father,[11] put it:

> We are just on the run from KFS so we cannot go and practice our culture, like going to perform the rituals. The ancestors give us blessings in living in our land, they give us our security. The living and the dead are bonded together, they coexist in the same land, and not giving them something – like pouring milk or honey on their graves – means they are hungry like we are. They are not at peace just as we are not at peace. (Eldoret, 21st April 2016)

At no point were the Sengwer consulted over the compensation, and at no point did they agree to this compensation process.[12] However, they were put under severe pressure to accept. The President and Deputy President, and the region's Senator all came to Eldoret and insisted there was no alternative. It was made abundantly clear that paramilitary force was going to be exercised against them if they refused. After being told by a trusted politician that the compensation

10 In 2009, the Government of Kenya had established the Embobut Task Force to look into the situation of the Sengwer evictions.

11 Kimaiyo has since become a leading figure in representing his community after having been badly wounded by KFS in April 2017. He was named Kenyan Human Rights Defender of the Year in 2017.

12 It should be noted that while Government and other non-Sengwer often claim they do not know how to consult the Sengwer, in fact the Sengwer of Embobut have a clear representative structure with 5 representatives from each of their 3 glades forming the 15 strong Embobut leadership, and with women and youth strongly represented.

was for the past harms they had experienced, and was not about their agreeing to leave their lands, many accepted the compensation. Many received nothing and much of the money was siphoned off by dominant non-Sengwer elites (this has been documented in reports; see, for example, Amnesty 2018: 7).

In January 2014 the mass evictions began. Sengwer spokesperson Yator Kiptum described it at the time:

> With the arrival of forest guards, families are running away from their homes. Eleven guards all armed with AK47 rifles were getting into peoples' houses. Homes are deserted. The guards shot one bullet in the air before [going] into the forest. Lots of confusion, fear, desperation and hopelessness is seen amongst community members. (10th January 2014, in Tickell 2014)[13]

In previous years homes had been burnt and then people had been able to return, often for up to a year, to continue their lives untroubled before the next eviction. However, beginning in January 2014, the evictions and harassment became intense and ongoing, with arrests and burnings a daily and weekly occurrence.

The particular impact this harassment is still having on the Sengwer women and children, is outlined in a 2016 report by Milka Chepkorir Kuto, a young Sengwer woman. Chepkorir Kuto describes the impact of the evictions on Sengwer women in Embobut, who, she says, are "often chased, while men are arrested by the guards during the eviction process." She says that they are particularly vulnerable to psychological torture, and to verbal, physical, and sexual abuse, at the hands of those evicting them; furthermore, they are especially vulnerable to illness and poverty following the destruction of their homes. Since they are not aware of their rights, they are not able to effectively challenge the evictions, or the abuse that they receive. Describing how the situation had worsened, she says that:

> The gender-based tolerance that previously favoured women against arrests had therefore changed … [as the] officers take advantage of the women's lesser ability to run and hide whenever they see them coming. Women are therefore arrested and their husbands called on phones to come pay some cash for the women to be released.

As most women have young children, they cannot afford to be held at the KFS camps overnight, or to be taken to the court the next day. Thus, community members are often forced to pay cash in order to get the women released. In this way, she suggests, women are being used by the officers to source money from the Sengwer community members (Chepkorir Kuto 2016: 6).

13 Tickell, Oliver. 2014. "Kenya – Forest People Facing Violent Eviction," *The Ecologist*, 9 janvier. https://theecologist.org/2014/jan/09/kenya-forest-people-facing-violent-evictionhttp://www.theecologist.org/News/news_analysis/2230122/kenya_forest_people_facing_violent_eviction.html (consulté le 26 janvier 2019).

Alternative futures: the government's or communities' pathways?

The mass evictions of January 2014 provoked international outcry, including an Avaaz petition against the evictions that gained almost 1 million signatures (at the end of the chapter we will see how the Sengwer engaged with the campaign to better achieve their objective of returning to their lands). The President of the World Bank, Jim Yong Kim, an anthropologist by training, acknowledged the Bank's responsibility to help address the situation and met with President Kenyatta. This led to a Colloquium at Eldoret in March 2015, convened and sponsored by the World Bank and including all of the primary role players in the crisis.[14] Organized with the Ministry of Environment, Water and Natural Resources, and presided over by the Permanent Secretary at the Ministry, this Colloquium brought the Sengwer and other forest communities together with KFS, and its parent Ministry. This Colloquium also included prominent participation by the main KFS development partner, the Finnish Government. The expressed aim was to bring communities and KFS together, in order to map a way forward – not only for the Sengwer of Embobut but for all ancestral forest peoples in Kenya whose lands have been taken over and declared protected areas.

In the days leading up to the Colloquium, KFS intensified its evictions, burnings, and arrests at Embobut. Based on my long-term experience with the Sengwer, this is something that often happens in the run up to such dialogues. I interpret this as an attempt to provoke the Sengwer into either backing out of such dialogues completely, or into engaging in them in an emotional way that makes them appear incapable of rational discussion. In this case, the KFS was claiming that there were no longer any Sengwer in Embobut (despite all the evidence to the contrary) and that thus the focus of the discussion should be on compensation, not on peoples' rights. In light of this, the Sengwer's presence and effective participation in the dialogue would certainly undermine the KFS argument.

At the Colloquium, the Permanent Secretary of the Ministry of Environment, Water and Natural Resources ridiculed them for wanting to retain their traditional way of life.[15] Despite these efforts to bully them into silence, the

14 The author attended this Colloquium which – among other more pressing matters – provided an opportunity for him to interview the then KFS Director, and meet with the then Permanent Secretary at the Ministry of Environment, Water and Natural Resources, as well as other key political players.

15 For example, in a room of 300 – mostly Government – people at the Colloquium on the 6th March 2015, the Permanent Secretary mocked the 30 Sengwer present for being so attached to their lands. In particular he mocked those Sengwer that he said believed they "must die for the forest." This was a reference to the Sengwer man who the previous day had threatened to pull the "emergency stop" lever in the helicopter – saying "Your bodies can be taken back to Nairobi, I will die on my ancestral lands." He said this when the Ministry official was refusing to land the helicopter to investigate – as the Government had promised they would – whether the Government had burnt 30 homes. They landed, witnessed the burnt homes, took photographs, but then the photographs were destroyed and the burnings denied, making it very hard for the Sengwer to remain in a "Dialogue" with those who were at the same time burning their homes.

Sengwer remained in the "dialogue." They were supported by the presentations from the World Bank and IUCN experts from around the world, which clearly demonstrated that securing such communities' tenure is the best way to secure indigenous forests. Even with this support, however, there was no shift in the approach of the KFS, the Ministry, or of governments and international bodies funding them – either at the Colloquium or since – these dynamics are further discussed below.

Despite the daily and weekly harassment that the Sengwer of Embobut experience, a large percentage of them have continually returned to stay on their lands. They are living in inadequate temporary shelters, such as under plastic tarpaulins that can be hidden from armed KFS guards during the day. They are being pursued and arrested on a daily basis by armed KFS guards, who demand bribes, and burn their homes and possessions – including school uniforms, school books, cooking utensils and bedding. Other non-Sengwer peoples were also evicted in January 2014 – these were people who had either been moved into Embobut by the Government, or had taken advantage of the Sengwer's previous eviction, and taken over land for cultivation. These peoples have not returned. That the Sengwer have insisted on returning – despite the ongoing harassment – highlights their commitment to their ancestral home.

Forest peoples and effective conservation

A key point made by the Sengwer, and in this chapter, is that these events are not only a violation of their rights – they have also led to increased deforestation and pressure on fragile ecosystems. The Sengwer say that this environmental destruction and degradation is a direct result of the denial of their rights to manage, protect and secure their way of life and their forests. These statements are supported by numerous recent scientific studies, which have shown that securing the land of forest peoples is the best way to protect indigenous forests and associated resources, like water (see, for example, Porter-Bolland et al. 2012; Seymour, La Vina, and Hite 2014). Current rights-based policies of pre-eminent global conservation bodies, such as the International Union for Conservation of Nature (IUCN 2012) and the World Wide Fund for Nature (WWF 2008), claim to be based on this science. At the Colloquium described above, all the IUCN representatives and global forestry experts brought in by the World Bank stated very clearly that the most effective way to secure indigenous forests globally, including in Africa, is to secure the community tenure rights of forest peoples on the condition that they protect their forests (Alden Wily 2018a, 2018b). These global policies also respond to years of pressure by indigenous peoples and their allies seeking to reverse centuries of dispossession and displacement.[16]

Furthermore, Kenya's 2010 constitution – in Article 63.2.d.ii (see below) – explicitly provides for the recognition of community lands required to make

16 See for example IUCN's Whakatane Mechanism. http://whakatane-mechanism.org/.

such an approach work (Alden Wily 2018c). Technically, current laws in Kenya, dating from British colonial law, forbid forest peoples to live within their lands when these have been gazetted as protected areas. However, the 2010 Constitution makes it clear that these laws have to be brought in line with the Constitution's recognition of such peoples' rights to secure their lives on their ancestral lands. Ironically, it was the appalling electoral violence accompanying the 2007 Presidential election in Kenya – violence that very much centered on politicians making use of peoples' sense of insecurity around land tenure – that led to the very progressive 2010 Constitution, which includes an article recognizing the community rights of hunter-gatherers (such as the Sengwer) to their ancestral lands.[17] I will return to this point below.

Contrary to both the scientific evidence and the Constitution, however, government agencies often use the pretext of "securing" indigenous forests to justify the eviction of forest peoples, and the imposition of paramilitary control. Both of these actions alienate peoples whose culture has depended on the forests, and leaves the forests in the hands of organizations and individuals who have no such long-term commitment or concern. To the contrary, their overriding motive is very often in seeking control over land to generate their own profits rather than to care for the forests. Indeed, as is evident elsewhere on the ground in Kenya, leaving such indigenous forest in the hands of the KFS can be a recipe for disaster. Often, they encourage what they call "Community Forest Associations" to move in and clear indigenous forest for temporary agriculture, on the pretext of regenerating the forest. This in turn allows KFS to claim that the only option is to turn areas of indigenous forest that were previously rich in biodiversity into areas of commercial forestry plantations that provide rich pickings – in terms of logging and charcoal burning – for the institution and for individuals within it.

A recent Task Force on Forest Resources Management and Logging Activities in Kenya established by the Government of Kenya to look into illegal logging found deep and widespread corruption in KFS – a finding that led to the suspension of the then KFS Director and the dismissal of numerous senior staff (Kenya Ministry of Environment and Forestry 2018). Importantly, this needs to be understood *not* primarily as an issue of corruption or incompetence, but as a result of the way that KFS has been structured. Furthermore, this structure is related to the approach of its primary donor agency, the Finnish Government. The Finnish embassy in Nairobi provided major funding and guidance for the KFS, through its project *Miti Mingi Maisha Bora* ("Many trees, good life"), which ran from 2009 to 2015 and sought to support Kenya's forest reform. The rationale for the project, described on the Embassy of Finland website, is

17 Article 63 of the 2010 Kenyan Constitution: "Community land shall vest in and be held by communities identified on the basis of ethnicity, culture or similar community of interest"; (2) and Community lands include: "(d) (ii) ancestral lands and lands traditionally occupied by hunter-gatherer communities." http://kenyalaw.org/kl/index.php?id=398.

to "reduce poverty through strengthening the forest sector in accordance with Kenya's development strategy Vision 2030."[18]

Toward this goal, the Finnish project has sought to mold the Kenya Forest Service as a self-standing commercial enterprise, encouraging large-scale plantations for profit.[19] Although this may appear to be a practical approach, in fact it seeks to transpose a model that may work well in Finland – where fast growing commercial plantations are the norm – to a Kenyan context where the forest is *not* fast growing, and where the biodiversity of indigenous forest is crucial. Furthermore, under this initiative, the KFS now has – as individuals and as an organization – a huge incentive not only to evict those who have sustained and lived with the forest, but also to destroy those indigenous forests in the pursuit of more immediately profitable, and ecologically impoverished, plantations.[20]

In 2013, the EU also granted further funding to KFS, in many ways picking up where the NRMP left off. Support for the WaTER project had as its aim the protection of the "water towers" (the forests) of the Cherangany Hills where the Sengwer live, and of Mt Elgon where the Chepkitale Ogiek live.[21] However, the World Bank project at least initially had the intention to secure the land rights of forest communities, rather than evicting them. In contrast, the EU project is simply focused on strengthening the KFS and similar agencies, and on livelihood projects for forest-adjacent communities. This project was suspended in 2018, citing "human rights abuses" following the killing of a Sengwer community member by a KFS guard (EU 2018).

An important question that all this raises is how forest peoples can most effectively influence those who are decision-makers in these processes. These include: the Finnish Government, which has been (de facto) funding, rather than challenging, the evictions and other abuses of power by the KFS; the EU, which continued to support the KFS and was stopped only when a Sengwer community member was killed; and the World Bank, which pulled back from an active role when its negative impact was made so clear by its own Inspection Panel – even though there was an express commitment of its President to continue to address these issues.

Whether one prioritizes the protection of the forests or the protection of human rights, the scientific evidence is clear that in cases like the Sengwer, these

18 Programme document: *Miti Mingi Maisha Bora: Support to Forest Sector Reform in Kenya. Implementation Phase (2009 – 2015).* http://www.finland.or.ke/public/default.aspx?contentid=271532&contentlan=2&culture=en-US (last accessed 10 February 2019).

19 See for example: https://um.fi/latest-funding-decisions/-/asset_publisher/SYmYYmTYh0sD/ahaKytInterventionType/id/1157004.

20 This is evident, for example, on the lower slopes of Mt Elgon where KFS has brought in farmers under the PELIS ("Shamba") system which is intended to enable farmers to temporarily farm while replanting forest in deforested areas, but here is being used to remove indigenous forest – leading to immediate revenue for KFS officers (for example, for making charcoal) – enabling indigenous forest to be replaced by commercial plantation forestry, under the guise of reforestation projects.

21 http://kefriwatertowers.org/.

protections are mutually reinforcing, rather than mutually exclusive. This argument is also the basis of the proposals made by the Sengwer to ensure the maintenance and ecological integrity of their ancestral lands, in exchange for the right to remain on these lands. However, when powerful role-players prioritize relationships with government bodies that are abusing their power, such arguments based on clear scientific evidence and on human rights do not work, because those government offices, and those prioritizing their relationship with such offices, are using their power to gain access to resources rather than to protect the environment or human rights. In such a context, the Sengwer, and those who support them, have no possibility for making themselves heard in this process.

The following section will examine the guiding principles that underlie these large-scale projects, tracing the apparent contradictions in the Kenyan legal framework to international discourses and policies.

Contradictions – from the global to the local

So far, this paper has described the details of the situation affecting the Sengwer in Kenya. This section examines contradictions inherent in Kenyan legislation, including the contradiction between the stated intention to protect the indigenous forests and the actual policies and actions that drive deforestation. Although the details are specific to Kenya, this section will show how this national context is situated within an overarching guiding global framework that is fraught with contradiction, and how these global patterns are played out within this national context, and these community members' lives.

Policy, law, and institutional power in Kenya

The most important legal frameworks governing the management of natural resources in Kenya over this period have been the Forest Act of 2005, which forbids communities from living on their ancestral lands, and the Wildlife Act of 2013, which prohibits their hunting and gathering and does not require the government to seek their Free Prior and Informed Consent (FPIC), as required by international law, when turning their land into "Protected Areas." Many forest communities invested a lot of time, effort, and hope in the development of a Community Land Act. This was one of the Acts that the August 2010 Constitution stipulated had to be developed and passed into law within 5 years (later extended to 6 years) – if this did not happen, it would trigger the dissolution of Parliament. It was the last such act to become law (in August 2016). Many see this delay as a reflection of the fact that recognizing communities' rights to their lands threatens the capture of lands by elites who have enormous clout in Parliament (Alden Wily 2018c).

Meanwhile, a new Forest Conservation and Management Act was also passed into law in August 2016 with almost no opportunity for input by forest-dwelling communities, this process included a review of the 2005 Forests Act, which was kept very much out of the public's eye.

On a more encouraging note, the new Forest Conservation and Management Act (7th September 2016) and the new Community Land Act (CLA, 21st September 2016) both provide for public lands to be transferred to community lands on a case by case basis. The CLA awaits the necessary regulations being issued to elaborate on the provisions, but in principle the Act outlines how communities can acquire formal title for community lands, derived from principles established in the 2010 Constitution (e.g. that community lands exist already and are community property, although held in trust presently by county governments until each community secures a formal title) and in the 2012 Land Act (e.g. that customary rights have equal legal force as freehold or leasehold rights).

Liz Alden Wily, an independent international expert on land tenure based in Nairobi, highlights the fact that, under the provisions of the CLA, title will be issued in the name of the community, and it does not need to form a legal entity such as a cooperative, society or interest association in order to qualify. Although a community title refers to the ultimate ownership of the entire land by the community, she points out that:

> families don't lose their rights to farm or house lands which they consider to be their private customary property. The CLA describes these as "customary rights of occupancy." As is the case in customary tenure, the community will uphold these and consider new applications. (Alden Wily 2016a: 3)

Meanwhile, the new Forest Conservation and Management Act of 2016 states that "Forests may be classified as public, community or private forests" (Article 30 (1)), but it then goes on to present a dilemma rather than a solution. On the one hand, in section 77 (a) it classifies "any land which immediately before the commencement of the Act, was gazetted or registered as a forest reserve … shall be deemed to be a public forest under this Act," while on the other hand in section 30 (3)(e) it classifies as community forests "forests on ancestral lands and lands traditionally occupied by hunter-gatherers."

In other words, by classifying the forests of people like the Sengwer as public lands to be controlled by KFS, it continues the practice of the old Forests Act of 2005, and follows Article 62 (1) (g) of the Constitution, which defines government forests as public land, and Article 62 (3) which vests these in the national government. Meanwhile, in classifying the lands (and by implication the forests) of groups such as the Sengwer as community lands, it restates the land rights of such traditional forest dwelling communities enshrined in Article 63 (2) (d) (ii) of the Constitution.[22]

22 It should be noted that Article 62 (1) (d) provides a route to resolving this situation in favour of communities when it states that Public land is "land in respect of which no individual or community ownership can be established by any legal process," and the Community Land Act (2016) can provide just such a legal process.

The third schedule to the Forest Conservation and Management Act, 2016, lists as gazetted public forests, those forests that are at the heart of the livelihoods, societies, and cultures of the traditional forest dwellers such as the Sengwer. Alden Wily makes the point forcefully in her comments on an earlier version of the Bill that (in this regard) is identical to the final act, when she says:

> The Bill stops short of enabling traditional forest communities to own precisely the forests whose conservation matters to them most, and to the Kenya public. Their ancestral lands continue to be listed as public forests vested in the Kenya Forest Service (s. 30 (1)). The Bill is silent where it should have provision for these important national forests to be transferred to status as community property (community lands) subject to conditions obliging the communities to actively conserve these forests. (Alden Wily 2016b: 3)

The two key ministries that were centrally involved in these legislative and policy processes were: the Ministry of Lands, in relation to the Community Land Bill,[23] and the Ministry of Environment, Water and Natural Resources, in relation to the Forest Conservation and Management Bill.

As noted above, the latter ministry has been overseeing the KFS and (until the 2017 elections) the Kenya Wildlife Service, who undertake the eviction and control aspects of the conservation process with the assistance of the police. These agencies also manage the compensation processes. The combination of these two processes – the eviction and control processes, and the compensation processes – creates a context that enables those within the structures, as well as dominant elites in forest-adjacent communities, to benefit twice. First, by siphoning off compensation that was supposed to reach forest-dwellers being evicted from their land (as noted in the previous section), and second, when those evictions remove the very communities most committed to stopping the exploitation of the forests by these elites.

Inherent contradictions in national and global policy

A sentence in a recent document for the EU-funded WaTER project serves to illustrate the nature of the contradiction that I wish to point to: “Climate change is estimated to cost Kenya’s economy as much as USD 500 million a year, equivalent to 2% of GDP hampering long-term growth” (EU 2016: 1). The justification of action on climate change because its impacts “hamper long-term growth” illustrates the flawed global logic at work. The assumption that

23 It should be noted that the National Land Commission has often been in conflict with the Ministry of Lands

we have to forever grow the economy in order to address poverty and improve lives, leads to the perpetuation of policies that devastate the environment, and to policies intended to impose control of that devastation. Furthermore, it rules out alternative, and more sustainable, approaches focused on de-growth, relocalization and a more equal distribution of resources rather than simply increased accumulation.

This larger global logic is evident in Kenya's "Vision 2030," which is presented as a national long-term development blueprint to transform Kenya into a newly industrializing, middle-income country providing a high quality of life to all its citizens by 2030 in a clean and secure environment (Government of Kenya 2016: 5).[24] This 2030 Vision, and World Bank and EU support for it, can be understood as reflecting a global preoccupation with accelerating economic growth through facilitating the growth of the private sector (often including sweeping land tenure reform which facilitates the privatization of collective land tenure systems); and with the parallel tactic of employing enforcement and restraint approaches, ostensibly to try to stem the inevitable environmental consequences of such a growth trajectory.

This broader policy framework is enacted through two approaches. First, an approach to local development and forest conservation that seeks to break peoples' connection to their lands in the name of (supposedly) improving their development prospects and protecting the forests. Second, it is mediated through kin and political networks (KNCHR and KLA 2006; Mutua 2008). In these systems, patronage and reward can redirect policies and practice to build and reward networks of political patronage, rather than to secure the objectives of the policy as it is conceived in the abstract, and conveyed on paper.

One of the key explanations for the failure of the World Bank – or the Finns through their MMMB project – to transform KFS's top-down enforcement and control approach to a participatory one is because their own top-down approach assumes that the problem is a weakness in the implementation by the KFS of participatory approaches. They see KFS as a "weak" institution in need of strengthening through more finance. A closer look reveals that, to the contrary, it has proved to be a very *strong* organization, one that continues to aggressively pursue not only an approach based on enforcement and control, but one that, from the top down, sees forest as a means for making money – both for the institution, and for private individuals within it (see KNCHR 2018).[25]

This broader political economy and policy analysis is in sharp contrast with the analytic starting point of the World Bank or the Finnish Government. This is

24 Government of Kenya 2016. Kenya Water Towers Agency Strategic Plan 2016–2020.

25 This was also reported by the Ministry of Environment and Forestry Taskforce to Inquire into Forest Resources Management and Logging Activities in Kenya, in a report on *Forest Resources Management and Logging Activities In Kenya – Findings And Recommendations*, April 2018 (NB the Ministry of Environment, Water and National Resources name was changed after the 2017 election to the Ministry of Environment and Forestry).

evident in, for example, the following extract from an evaluation that the Finns carried out of their funding for KFS:

> The Forest Act (GoK 2005) established the Kenya Forest Service in February 2007 which is a semi-autonomous institution governed by an independent board. KFS aims to become a financially viable institution that sustainably manages Kenya's forest resources for the benefit of the State and Kenyans. The Forest Act also sets up a framework for participatory forest management by creating Community Forest Associations (CFAs) adjacent to government forest reserves. The Act also allows for the development of management agreements, concessions and partnerships between KFS and the private sector regarding the long-term management of forest plantations.
>
> Participatory forest management (PFM) is yet to effectively take off in Kenya ... several PFM issues remain unresolved which include policy position on suitability of PFM for different forest types (plantations, indigenous forests), land tenure arrangements (state forest reserves, trust land) and policy position on how benefits/costs are shared between different parties. (Ministry for Foreign Affairs of Finland 2010: 4)

The "several PFM issues" that "remain unresolved" are presented as technical and policy issues, thereby ignoring the fundamental, structural issues of power and marginalization. These get expressed in a variety of ways. As I have described above, the institutional culture of KFS is focused on extracting benefits for individuals in the KFS, and the institution itself, at the expense of forest communities and indigenous forests. Finnish funding has helped to promote Community Forest Associations (CFAs); however, these can actually be highly counterproductive. Extensive literature on commons regimes has shown that, unless a community has long-term ownership rights to their resources then it is hard to take a long-term sustainable approach to those resources (Ostrom 1990; The Ecologist 1995; Chhatre and Agrawal 2009; Seymour, La Vina, and Hite 2014). The CFA approach is specifically designed to benefit communities "adjacent to government forest reserves." (KNCHR 2018: 58–60) Forest *dwelling* communities such as the Sengwer or the Ogiek of Mt Elgon are not "adjacent" to the forest, they have strong cultural, social and livelihood relations with their forests and wish to continue to sustain those forests and be sustained by them. These are the same people whose presence is criminalized by the interlinking set of institutional and legal arrangements described above.

These arrangements also provide the means for the dominant members of adjacent communities and the wider society (including KFS) to extract maximum resources from forests without consideration for the forests' long-term well-being. These structures and processes thus marginalize – and even render invisible – the peoples who have historically depended on, and been sustained by, these forests. This "invisibility" is evident in the project documentation for the EU WaTER project, which did not include any reference to the troublesome existence of forest-dwelling communities themselves.

Forest peoples' solutions

Today the indigenous forest communities of Kenya are connected through their Forest Indigenous Peoples Network (FIPN).[26] In a presentation given by traditional forest dwelling communities to the National Land Commission (NLC)[27] Task Force on Historical Injustices in Nairobi on the 11th September 2014, the forest dwelling communities described themselves as follows:

> 1 We are self-identified traditional Forest Dweller Communities who share common historical and present land grievances.
> 2 We have always depended on our forests and we still do to this day.
> 3 We are very severely marginalized: our rights to our lands and resources have not been recognized and respected by the government and dominant neighboring peoples who have encroached on our land, and continued that marginalization and discrimination.
> 4 We are the indigenous forest peoples of Kenya. Although we recognize all Kenyans as indigenous to their area, unlike others we define ourselves as indigenous peoples according to both (i) our historical and current dependence on our forests and (ii) our being structurally marginalized because of that dependence and because of our traditional livelihoods and social structures that are part of our dependence on the forests (as made clear in the African Human and Peoples Rights Commission definition). (FIPN 2014: 1)

They expressed as their main demands:

> 1 To be acknowledged as traditional forest dweller communities
> 2 To have our principle lands, *our forests*, returned to us under community land titles
> 3 To have the right to conserve our forestlands in the interests of the nation, and so that water can flow again from our forests. (FIPN 2014: 2)

They state their proposal in very simple terms:

> The conflict between the demands of forest conservation and our demand that our land rights be recognised **need not exist**. Our proposal is that: In return for restitution of our customary forestlands through a transfer from public to community land status, we are willing to be legally bound to rehabilitate, conserve, and manage our forests for the people of Kenya. (FIPN 2014: 3)

26 FIPN has thus far been refused registration as an NGO by the board that oversees NGO registrations in Kenya.

27 The NLC is tasked by the 2010 Constitution with resolving such situations. In November 2015 the NLC came to the Ogiek at Chepkitale, Mt Elgon (FPP 2013). The next NLC ground visit was supposed to be to the Sengwer communities in Embobut. However, KFS refused the NLC permission to meet with the Sengwer on their ancestral lands.

They conclude that this would be "win-win for land rights and conservation":

> The best solution to conservation and water tower protection and rehabilitation lies in meeting our land rights on condition of us protecting those forests. We historically protected those forests and we can do this again. This includes protecting against wrongful occupation and use by outsiders, against clearing and degrading practices, and actions to rehabilitate the forest. We want the bees, the wildlife, the canopy of trees, the diversity of trees and plants, and the water to come back. Our culture and our own forest-based livelihood depend upon this." (FIPN 2014: 3)

The challenge of indigenous peoples in Africa: why does it matter?

KFS, their parent ministry, and other State authorities have often insisted that they are not burning Sengwer homes, sometimes by stating that there are no homes there to be burnt. As described above, these denials played a large part in making dialogue impossible at the World Bank Colloquium. In January 2014, the County Commissioner originally denied that KFS forest guards were burning homes during the mass evictions, and accused the Sengwer of burning their own homes. He later admitted that KFS *had* been burning homes and that KFS would now demolish what remained of the homes. The County Commissioner (who played a central role in coordinating the evictions) confirmed that houses were being burnt and that the government would continue doing this, stating:

> It may seem wrong and primitive to burn houses, but gentlemen, look, we have to face the reality in this one and tell our people that the forest is out of bounds henceforth. (Suter 2013)

By February 2016, the KFS was insisting that that no Sengwer remained in Embobut. This was their grounds for stopping the NLC from going to Embobut to meet with Sengwer communities on their lands. In this way, they sought to make the issue one of compensation and reforestation rather than one of recognition of Sengwer land rights. KFS agents themselves, however, record great numbers of cases of Sengwer whom they have arrested and charged for being in Embobut; between June and September 2015, 21 such cases were recorded in court in Iten.

Do indigenous peoples exist in Africa?

The World Bank, Equator Banks,[28] and other investment banks increasingly have what are referred to as "indigenous peoples' safeguards" which they are required

28 Banks committed to the Equator principles, http://equator-principles.com/.

to enact in areas where such populations are identified as being affected, in order for funding to be provided, or maintained. An emerging pattern in African contexts is increasingly narrow readings of the safeguard application text, resulting in a determination that there are no indigenous peoples present – and thus the safeguards do not apply. If the term "indigenous peoples" is not in use in a given country, alternate indicators (such as customary governance, or other associated issues that would require protection under the indigenous peoples safeguards) may not be recognized, regardless of the land tenure system at play.

Many African governments have been pushing to be able to opt out of the new indigenous peoples' safeguard that is being developed (and that will replace the World Bank's Operation Policy 4.20), claiming that it shouldn't apply in Africa. One reason given for this is that such considerations trigger ethnic tension. However, the African Commission on Human and Peoples' Rights (ACHPR) is clear that it is the *denial* of peoples' rights that causes conflict, not the attempt to secure them (ACHPR 2006: 12). A different interpretation of their reticence is that adopting such safeguards would mean that funding from the World Bank and others would be threatened whenever such projects failed to recognize indigenous peoples' rights.[29]

Resistance to the concept of indigeneity is a common pattern in Africa (see also Hays, this volume). The ACHPR does, however, describe "overall characteristics" of groups that identify themselves as indigenous peoples: "their cultures and ways of life differ considerably from the dominant society, and that their cultures are under threat, in some cases to the point of extinction" (ACHPR 2006: 10). Furthermore, the Commission notes that a key characteristic of indigenous peoples in Africa is that their "particular way of life depends on access and rights to their traditional lands and the natural resources thereon" (ibid).

The ACHPR makes the crucial point that "indigenous peoples" is an important analytic category in Africa because it describes the *structural* position of certain groups who are dependent on, but often dispossessed of, their ancestral lands and resources, and who also experience severe discrimination. The document describes how their dependence, and resource use, differs from the majority population; when this difference is rendered as "backwards" their livelihood patterns and social and cultural ways of organizing are seen as "inferior": "they suffer from discrimination as they are regarded as less developed and less advanced than other more dominant sectors of society" (ACHPR 2006: 10).

29 Ironically, the World Bank's new Environment and Social Standards (ESS7) under the Environmental and Social Framework approved in 2016 refer to "Indigenous Peoples/Sub-Saharan African Historically Underserved Traditional Local Communities" http://pubdocs.worldbank.org/en/276101511809520481/ESS7-FactSheet-WB-ESF.pdf (accessed 10 February 2019). Although, elsewhere in the world, that expanded category might be a way of watering down indigenous peoples' rights, in the African context it could allow communities to circumvent the block objection of many African governments that in Africa, all are indigenous, so no particular consideration is needed for the structurally disadvantaged who seek redress through calling themselves indigenous peoples.

However, the ACHPR doesn't clearly develop an analysis recognizing that this discrimination is specifically founded in others' prejudice against their livelihood systems, and that this prejudice is used to justify dispossession. Furthermore, this discrimination and dispossession is more fundamentally based on denying that indigenous peoples exist at all, or on defining them as impoverished subsets of dominant ethnic groups. Thus, the discrimination is able to continue through a sleight of hand that scolds them for being backward, and then silences them by claiming they aren't even there.

This is evident in the case of the Sengwer. The government denies they exist, denies that they are a *people* (rather than backward and poor members of more powerful peoples), denies that they are in Embobut, and actively burns their homes. At the same time, the government authorities deny that they are burning their homes. This combination of discrimination against them, and outright denial of their existence as indigenous peoples, is what needs to be addressed.

Meanwhile, more powerful peoples can claim to speak for the most marginalized, thus becoming intermediaries between them and outsiders. This allows such groups to channel to themselves resources that are supposed to address the situation of the poorest groups, resulting in further marginalization of the Sengwer and other similar groups. This happens at multiple levels. The examples of Finnish funding for KFS's Community Forest Associations, the EU support of the KFS, and the World Bank's NRMP livelihood projects, are all examples of projects that appear to enable community benefit, while actually enabling elites to capture forest peoples' resources. Indigenous Peoples Organisations (IPOs) can also create this effect, when indigenous pastoralist groups (who, although marginalized by the mainstream, themselves have often marginalized the forest peoples) sometimes claim to represent both pastoralists and forest hunter gatherers, thus rendering forest peoples invisible.

Global discourse, national impacts, local realities

Another example of disjuncture between international intentions and national and local consequences is provided by a petition that circulated in January 2014. Avaaz – the international online campaign organization – wanted to launch a signature campaign against the Kenyan Government for burning Sengwer homes.[30] It took huge effort on the part of communities and their supporters to persuade Avaaz to direct their campaign at the World Bank, who acknowledges that such people exist, rather than at the Kenyan Government, who could use any such campaign directed against them to instead proclaim themselves as victims of a global campaign.

International campaigning organizations like Avaaz, although well intended, can sometimes address such issues in isolation, neglecting to address

30 *Before the last home is torched.* http://www.avaaz.org/en/stop_the_forced_evictions_loc_kenya_pa_uk/?bHTAbab&v=35531 (last accessed 30 November 2018).

the structural issues. This can give the impression that the overall system is fine and we just need to tackle the few exceptions. There are good reasons for this approach; it can seem more efficient to portray a particular company, project, or government as out of line with the overall positive rights-based narrative, rather than addressing the need to structurally change the whole system. As evident in many African states' responses to the new World Bank safeguards, there is an attempt to evade the issue of structural discrimination, through the argument that indigenous peoples' rights privilege small groups of citizens who already have the full protection of the law like all other citizens, and that applying such rights will cause ethnic tension.

In Africa, as I have described above, the usefulness of an "indigenous peoples' rights" approach is highly contested; researchers working with this issue also have different perspectives on it. It is critical to keep in mind the foundations of the category and the kind of discrimination these rights are designed to address. The Sengwer and other current or former hunters and gatherers are peoples practicing livelihood systems that involve a deep, particular connection to place that is different from that which the majority practice – and the deep discrimination against those practicing such systems is the very basis of the category "indigenous" and the reason that their rights have to be asserted. Without specific attention to indigenous peoples' rights, such peoples are not just discriminated against, they are rendered invisible. This allows powerful social actors to extend the privileges of their positions under the guise of "equal treatment" of all ethnic groups.

Conclusions

Recognizing the specific ways in which international involvement in indigenous peoples' situations can negatively impact on their situation on the ground in Africa is a critical aspect of effective action contesting violations of indigenous peoples' rights. In this chapter I have described how well-intentioned international projects can have devastating effects. Other forms of international campaigns are also vulnerable to misinterpretation of local dynamics. Furthermore, when such efforts address specific cases as if they were isolated incidents, it distracts us from the global structural dynamics that allow for continued discrimination against indigenous peoples like the Sengwer. Addressing this structural discrimination is the only way to achieve real progress in advancing their human rights.

However, the Sengwer are not fighting only for their own sake, nor only for their rights to remain in the forest and protect their economic subsistence. Just as those in the global north often express their concern for the long-term well-being of all by reference to future generations, the Sengwer express their concern through their obligation to their ancestors to continue to care for their lands. Their predicament exemplifies the deep contradictions that inhabit the global governance of land and the environment, at a time when global efforts have to focus on both the sustainability of livelihoods in relation to the carrying capacity of the planet and the protection of distinct cultures.

The Sengwer possess the knowledge and capacity to keep the forest alive, but they are confronted with a practice of brutal dispossession, including through eviction and the burning of their homes – all in the name of "conservation." Perhaps the most important aspect of their predicament that needs to be grasped is that supporting such marginalized peoples in their efforts to secure their rights to their lands does not undermine the equal treatment of others. It is part of a process of ensuring equal treatment for all; and it supports the maintenance of indigenous forests on which the Sengwer, their downstream farming neighbors, and ultimately all of us depend.

References

ACHPR (African Commission on Human and Peoples' Rights). 2006. *Indigenous Peoples in Africa: The Forgotten Peoples?* Banjul, Copenhagen: IWGIA and ACHPR.

Alden Wily, Liz. 2016a. "The National Constitution and Forest Dweller Land Rights in Kenya." *Expert Evidence Submitted to Eldoret High Court*, February 2016. https://www.forestpeoples.org/en/topics/rights-land-natural-resources/publication/2016/national-constitution-and-forest-dweller-land- (accessed 24 Febrary 2019).

Alden Wily, Liz. 2016b. "Note for Communities Following the Enactment of the Community Land Act, No. 27 of 2016." 9 October 2016.

Alden Wily, Liz. 2018a. "Community Property in Africa." June 2018. http://www.forestpeoples.org/en/node/50264 (accessed 28 January 2019).

Alden Wily, Liz. 2018b. "Community Property around the World." June 2018. http://www.forestpeoples.org/en/node/50264 (accessed 28 January 2019).

Alden Wily, Liz. 2018c. "Risks to the Sanctity of Community Land in Kenya: A Critical Assessment of New Legislation with Reference to Forestlands." *Land Use Policy* 75: 661–672.

Amnesty International. 2018. "Families Torn Apart: Forced Eviction of Indigenous Peoples in Embobut Forest, Kenya." https://www.amnesty.org/en/documents/afr32/8340/2018/en/ (accessed 28 January 2019).

Cavanagh, Connor J. 2016. "Anthropos into Humanitas: Civilizing Violence, Scientific Forestry, and the 'Dorobo Question' in Eastern Africa." *Environment and Planning D: Society and Space* 35 (4): 694–713.

Chhatre, Ashwini, and Arun Agrawal. 2009. "Trade-offs and Synergies between Carbon Storage and Livelihood Benefits from Forest Commons." *Proceedings of the National Academy of Sciences of the USA*. 106 (42): 17667–17669.

Chepkorir Kuto, Milka. 2016. *Sengwer Women's Experience of Evictions and their Involvement in the Struggle for Sengwer Land Rights*. Moreton-in-Marsh: Forest Peoples' Programme. https://www.forestpeoples.org/sites/default/files/publication/2016/10/sengwerwomenreportweb.pdf (accessed 24 February 2019).

The Ecologist. 1995. "The Commons: Where the Community has Authority." In *The Earthscan Reader in Sustainable Development*, edited by John Kirkby, Phil O'Keefe, and Lloyd Timberlake, 227–237. London: Earthscan.

EU (European Union). 2016. "Action Fiche For Kenya's Water Tower Protection and Climate Change (WaTER) Programme." Ref. Ares (2016)3622371-19/07/2016.

EU (European Union). 2018. "EU Suspends Its Support for Water Towers in View of Reported Human Rights Abuses." *Delegation of the European Union to Kenya: Press Release*, 17 January. https://eeas.europa.eu/delegations/kenya/38343/eu-suspends-its-support-water-towers-view-reported-human-rights-abuses_en (consulted 26 January 2019).

FIPN (Forest Indigenous Peoples Network). 2014. "Forest Dwelling Communities Position Statement: Securing Our Rights, Our Lands and Our Forests." Presented to the National Land Commission Task Force on Historical Land Injustices, Nairobi, 11 September.

FPP (Forest Peoples Programme). 2013. *Chepkitale Ogiek Community Document their Customary Bylaws for the First Time in Order to Ensure the Continued Conservation of their Ancestral Lands and Natural Resources* (26 November). Moreton-in-Marsh: Forest Peoples Programme. http://whakatane-mechanism.org/news/201311chepkitale-ogiek-community-document-their-customary-bylaws-first-time-order-ensure (accessed 26 January 2019).

FPP (Forest Peoples Programme). 2016. *Illegal and Forceful Evictions of the Sengwer Indigenous People from their Ancestral Lands in the Cherangany Hills, Kenya*. Moreton-in-Marsh: Forest Peoples Programme https://www.forestpeoples.org/en/featured-topic/illegal-and-forceful-evictions-sengwer-indigenous-people-their-ancestral-lands (accessed 26th January, 2019).

IUCN (International Union for the Conservation of Nature). 2012. "International Union for Conservation of Nature Submission to the 11th Session of the United Nations Permanent Forum on Indigenous Issues." *New York City*, 7–18 May. https://www.iucn.org/sites/dev/files/content/documents/iucn_unpfii_submission_11th_session.pdf (accessed 10 February 2019).

Kenya Ministry of Environment and Forestry. 2018. *Taskforce Report on Forest Resources Management and Logging Activities in Kenya*. http://www.environment.go.ke/wp-content/uploads/2018/05/Task-Force-Report.pdf (accessed 4 April 2019)

Kiprop, Jonah, Violet Oriwo, Meshak Muga, Roxventa Othim, and Collins Obonyo. 2017. *Assessment of Indigenous Technical Knowledge on Production and Utilization of Non-Wood Forest Products (NWFPs) in Cherangany and Mt. Elgon Water Towers of Kenya*. Nairobi: Kenya Forestry Research Institute (published as Component 4: *Science to Inform Design of Community-Level Actions and Policy Decisions*, in a series to inform the Kenya's Water Towers Protection and Climate Change Mitigation and Adaptation (WaTER) Programme).

KNCHR (Kenya National Commission on Human Rights). 2018. *An Interim Report of the High-level Independent Fact-finding Mission to Embobut Forest in Elgeyo Marakwet County*. A Kenya National Commission on Human Rights Report. https://eeas.europa.eu/sites/eeas/files/report_knchr-_14_june-official_0.pdf (accessed 10 February 2019).

KNCHR (Kenya National Commission on Human Rights) and KLA (Kenya Land Alliance). 2006. *Unjust Enrichment: The Making of Land Grabbing Millionaires*. Nairobi: KNCHR and KLA. http://www.knchr.org/Portals/0/EcosocReports/Unjust%20Enrichment%20Volume%201.pdf (accessed 10 February 2019).

Ministry for Foreign Affairs of Finland. 2010. *Finnish Support to Forestry and Biological Resources (1. Kenya, 3. Tanzania, 4. Zambia)*. Evaluation Report 2010:5/II. Available at: https://um.fi/documents/384998/385866/parts__1__kenya__3__tanzania__4__zambia (accessed 10 February 2019).

Mutua, Makau. 2008. *Kenya's Quest for Democracy: Taming Leviathan (Challenge and Change in African Politics)*. Boulder, CO: Lynne Rienner Publishers.

Ostrom, Elinor. 1990. *Governing the Commons: The Evolution of Institutions for Collective Action*. Cambridge: Cambridge University Press.

Porter-Bolland, Luciana, Eduard Ellis, Manuel Guariguata, Isabel Ruiz-Mallén, Simoneta Negrete-Yankelevich, and Victoria Reyes-García. 2012. "Community Managed Forests and Forest Protected Areas: An Assessment of their Conservation Effectiveness across the Tropics." *Forest Ecology and Management* 268: 6–17.

Schmidt-Soltau, Kai. 2006. *Kenya – Natural Resource Management Project: Indigenous Peoples Planning Framework*. Washington, DC; World Bank.

Seymour, Francis, Tony La Vina, and Kristin Hite. 2014. *Evidence Linking Community Level Tenure and Forest Condition: An Annotated Bibliography*. Climate and Land Use Alliance. http://www.climateandlandusealliance.org/wp-content/uploads/2015/08/Community_level_tenure_and_forest_condition_bibliography.pdf (accessed 26 January 2019).

Suter, Philemon. 2013. "Politicians 'See' Pain of Evictees as Squatters' Houses Go Up in Flames." *Daily Nation*, 26 January 2013. http://www.nation.co.ke/news/politics/houses-go-up-in-flames/-/1064/2160528/-/okmsvi/-/index.html (accessed 29 January 2019).

WBIP (World Bank Inspection Panel). 2014. "Kenya – Natural Resources Management Project: Request for Inspection." Submitted on 2 January 2013. Washington, DC: World Bank.

WWF (World Wide Fund for Nature) International. 2008. *Indigenous Peoples and Conservation: WWF Statement of Principles*. Gland: WWF International.

11 Redefining university research enterprises

Partnership and collaboration in Laxyuup Gitxaała

Charles R. Menzies and Caroline F. Butler

Introduction

Partnerships and collaboration between universities and indigenous communities have become the standard approach for most university-involved research projects in Canada. While forms of research collaboration have long been part of anthropological research (Menzies 2015) the power dynamics of such collaborations have typically remained unbalanced, tilted in favor of the non-indigenous university-based researcher (La Salle 2010). With the growth of autonomous indigenous research agencies and a modest expansion in indigenous research faculty numbers the power imbalance has begun to shift to greater equity.

This chapter describes a collaborative project between the University of British Columbia (UBC) and Gitxaała Nation. It explores how our ongoing collaboration personally (as researchers) and, more critically, structurally (as institutions) can potentially play a role in redefining the university research enterprise. We draw upon our history of collaboration in research over the last fifteen years. The nature and extent of our collaboration has shifted as our relationship changed from teacher/student, to colleagues, and then to representatives of collaborating agencies. At the core has been a combined intent to engage in research and teaching practice that provides useful research for Gitxaała Nation and that also speaks to a wider world of scholarship.

The University of British Columbia and Gitxaała Nation partnership

This Nation-Institution partnership is one of extremes. UBC is the largest university in the province, with almost 55,000 students and 5,000 faculty at its Vancouver campus, a research budget of $580 million and over 3,000 yearly research partnerships, agreements and contracts.[1] Gitxaała Nation has approximately 1,900 citizens, 450 of whom live in the village of Lach Klan (Kitkatla BC), which is accessible by boat or floatplane from Prince Rupert. The Nation holds territory on the North Coast of British Columbia, stretching from Prince Rupert, south

1 https://www.ubc.ca/about/facts.html.

to Aristazabal Island. It is governed by a table of *Smgigyet* (hereditary chiefs) and *Sigidmhanaa* (matriarchs), who provide the mandate for territorial issues, and an elected Chief and Council who manage the administrative functions of the band and enact the mandate of hereditary table.

The UBC-Gitxaała Nation partnership emerged out of a longstanding research collaboration initiated in 2001 (Butler 2004; Lewis 2004; Menzies 2004). Charles Menzies, an anthropologist at UBC, and a member of Gitxaała Nation who grew up in Prince Rupert, came "home" to conduct research with and for Gitxaała Nation. Caroline Butler began working with the community as a graduate research assistant while doing her doctoral research on commercial fisheries in Prince Rupert. Over the life of our collaborative venture a multitude of sub-projects, consultancies, and student projects have been developed. The initial collaborative framework started from a researcher-initiated program designed to complement and extend Gitxaała Nation's ongoing research needs in relation to treaty negotiations and aboriginal rights and title litigation[2] (see Menzies 2004). There are several salient features to this process. There must be recognition of the need for prior informed consent given by the community for conducting research. This process involves multiple levels, including administrative (the elected council), hereditary (the traditional government), and individual (research participants). Furthermore, it must be recognized that "prior informed consent" in fact requires an ongoing process of renegotiation, which means that the researchers have to regularly present their results and new questions according to the development of their investigations. Also crucial is an acknowledgement of Gitxaała ownership of intellectual property, and the fundamental principle that authority and control over the framework resides within the First Nation. Hence, the research presents some characteristics, particularly for what regards intellectual property rights.

Charles Menzies' own subject location as both Gitxaała member and university researcher complicates and disrupts the normative approach of university-led community research, in which the researcher typically self-presents as a non-indigenous "expert" on indigenous peoples. The mainstream narrative of collaborative research has assumed that non-indigenous researchers are at the core of the endeavor linked to the research university. The dominance of the normative model is clear when one reviews the literature on community-based and participatory research methods. These methods are designed to resolve the methodological problems associated with an assumed power imbalance tilted toward the university-based non-indigenous researcher. Although the situation is starting to shift, in most parts of the world, the majority of university researchers studying indigenous communities are not indigenous themselves. This fact (consciously or otherwise) has shaped the discussion on collaborative research toward

2 As a First nation with Aboriginal rights not ceded or extinguished through a treaty, the Nation is required in many intergovernmental processes to document its land use and territorial occupation, and to prove its claim to an area in order to participate in environmental assessments, co-management or any negotiations with other governments and/or industry.

consideration of the power of the researcher versus the presumed lack of power of the researched. This is not surprising as it follows the topography of debates within mainstream anthropology over the past several decades, in which giving voice to the voiceless is considered a critical principle of anthropology (Marcus and Fisher 1986). Debates over the presumed power of the anthropologist reflect an underlying colonial history of anthropology (Asad 1973, Gough 1968). Despite a turn in political anthropology in the 1990s (see Bellier 2015) the majority of studies (irrespective of their liberal values) still presume that indigenous communities lack power, authority, and the ability to speak for themselves. By virtue of his being a Gitxaała member and the university research Menzies' subject location troubles the normative model of university expert seeking out community-based indigenous partners in collaboration.

In addition to questions of power, the mainstream narrative of collaborative research also engages the idea of *capacity building*. Underlying this narrative is an assumption that capacity in indigenous communities needs to be "developed" or "improved." This reflects a Eurocentric and bureaucratic understanding of capacity that recognizes particular realms of competence and ways of doing things that are different from, but not inherently superior to, indigenous ways of organizing activities and people. This understanding can be inverted by recentering indigenous society and governance. If technical knowledge and competence in First nations social, political, linguistic (etc.) practices is prioritized, then it is the universities, government, and business enterprises that have the real "capacity deficit." The observation of intergovernmental and consultative processes often illustrates that non-indigenous researchers and regulators lack fundamental competencies in relation to understanding First Nations practices, histories, expectations, and technical competencies. We will argue that Gitxaała Nation has worked to build this capacity within the university through collaborative research, and through the ongoing training of *K'msiwah* (Euro-Canadian, "ghost people") staff. Caroline Butler, one of the authors, is an example of such a person; her subject location as a non-indigenous researcher working within Gitxaała's research agency, Gitxaała Environmental Monitoring (GEM), reflects the trend over the last four decades of First Nations hiring trained outsiders for in-house research activities.

Our research collaboration has developed through unsettling and an inverting of the normative frame, and expectations based in it. We confront it both personally and structurally. We confront the assumptions buried within the supposedly neutral concept of "capacity." It is exactly because this normative frame is so powerful that we need to constantly remind non-indigenous partners of the real, existing capacity within indigenous communities, and make them (non-indigenous partners) aware of their own needs for capacity development.

University-led, community-based: early collaborative research projects 2001–2010

Gitxaała Nation has had hosted relatively little ethnographic research over the course of its encounter with the *K'msiwah* world. William Beynon interviewed

Gitxaała Elders in 1916 as part of his fieldwork for Marius Barbeau. Beynon was a Tsimshian ethnographer who worked as a translator and co-ethnographer for many early twentieth century anthropologists including Franz Boas. Marius Barbeau played a pivotal role in Canadian anthropology as the lead ethnographer of what is today call the Canadian Museum of History. During the course of his work Beynon recorded *adaawx* (oral histories) and mapped hunting territories. Gitxaała citizens, familiar with Beynon and Barbeau's work, tend to consider it incomplete and lacking in accuracy. Nonetheless, the Beynon texts have been regularly cited by ethnographers, historians, and government regulators (for detailed discussion, see Menzies 2016: 20–25), and have become the foundation of non-indigenous definitions of the Gitxaała, and their rights and identity in relationship to their neighboring First Nations. There were few outside researchers throughout the rest of the twentieth century (Menzies 2016). When indigenous nations on the North Coast of British Columbia began to discuss collaborating for land claims in the 1980s, James McDonald of the University of Northern British Columbia documented parts of this process, in association with a regional Tribal Council. Academic partnerships did not flourish; to the contrary, research was sometimes exploitative. In particular, a study by the federal Department of Fisheries mapping abalone[3] harvesting areas led to the release of Gitxaała information to commercial harvesters; this resulted in a long-term distrust of external research (see Menzies 2004, 2010, 2015).

Internal research for rights and title purposes has had greater support from the community. Beginning in the 1990s, Gitxaała and four other First Nations in the region formed the "Tsimshian Tribal Council" (TTC) and collaborated for over a decade on a comprehensive claim through the BC Treaty Process.[4] Several kinds of research were conducted as a part of this process, including historical and genealogical research carried out by TTC staff. In the early 1990s, Gitxaała members conducted their own traditional use study, and further mapped Gitxaała land use in the early 2000s as part of the provincial land use planning process; for both projects non-indigenous consultants were contracted to do the mapping.

Menzies approached Gitxaała Nation in 2001 with funding from the Province of British Columbia's funding agencies, Forests Renewal BC, and Fisheries Renewal BC, for projects on Gitxaała resource use and management (Menzies 2016). Any project, whether initiated by a community member or an outsider, requires seeking formal permission through culturally relevant protocols (Menzies 2004). That he was, in addition to being a community member, a faculty member at a research university further complicated the situation. As noted in our documentary, *Returning to Gitxaała* (Menzies, Rashleigh, and

3 Abalone is a mollusk and a cultural significant species for Gitxaała (see Menzies 2004, 2010, 2015).

4 Starting in the 1970s Canada has entertained two general types of land claims: comprehensive claims which are designed to result in treaties to extinguish all outstanding rights and title issues with a particular First nation, and; specific claims that deal with a failure by Canada to fulfill obligations under existing treaties, other agreements, or as defined in the Indian Act of Canada.

Butler 2005), Menzies was simultaneously seen in Gitxaała as an official agent of the University of British Columbia and as a community member. Occupying this kind of dual role is something that non-indigenous researchers do not experience. These projects initiated a decade of collaborative community-based research documenting Gitxaała patterns of resource harvesting and traditions of habitat and population enhancement, and adaptations to climate change.

These early projects followed a classic collaborative model. The projects were approved by the elected Chief and Council, and managed by the Treaty Coordinator, the Gitxaała staff member tasked with organizing community and collaborative research on land use and rights. Information about these projects was conveyed through public meetings held in the community. The projects were generally well-received by community members. For the research,[5] a university researcher (in this case, Menzies or Butler) was paired with a community-based researcher who scheduled, facilitated, and where necessary, translated interviews. Gitxaała researchers were identified by the Treaty Coordinator for their *Sm'algyax* (Gitxaała's language) language skills and community relationships. It was important for the Gitxaała researcher to be a fluent-speaker of the Gitxaała language, and in good standing with other community members, in order for them to be able to successfully recruit research participants, create a comfortable interview dynamic, and guide the UBC researchers on Gitxaała protocol and culture.

The legacy of the abalone research resulted in limitations to our research. Community elders would not initially sanction field site visits, and the mapping of harvesting sites, due to concerns regarding the publication of spatial data by any external institution. Furthermore, information regarding traditional medicines was considered too sensitive to document through the collaborative model. These components of Gitxaała resource use were thus not part of the early collaborative research. However, the early projects did result in the documentation of species used, seasonality, and the *ayaawx* (laws) regarding the respectful harvest of resources. Research products included educational videos and elementary and high school curriculum, as well as more standard reports and academic publications.[6]

Lessons learned

This phase of research was both productive and limited. The collaborative relationship between Gitxaała and UBC was established and refined according to community priorities and protocols, but the development of meaningful trust took a full decade. Menzies (2004) has discussed the high degree of community control over

5 We use the term research to cover all forms of social science research that we engage in, whether by means of participant observations, structured interviews, videography, landscape archaeology, or more technocratic applied policy-oriented work. While each particular project has it's own research methods, we prefer not to differentiate by to discuss the generic act of engaging in research as a form of inquiry and analysis.

6 See http://www.ecoknow.ca (accessed 24 February 2019)

the research in terms of design and approval. Individual and leadership approvals of draft products and the use of community knowledge were essential. The lowest comfort level regarding research topics and publication was used – only material with which everyone was comfortable was made public. Thus, while each research participant approved the material from their own interview(s), or removed information they decided should not be in the report/papers, members of the Elected Band Council and hereditary leaders also reviewed the final products. Where any hereditary leader expressed concern about content being made public, that material was removed and archived for community use.

Despite Menzies' personal connection to the community, and the approval of the research by the leadership, there persisted for many years a basic distrust of any research associated with an external institution such as UBC. This resulted in a very slow advancement of the research from the margins to the center of Gitxaała knowledge and power. In the early years, only a few of the high-ranking knowledge holders of the community participated in the research and these had direct family ties to either Menzies or the community researchers. As community confidence in the research relationship and community approval of the early research products grew, more *Smgigyet* and *Sigidmhanaa* agreed to be interviewed. Menzies' position within the community was being shifted through the act of collaborative research. Having grown up outside of the village, the community-based research activities extended his personal connections beyond his Gitxaała family to many of the elders, hereditary leaders, and harvesters in Lach Klan. He was increasingly directed in his research activities by the elders, who shared with him their priorities for documentation and archaeological surveys. It was a decade of proving worth and earning trust. It was also a decade of Gitxaała hereditary leaders internally negotiating and debating the value of written documentation within an oral system of governance and cultural learning.

Internal applied research: 2009

During the early phase of the UBC research, the Gitxaała government's Resource Management and Treaty Departments were engaged in detailed documentation on behalf of Gitxaała, in particular research on cultural sites, land use, and laws. Several years later Gitxaała withdrew completely from the treaty process. While there was initial excitement about the opportunities for modern treaties that were established in the late twentieth century,[7] as the Nisga'a treaty was negotiated and the reality of extinguishing title became clear, Gitxaała leaders became skeptical of the value of continuing in the treaty process. After the Nation withdrew from treaty research and negotiations in 2004, there was a lull in internal research. Increasing interest in resource development in Gitxaała Territory initiated a new

7 The Calder Case 1973 brought to trial by a Nisga'a First Nation claim, established that Aboriginal title had not been extinguished in areas of Canada where treaties had not been signed. This started a modern land claims and treaty process with Nations in the territories in the north of Canada and British Columbia.

phase of applied research by the Nation, however, and by 2009, there were proposals for several windfarms, Liquid Natural Gas (LNG) pipelines and export terminals, a container port expansion, and a gold mine within Gitxaała Territory.

In 2006, Gitxaała Environmental Monitoring (GEM) was initiated with external consultants, to commence the research and monitoring work that was required by the resource development proposals in the region at that time, specifically windfarms. The vision for the department was reworked in 2009, with the establishment of an office in Prince Rupert, and the hiring of a full-time Environmental Assessment Coordinator. Butler was brought on part-time to facilitate the community-based research such as Traditional Use Studies.[8] The Gitxaała Fisheries Department moved to the GEM office in 2010, creating a resource management and research hub for Gitxaała Nation.

Currently, GEM consists of an Environmental Assessment (EA) Manager, an EA Coordinator, and a Heritage Research Coordinator (Butler). Several community researchers and *Sm'algyax* interpreters work for the cultural heritage program on a project by project basis. The Fisheries Manager and one of the Fisheries technicians also work out of the Prince Rupert office, so while GEM and Gitxaała Fisheries are two separate departments, they are closely linked in terms of research, programming, and activities.

GEM engages in Environmental Assessments on behalf of the Nation, responds to provincial referrals,[9] and also secures funding for community heritage research priorities such as language revitalization and the documentation of Gitxaała *ayaawx* (laws), and the creation of a community archive. As part of the EA process, GEM has conducted, with the support of consultants, Gitxaała Use Studies, socio-economic surveys, habitat mapping, and documentation of travel routes and fishing gear placement along proposed tanker routes. The socio-economic reports outline the potential impacts of projects on Gitxaała resource use, marine travel, access to social services, and employment (Calliou Group 2015). A health impact assessment in 2016[10] further explored the specific health and wellbeing impacts of rapid industrialization from Liquid Natural Gas development in the Prince Rupert area.

The collaboration with UBC extends to this very applied aspect of the Nation's work. Menzies has been called upon to provide expert testimony, review regulatory documents, and write reports, particularly regarding Gitxaała's historical settlements and rights. He works directly with GEM and Gitxaała's legal counsel

8 Traditional Use Studies produce spatial datasets documenting community land and marine use, harvesting areas, cultural, spiritual and historical sites. These are very common for Environmental Assessments, and land claims.

9 When the government of British Columbia receives an application for a land use tenure, or small-scale development on Provincial Crown land, the proposal is forwarded to the First Nation(s) within whose territory the activity falls. The First Nation responds with its concerns regarding impacts for BC to consider when approving the project.

10 The report Commissioned by Gitxaala Environmental Monitoring in July 2016 was conducted by Janis Shandro and entitled *Potential Risks, Impacts and Opportunities of the Aurora LNG Project for Gitxaala Nation.*

to provide this service. For example, when Enbridge proposed the Northern Gateway project to pipe oil from Alberta to Kitimat BC, and have oil tankers transverse Gitxaała territorial waters, Menzies wrote a report on Gitxaała governance and territory to support the Nation's legal arguments regarding the project's impact on Gitxaała Aboriginal rights and title.

Menzies is also called upon to contribute to the community heritage projects. The UBC Ethnographic Film Unit provides in-kind contributions to the video projects initiated by GEM, including the development of Sm'algyax language videos and participatory film making projects involving Gitxaała youth. Menzies provides guidance and advice on community historical research, and is the community's expert on the historical materials on Gitxaała produced by Beynon and Barbeau in the early twentieth century.

Menzies, and others at the UBC Anthropology Department, have thus become resources that contribute directly to the non-academic research required by Gitxaała. Menzies' work as an expert witness for the Nation was an important part of their success in documenting their rights. Through Menzies' work on community heritage projects UBC makes a direct contribution to research and documentation for community use.

Service learning to apprenticeship: student research

In one of our early collaborations, we co-taught two graduate field schools in 2006 and 2007 (see Menzies and Butler 2011). Our courses followed a standard service-learning approach in which student research projects were developed within community through a consultative process and then students were paired up with projects in accord with their individual interests. This model has been effective in meeting student learning needs and moderately effective in meeting community expectations. However, we came to view the underlying model as problematic as the frame still focused research inward onto the community as an object of study. Given the pressure on Gitxaała from increasing industrial developments, and thus the importance of high-quality research to support and define Gitxaała rights and title, student research – however well meaning – is insufficient; professional work directly controlled by the Nation is essential. The research projects for such work need to be service-based, not collaborative. While the students did produce projects of interest to community, such as profiles of Elders, assessments of service gaps, they were unable to produce products of direct relevance to the most pressing issues facing the Nation.

Furthermore, the field school model has its flaws from a community perspective. Having six graduate students descend on the community for a month is intrusive and disruptive. At the same time, the research period is too brief to result in projects of any real depth or nuance. In addition, there are too many students to adequately supervise and fully guide their engagement with community members. Our community researchers were stretched quite thin to provide supervision for all interviews and other research activities.

There still remains a place and a need for student research, but we have developed a summer internship program to facilitate graduate student projects. This approach parallels longstanding models of cooperative learning and work semesters. It places the student, usually non-indigenous, into a work-like setting within which they conduct research under the authority and jurisdiction of Gitxaała. The student provides subsidized labor to the GEM office for any work that is needed. The GEM office then facilitates access to community members, staff, and leadership, for the student's thesis research. We supervise these graduate research projects under the authority of the university, which ultimately necessitates the production of two unique work products: a research report for Gitxaała and a thesis for UBC. The individual graduate students are more productive, and less overwhelming to the community. They have the opportunity to build more direct and meaningful relationships with Gitxaała individuals and families, and have the time to do research and work of value to GEM and the Nation. The research internship has proven useful and beneficial to all involved, but is, essentially, a by-product of the primary collaboration not a key focus or intent.

The direction of our deployment of student researchers was realigned to focus on external agencies, processes, and people that Gitxaała needed to understand more fully. Research on Gitxaała in support of rights and title was carefully brought under the direct control and authority of the internal structures of Gitxaała nation. Out of this process we developed a series of research internships that produced theses focused on topics of practical use for Gitxaala, for example, provincial forestry policy (Rogers 2007), marine use planning (Moffitt 2012), and wind farms (Rodman 2013).

The two most recent graduate students have been directed toward topics that do focus on engagement with community members and Gitxaała themes, but that are directly relevant to questions posed by resource development. One student explored the meaning of food security to Gitxaała citizens, focusing on issues of cultural security, social wellbeing, and food sovereignty (Gendron 2016). In 2015, a student worked with community members who have been directly involved in GEM's Environmental Assessment research, and the provision of testimony to the Northern Gateway Joint Review Panel. She asked them about contemporary Gitxaała identity in the context of resource development and threats to territory (Laforest 2017). These are projects that have direct relevance to GEM's documentation of project impacts, but that are not compatible with the rather rapid research methods required to meet EA process deadlines. The current structure for student research thus provides the opportunity to explore some of the more nuanced ethnographic and socio-economic questions posed by resource development in Gitxaała territory.

Current Laxyuup-Gitxaała partnership

During the last few years UBC-Gitxaała projects have focused on archaeological work in key settlement sites, reflecting the Nation's concerns regarding the potential impacts of development, and the documentation of historical residency. Gitxaała Nation initiated a collaborative archaeology research project with UBC to explore resource use and settlement patterns. Since 2009 we have documented a series of Gitxaała villages and occupation sites. Many of these places, while known within Gitxaała, had not been documented in official databases. As a result of increased large ship traffic and related industrial developments, Gitxaała Nation has taken a proactive approach to get out in front of the developments to record and document our own history. The most recent UBC project has explored the alpine hunting territories of Gitxaała *walps* (matrilineal property holding corporate groups). This work seeks to document the ways in which the non-coastal parts of the territory were accessed and used. The pursuit of mountain goats for food and materials production has been a central theme of investigation.

A current tension in our present work is finding the balance between academic research and the current priorities of the community. When Menzies recently proposed an extension of his research in Gitxaała's alpine territories, Butler's response was "what's in it for us?" In this section, we reflect on this particular discussion as it points to some of the shifting dynamics in the research relationship.

When assessing prospective research topics and projects, we move ironically between subject positions. Butler is required to take the "insider" position, as GEM staff, querying the value of Menzies' academic proposal to Gitxaała Nation research priorities and community needs. In this case, Butler suggested making links between the project and Gitxaała's marine plan implementation, by including fieldtrips for youth to the alpine hunting territories as a component of the project. One of her current roles in the collaboration is to look for ways to tie the ongoing university-based use and occupancy research directly to the immediate research and programming activities of the GEM office. While the big picture value of Menzies' research is directly linked to the Nation's documentation of rights and title through historical use, Butler is tasked with pushing for the more direct utility of these projects to community needs. The insider/outsider dynamic becomes somewhat muddled when a non-indigenous staff member is asking a community member to rationalize his academic research.

Second, this exchange points to the fact that Gitxaała Nation is not passive in its acceptance of research proposals. GEM and the Gitxaała Fisheries Department are often approached by university researchers or other Nations and/or First Nations organizations seeking research partnerships. Gitxaała Nation is discerning about such opportunities; only research of direct utility to current Gitxaała priorities is undertaken or approved. While the Gitxaała-UBC partnership is longstanding, and while Menzies is a community member and respected Gitxaała scholar, his projects continue to be negotiated and shaped by the Nation's evolving needs and positions. Concerns regarding research fatigue are a major part of this decision-making. The ongoing need of the GEM office and the Fisheries Department to engage Gitxaała citizens in EA-related research means that the impact of other, perhaps less pressing research on community willingness to participate in internal projects must be considered. This research triage is another burden of the industrial development boom in the region – the need to sometimes limit research in order to preserve community goodwill and interest.

These issues reflect the need to develop a balanced community-oriented research agenda. The long-term benefits of extensive ethnographic documentation (such as the goat project) provide a counterpoint to the reactive project-based TUS mapping that GEM must regularly produce. The UBC collaboration and external funding provide the opportunity to use more classic ethnographic methods and explore topics and parts of the territory that are not prioritized in EA-related investigations. Scoping research priorities that reflect immediate technical needs posed by industrial development threats or economic development opportunities *and* immediate community priorities for language education and revitalization of traditional governance structures is imperative. And where possible, finding ways to create cultural products for community use from EA-based research redeems the repetitive burden of project specific research. The Fisheries Program recently facilitated development of bilingual Sm'algyax/English children's books that were drawn from stories Elders told during interviews during the last 15 years of research.

The most direct benefit from an academic – community collaboration can be built through strategic planning. GEM has been unable to truly take advantage of the opportunities offered by this longstanding personal and institutional collaboration because of the constant reactive state of GEM research. The flurry of LNG, Enbridge and other development proposals has resulted in the GEM office being limited to initiating research that reflects the requirements of EAs and regulatory engagement. There are plans for a strategic planning session to collaboratively identify research priorities associated with rights and title, the impacts of resource development, language revitalization, and cultural programming. This will allow Gitxaała Nation to get out in front of the research process and propose relevant and priority research topics to UBC Anthropology, and to solicit academic partnerships with other departments and institutions to achieve the research outcomes identified by Gitxaała Nation.

Essentially, Gitxaała Nation leadership wants to turn the research process on its head. Rather than having external researchers approach GEM with project proposals, often with funding in place, looking for a host community, Gitxaała Nation wants to develop a list of projects, and seek out preferred partners by creating an inventory of academic experts. There are a number of priority areas where research planning needs to occur. The gathering of baseline data for monitoring the cumulative effects of industrial development is a regional priority for the North Coast of BC, and GEM has already identified Gitxaała-specific values and associated indicators. The implementation of the Gitxaała Marine Use Plan requires both ecological and cultural research. Finally, Gitxaała Elders have a long list of cultural and language documentation priorities, for the creation of Gitxaała curriculum and revitalization programming. These priorities need to be operationalized into projects that can be used to guide graduate student acceptance and establish institutional research partnerships. Essentially, GEM envisions academic institutions as service providers or consultants who will provide research services through trade rather than remuneration. Access to community knowledge and capacity, within strict research protocol agreements, will be bartered for research services.

In preparation for this research model, GEM is developing both internal and external research protocols that formalize the process of research with Gitxaała Nation. The internal protocols reflect the need to coordinate the research activities of the Nation's departments. Various programs are engaged in research to support the implementation of the Wellness Plan, the Marine Use Plan, and various community programs. The internal research protocol ensures that all existing resources and materials are available to the Nation's researchers, all materials are archived for future use, and that published materials are consistent and approved.

The external research protocol is based on the collaborative model developed by Menzies (2004). A process of consultation and research proposal approval is being formalized through the certification process of the Nation. GEM oversight of the research activities and GEM and Leadership approval of draft products will be a formal requirement of research partnership. Individual approval of all contributed material in context remains a critical component of the research process.

Capacity

As described early on in this chapter, community-based research projects have always followed a model where a university researcher is paired with a community researcher to conduct interviews and other research activities. This was understood as facilitating skills sharing and capacity building – on both sides. The university researcher held a certain set of skills and knowledge, such as methodology, documentation and recording, and ethnographic analysis, and the community researcher held a different set, such as language fluency, cultural protocols, and personal and family histories.

Most discussions of collaborative research models seem to differentiate between capacity and knowledge – conceptualizing them as one-way streets running in opposite directions. Capacity runs from the university to the community, transferring "western" skills to community members. And knowledge (you can read this as cultural understanding, data, or material), is channeled from the community to the university.

From a Gitxaała perspective, capacity building has gone in the opposite direction – it is the Nation that has been building capacity at UBC for over a decade. Through supporting the research activities of Menzies, Gitxaała has enhanced the career of a Gitxaała anthropologist, providing UBC with an indigenous academic with significant field expertise and publications. The Nation has sponsored the MA research of ten non-Gitxaała UBC students, and provided field research experience to over a dozen others through fieldschools and research assistant positions. Their experience working in Gitxaała territory and directly engaging with community members has provided them with the skills and the publications required to launch their careers in both academic and applied settings.

This process of capacity building fostered by Gitxaała can also be seen within the context of wider community-government, and community-industry, relations. Many times, government and business officials assume they need to "educate" indigenous communities. Very often one of the promises they make is to contribute to "capacity building" within Gitxaała through the provisions of skills and job training. Skills and job training are certainly very useful. However, what tends to happen is that those programs do not meet expectations. However, through the process of interacting with Gitxaała the outside officials have their own capacity built as they learn about indigenous cultures, organizations, and protocols, and ultimately become more effective at their job of setting up opportunities for non-indigenous peoples to extract resources, value, and knowledge from our indigenous communities. In this normative frame, capacity building remains part of the colonial process of disposition that began with our land and continues with our knowledge. By striving to take control over the process of research and establishing protocol agreements Gitxaała is working to undermine the negative unidirectional aspect of knowledge extraction.

It is important to note that Gitxaała community researchers have always spoken positively of their experiences working on the collaborative research projects coordinated with UBC. They emphasize how much they have learned, and how it changed how they understood their community and history – through conversations with their Elders. Every community researcher has expressed joy at the extra, direct, and intimate opportunity to listen to their Elders and ask them questions that our research process provides to them. Because of the way Gitxaała retains control over the research process the direct benefit of research, in terms of capacity building and knowledge acquisition, remains an internal process. This is especially important for community members, as the older forms of university research simply removed knowledge from the community without providing any effective benefits in return.

Research facilitator and Sm'algyax expert Ernie Bolton worked on GEM-UBC projects for a decade, and more recently with TUS consultants on EA-focused documentation. He has invested a dozen years in training Butler on protocol and etiquette, social relationships and responsibilities, and the methodological intricacies specific to research in Laxyuup Gitxaała. Bolton welcomes the opportunity provided by the research to speak with Smgigyet and Elders about Gitxaała culture and history, and to enhance his already expansive cultural knowledge. The skills Bolton and other Gitxaała researchers have acquired or enhanced through the collaborative project, through engaging with university researchers, are primarily those related to training and teaching outsiders. The very real social liability posed by an outside researcher in Gitxaała society has required significant work.

From a Gitxaała Nation perspective, valuable skills for researchers are the ability to understand the community's needs and priorities, and to navigate Gitxaała social relationships. In this way, Butler's long apprenticeship with Bolton in Lach Klan is far more relevant to GEM's immediate needs than her academic apprenticeship with Menzies at UBC. UBC credentials are of a particular value, but it is the hands-on training in a totally different realm that is valued by Gitxaała. GEM staff and community members constantly joke that Butler is a "work in progress" but "coming along nicely." Greater value is placed on the skills and knowledge contributed by the community, than the capacity developed by *K'msiwah* institutions. The community sees itself as investing in the task of building capacity and enhancing skills by educating *K'msiwah* staff and other researchers – to a point.

For Butler, the ongoing apprenticeship with Gitxaała Nation has contributed significantly to her understanding of Gitxaała culture, but one that is bounded by community's emphasis on its necessary and deliberate incompleteness. Sixteen years of research, regular community engagement and ongoing direction from leadership allows her to identify Gitxaała values and concerns in an EA or marine planning context with other governments or technical staff working for other First Nations. However, the vigilance of Gitxaała Elders in protecting their cultural patrimony from outsiders means that even community-controlled research is met with questions and skepticism, and Butler's right to document their knowledge – even as their employee – is never a given. A large part of her capacity building is an enhanced understanding of her own "whiteness," and what that means to Gitxaała people, and her own implication in modern forms of colonial intrusion. Gitxaała Nations' very need of an in-house anthropologist is wrapped in the burden of Gitxaała having to prove their Aboriginal title, save their language, and find ways to protect their resources.

Butler has shifted from a student researcher to an employee, which retains the value of Gitxaała's investment in the original UBC collaboration. However, it is important to note that Gitxaała generally retains very little in terms of "capacity" developed from the collaborative partnership on academic projects. The reports and academic materials are useful, but realistically, the students and UBC benefit more directly than the community. The more direct benefits to community come from the ability to leverage the power associated with Menzies' academic credentials for Gitxaała's engagement with government and industry.

It is important to conceptualize Gitxaała as a patient host of academic research, not as the passive grateful recipient of it. Academic research is a means to an end, which is often not actually the direct product of the research. The overall research collaboration is of value to the community, but not all aspects of it are of equal value or even high value to Gitxaała. Gitxaała has chosen to engage in research projects and host field schools and summer students, in order to build institutional expertise on Gitxaała culture. And to establish a set of relationships that allow Gitxaała to call on that expertise for its own purposes.

Conclusions

The Gitxaała-UBC collaboration illustrates the evolving nature of community and university research relationships and the ways in which researcher positions, community policies, and the relative benefits of research are constantly shifting and renegotiated. By taking a Gitxaała-centric perspective on research, definitions of capacity, of value and of collaboration are reworked to highlight and support community skills, priorities, and control. The university becomes a hive of worker bees who can be mobilized by Gitxaała as tools for sovereignty.

The early collaborative research initiated by Menzies was both innovative and traditional. It followed a standard collaborative model, but set a high standard for multi-leveled community approval. As the partnership became more established, the commitment allowed Gitxaała to increasingly shape the research themes and products toward community priorities. The association with UBC has supported Gitxaała's ability to be discerning and proactive about research opportunities. The Nation's experience in collaborative research has set the bar high in terms of approving projects of clear value with relevant methodologies. Essentially, the relationship has developed in way that has resulted in a truly empowered collaborative model where Gitxaała even probes the focus and designs of Menzies' projects, and holds all potential research partners to the guidelines he has set. Good collaborative research thus results in the researchers becoming disempowered. This is perhaps why most collaborative structures only get partway there.

The partnership increased both internal and external capacity. Menzies' academic career was supported and enhanced by his community, building a critical resource for Gitxaała Nation's advancement of its sovereignty through litigation, regulatory processes, and development agreements. External capacity was built by training UBC researchers, but transformed into internal capacity by hiring Butler to work directly for the Nation. Gitxaała approaches all research with an evaluative lens, calculating whether the investment in the researcher, and contribution to the research, is balanced by either a direct benefit in terms of the research products, or a broader benefit in terms of the greater relationship with UBC (or other institution). Gitxaała Nation is thus strategic about research, evaluating the long-term and auxiliary benefits of collaboration.

Research on and in support of indigenous peoples' rights is a critical part of anthropology's involvement in the decolonizing project. However, the sovereigntist focus and intent of this type of research is not enough to ensure its meaningful contribution to the advancement of indigenous aspirations. The structure and power dynamics of our research must bend to the will and mandate of the communities for whom we work. For how can we document indigenous land rights if we cannot concede a community's jurisdiction over our research?

References

Asad, Talal, ed. 1973. *Anthropology and the Colonial Encounter.* London: Ithaca Press; Atlantic Highlands, NJ: Humanities Press.

Bellier, Irene. 2015. "A Political Anthropologist's Journey from the Local to the Global: An Interview with Irene Bellier." (CNRS-EHESS) by Susana Narodsky and Margaret Buckner, *American Anthropologist* 117 (3): 576–586, doi:10.1111/aman.12298.

Butler, Caroline F. 2004. "Researching Traditional Ecological Knowledge for Multiple Uses." *Canadian Journal of Native Education* 28 (1): 33–48.

Calliou Group. 2015. *Gitxaala Nation Socio-economic Report: Port Edward Area LNG Projects.* Report Commissioned by Gitxaala Environmental Monitoring, Gitxaala Nation, July 2015.

Gendron, Danielle Renee. 2016. *Eating Gitxaała, Being Gitxaała: Food and Cultural Security*. Electronic Theses and Dissertations (ETDs) 2008+, University of British Columbia. doi:10.14288/1.0300278.

Gough, Kathleen. 1968. "New Proposals for Anthropologists." *Current Anthropology* 9 (5): 403–435.

Laforest, Marie-Élise Carmel. 2017. *Gitxaała Sovereignty: Indigenous Governance and Industrial Development*. Electronic Theses and Dissertations (ETDs) 2008+, University of British Columbia. doi:10.14288/1.0343646.

La Salle, Marina. 2010. "Community Collaboration and Other Good Intentions." *Archaeologies: The Journal of the World Archaeological Congress* 6 (3): 401–422.

Lewis, John [Wuyee Wi Medeek]. 2004. "Forests for the Future: The View from Gitkxaala." *Canadian Journal of Native Education* 28 (1), 8–14.

Marcus, George, and Michael Fisher. 1986. *Anthropology as Cultural Critique: An Experimental Moment in the Human Sciences*. Chicago, IL: University of Chicago Press.

Menzies, Charles R. 2004. "Putting Words into Action: Negotiating Collaborative Research in Gitxaała." *Canadian Journal of Native Education* 27 (3): 15–32.

Menzies, Charles R. 2010. "Dm sibilhaa'nm da laxyuubm Gitxaała: Picking Abalone in Gitxaała Territory." *Human Organization* 69 (3): 213–220.

Menzies, Charles R. 2015. "Revisiting 'Dm sibilhaa'nm da laxyuubm Gitxaała (Picking Abalone in Gitxaała Territory)': Vindication, Appropriation, and Archaeology." *BC Studies* 187 (Autumn): 129–153.

Menzies, Charles R. 2016. *People of the Saltwater: An Ethnography of the Git lax m'oon*. Lincoln. University of Nebraska Press.

Menzies, Charles R., and Caroline F. Butler. 2011. "Collaborative Service Learning and Anthropology with Gitxaała Nation." with reflections by Solen Roth, Natalie J. K. Baloy, Robin Anderson, Jennifer Wolowic, Oralia Gómez-Ramírez, and concluding comments by Nees Ma'Outa (Clifford White) *Collaborative Anthropologies* 4: 169–242.

Menzies, Charles R., Jennifer Rashleigh, and Caroline Butler. 2005. "Returning to Gitxaala." *A Production of the Ethnographic Film Unit at UBC*. Video: 25 minutes.

Moffitt, Morgan E. 2012. *Gitxaała Marine Use Planning: Making Indigenous Jurisdiction in Contemporary Aboriginal-state Relations*. University of British Columbia. Retrieved from https://open.library.ubc.ca/cIRcle/collections/24/items/1.0073339.

Rodman, Lauren S. 2013. *Spinning Wind into Power: Industry and Energy in Gitxaała Nation, British Columbia*. University of British Columbia. Retrieved from https://open.library.ubc.ca/cIRcle/collections/24/items/1.0073866

Rogers, Jessica. 2007. *Reshaping Crown-First Nation Relationships Amid Changing Contexts: An Examination of the Intersection between the Crown's Promise of a New Relationship and the Implementations of the Forest and Range Agreement*. University of British Columbia. Retrieved from https://open.library.ubc.ca/cIRcle/collections/831/items/1.0101131.

Index

Note: Page numbers followed by "n" denote footnotes.

www.ingramcontent.com/pod-product-compliance
Ingram Content Group UK Ltd.
Pitfield, Milton Keynes, MK11 3LW, UK
UKHW022013180926
475701UK00003B/346
9781032088525